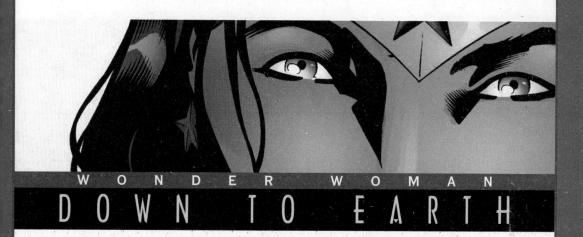

WONDER WOMAN
DOWN TO EARTH

WONDER WOMAN
DOWN TO EARTH

GREG RUCKA WRITER

DREW JOHNSON PENCILLER

RAY SNYDER INKER

RICHARD & TANYA HORIE **TRISH MULVIHILL** COLORISTS

TODD KLEIN LETTERER

ERIC SHANOWER ART ON MEDIA COVERAGE OF REFLECTIONS

WONDER WOMAN CREATED BY WILLIAM MOULTON MARSTON

Dan DiDio VP-Editorial
Ivan Cohen Editor-original series
Anton Kawasaki Editor-collected edition
Robbin Brosterman Senior Art Director
Paul Levitz President & Publisher
Georg Brewer VP-Design & Retail Product Development
Richard Bruning Senior VP-Creative Director
Patrick Caldon Senior VP-Finance & Operations
Chris Caramalis VP-Finance
Terri Cunningham VP-Managing Editor
Alison Gill VP-Manufacturing
Rich Johnson VP-Book Trade Sales
Hank Kanalz VP-General Manager, WildStorm
Lillian Laserson Senior VP & General Counsel
Jim Lee Editorial Director-WildStorm
David McKillips VP-Advertising & Custom Publishing
John Nee VP-Business Development
Gregory Noveck Senior VP-Creative Affairs
Cheryl Rubin VP-Brand Management
Bob Wayne VP-Sales & Marketing

WONDER WOMAN: DOWN TO EARTH

DC Comics, 1700 Broadway, New York, NY 10019
A Warner Bros. Entertainment Company
Printed in Canada. First Printing.
ISBN: 1-4012-0226-8

Special thanks to Matthew Clark, Rick Burchett and Trish Mulvihill
Interior color separations by WildStorm FX
Cover art by Greg Land and Matt Ryan.
Cover color by Justin Ponsor.

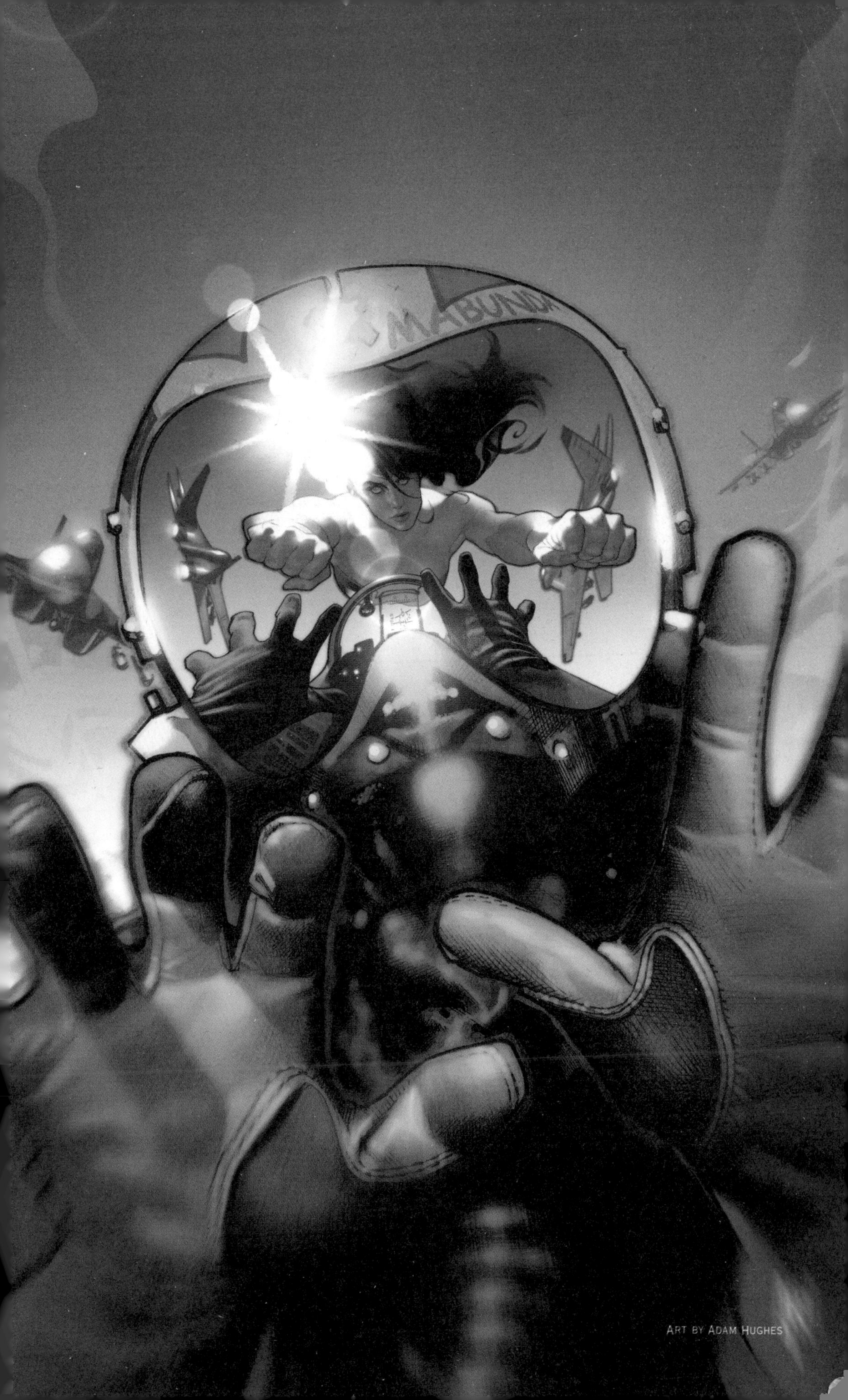
MABUNDA

ART BY ADAM HUGHES

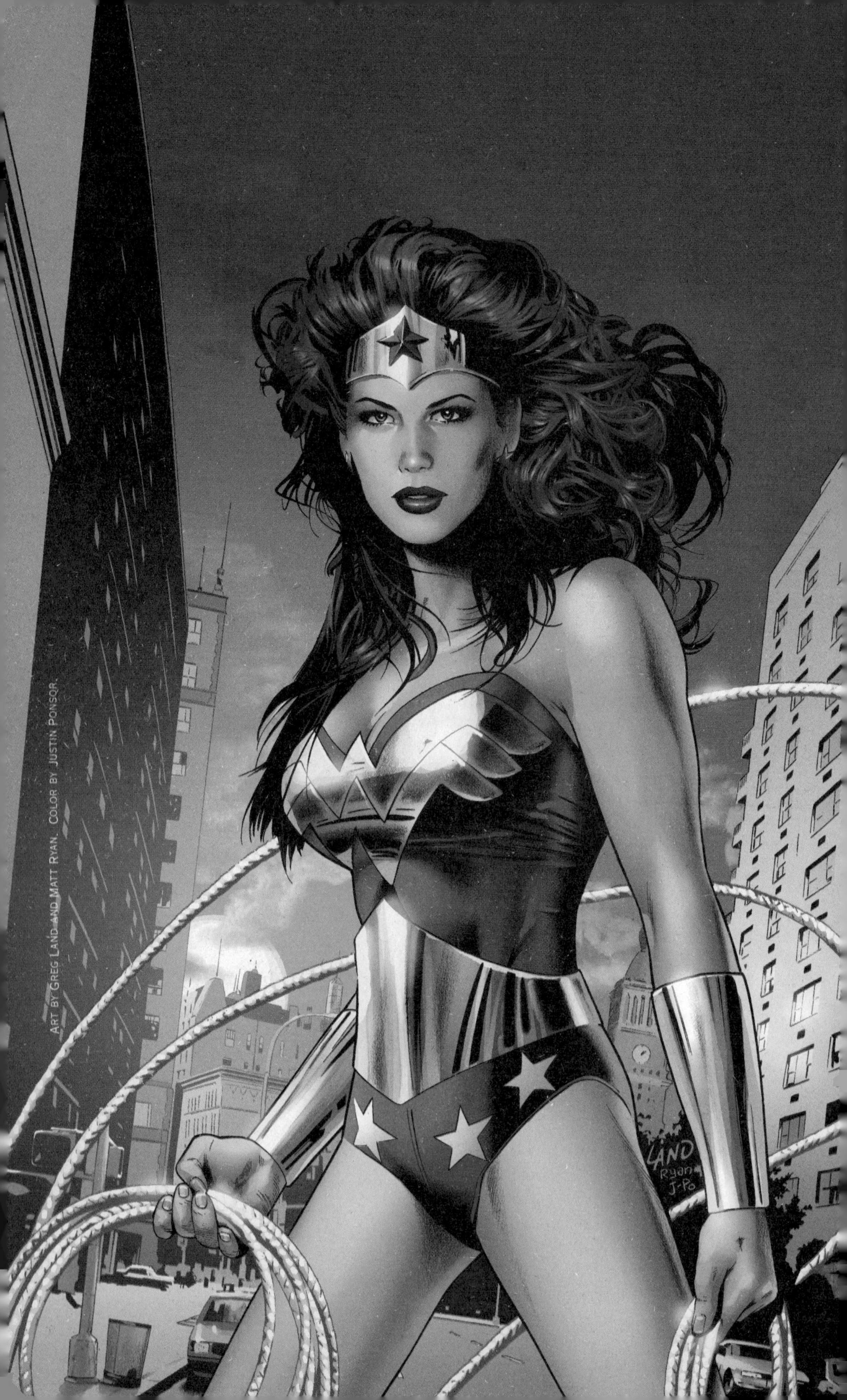
LAND
Ryan
J-Po

ART BY GREG LAND AND MATT RYAN. COLOR BY JUSTIN PONSOR.

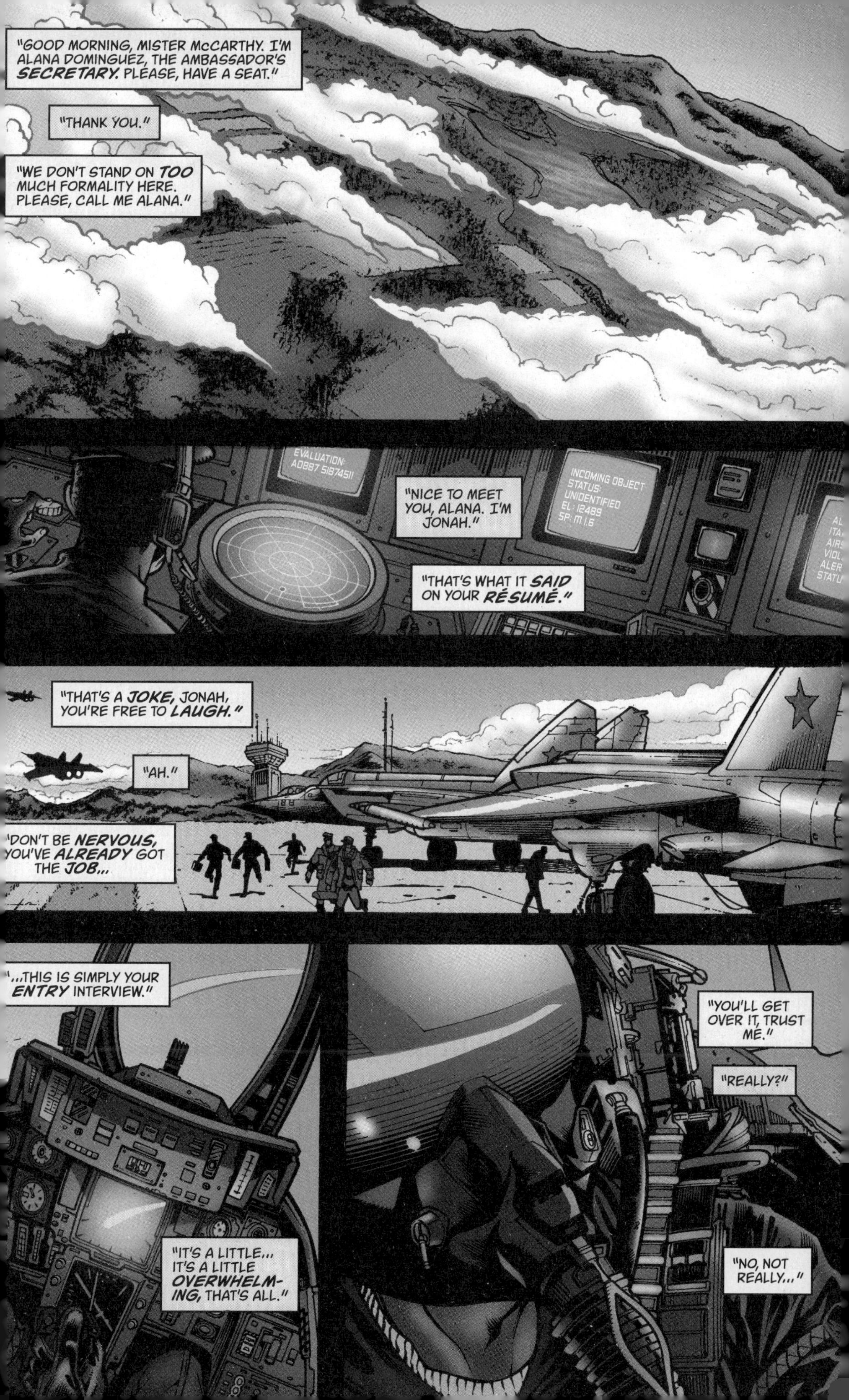
"GOOD MORNING, MISTER McCARTHY. I'M ALANA DOMINGUEZ, THE AMBASSADOR'S SECRETARY. PLEASE, HAVE A SEAT."
"THANK YOU."
"WE DON'T STAND ON TOO MUCH FORMALITY HERE. PLEASE, CALL ME ALANA."
EVALUATION:
"NICE TO MEET YOU, ALANA. I'M JONAH."
INCOMING OBJECT STATUS: UNIDENTIFIED EL: 12489 SP: M 1.6
"THAT'S WHAT IT SAID ON YOUR RÉSUMÉ."
"THAT'S A JOKE, JONAH, YOU'RE FREE TO LAUGH."
"AH."
"DON'T BE NERVOUS, YOU'VE ALREADY GOT THE JOB...
"...THIS IS SIMPLY YOUR ENTRY INTERVIEW."
"IT'S A LITTLE... IT'S A LITTLE OVERWHELMING, THAT'S ALL."
"YOU'LL GET OVER IT, TRUST ME."
"REALLY?"
"NO, NOT REALLY..."

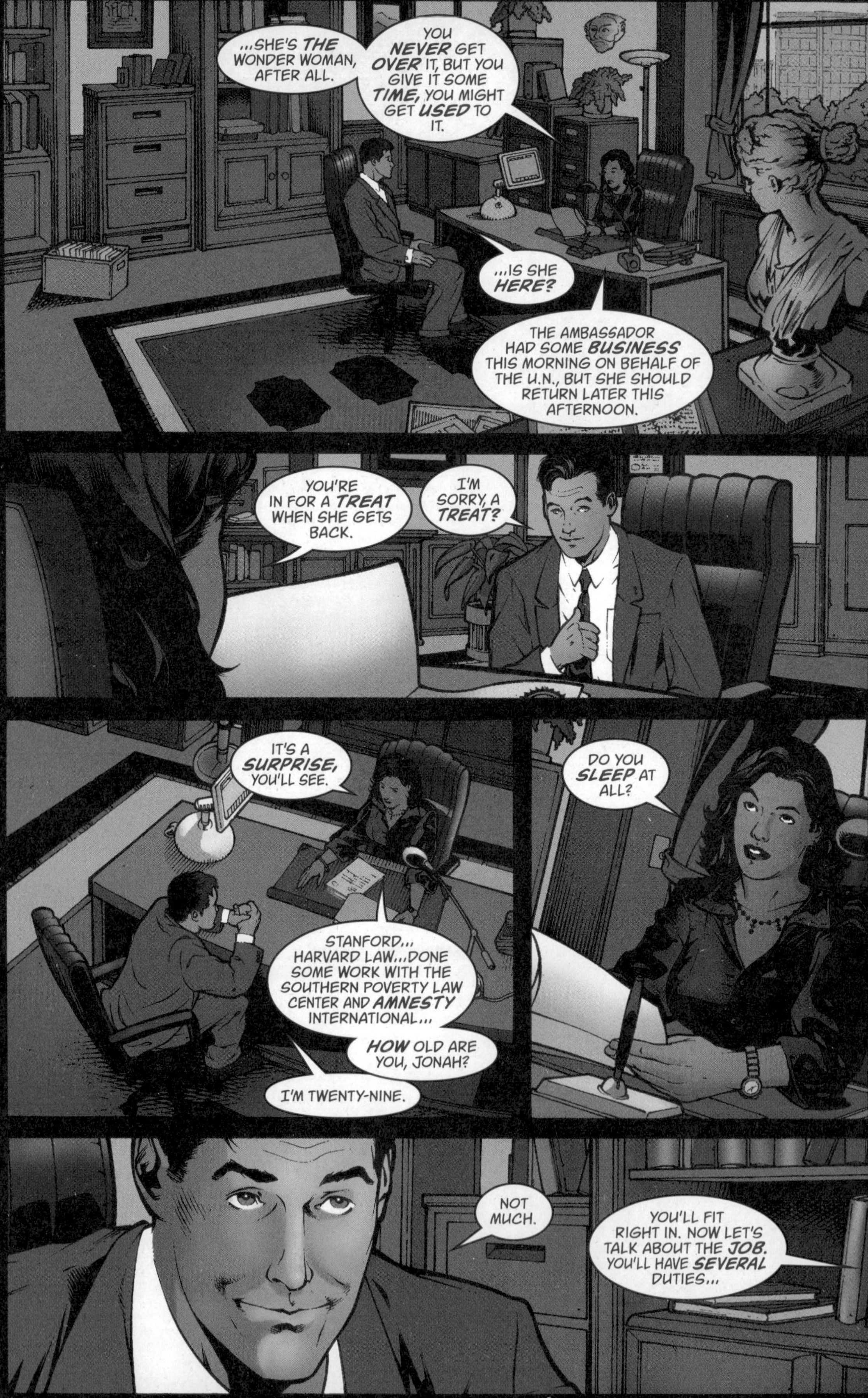
...SHE'S THE WONDER WOMAN, AFTER ALL.
YOU NEVER GET OVER IT, BUT YOU GIVE IT SOME TIME, YOU MIGHT GET USED TO IT.
...IS SHE HERE?
THE AMBASSADOR HAD SOME BUSINESS THIS MORNING ON BEHALF OF THE U.N., BUT SHE SHOULD RETURN LATER THIS AFTERNOON.
YOU'RE IN FOR A TREAT WHEN SHE GETS BACK.
I'M SORRY, A TREAT?
IT'S A SURPRISE, YOU'LL SEE.
STANFORD... HARVARD LAW...DONE SOME WORK WITH THE SOUTHERN POVERTY LAW CENTER AND AMNESTY INTERNATIONAL...
HOW OLD ARE YOU, JONAH?
I'M TWENTY-NINE.
DO YOU SLEEP AT ALL?
NOT MUCH.
YOU'LL FIT RIGHT IN. NOW LET'S TALK ABOUT THE JOB. YOU'LL HAVE SEVERAL DUTIES...

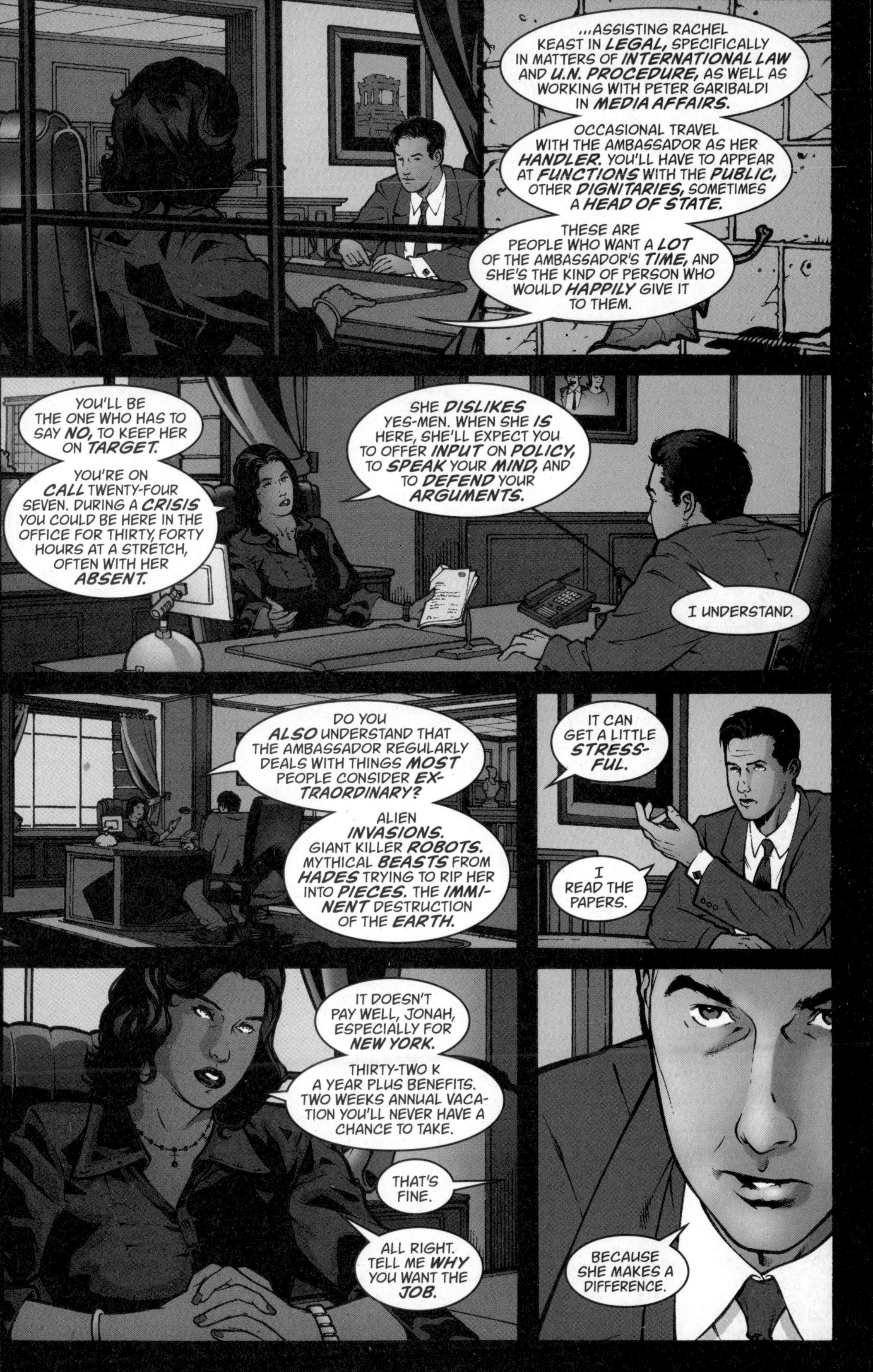
...ASSISTING RACHEL KEAST IN LEGAL, SPECIFICALLY IN MATTERS OF INTERNATIONAL LAW AND U.N. PROCEDURE, AS WELL AS WORKING WITH PETER GARIBALDI IN MEDIA AFFAIRS.
OCCASIONAL TRAVEL WITH THE AMBASSADOR AS HER HANDLER. YOU'LL HAVE TO APPEAR AT FUNCTIONS WITH THE PUBLIC, OTHER DIGNITARIES, SOMETIMES A HEAD OF STATE.
THESE ARE PEOPLE WHO WANT A LOT OF THE AMBASSADOR'S TIME, AND SHE'S THE KIND OF PERSON WHO WOULD HAPPILY GIVE IT TO THEM.
YOU'LL BE THE ONE WHO HAS TO SAY NO, TO KEEP HER ON TARGET.
YOU'RE ON CALL TWENTY-FOUR SEVEN. DURING A CRISIS YOU COULD BE HERE IN THE OFFICE FOR THIRTY, FORTY HOURS AT A STRETCH, OFTEN WITH HER ABSENT.
SHE DISLIKES YES-MEN. WHEN SHE IS HERE, SHE'LL EXPECT YOU TO OFFER INPUT ON POLICY, TO SPEAK YOUR MIND, AND TO DEFEND YOUR ARGUMENTS.
I UNDERSTAND.
DO YOU ALSO UNDERSTAND THAT THE AMBASSADOR REGULARLY DEALS WITH THINGS MOST PEOPLE CONSIDER EX-TRAORDINARY?
ALIEN INVASIONS. GIANT KILLER ROBOTS. MYTHICAL BEASTS FROM HADES TRYING TO RIP HER INTO PIECES. THE IMMI-NENT DESTRUCTION OF THE EARTH.
IT CAN GET A LITTLE STRESS-FUL.
I READ THE PAPERS.
IT DOESN'T PAY WELL, JONAH, ESPECIALLY FOR NEW YORK.
THIRTY-TWO K A YEAR PLUS BENEFITS. TWO WEEKS ANNUAL VACA-TION YOU'LL NEVER HAVE A CHANCE TO TAKE.
THAT'S FINE.
ALL RIGHT. TELL ME WHY YOU WANT THE JOB.
BECAUSE SHE MAKES A DIFFERENCE.

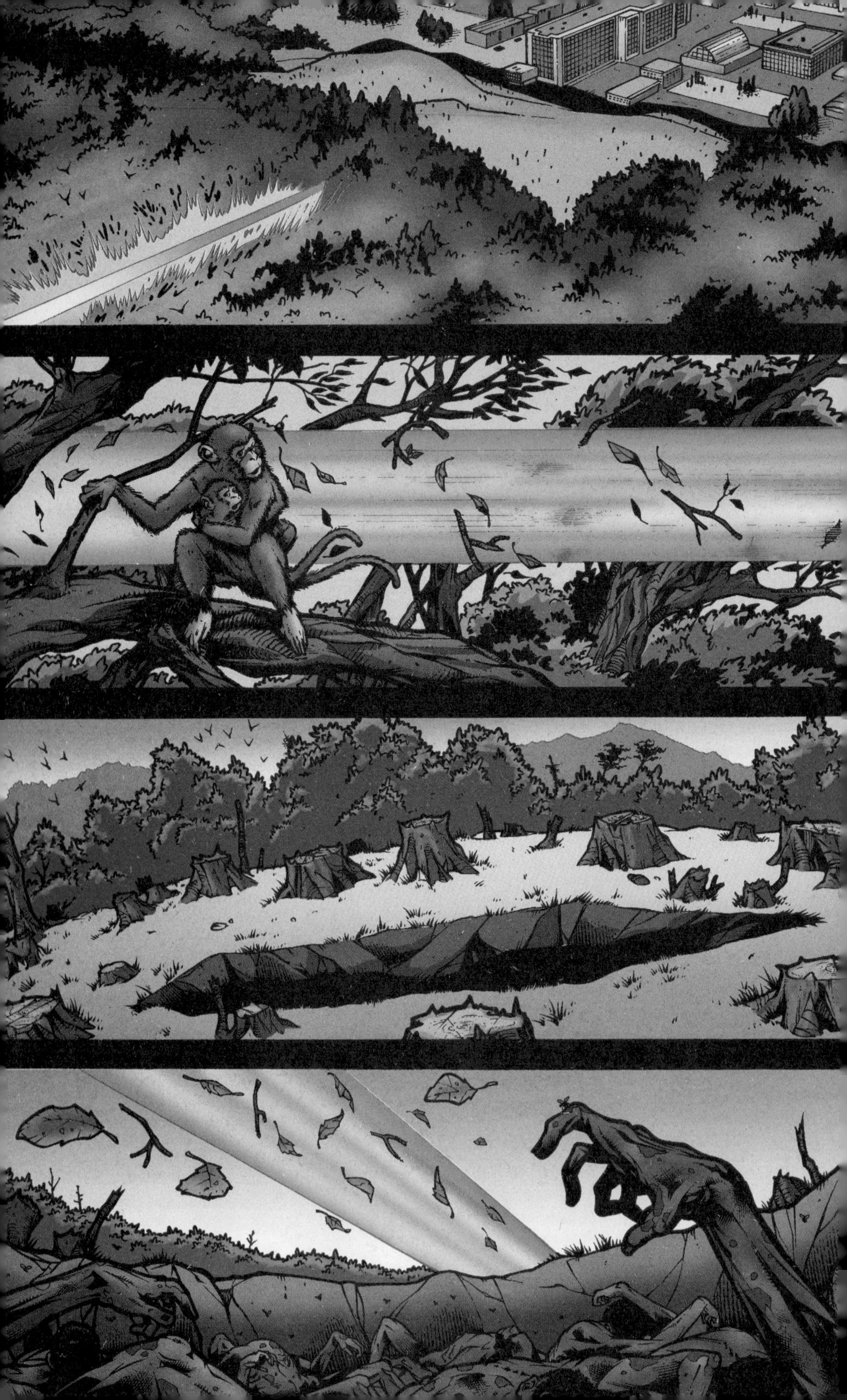

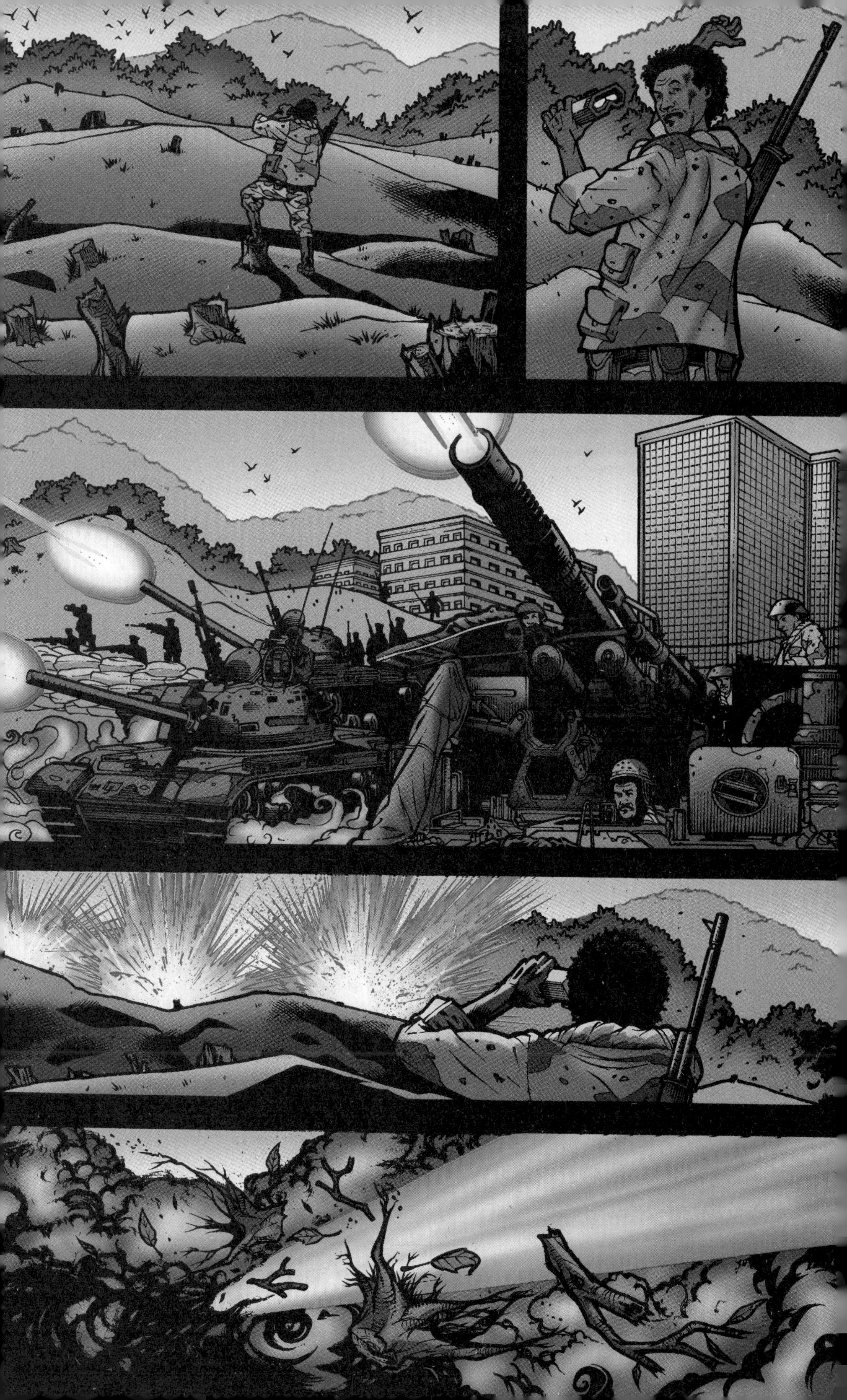

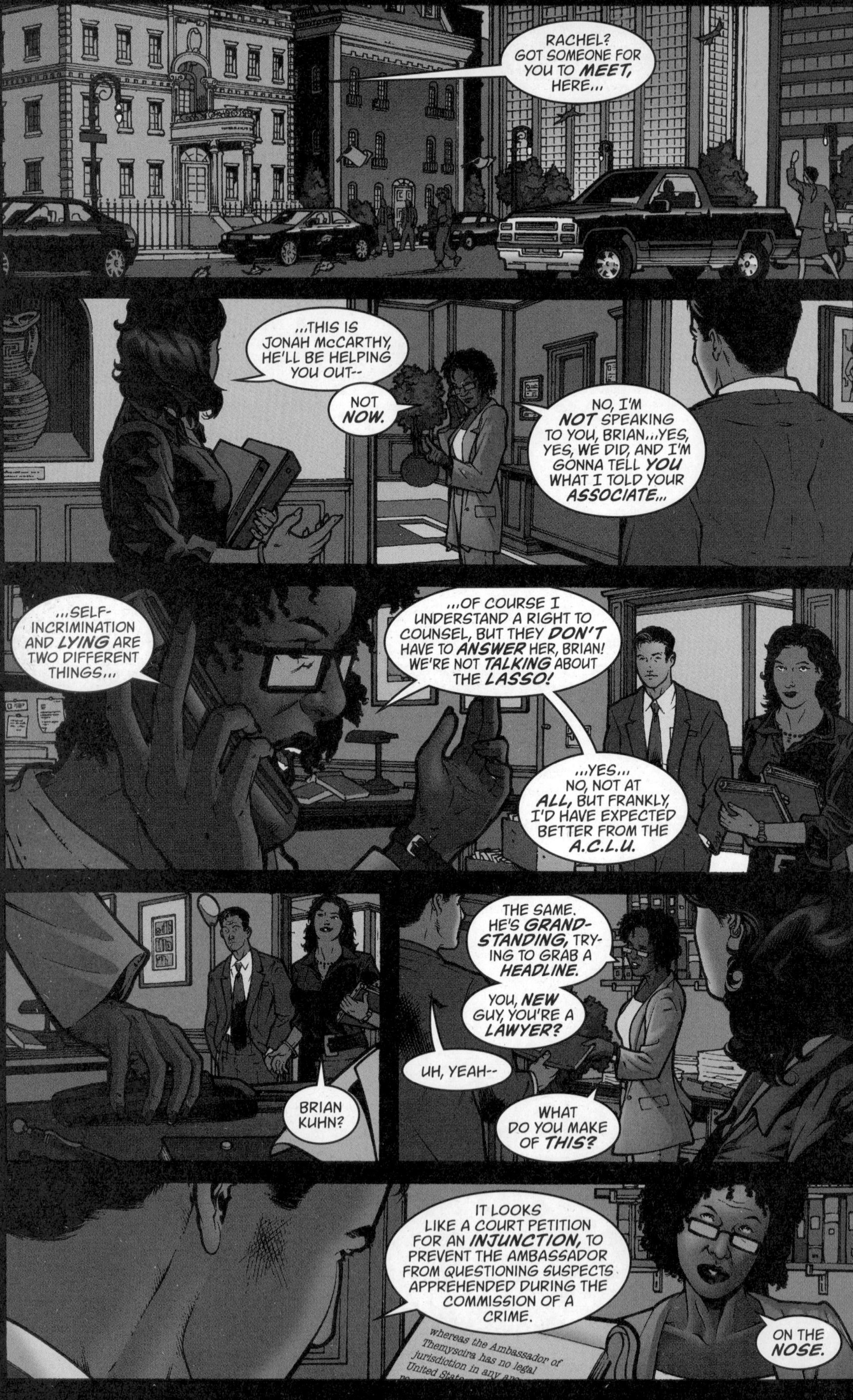

RACHEL? GOT SOMEONE FOR YOU TO MEET, HERE...
...THIS IS JONAH McCARTHY, HE'LL BE HELPING YOU OUT--
NOT NOW.
NO, I'M NOT SPEAKING TO YOU, BRIAN...YES, YES, WE DID, AND I'M GONNA TELL YOU WHAT I TOLD YOUR ASSOCIATE...
...SELF-INCRIMINATION AND LYING ARE TWO DIFFERENT THINGS...
...OF COURSE I UNDERSTAND A RIGHT TO COUNSEL, BUT THEY DON'T HAVE TO ANSWER HER, BRIAN! WE'RE NOT TALKING ABOUT THE LASSO!
...YES... NO, NOT AT ALL, BUT FRANKLY, I'D HAVE EXPECTED BETTER FROM THE A.C.L.U.
BRIAN KUHN?
THE SAME. HE'S GRAND-STANDING, TRY-ING TO GRAB A HEADLINE.
YOU, NEW GUY, YOU'RE A LAWYER?
UH, YEAH--
WHAT DO YOU MAKE OF THIS?
IT LOOKS LIKE A COURT PETITION FOR AN INJUNCTION, TO PREVENT THE AMBASSADOR FROM QUESTIONING SUSPECTS APPREHENDED DURING THE COMMISSION OF A CRIME.
whereas the Ambassador of
Themyscira has no legal
jurisdiction in any
ON THE NOSE.

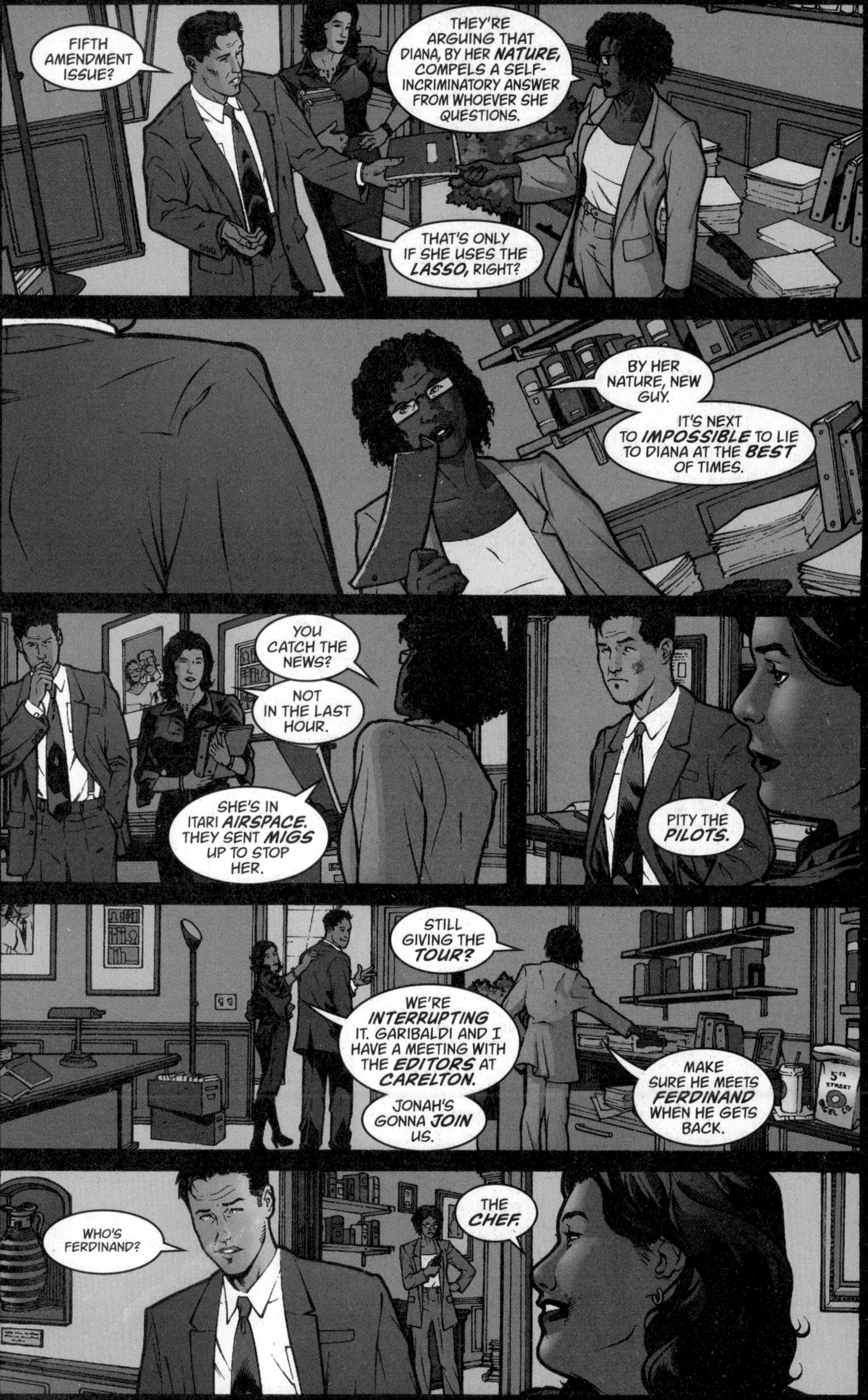
FIFTH AMENDMENT ISSUE?
THEY'RE ARGUING THAT DIANA, BY HER NATURE, COMPELS A SELF-INCRIMINATORY ANSWER FROM WHOEVER SHE QUESTIONS.
THAT'S ONLY IF SHE USES THE LASSO, RIGHT?
BY HER NATURE, NEW GUY.
IT'S NEXT TO IMPOSSIBLE TO LIE TO DIANA AT THE BEST OF TIMES.
YOU CATCH THE NEWS?
NOT IN THE LAST HOUR.
SHE'S IN ITARI AIRSPACE. THEY SENT MIGS UP TO STOP HER.
PITY THE PILOTS.
STILL GIVING THE TOUR?
WE'RE INTERRUPTING IT. GARIBALDI AND I HAVE A MEETING WITH THE EDITORS AT CARELTON.
JONAH'S GONNA JOIN US.
MAKE SURE HE MEETS FERDINAND WHEN HE GETS BACK.
5TH STREET BAGEL CO.
WHO'S FERDINAND?
THE CHEF.

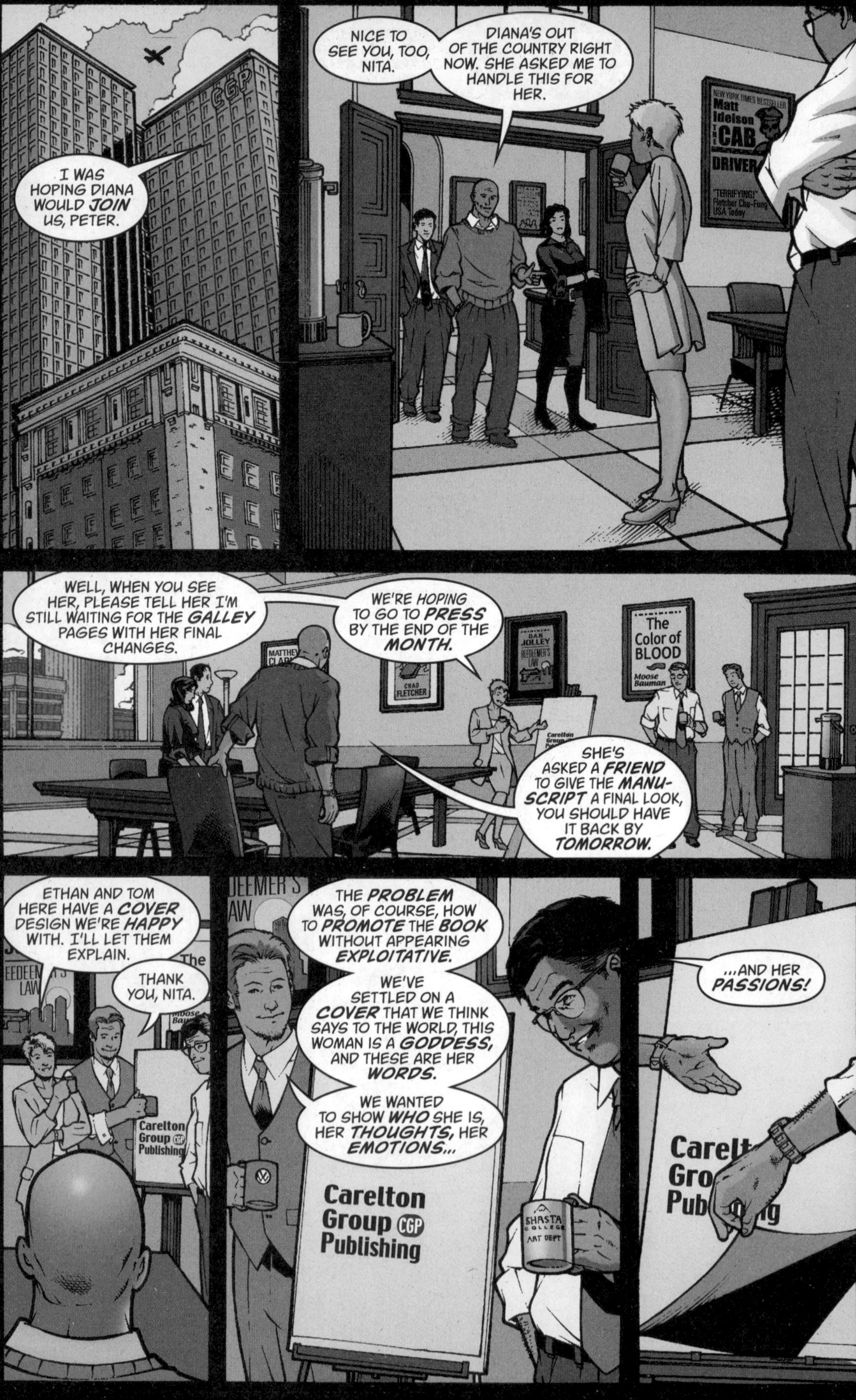
I WAS HOPING DIANA WOULD JOIN US, PETER.
NICE TO SEE YOU, TOO, NITA.
DIANA'S OUT OF THE COUNTRY RIGHT NOW. SHE ASKED ME TO HANDLE THIS FOR HER.
NEW YORK TIMES BESTSELLER Matt Idelson THE CAB DRIVER "TERRIFYING!" Fletcher Chu-Fong USA Today
WELL, WHEN YOU SEE HER, PLEASE TELL HER I'M STILL WAITING FOR THE GALLEY PAGES WITH HER FINAL CHANGES.
WE'RE HOPING TO GO TO PRESS BY THE END OF THE MONTH.
CHAD FLETCHER
DAN JOLLEY REDEEMER'S LAW
The Color of BLOOD Moose Bauman
SHE'S ASKED A FRIEND TO GIVE THE MANU-SCRIPT A FINAL LOOK, YOU SHOULD HAVE IT BACK BY TOMORROW.
ETHAN AND TOM HERE HAVE A COVER DESIGN WE'RE HAPPY WITH. I'LL LET THEM EXPLAIN.
THANK YOU, NITA.
Carelton Group CGP Publishing
THE PROBLEM WAS, OF COURSE, HOW TO PROMOTE THE BOOK WITHOUT APPEARING EXPLOITATIVE.
WE'VE SETTLED ON A COVER THAT WE THINK SAYS TO THE WORLD, THIS WOMAN IS A GODDESS, AND THESE ARE HER WORDS.
WE WANTED TO SHOW WHO SHE IS, HER THOUGHTS, HER EMOTIONS...
Carelton Group CGP Publishing
...AND HER PASSIONS!
SHASTA COLLEGE ART DEPT

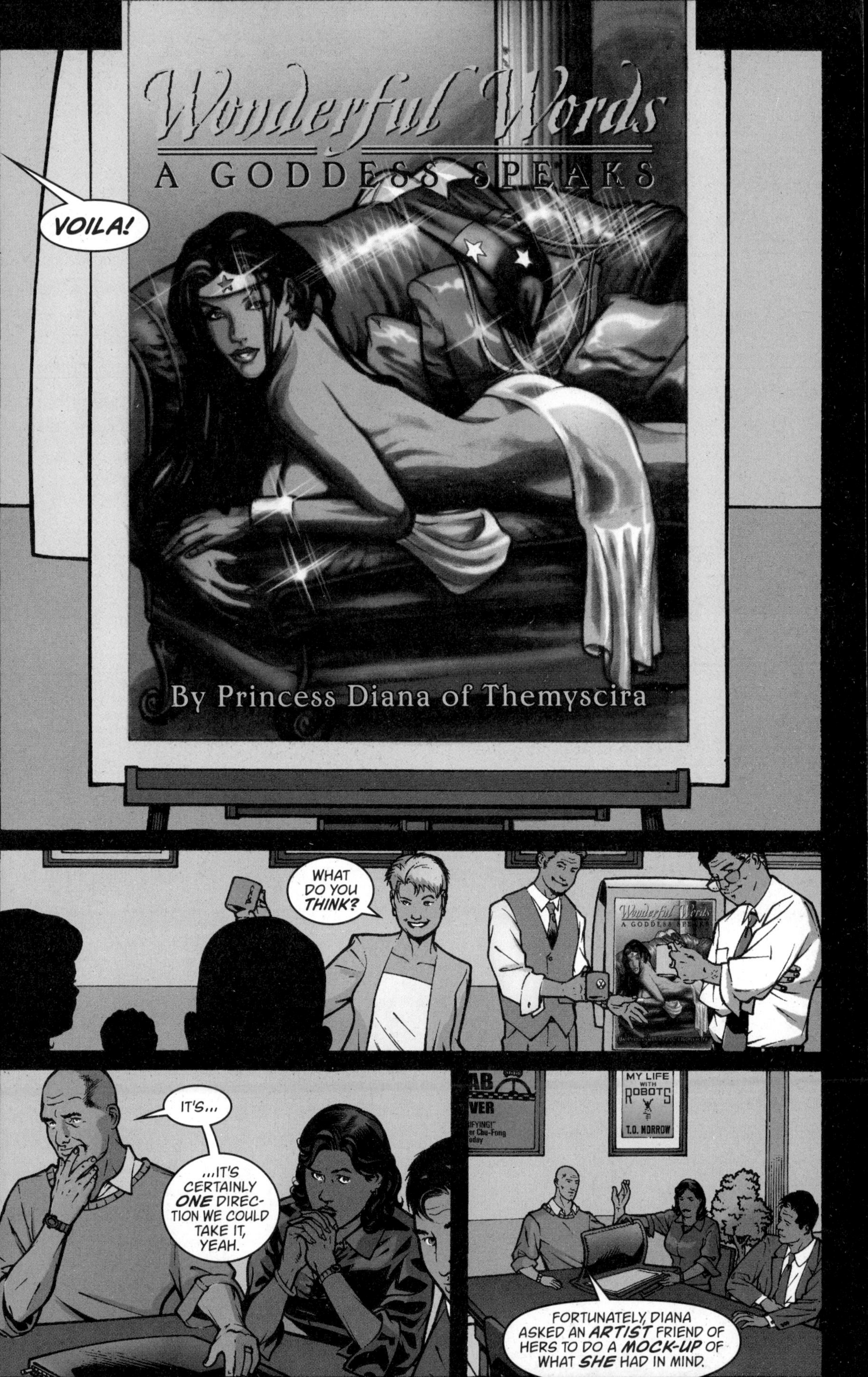
Wonderful Words
A GODDESS SPEAKS
VOILA!
By Princess Diana of Themyscira
WHAT DO YOU THINK?
Wonderful Words
A GODDESS SPEAKS
IT'S...
...IT'S CERTAINLY ONE DIRECTION WE COULD TAKE IT, YEAH.
MY LIFE WITH ROBOTS
T.O. MORROW
FORTUNATELY, DIANA ASKED AN ARTIST FRIEND OF HERS TO DO A MOCK-UP OF WHAT SHE HAD IN MIND.

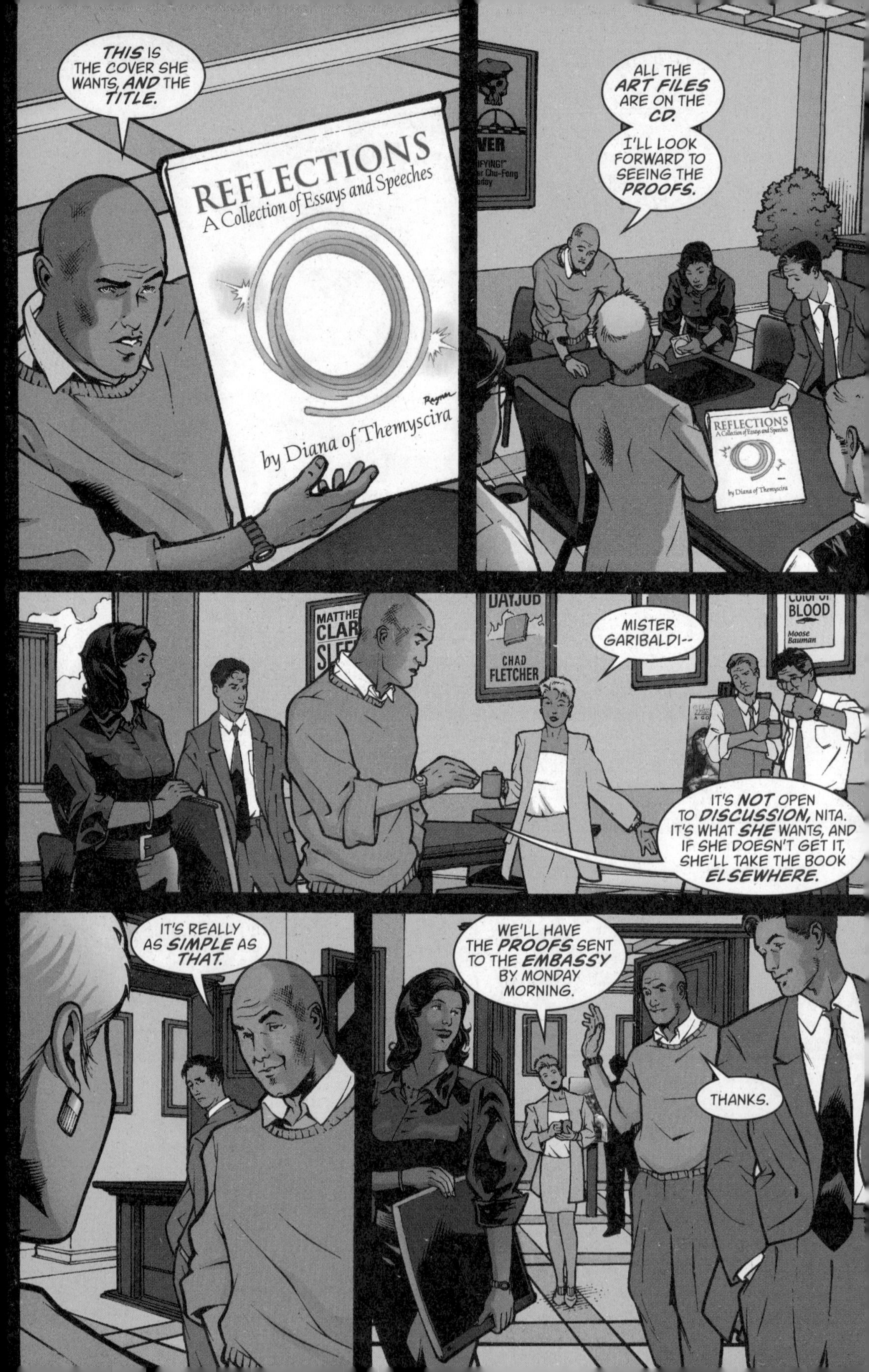
THIS IS THE COVER SHE WANTS, AND THE TITLE.
REFLECTIONS
A Collection of Essays and Speeches
by Diana of Themyscira
ALL THE ART FILES ARE ON THE CD.
I'LL LOOK FORWARD TO SEEING THE PROOFS.
DAYJOB
CHAD FLETCHER
BLOOD
Moose Bauman
MISTER GARIBALDI--
IT'S NOT OPEN TO DISCUSSION, NITA. IT'S WHAT SHE WANTS, AND IF SHE DOESN'T GET IT, SHE'LL TAKE THE BOOK ELSEWHERE.
IT'S REALLY AS SIMPLE AS THAT.
WE'LL HAVE THE PROOFS SENT TO THE EMBASSY BY MONDAY MORNING.
THANKS.

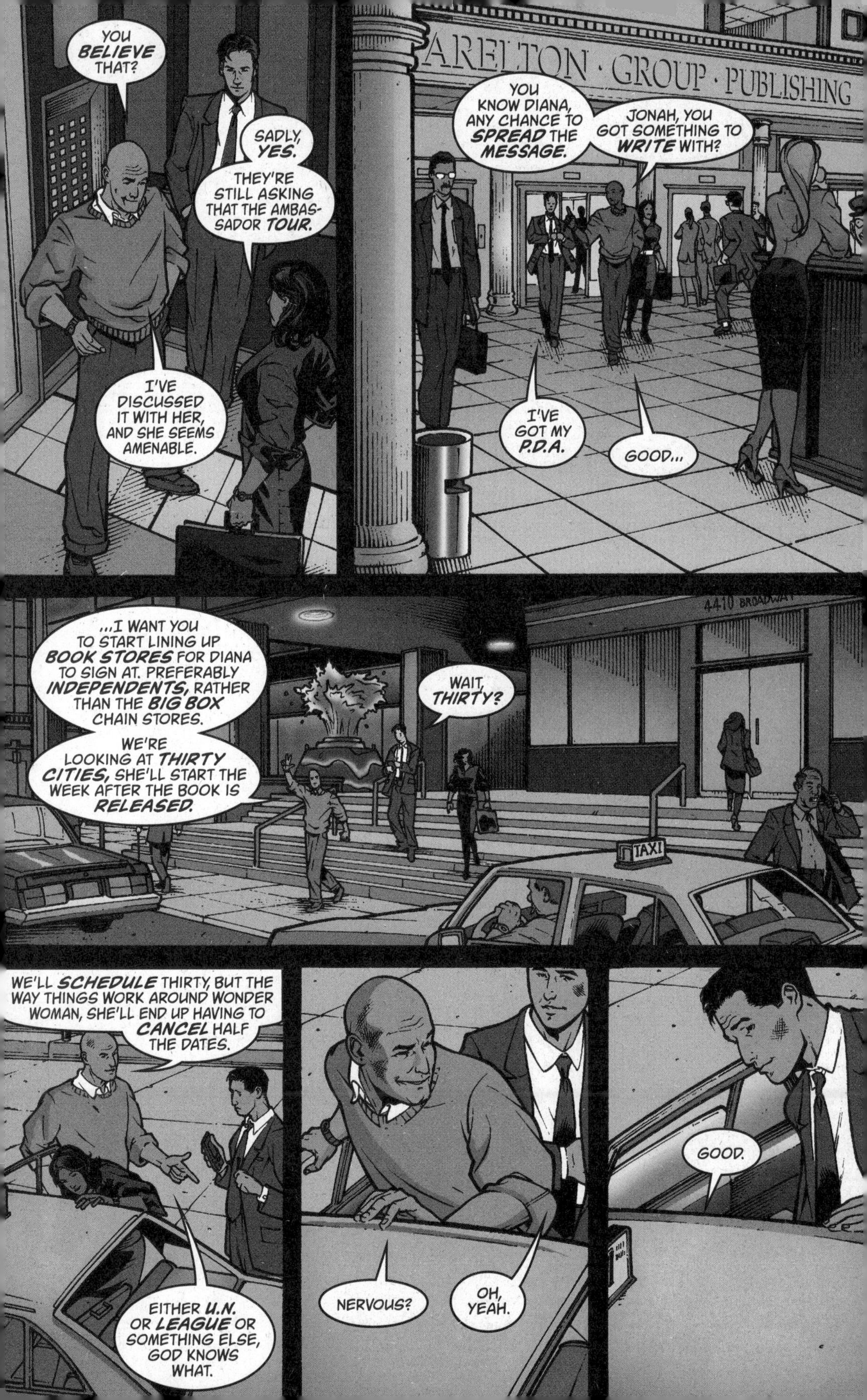

YOU BELIEVE THAT?
SADLY, YES.
THEY'RE STILL ASKING THAT THE AMBASSADOR TOUR.
I'VE DISCUSSED IT WITH HER, AND SHE SEEMS AMENABLE.
ARELTON · GROUP · PUBLISHING
YOU KNOW DIANA, ANY CHANCE TO SPREAD THE MESSAGE.
JONAH, YOU GOT SOMETHING TO WRITE WITH?
I'VE GOT MY P.D.A.
GOOD...
4410 BROADWAY
...I WANT YOU TO START LINING UP BOOK STORES FOR DIANA TO SIGN AT. PREFERABLY INDEPENDENTS, RATHER THAN THE BIG BOX CHAIN STORES.
WE'RE LOOKING AT THIRTY CITIES, SHE'LL START THE WEEK AFTER THE BOOK IS RELEASED.
WAIT, THIRTY?
TAXI
WE'LL SCHEDULE THIRTY, BUT THE WAY THINGS WORK AROUND WONDER WOMAN, SHE'LL END UP HAVING TO CANCEL HALF THE DATES.
EITHER U.N. OR LEAGUE OR SOMETHING ELSE, GOD KNOWS WHAT.
NERVOUS?
OH, YEAH.
GOOD.

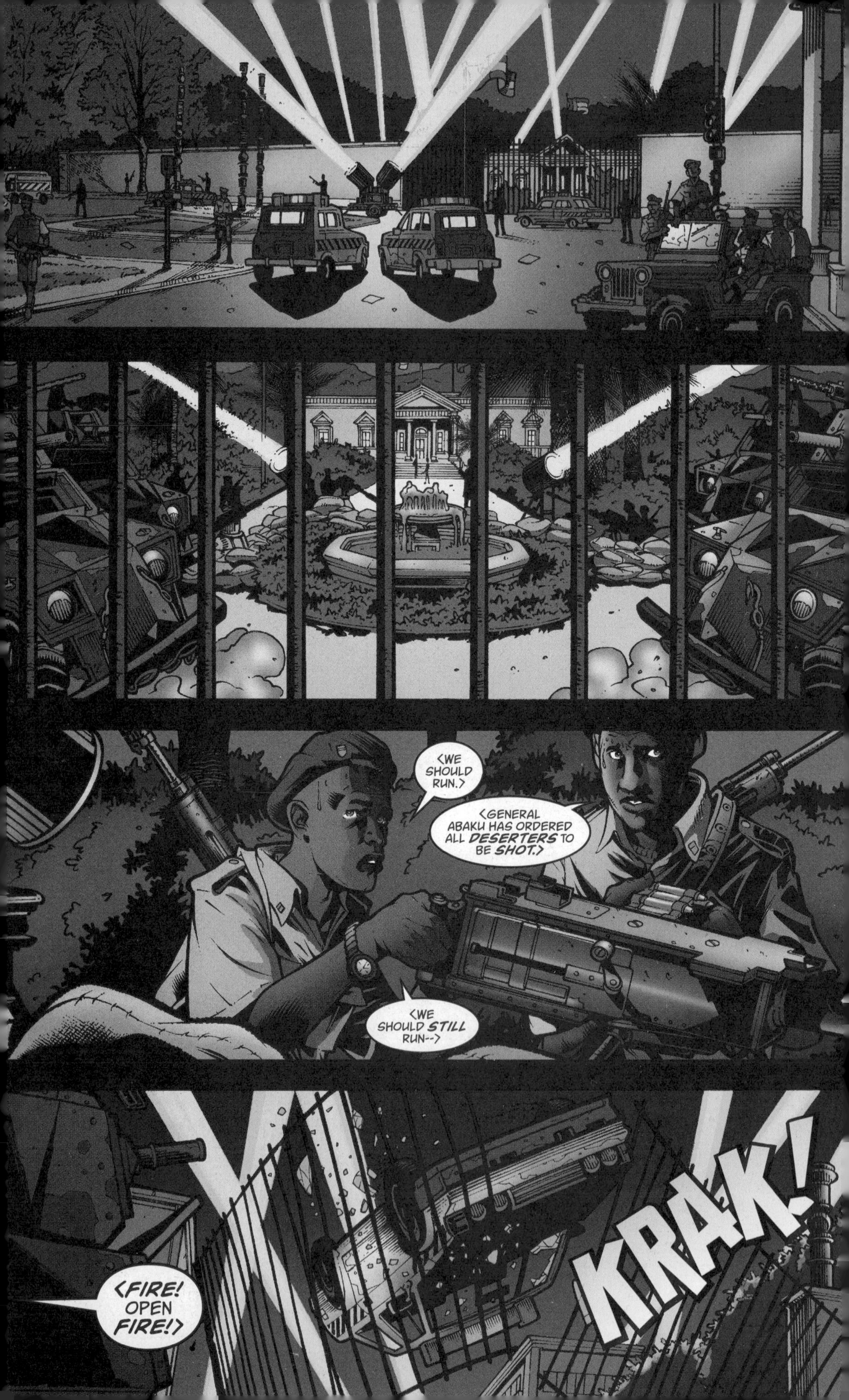
<WE SHOULD RUN.>
<GENERAL ABAKU HAS ORDERED ALL DESERTERS TO BE SHOT.>
<WE SHOULD STILL RUN-->
<FIRE! OPEN FIRE!>
KRAK!

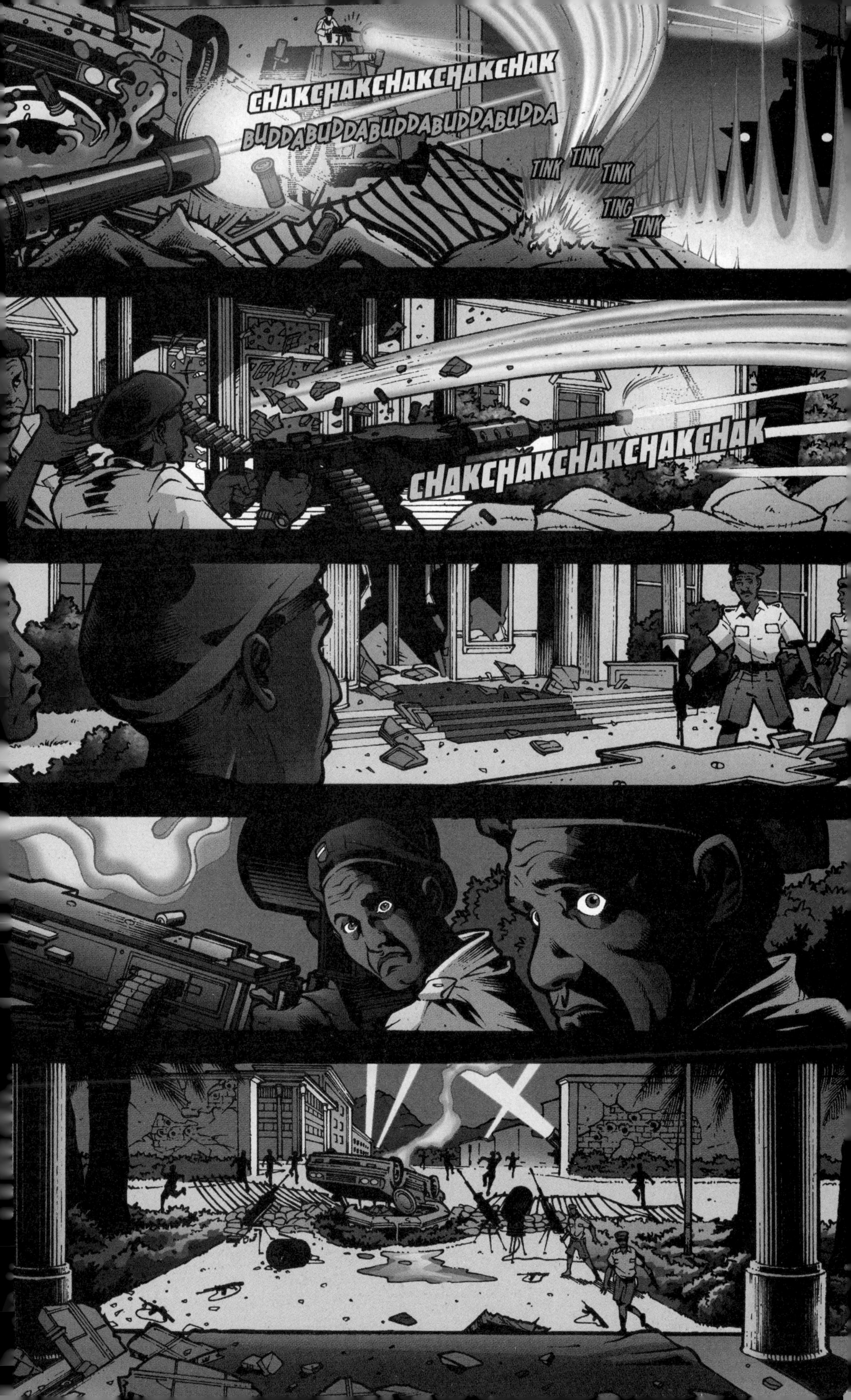
CHAKCHAKCHAKCHAKCHAK
BUDDABUDDABUDDABUDDABUDDA
TINK
TINK
TINK
TING
TINK
CHAKCHAKCHAKCHAKCHAK

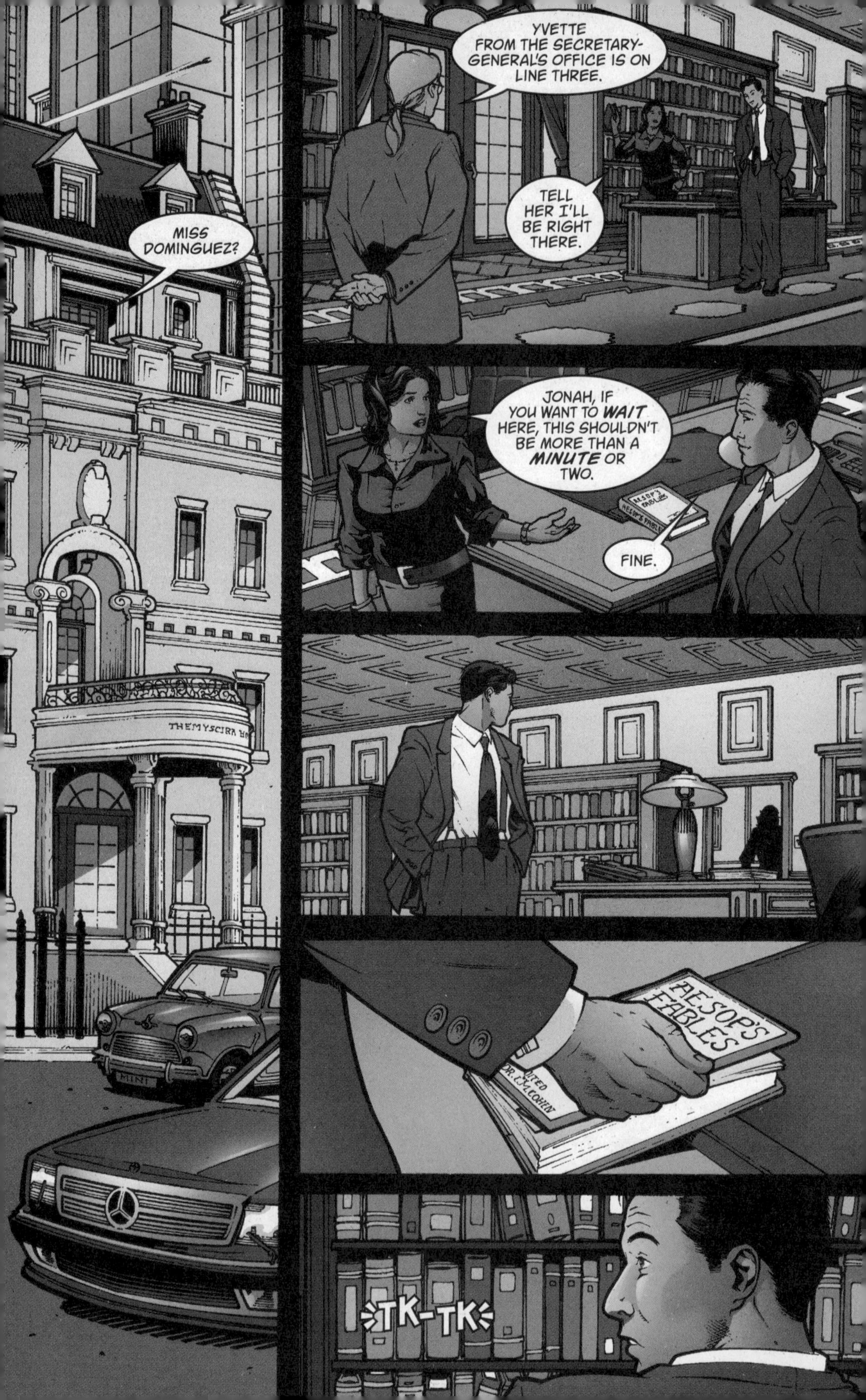
MISS DOMINGUEZ?
THEMYSCIRA
YVETTE FROM THE SECRETARY-GENERAL'S OFFICE IS ON LINE THREE.
TELL HER I'LL BE RIGHT THERE.
JONAH, IF YOU WANT TO WAIT HERE, THIS SHOULDN'T BE MORE THAN A MINUTE OR TWO.
FINE.
AESOP'S FABLES
TK-TK

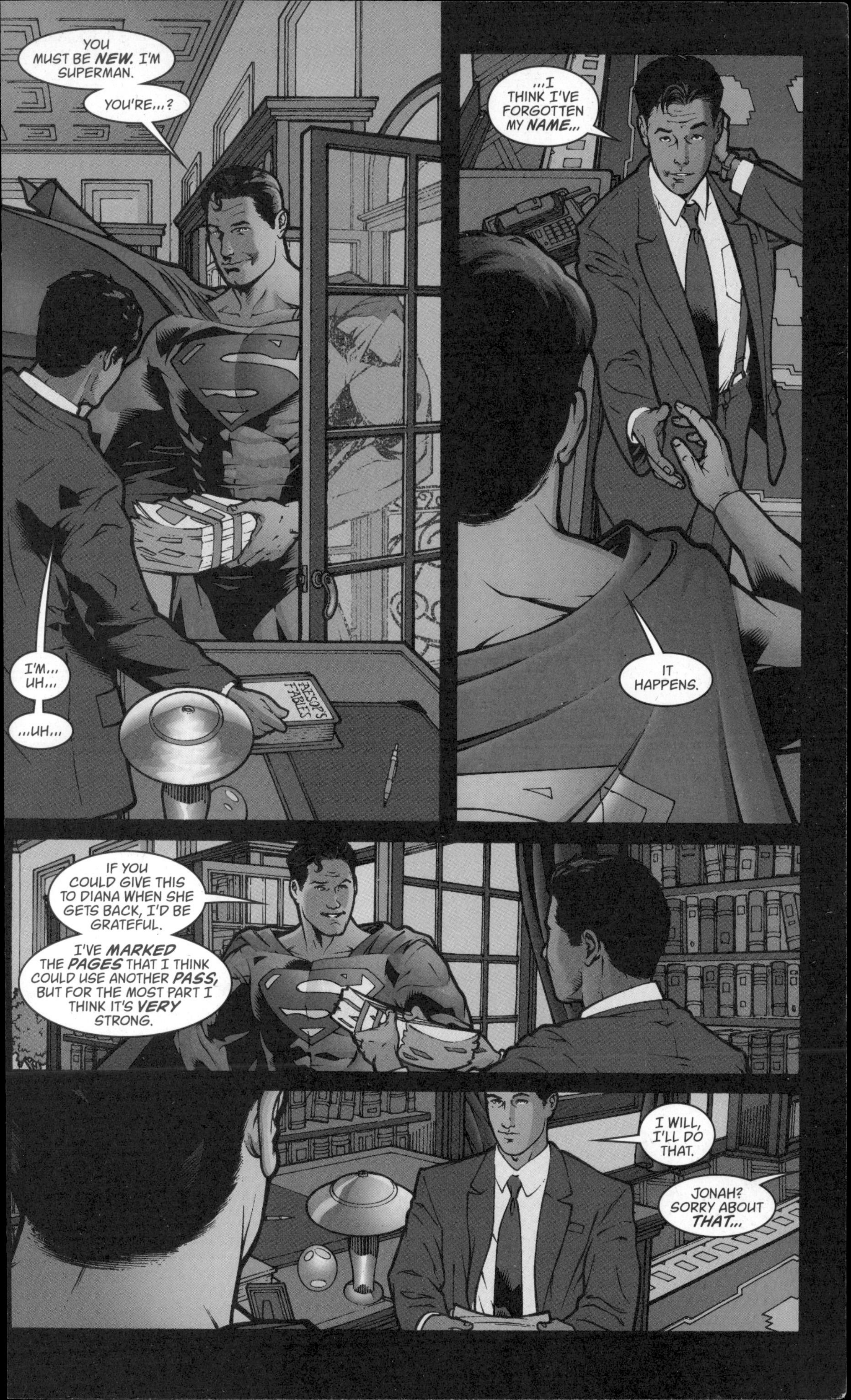
YOU MUST BE NEW. I'M SUPERMAN.
YOU'RE...?
I'M... UH...
...UH...
AESOP'S FABLES
...I THINK I'VE FORGOTTEN MY NAME...
IT HAPPENS.
IF YOU COULD GIVE THIS TO DIANA WHEN SHE GETS BACK, I'D BE GRATEFUL.
I'VE MARKED THE PAGES THAT I THINK COULD USE ANOTHER PASS, BUT FOR THE MOST PART I THINK IT'S VERY STRONG.
I WILL, I'LL DO THAT.
JONAH? SORRY ABOUT THAT...

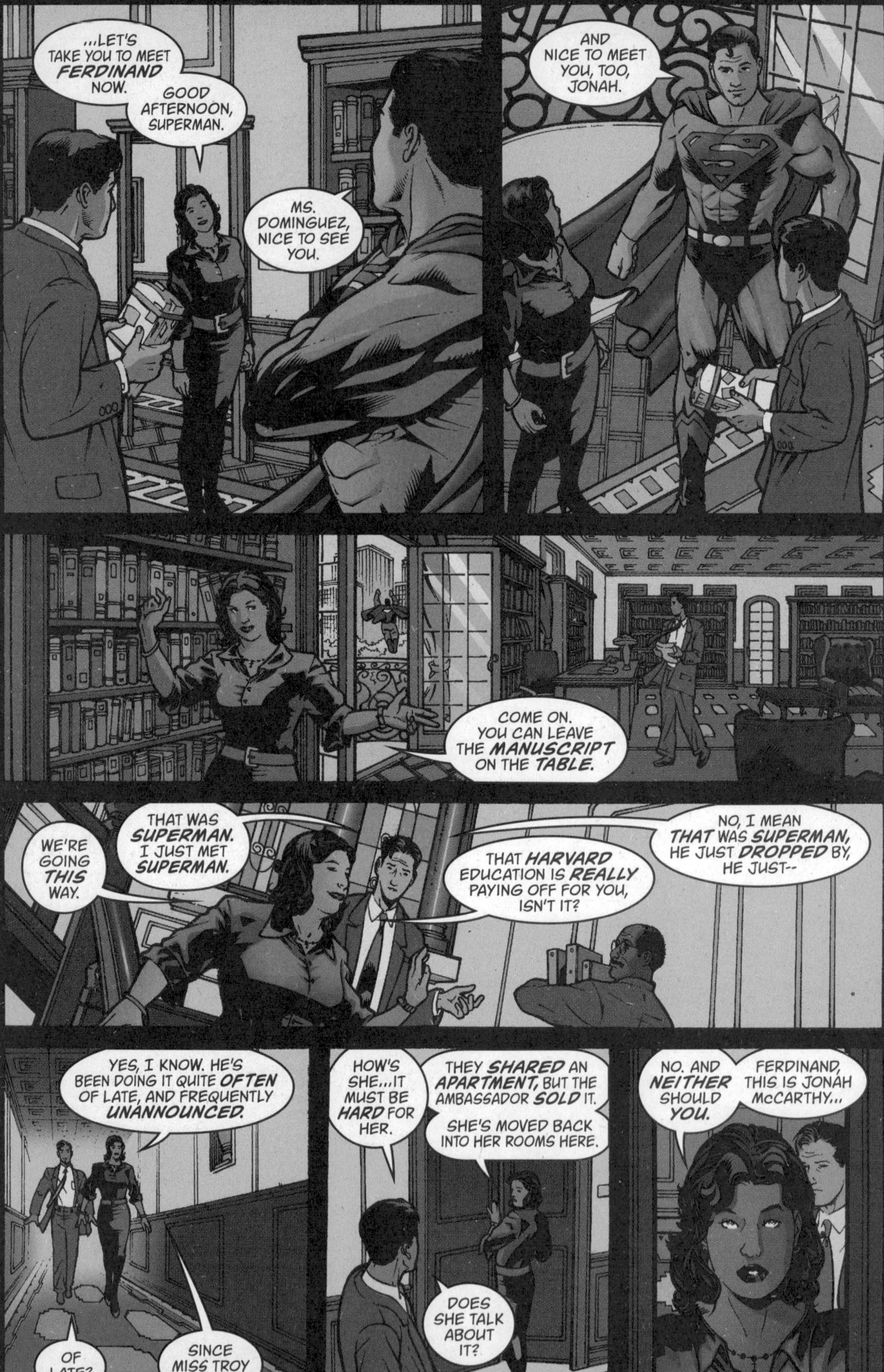
...LET'S TAKE YOU TO MEET FERDINAND NOW.
GOOD AFTERNOON, SUPERMAN.
MS. DOMINGUEZ, NICE TO SEE YOU.
AND NICE TO MEET YOU, TOO, JONAH.
COME ON. YOU CAN LEAVE THE MANUSCRIPT ON THE TABLE.
WE'RE GOING THIS WAY.
THAT WAS SUPERMAN. I JUST MET SUPERMAN.
THAT HARVARD EDUCATION IS REALLY PAYING OFF FOR YOU, ISN'T IT?
NO, I MEAN THAT WAS SUPERMAN, HE JUST DROPPED BY, HE JUST--
YES, I KNOW. HE'S BEEN DOING IT QUITE OFTEN OF LATE, AND FREQUENTLY UNANNOUNCED.
OF LATE?
SINCE MISS TROY DIED.
HOW'S SHE...IT MUST BE HARD FOR HER.
THEY SHARED AN APARTMENT, BUT THE AMBASSADOR SOLD IT.
SHE'S MOVED BACK INTO HER ROOMS HERE.
DOES SHE TALK ABOUT IT?
NO. AND NEITHER SHOULD YOU.
FERDINAND, THIS IS JONAH McCARTHY...

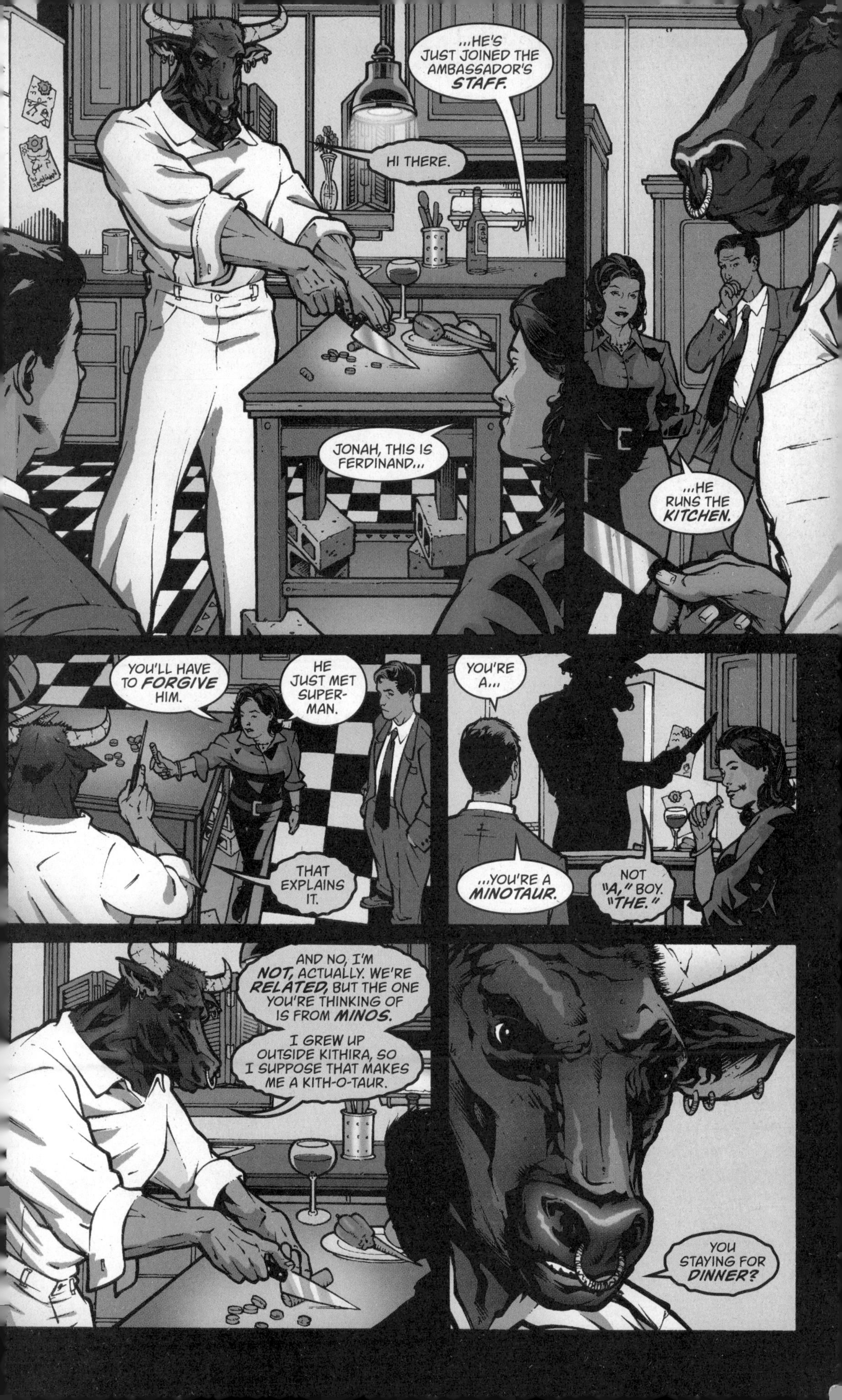
...HE'S JUST JOINED THE AMBASSADOR'S STAFF.
HI THERE.
JONAH, THIS IS FERDINAND...
...HE RUNS THE KITCHEN.
YOU'LL HAVE TO FORGIVE HIM.
HE JUST MET SUPER-MAN.
THAT EXPLAINS IT.
YOU'RE A...
...YOU'RE A MINOTAUR.
NOT "A," BOY. "THE."
AND NO, I'M NOT, ACTUALLY. WE'RE RELATED, BUT THE ONE YOU'RE THINKING OF IS FROM MINOS.
I GREW UP OUTSIDE KITHIRA, SO I SUPPOSE THAT MAKES ME A KITH-O-TAUR.
YOU STAYING FOR DINNER?

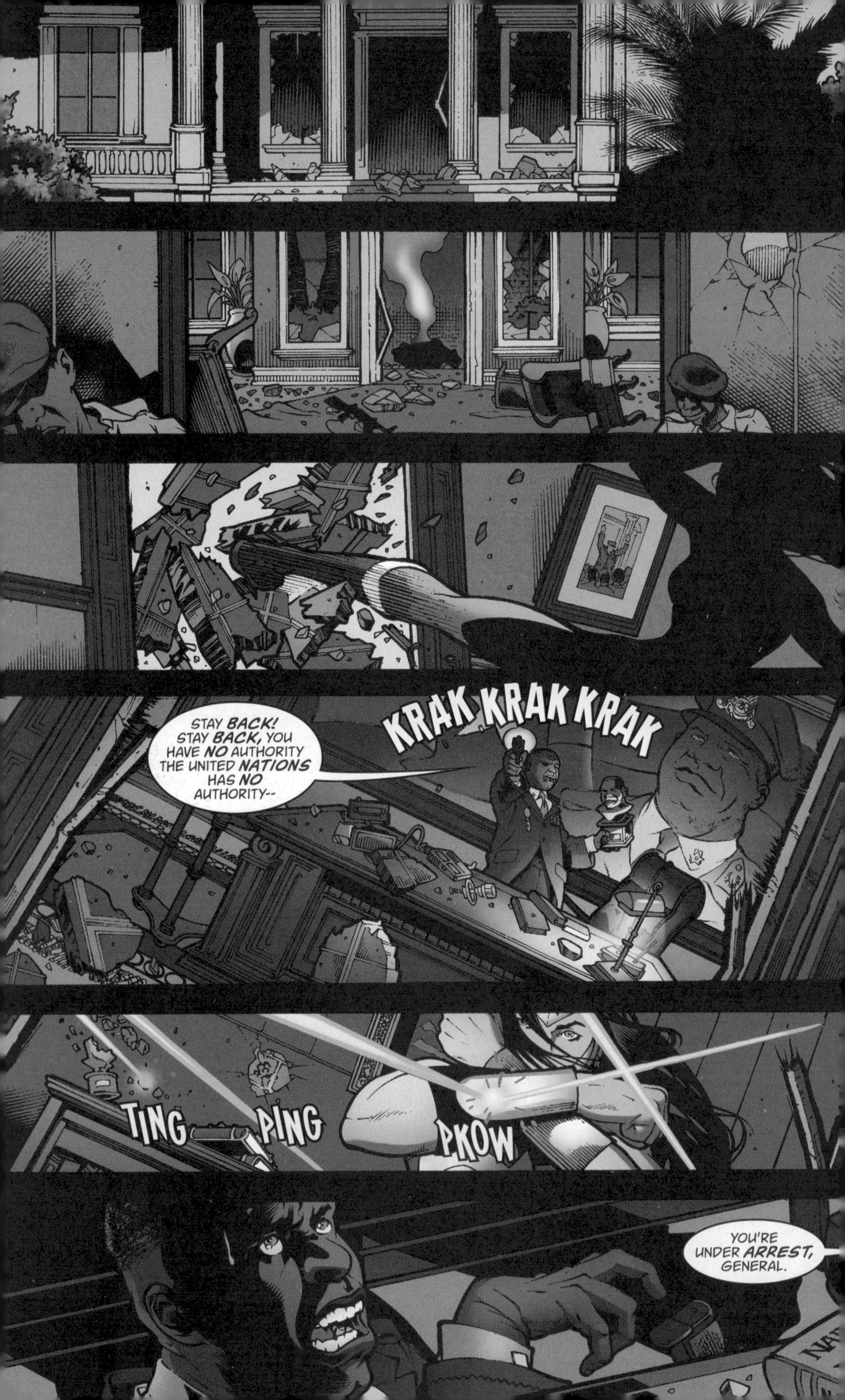
KRAK KRAK KRAK
STAY BACK! STAY BACK, YOU HAVE NO AUTHORITY THE UNITED NATIONS HAS NO AUTHORITY--
TING
PING
PKOW
YOU'RE UNDER ARREST, GENERAL.

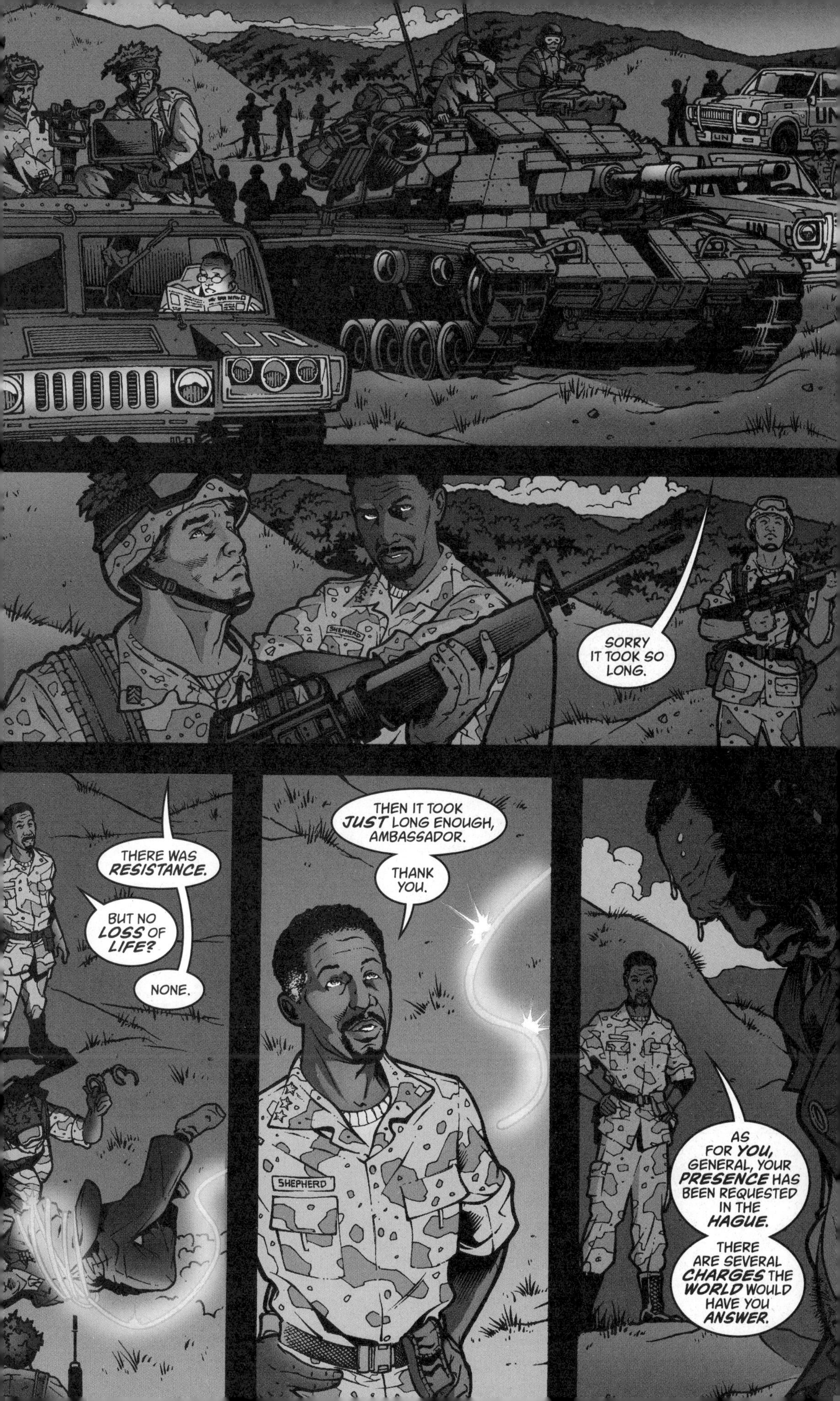
UN
UN
UN
UN
SHEPHERD
SORRY IT TOOK SO LONG.
THERE WAS RESISTANCE.
BUT NO LOSS OF LIFE?
NONE.
THEN IT TOOK JUST LONG ENOUGH, AMBASSADOR.
THANK YOU.
SHEPHERD
AS FOR YOU, GENERAL, YOUR PRESENCE HAS BEEN REQUESTED IN THE HAGUE.
THERE ARE SEVERAL CHARGES THE WORLD WOULD HAVE YOU ANSWER.

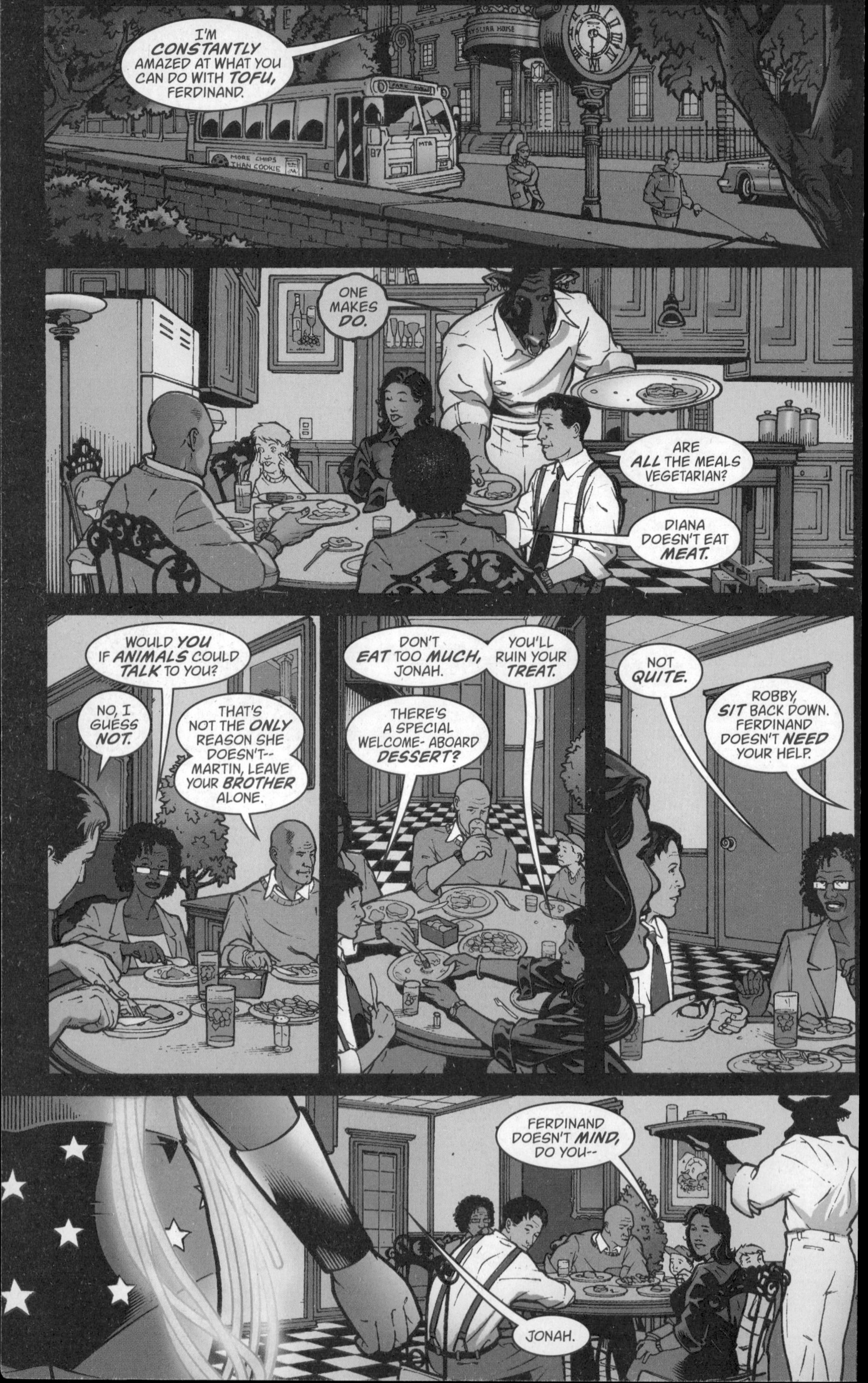
I'M CONSTANTLY AMAZED AT WHAT YOU CAN DO WITH TOFU, FERDINAND.
MORE CHIPS THAN COOKIE
ONE MAKES DO.
ARE ALL THE MEALS VEGETARIAN?
DIANA DOESN'T EAT MEAT.
WOULD YOU IF ANIMALS COULD TALK TO YOU?
NO, I GUESS NOT.
THAT'S NOT THE ONLY REASON SHE DOESN'T-- MARTIN, LEAVE YOUR BROTHER ALONE.
DON'T EAT TOO MUCH, JONAH.
YOU'LL RUIN YOUR TREAT.
THERE'S A SPECIAL WELCOME- ABOARD DESSERT?
NOT QUITE.
ROBBY, SIT BACK DOWN. FERDINAND DOESN'T NEED YOUR HELP.
FERDINAND DOESN'T MIND, DO YOU--
JONAH.

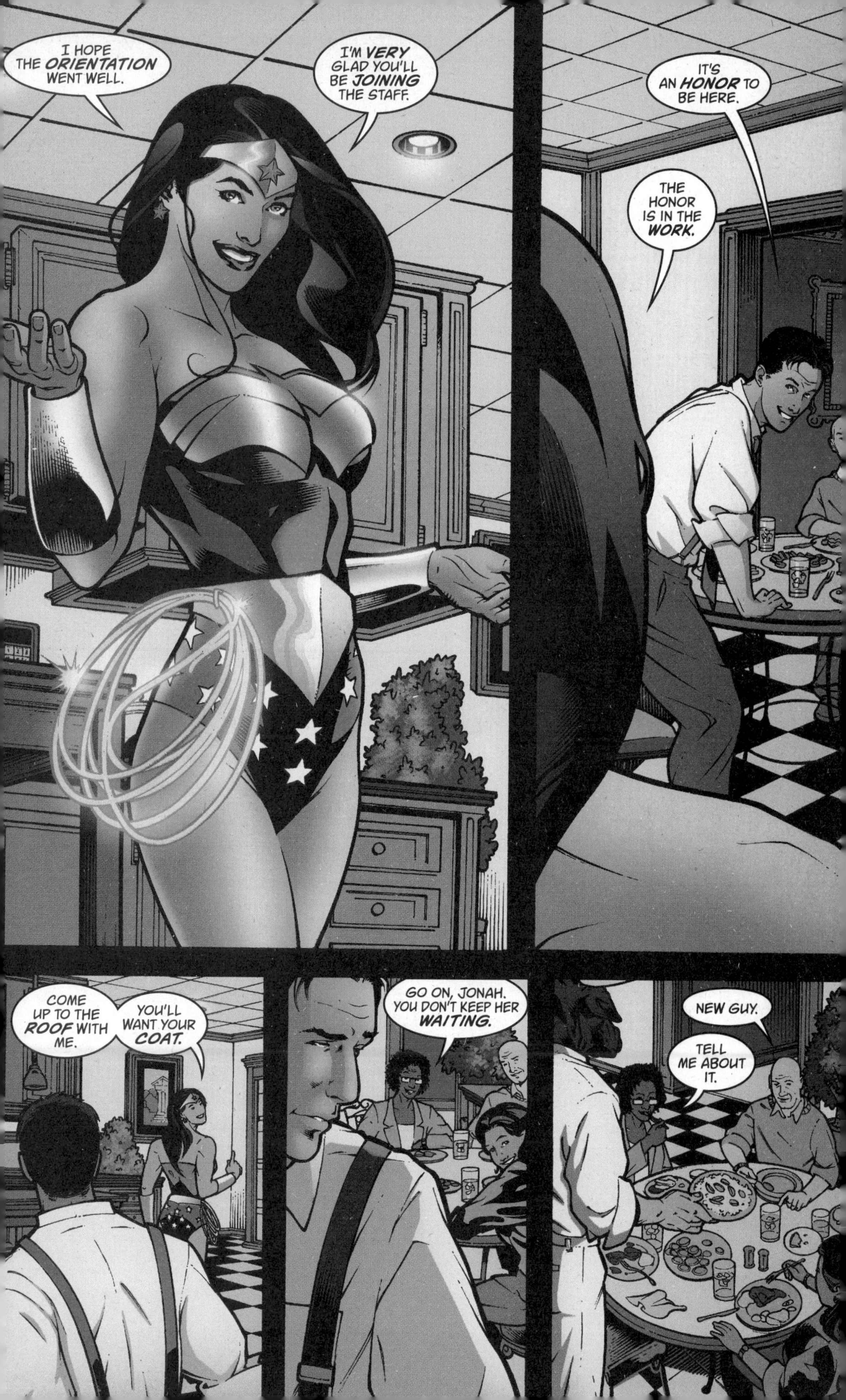
I HOPE THE ORIENTATION WENT WELL.
I'M VERY GLAD YOU'LL BE JOINING THE STAFF.
IT'S AN HONOR TO BE HERE.
THE HONOR IS IN THE WORK.
COME UP TO THE ROOF WITH ME.
YOU'LL WANT YOUR COAT.
GO ON, JONAH. YOU DON'T KEEP HER WAITING.
NEW GUY.
TELL ME ABOUT IT.

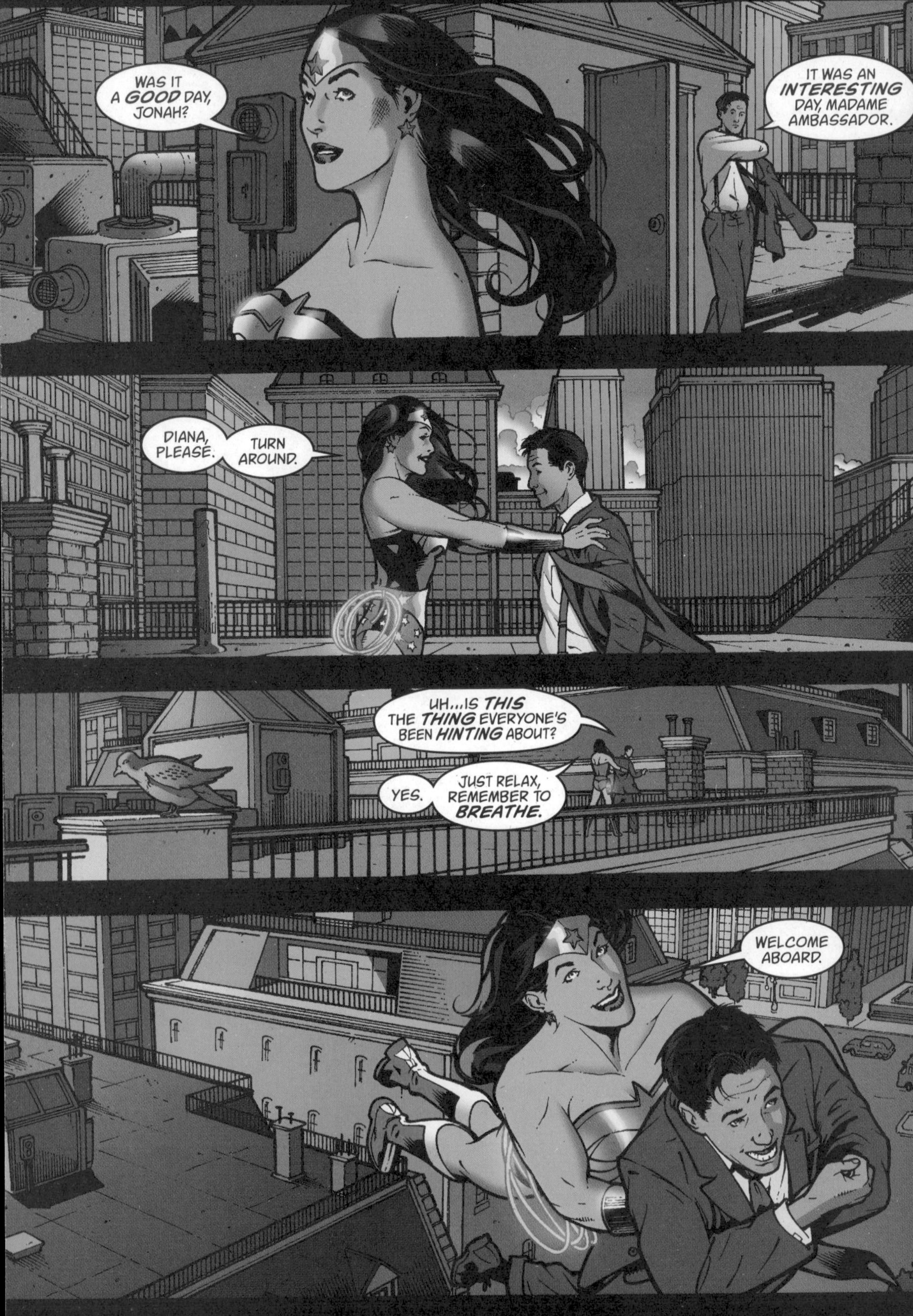

WAS IT A GOOD DAY, JONAH?
IT WAS AN INTERESTING DAY, MADAME AMBASSADOR.
DIANA, PLEASE.
TURN AROUND.
UH...IS THIS THE THING EVERYONE'S BEEN HINTING ABOUT?
YES.
JUST RELAX, REMEMBER TO BREATHE.
WELCOME ABOARD.

ART BY ADAM HUGHES

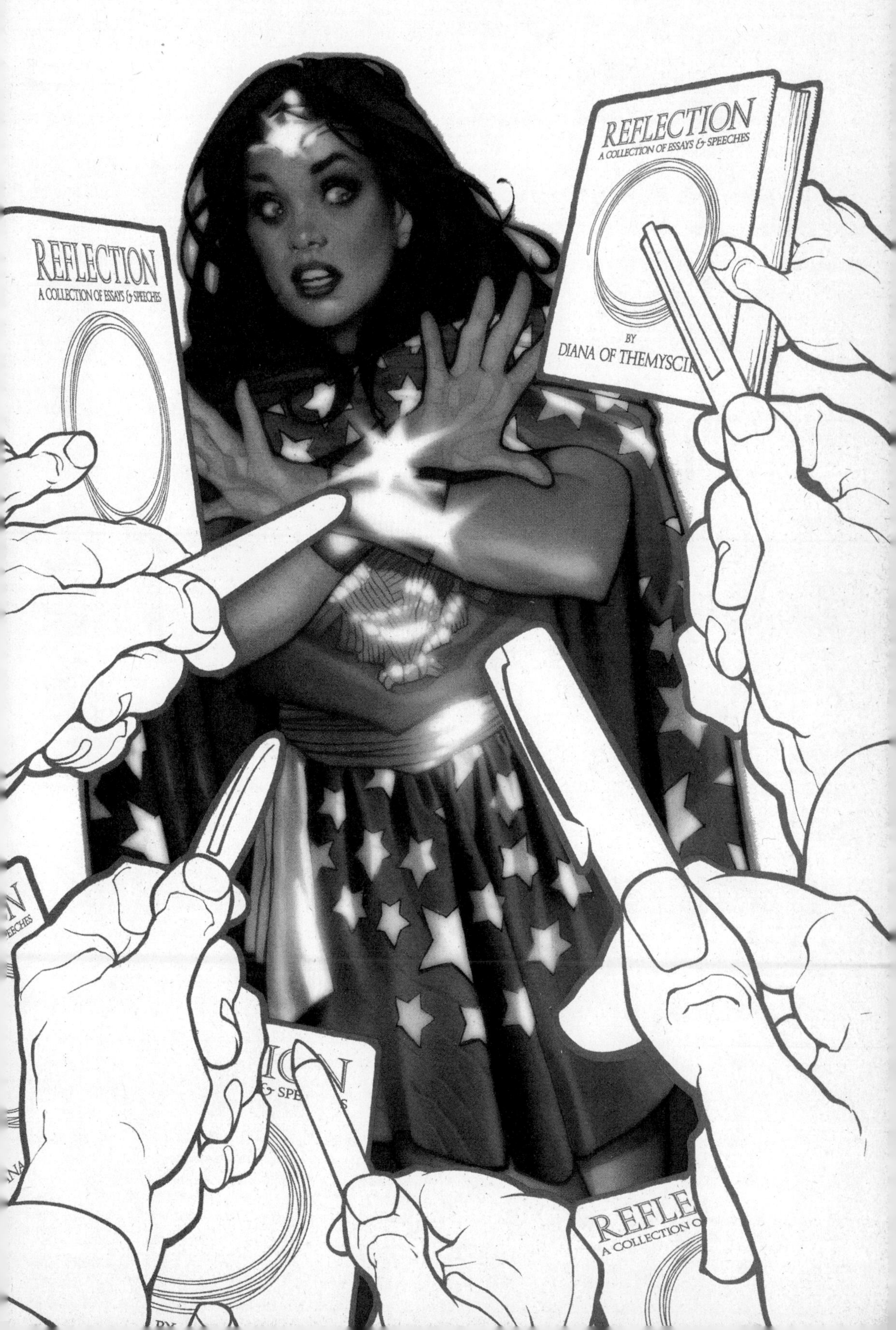

REFLECTION
A COLLECTION OF ESSAYS & SPEECHES
REFLECTION
A COLLECTION OF ESSAYS & SPEECHES
BY
DIANA OF THEMYSCI

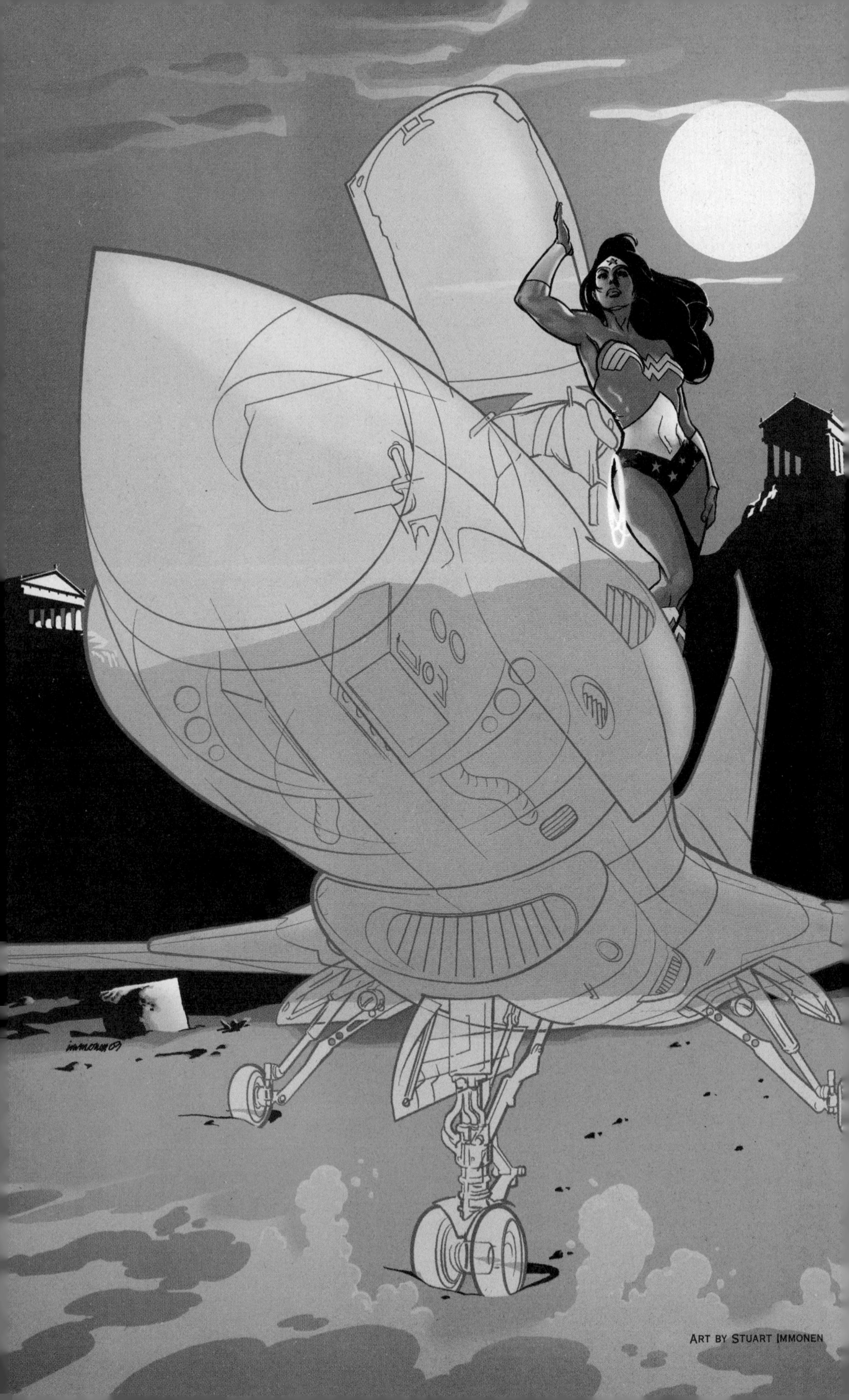

ART BY STUART IMMONEN

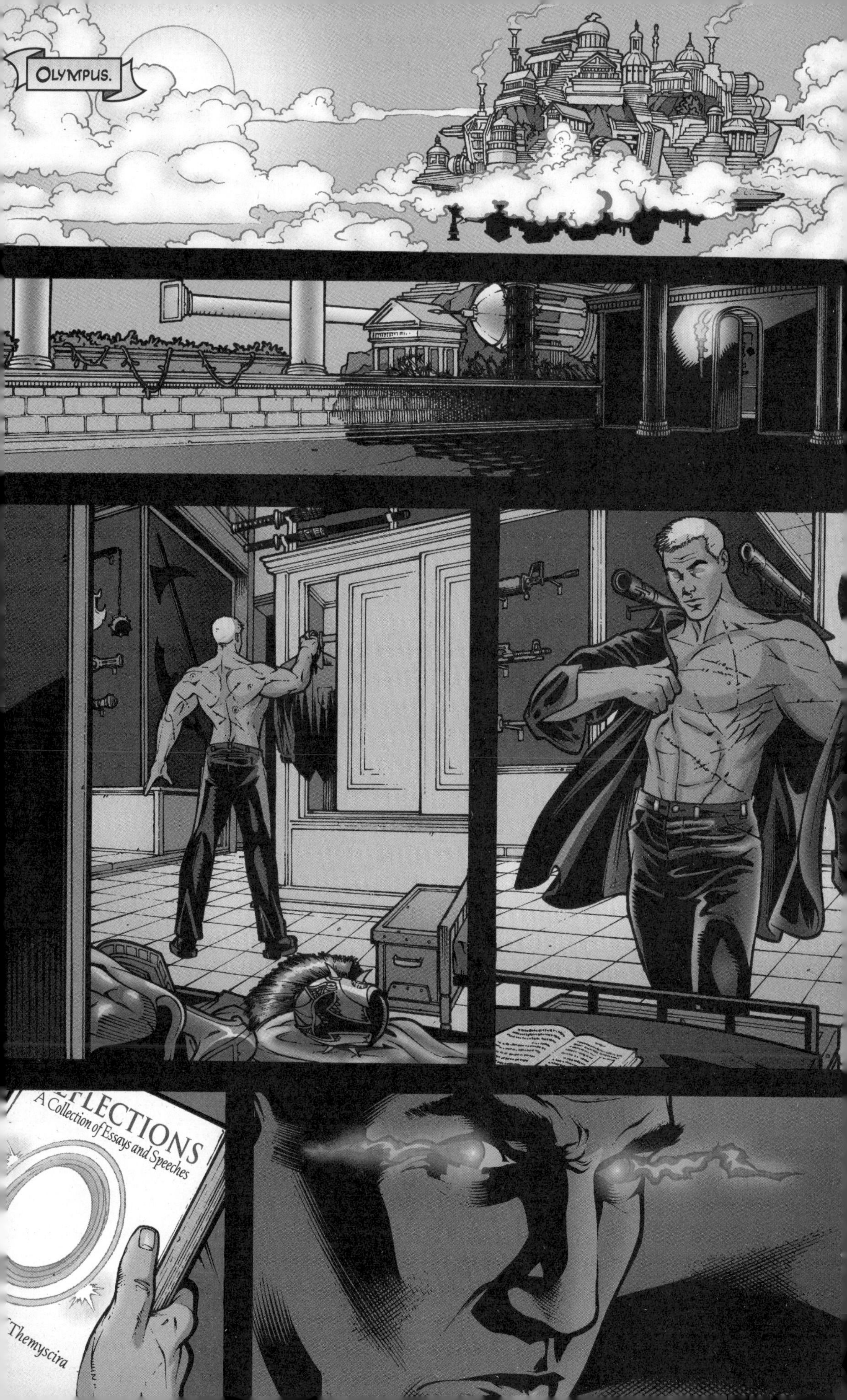
OLYMPUS.
EFLECTIONS
A Collection of Essays and Speeches
Themyscira

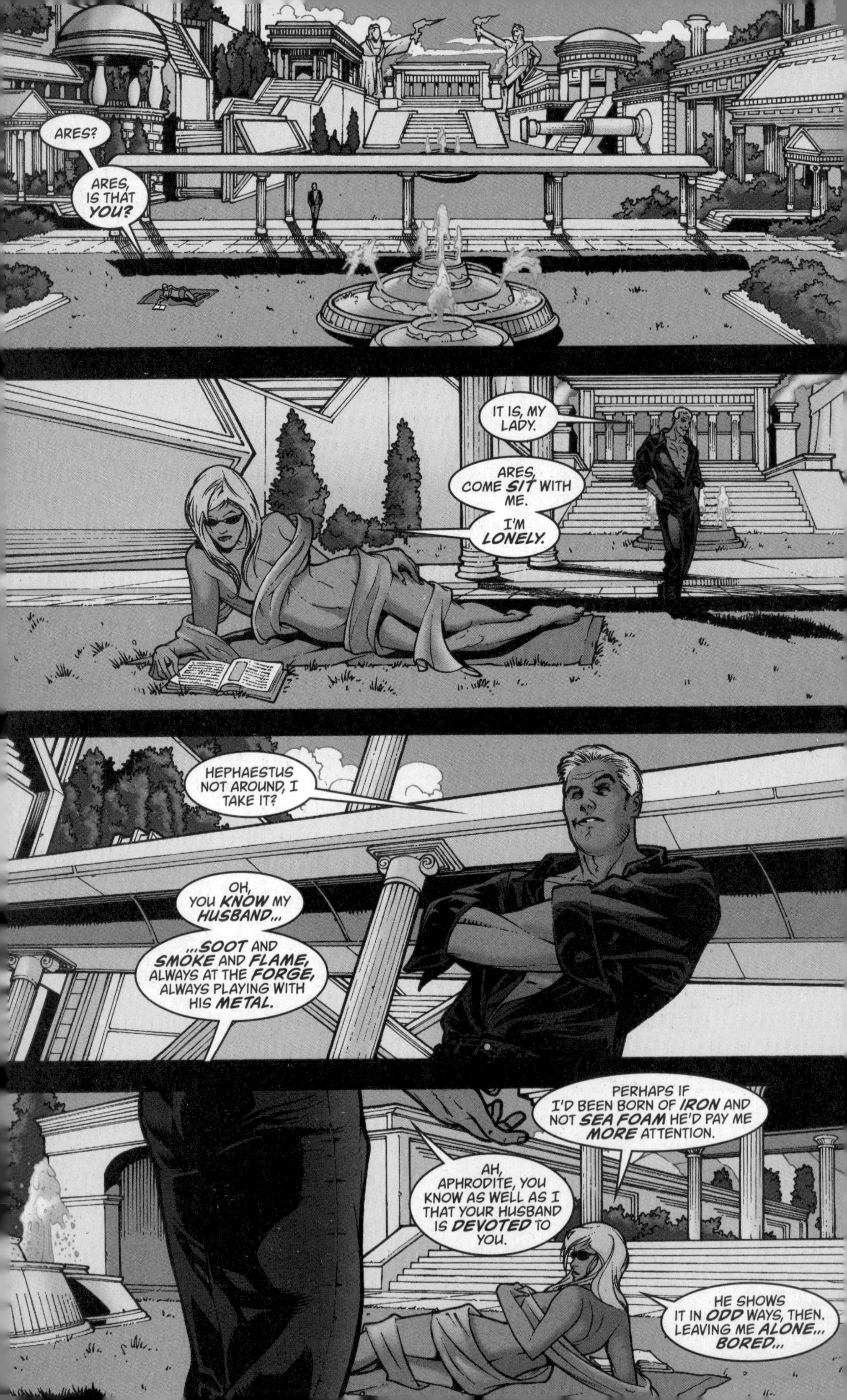
ARES?
ARES, IS THAT YOU?
IT IS, MY LADY.
ARES, COME SIT WITH ME.
I'M LONELY.
HEPHAESTUS NOT AROUND, I TAKE IT?
OH, YOU KNOW MY HUSBAND...
...SOOT AND SMOKE AND FLAME, ALWAYS AT THE FORGE, ALWAYS PLAYING WITH HIS METAL.
PERHAPS IF I'D BEEN BORN OF IRON AND NOT SEA FOAM HE'D PAY ME MORE ATTENTION.
AH, APHRODITE, YOU KNOW AS WELL AS I THAT YOUR HUSBAND IS DEVOTED TO YOU.
HE SHOWS IT IN ODD WAYS, THEN. LEAVING ME ALONE... BORED...

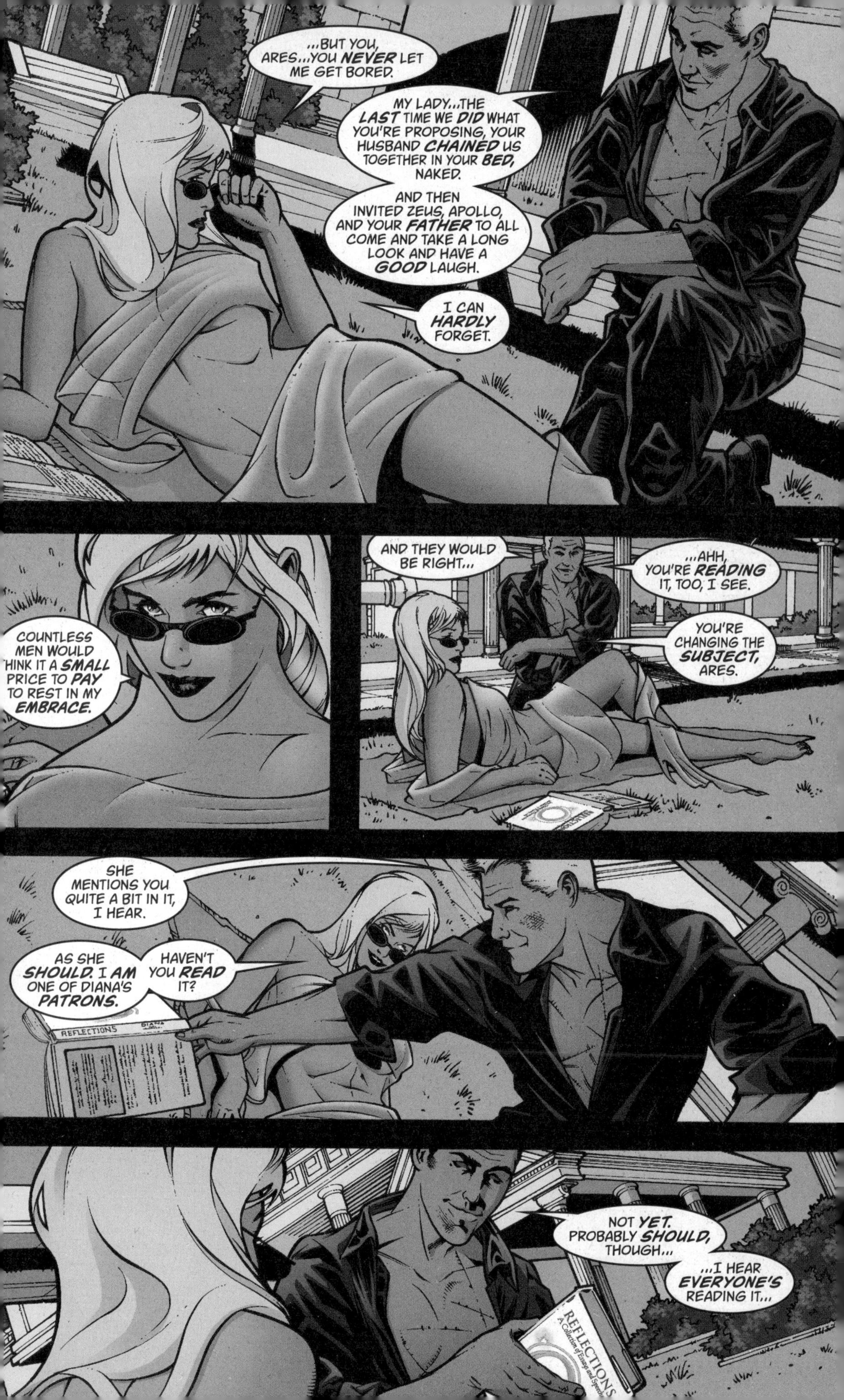

...BUT YOU, ARES...YOU NEVER LET ME GET BORED.
MY LADY...THE LAST TIME WE DID WHAT YOU'RE PROPOSING, YOUR HUSBAND CHAINED US TOGETHER IN YOUR BED, NAKED.
AND THEN INVITED ZEUS, APOLLO, AND YOUR FATHER TO ALL COME AND TAKE A LONG LOOK AND HAVE A GOOD LAUGH.
I CAN HARDLY FORGET.
COUNTLESS MEN WOULD HINK IT A SMALL PRICE TO PAY TO REST IN MY EMBRACE.
AND THEY WOULD BE RIGHT...
...AHH, YOU'RE READING IT, TOO, I SEE.
YOU'RE CHANGING THE SUBJECT, ARES.
SHE MENTIONS YOU QUITE A BIT IN IT, I HEAR.
AS SHE SHOULD. I AM ONE OF DIANA'S PATRONS.
HAVEN'T YOU READ IT?
REFLECTIONS
DIANA
NOT YET. PROBABLY SHOULD, THOUGH...
...I HEAR EVERYONE'S READING IT...
REFLECTIONS

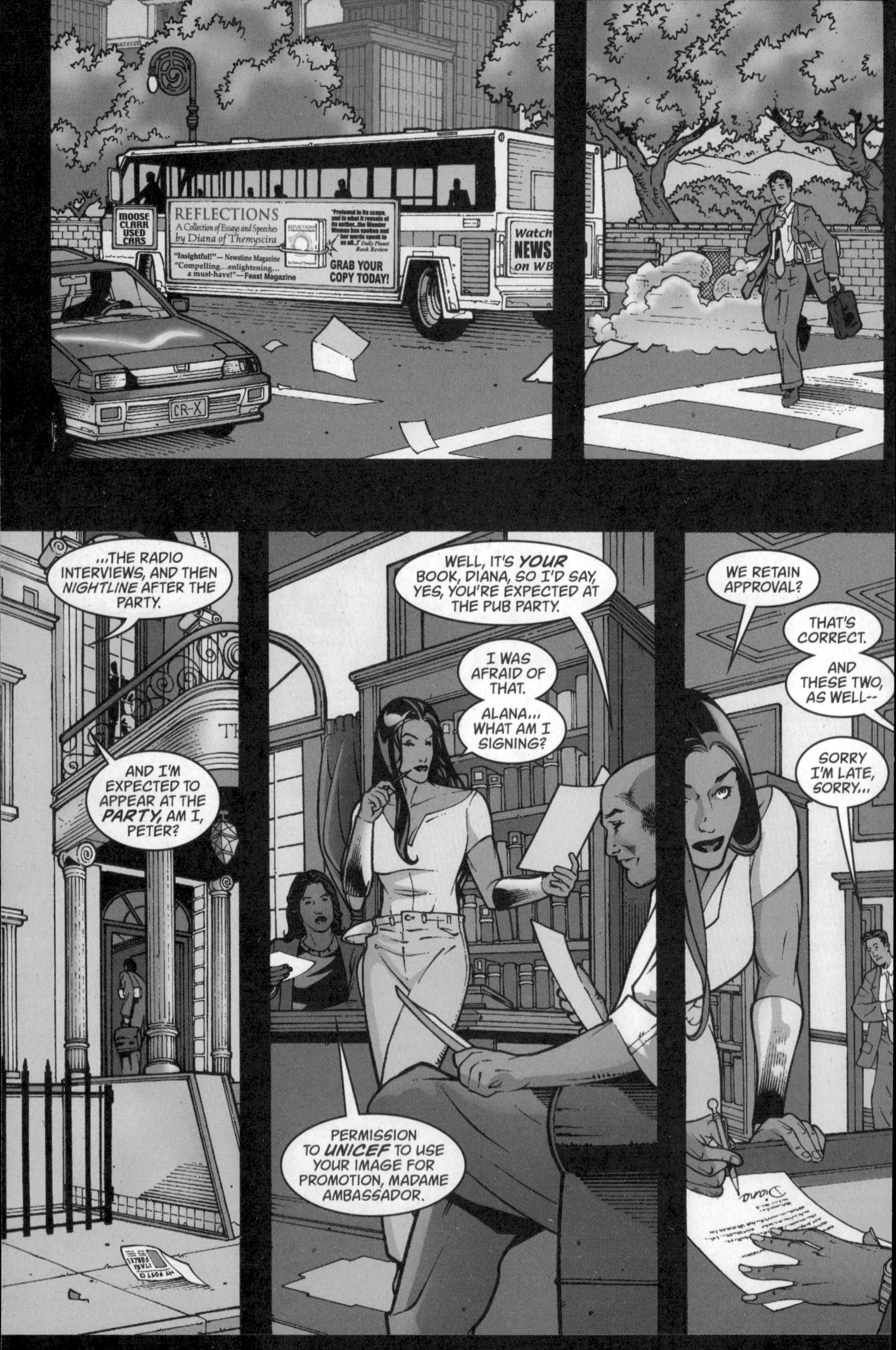
MOOSE CLARK USED CARS
REFLECTIONS
A Collection of Essays and Speeches
by Diana of Themyscira
"Insightful!"— Newstime Magazine
"Compelling...enlightening... a must-have!"—Feast Magazine
"Profound in its scope, and in what it reveals of its author...the Wonder Woman has spoken and her words speak to us all...!" Daily Planet Book Review
GRAB YOUR COPY TODAY!
Watch NEWS on WB
CR-X
...THE RADIO INTERVIEWS, AND THEN NIGHTLINE AFTER THE PARTY.
AND I'M EXPECTED TO APPEAR AT THE PARTY, AM I, PETER?
WELL, IT'S YOUR BOOK, DIANA, SO I'D SAY, YES, YOU'RE EXPECTED AT THE PUB PARTY.
I WAS AFRAID OF THAT.
ALANA... WHAT AM I SIGNING?
PERMISSION TO UNICEF TO USE YOUR IMAGE FOR PROMOTION, MADAME AMBASSADOR.
WE RETAIN APPROVAL?
THAT'S CORRECT.
AND THESE TWO, AS WELL--
SORRY I'M LATE, SORRY...

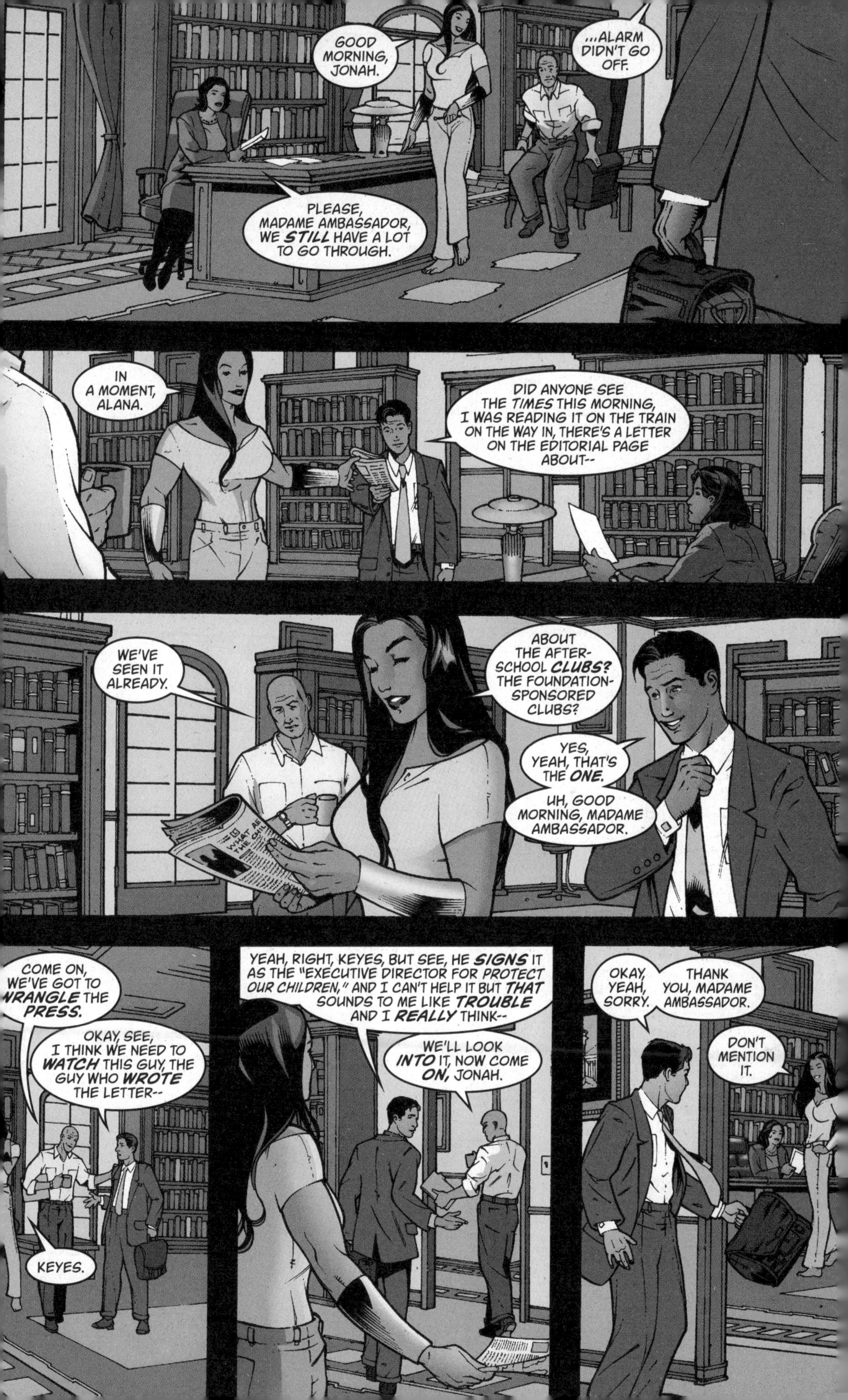
GOOD MORNING, JONAH.
...ALARM DIDN'T GO OFF.
PLEASE, MADAME AMBASSADOR, WE STILL HAVE A LOT TO GO THROUGH.
IN A MOMENT, ALANA.
DID ANYONE SEE THE TIMES THIS MORNING, I WAS READING IT ON THE TRAIN ON THE WAY IN, THERE'S A LETTER ON THE EDITORIAL PAGE ABOUT--
WE'VE SEEN IT ALREADY.
ABOUT THE AFTER-SCHOOL CLUBS? THE FOUNDATION-SPONSORED CLUBS?
YES, YEAH, THAT'S THE ONE.
UH, GOOD MORNING, MADAME AMBASSADOR.
COME ON, WE'VE GOT TO WRANGLE THE PRESS.
OKAY, SEE, I THINK WE NEED TO WATCH THIS GUY, THE GUY WHO WROTE THE LETTER--
KEYES.
YEAH, RIGHT, KEYES, BUT SEE, HE SIGNS IT AS THE "EXECUTIVE DIRECTOR FOR PROTECT OUR CHILDREN," AND I CAN'T HELP IT BUT THAT SOUNDS TO ME LIKE TROUBLE AND I REALLY THINK--
WE'LL LOOK INTO IT, NOW COME ON, JONAH.
OKAY, YEAH, SORRY.
THANK YOU, MADAME AMBASSADOR.
DON'T MENTION IT.

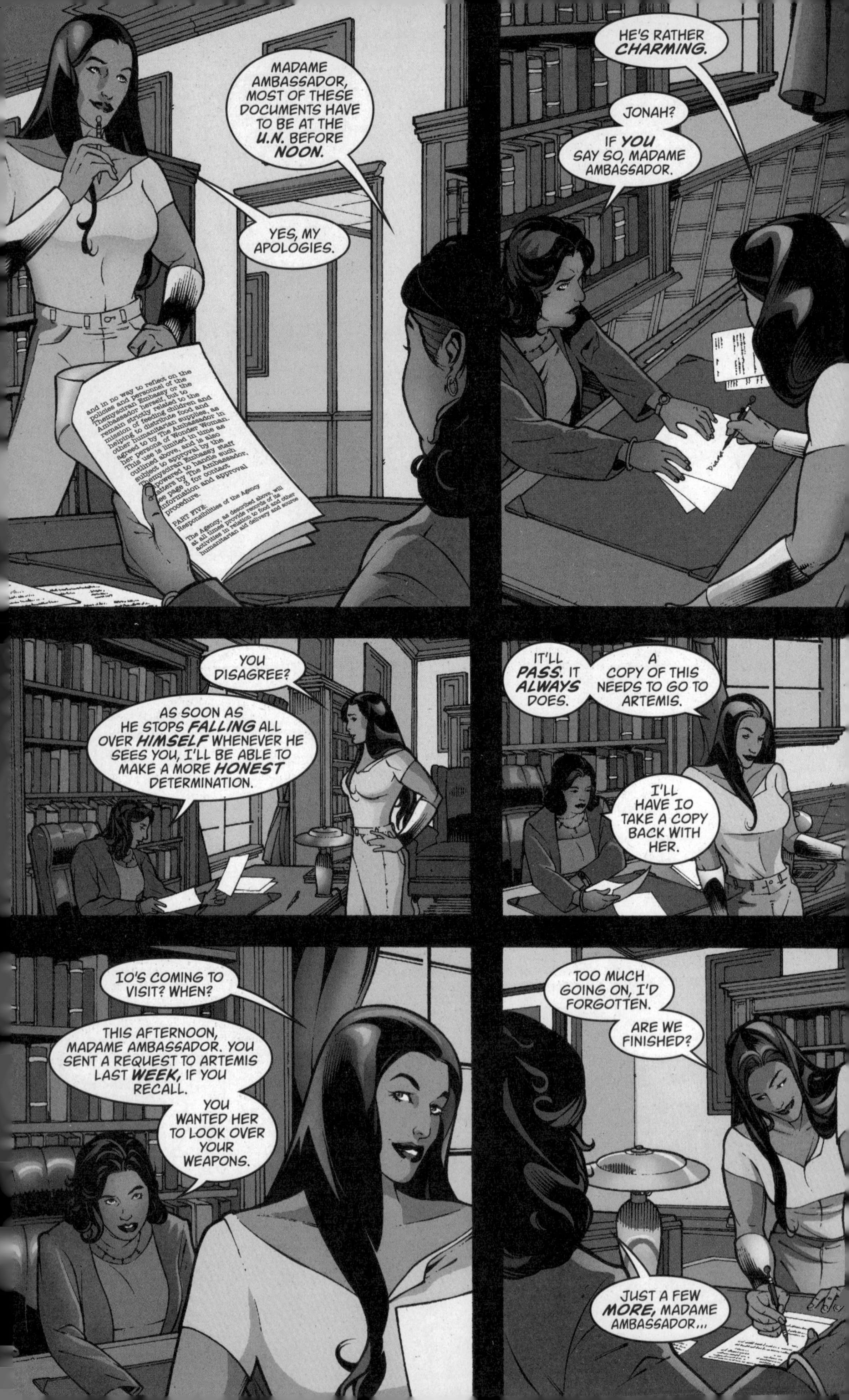
MADAME AMBASSADOR, MOST OF THESE DOCUMENTS HAVE TO BE AT THE U.N. BEFORE NOON.
YES, MY APOLOGIES.
HE'S RATHER CHARMING.
JONAH?
IF YOU SAY SO, MADAME AMBASSADOR.
YOU DISAGREE?
AS SOON AS HE STOPS FALLING ALL OVER HIMSELF WHENEVER HE SEES YOU, I'LL BE ABLE TO MAKE A MORE HONEST DETERMINATION.
IT'LL PASS. IT ALWAYS DOES.
A COPY OF THIS NEEDS TO GO TO ARTEMIS.
I'LL HAVE IO TAKE A COPY BACK WITH HER.
IO'S COMING TO VISIT? WHEN?
THIS AFTERNOON, MADAME AMBASSADOR. YOU SENT A REQUEST TO ARTEMIS LAST WEEK, IF YOU RECALL.
YOU WANTED HER TO LOOK OVER YOUR WEAPONS.
TOO MUCH GOING ON, I'D FORGOTTEN.
ARE WE FINISHED?
JUST A FEW MORE, MADAME AMBASSADOR...

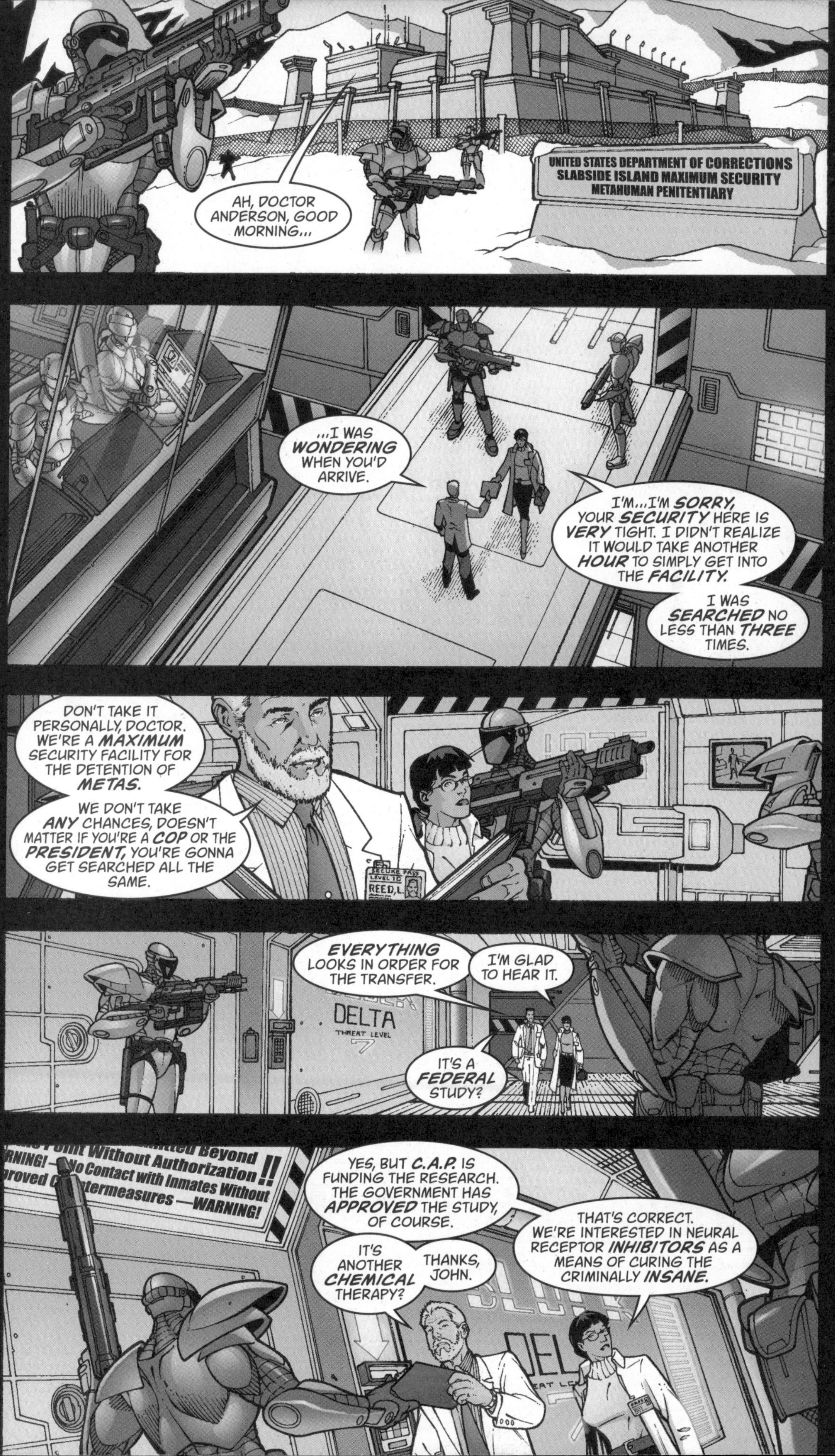
UNITED STATES DEPARTMENT OF CORRECTIONS
SLABSIDE ISLAND MAXIMUM SECURITY
METAHUMAN PENITENTIARY
AH, DOCTOR ANDERSON, GOOD MORNING...
...I WAS WONDERING WHEN YOU'D ARRIVE.
I'M...I'M SORRY, YOUR SECURITY HERE IS VERY TIGHT. I DIDN'T REALIZE IT WOULD TAKE ANOTHER HOUR TO SIMPLY GET INTO THE FACILITY.
I WAS SEARCHED NO LESS THAN THREE TIMES.
DON'T TAKE IT PERSONALLY, DOCTOR. WE'RE A MAXIMUM SECURITY FACILITY FOR THE DETENTION OF METAS.
WE DON'T TAKE ANY CHANCES, DOESN'T MATTER IF YOU'RE A COP OR THE PRESIDENT, YOU'RE GONNA GET SEARCHED ALL THE SAME.
SECURE PASS
LEVEL 10
REED, L.
EVERYTHING LOOKS IN ORDER FOR THE TRANSFER.
I'M GLAD TO HEAR IT.
DELTA
THREAT LEVEL
7
IT'S A FEDERAL STUDY?
No Contact with Inmates Without
WARNING!
YES, BUT C.A.P. IS FUNDING THE RESEARCH. THE GOVERNMENT HAS APPROVED THE STUDY, OF COURSE.
THAT'S CORRECT. WE'RE INTERESTED IN NEURAL RECEPTOR INHIBITORS AS A MEANS OF CURING THE CRIMINALLY INSANE.
IT'S ANOTHER CHEMICAL THERAPY?
THANKS, JOHN.

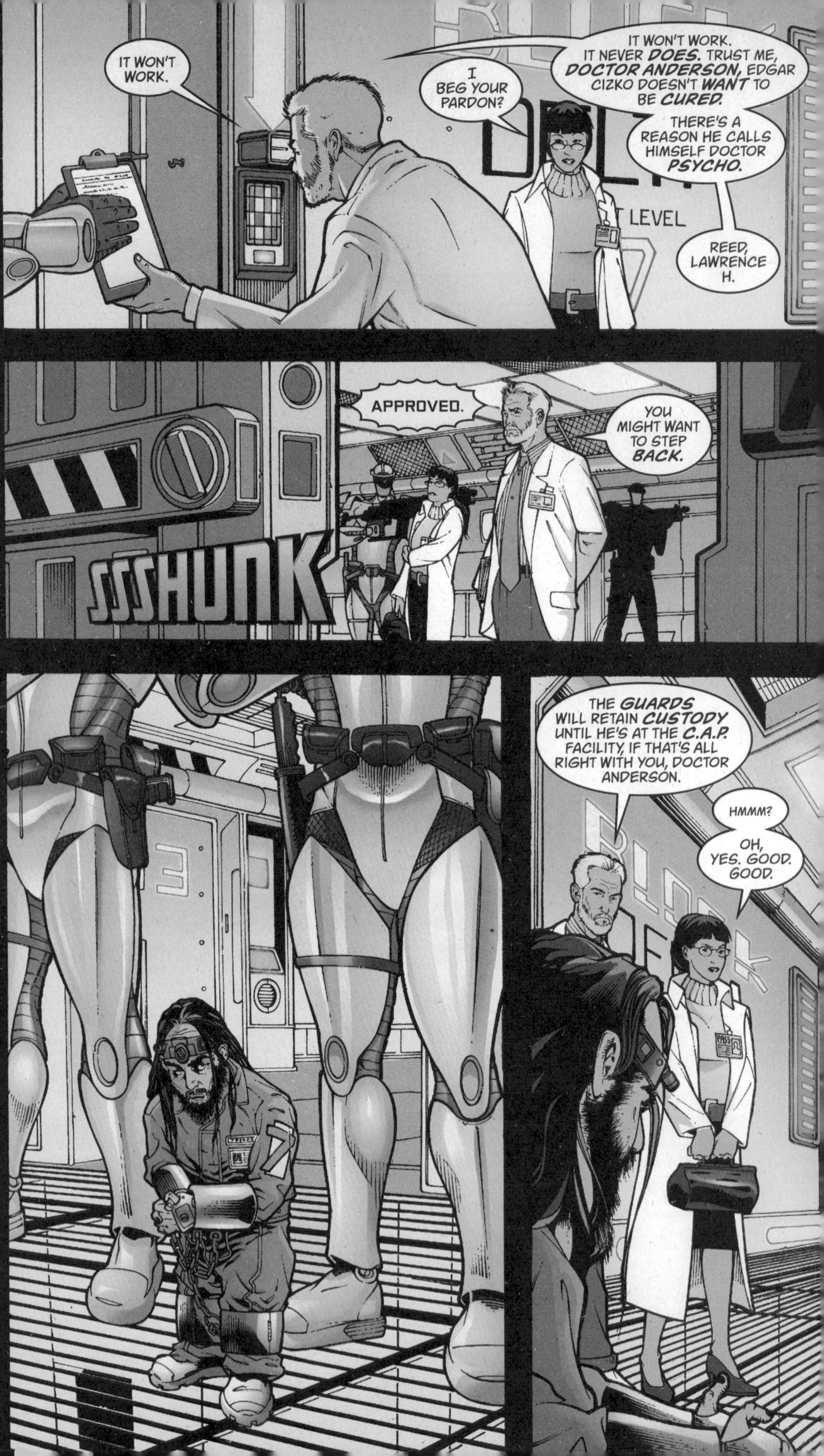

IT WON'T WORK.
I BEG YOUR PARDON?
IT WON'T WORK. IT NEVER DOES. TRUST ME, DOCTOR ANDERSON, EDGAR CIZKO DOESN'T WANT TO BE CURED.
THERE'S A REASON HE CALLS HIMSELF DOCTOR PSYCHO.
REED, LAWRENCE H.
APPROVED.
YOU MIGHT WANT TO STEP BACK.
SSSHUNK
THE GUARDS WILL RETAIN CUSTODY UNTIL HE'S AT THE C.A.P. FACILITY, IF THAT'S ALL RIGHT WITH YOU, DOCTOR ANDERSON.
HMMM?
OH, YES. GOOD. GOOD.

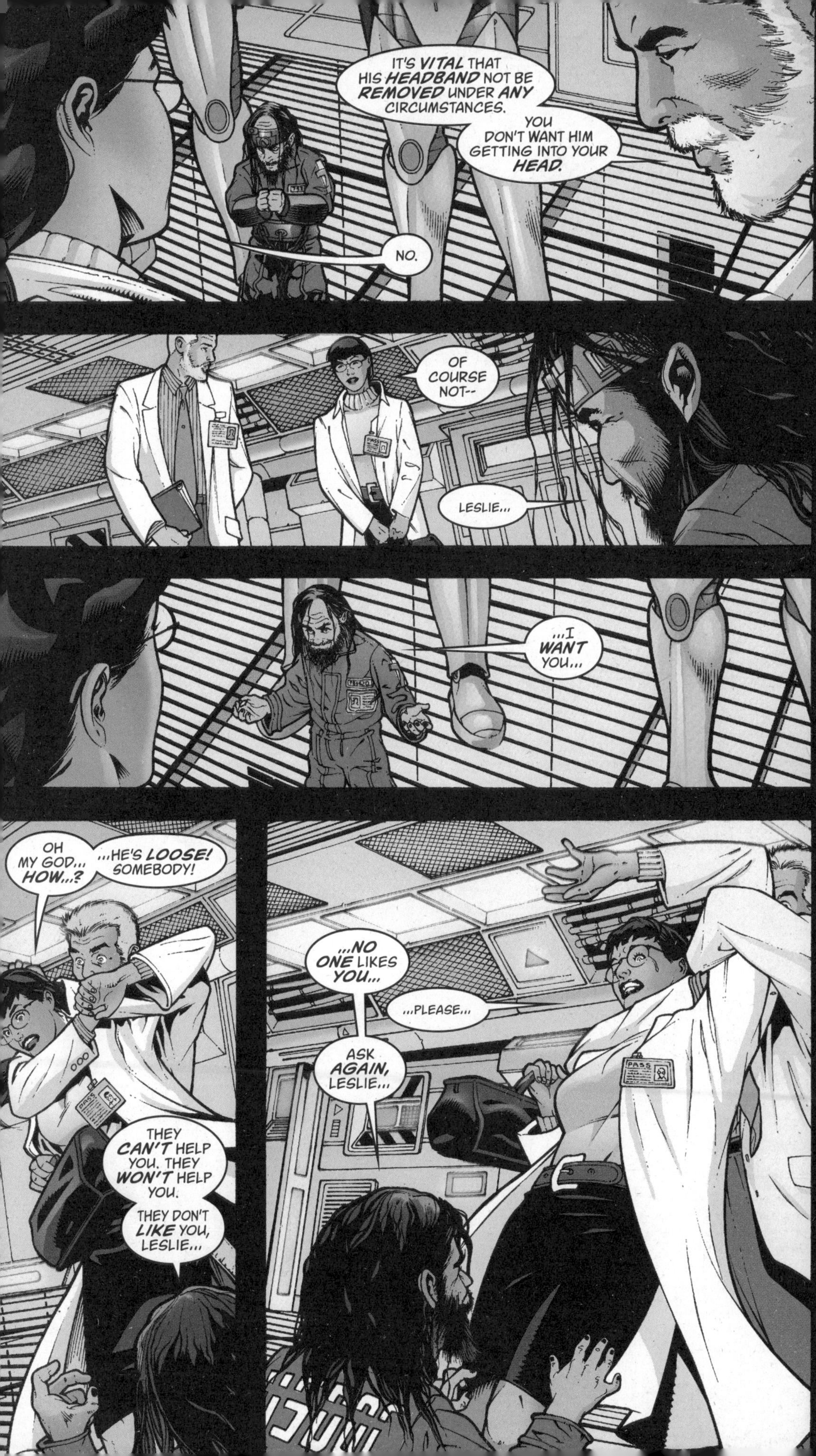
IT'S VITAL THAT HIS HEADBAND NOT BE REMOVED UNDER ANY CIRCUMSTANCES.
YOU DON'T WANT HIM GETTING INTO YOUR HEAD.
NO.
OF COURSE NOT--
LESLIE...
...I WANT YOU...
OH MY GOD... HOW...?
...HE'S LOOSE! SOMEBODY!
THEY CAN'T HELP YOU. THEY WON'T HELP YOU.
THEY DON'T LIKE YOU, LESLIE...
...NO ONE LIKES YOU...
...PLEASE...
ASK AGAIN, LESLIE...

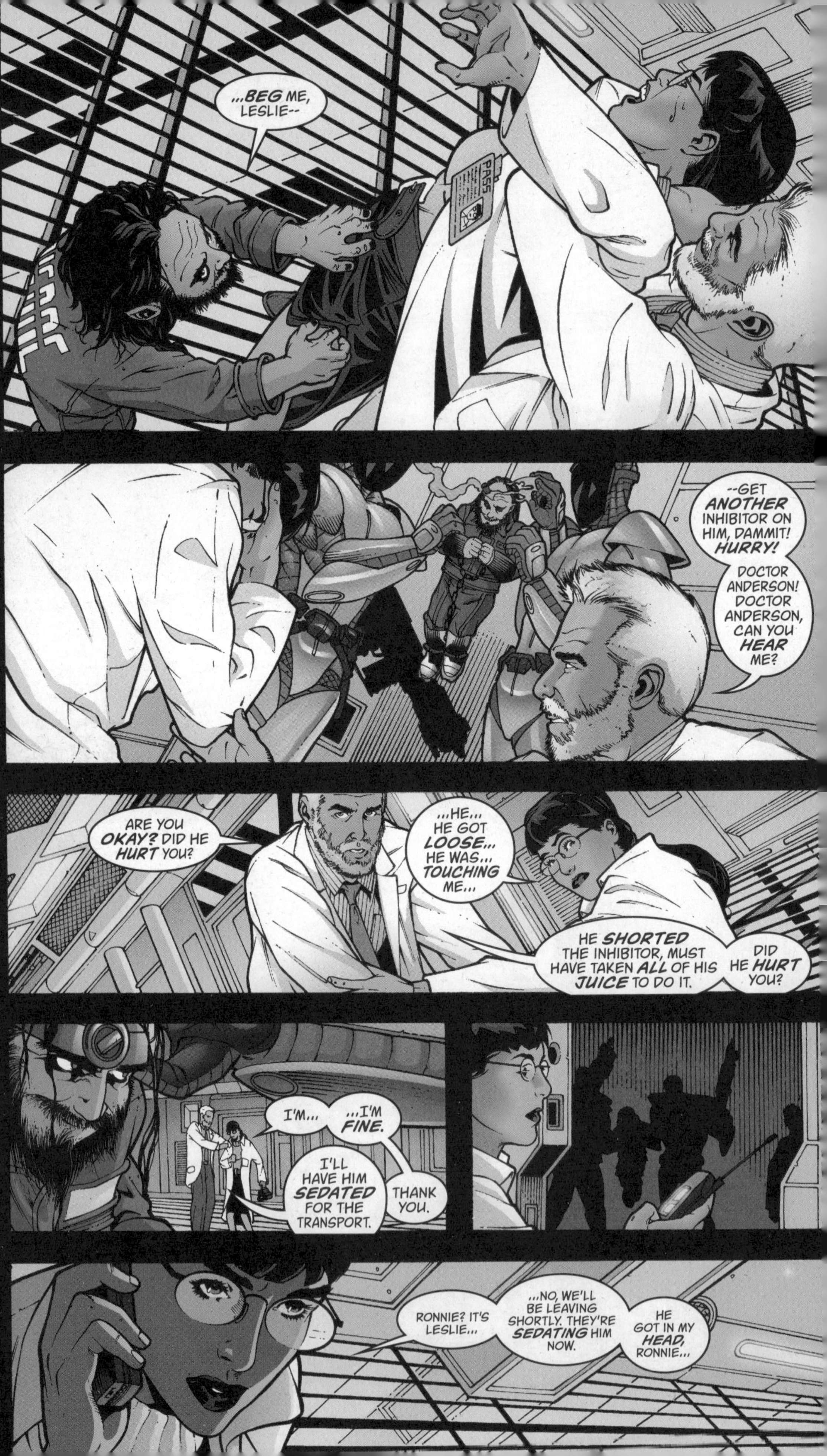

...BEG ME, LESLIE--
--GET ANOTHER INHIBITOR ON HIM, DAMMIT! HURRY!
DOCTOR ANDERSON! DOCTOR ANDERSON, CAN YOU HEAR ME?
ARE YOU OKAY? DID HE HURT YOU?
...HE... HE GOT LOOSE... HE WAS... TOUCHING ME...
HE SHORTED THE INHIBITOR, MUST HAVE TAKEN ALL OF HIS JUICE TO DO IT.
DID HE HURT YOU?
I'M...
...I'M FINE.
I'LL HAVE HIM SEDATED FOR THE TRANSPORT.
THANK YOU.
RONNIE? IT'S LESLIE...
...NO, WE'LL BE LEAVING SHORTLY. THEY'RE SEDATING HIM NOW.
HE GOT IN MY HEAD, RONNIE...

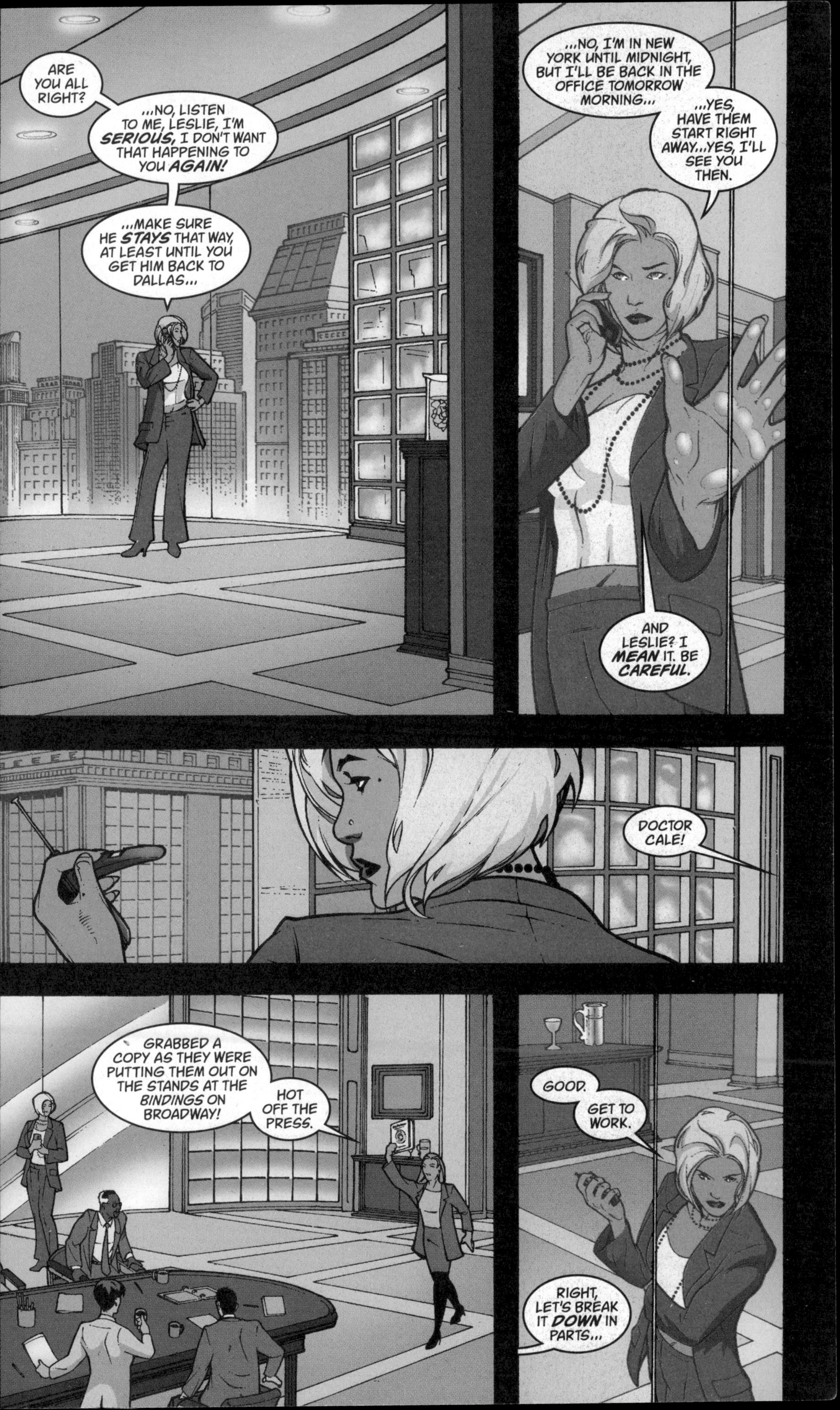
ARE YOU ALL RIGHT?
...NO, LISTEN TO ME, LESLIE, I'M *SERIOUS,* I DON'T WANT THAT HAPPENING TO YOU *AGAIN!*
...MAKE SURE HE *STAYS* THAT WAY, AT LEAST UNTIL YOU GET HIM BACK TO DALLAS...
...NO, I'M IN NEW YORK UNTIL MIDNIGHT, BUT I'LL BE BACK IN THE OFFICE TOMORROW MORNING...
...YES, HAVE THEM START RIGHT AWAY...YES, I'LL SEE YOU THEN.
AND LESLIE? I *MEAN* IT. BE *CAREFUL.*
DOCTOR CALE!
GRABBED A COPY AS THEY WERE PUTTING THEM OUT ON THE STANDS AT THE *BINDINGS* ON BROADWAY!
HOT OFF THE PRESS.
GOOD.
GET TO WORK.
RIGHT, LET'S BREAK IT *DOWN* IN PARTS...

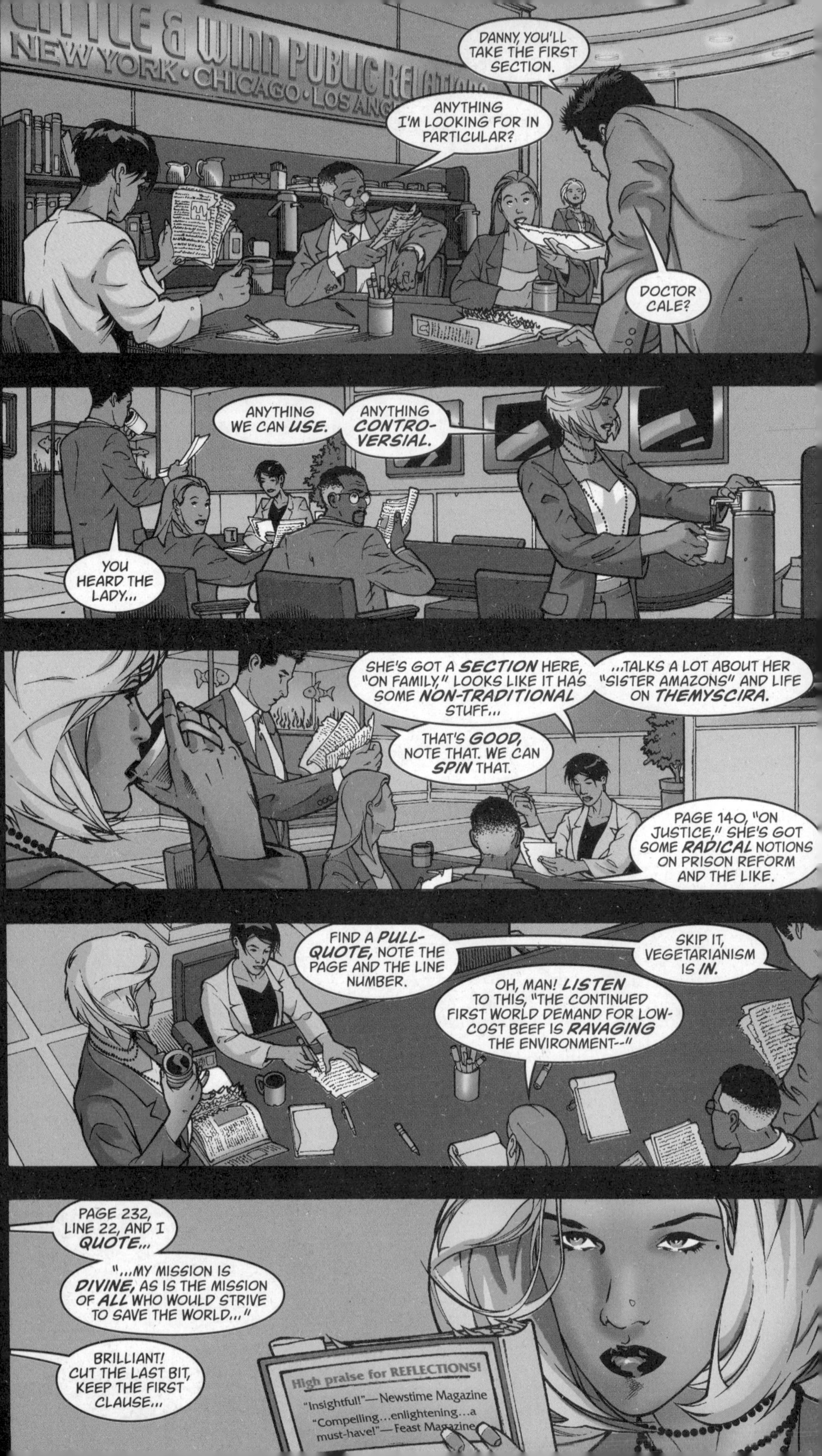

NEW YORK · CHICAGO · LOS ANG
DANNY, YOU'LL TAKE THE FIRST SECTION.
ANYTHING I'M LOOKING FOR IN PARTICULAR?
DOCTOR CALE?
ANYTHING WE CAN **USE.**
ANYTHING **CONTROVERSIAL.**
YOU HEARD THE LADY...
SHE'S GOT A **SECTION** HERE, "ON FAMILY," LOOKS LIKE IT HAS SOME **NON-TRADITIONAL** STUFF...
...TALKS A LOT ABOUT HER "SISTER AMAZONS" AND LIFE ON **THEMYSCIRA.**
THAT'S **GOOD,** NOTE THAT. WE CAN **SPIN** THAT.
PAGE 140, "ON JUSTICE," SHE'S GOT SOME **RADICAL** NOTIONS ON PRISON REFORM AND THE LIKE.
FIND A **PULL-QUOTE,** NOTE THE PAGE AND THE LINE NUMBER.
SKIP IT, VEGETARIANISM IS **IN.**
OH, MAN! **LISTEN** TO THIS, "THE CONTINUED FIRST WORLD DEMAND FOR LOW-COST BEEF IS **RAVAGING** THE ENVIRONMENT--"
PAGE 232, LINE 22, AND I **QUOTE...**
"...MY MISSION IS **DIVINE,** AS IS THE MISSION OF **ALL** WHO WOULD STRIVE TO SAVE THE WORLD..."
BRILLIANT! CUT THE LAST BIT, KEEP THE FIRST CLAUSE...
High praise for REFLECTIONS!
"Insightful!"—Newstime Magazine
"Compelling...enlightening...a must-have!"—Feast Magazine

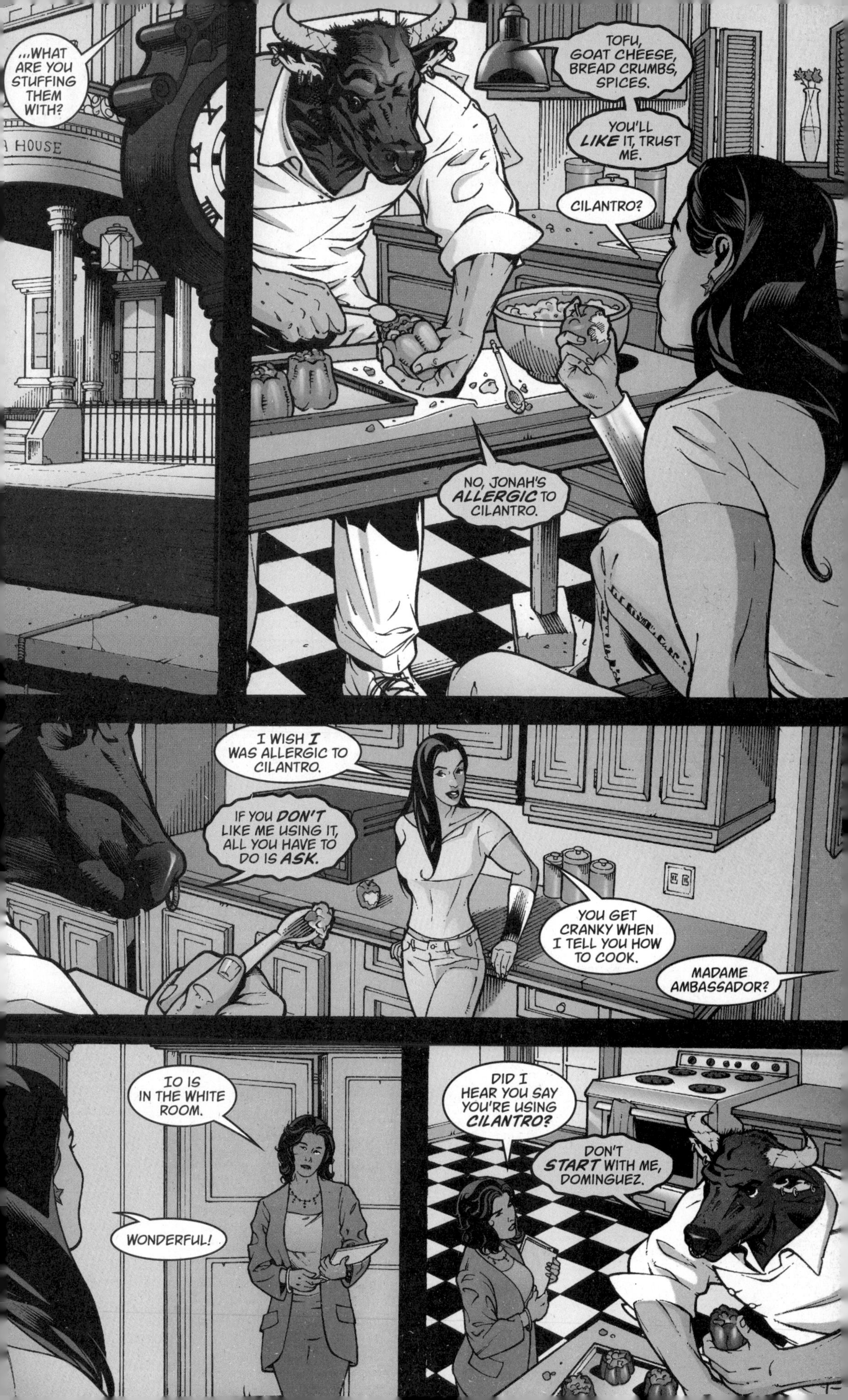
...WHAT ARE YOU STUFFING THEM WITH?
TOFU, GOAT CHEESE, BREAD CRUMBS, SPICES.
YOU'LL LIKE IT, TRUST ME.
CILANTRO?
NO, JONAH'S ALLERGIC TO CILANTRO.
I WISH I WAS ALLERGIC TO CILANTRO.
IF YOU DON'T LIKE ME USING IT, ALL YOU HAVE TO DO IS ASK.
YOU GET CRANKY WHEN I TELL YOU HOW TO COOK.
MADAME AMBASSADOR?
IO IS IN THE WHITE ROOM.
WONDERFUL!
DID I HEAR YOU SAY YOU'RE USING CILANTRO?
DON'T START WITH ME, DOMINGUEZ.

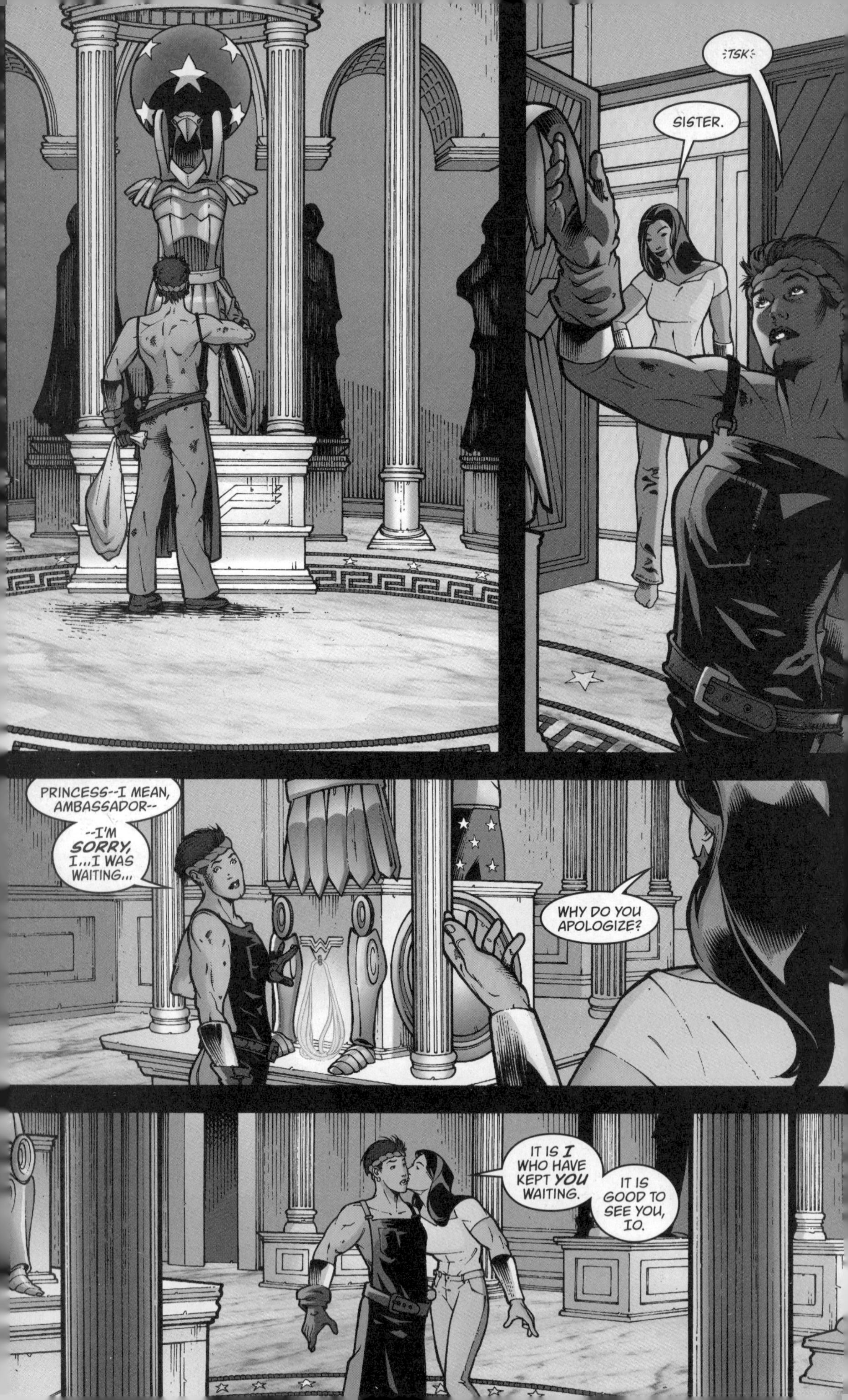

TSK
SISTER.
PRINCESS--I MEAN, AMBASSADOR--
--I'M SORRY, I...I WAS WAITING...
WHY DO YOU APOLOGIZE?
IT IS I WHO HAVE KEPT YOU WAITING.
IT IS GOOD TO SEE YOU, IO.

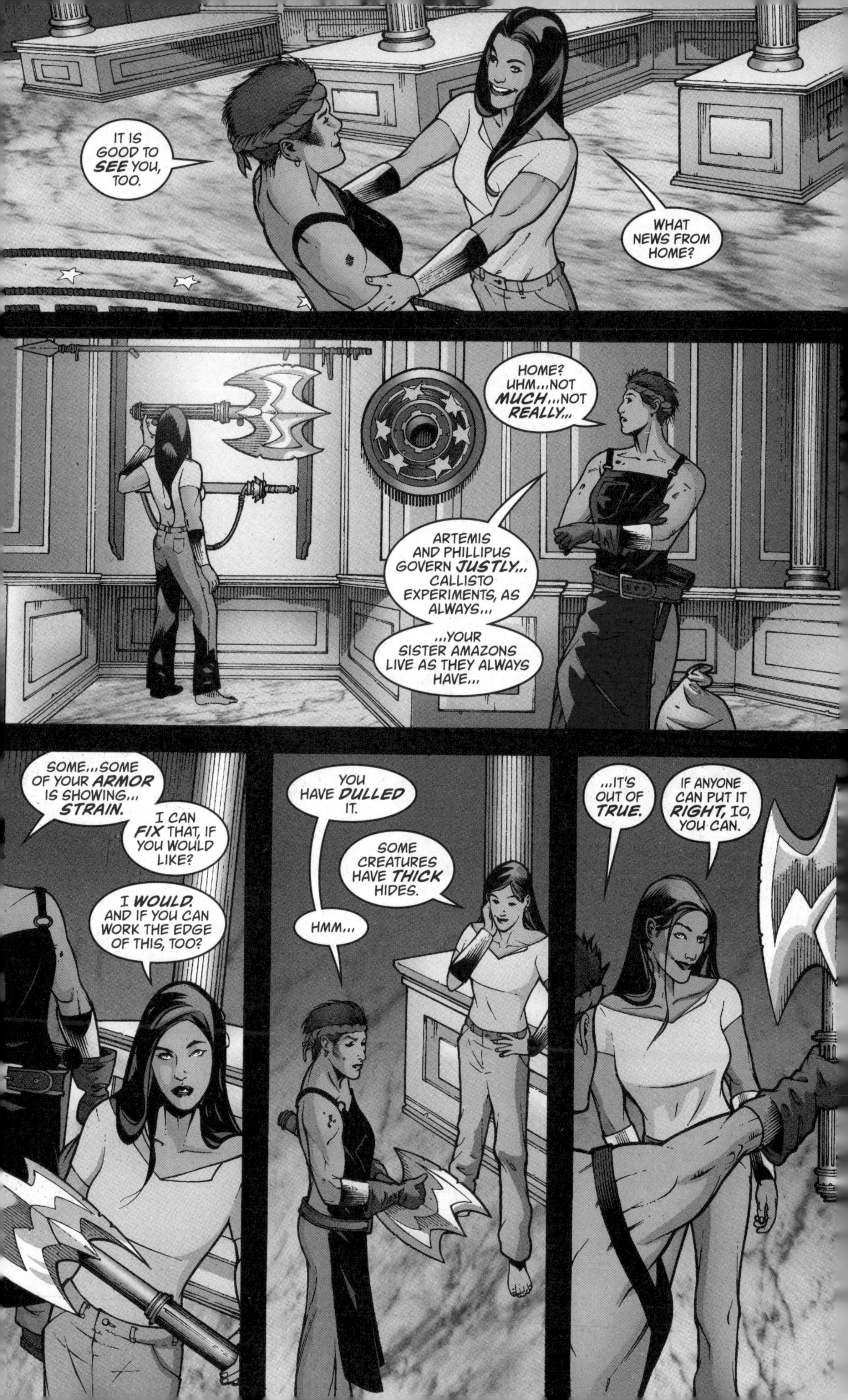
IT IS GOOD TO SEE YOU, TOO.
WHAT NEWS FROM HOME?
HOME? UHM...NOT MUCH...NOT REALLY...
ARTEMIS AND PHILLIPUS GOVERN JUSTLY... CALLISTO EXPERIMENTS, AS ALWAYS...
...YOUR SISTER AMAZONS LIVE AS THEY ALWAYS HAVE...
SOME...SOME OF YOUR ARMOR IS SHOWING... STRAIN.
I CAN FIX THAT, IF YOU WOULD LIKE?
I WOULD. AND IF YOU CAN WORK THE EDGE OF THIS, TOO?
YOU HAVE DULLED IT.
SOME CREATURES HAVE THICK HIDES.
HMM...
...IT'S OUT OF TRUE.
IF ANYONE CAN PUT IT RIGHT, IO, YOU CAN.

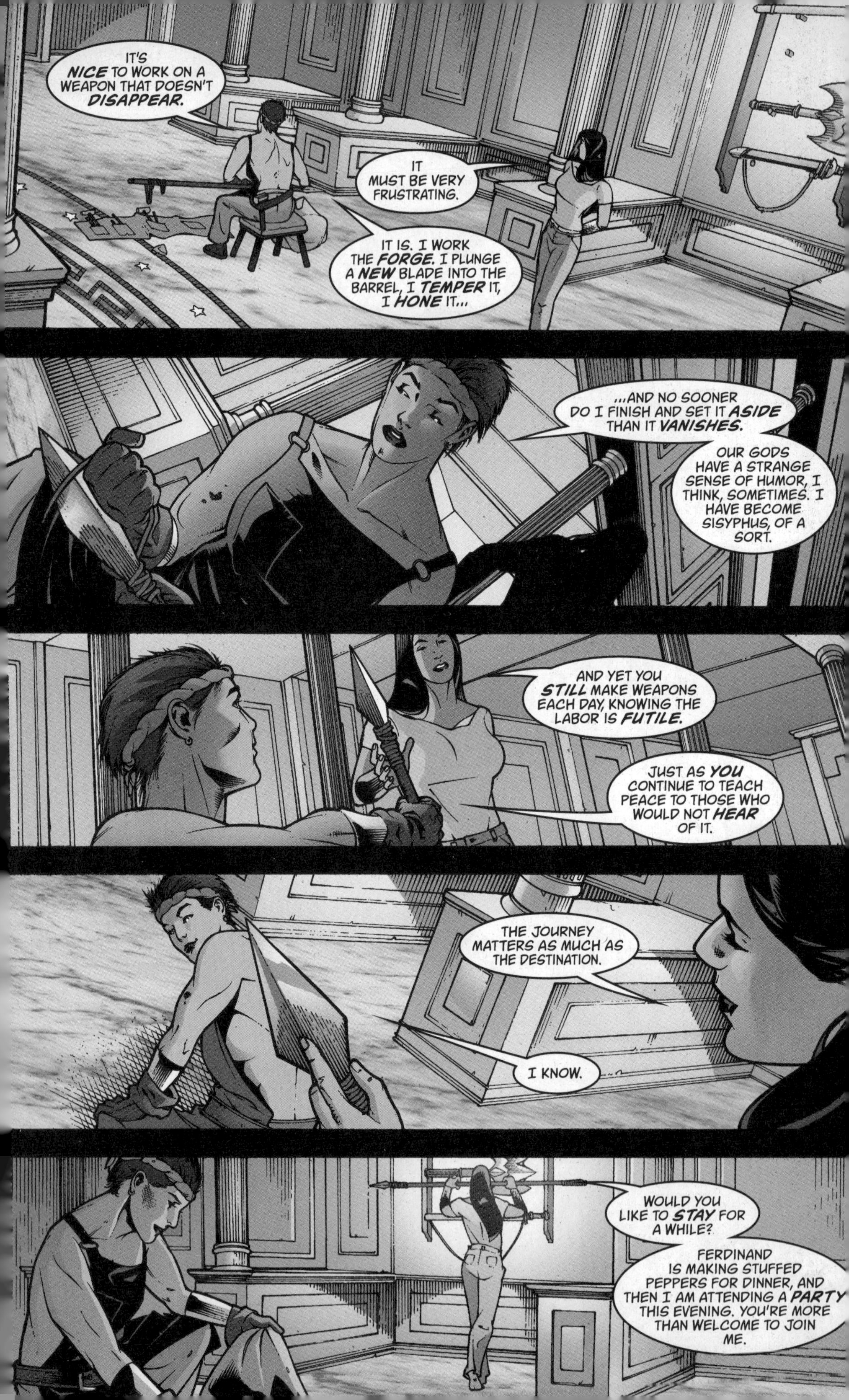
IT'S NICE TO WORK ON A WEAPON THAT DOESN'T DISAPPEAR.
IT MUST BE VERY FRUSTRATING.
IT IS. I WORK THE FORGE. I PLUNGE A NEW BLADE INTO THE BARREL, I TEMPER IT, I HONE IT...
...AND NO SOONER DO I FINISH AND SET IT ASIDE THAN IT VANISHES.
OUR GODS HAVE A STRANGE SENSE OF HUMOR, I THINK, SOMETIMES. I HAVE BECOME SISYPHUS, OF A SORT.
AND YET YOU STILL MAKE WEAPONS EACH DAY, KNOWING THE LABOR IS FUTILE.
JUST AS YOU CONTINUE TO TEACH PEACE TO THOSE WHO WOULD NOT HEAR OF IT.
THE JOURNEY MATTERS AS MUCH AS THE DESTINATION.
I KNOW.
WOULD YOU LIKE TO STAY FOR A WHILE?
FERDINAND IS MAKING STUFFED PEPPERS FOR DINNER, AND THEN I AM ATTENDING A PARTY THIS EVENING. YOU'RE MORE THAN WELCOME TO JOIN ME.

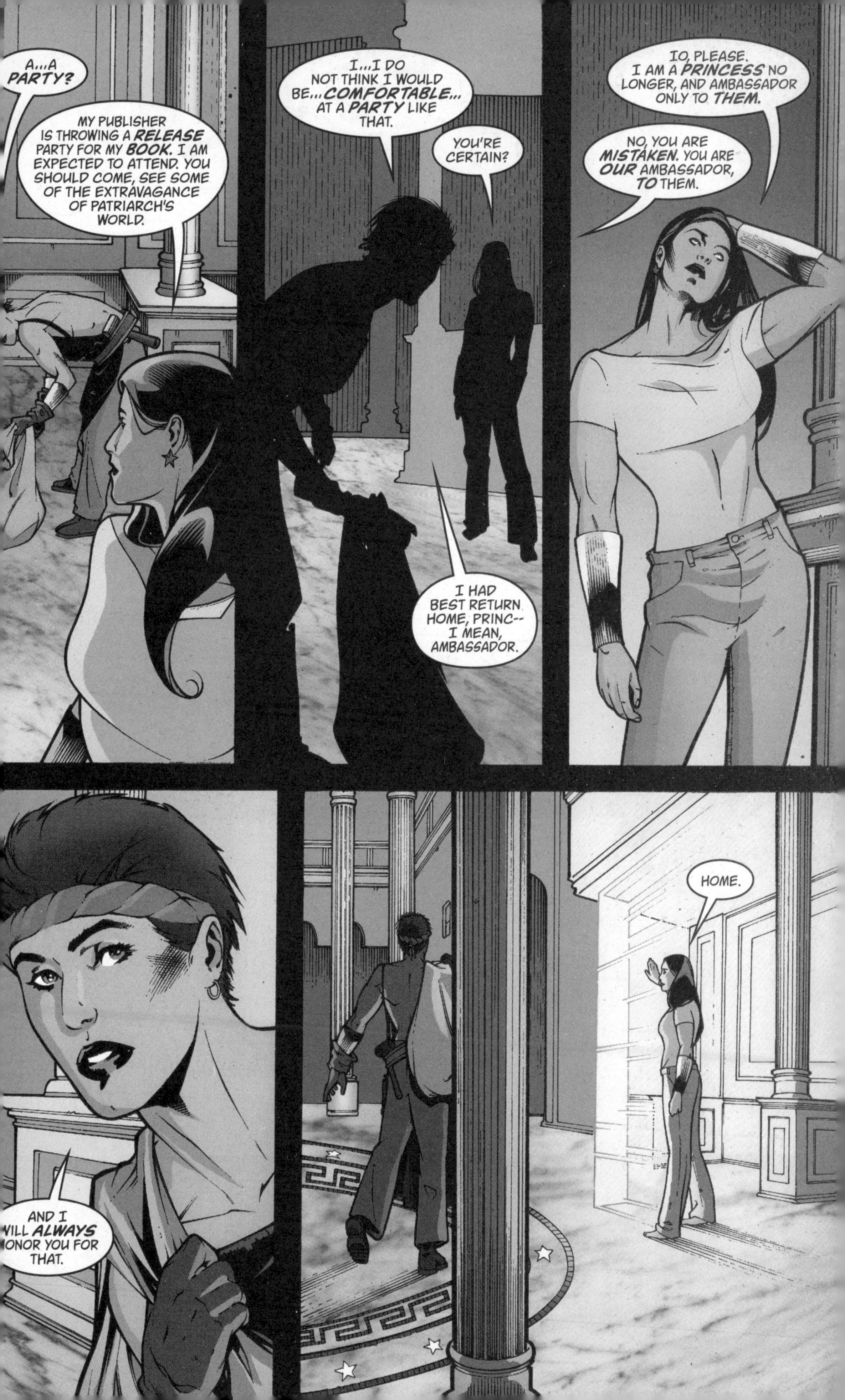
A...A PARTY?
MY PUBLISHER IS THROWING A RELEASE PARTY FOR MY BOOK. I AM EXPECTED TO ATTEND. YOU SHOULD COME, SEE SOME OF THE EXTRAVAGANCE OF PATRIARCH'S WORLD.
I...I DO NOT THINK I WOULD BE...COMFORTABLE... AT A PARTY LIKE THAT.
YOU'RE CERTAIN?
I HAD BEST RETURN HOME, PRINC-- I MEAN, AMBASSADOR.
IO, PLEASE. I AM A PRINCESS NO LONGER, AND AMBASSADOR ONLY TO THEM.
NO, YOU ARE MISTAKEN. YOU ARE OUR AMBASSADOR, TO THEM.
AND I WILL ALWAYS HONOR YOU FOR THAT.
HOME.

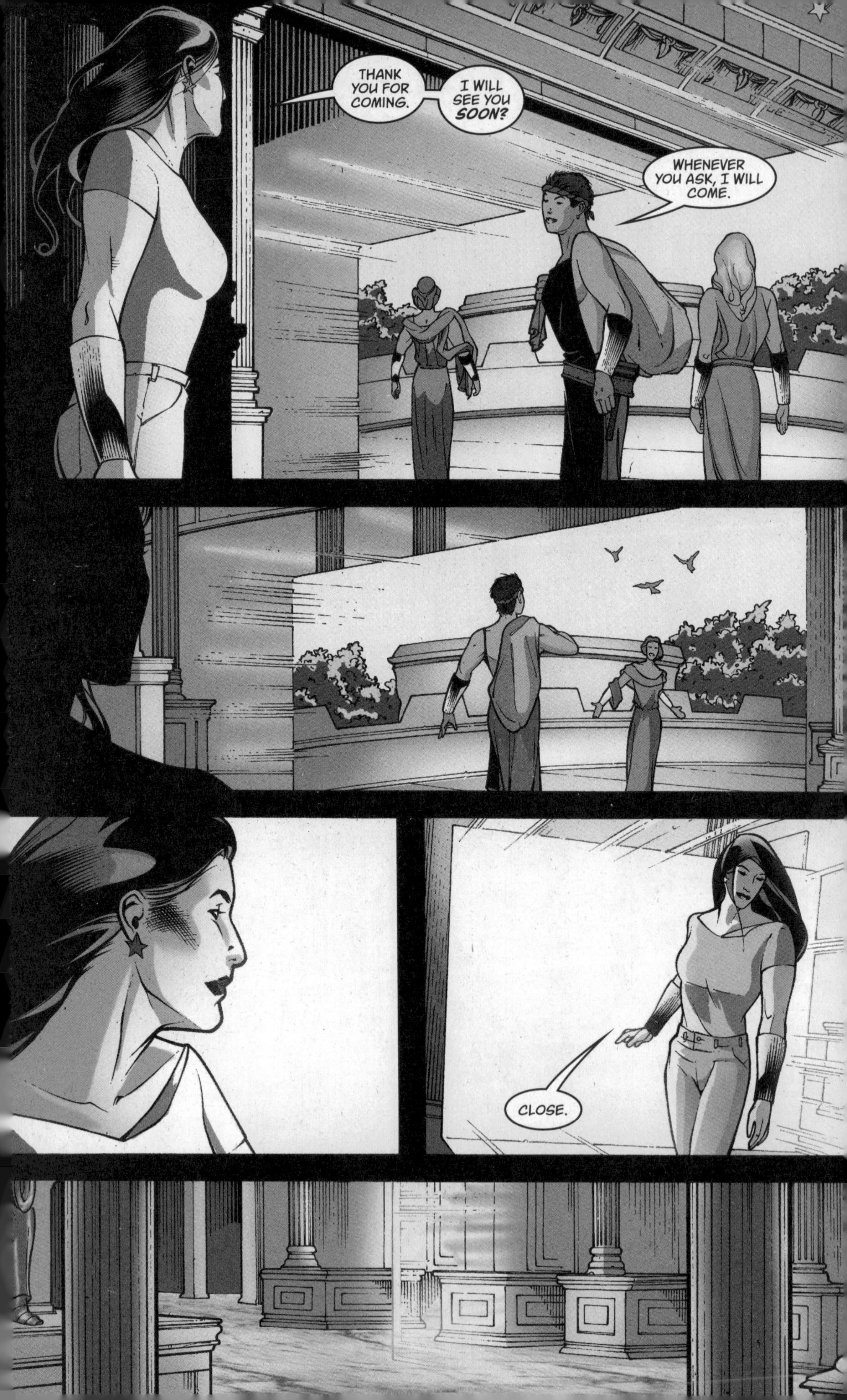
THANK YOU FOR COMING.
I WILL SEE YOU SOON?
WHENEVER YOU ASK, I WILL COME.
CLOSE.

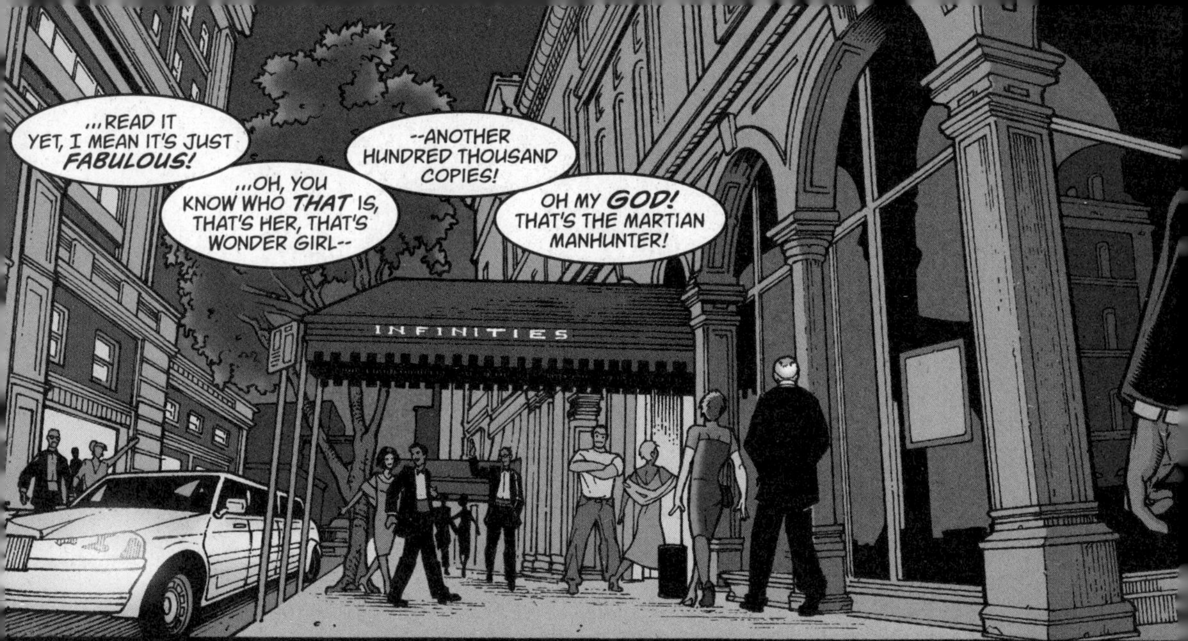
...READ IT YET, I MEAN IT'S JUST **FABULOUS!**
...OH, YOU KNOW WHO **THAT** IS, THAT'S HER, THAT'S WONDER GIRL--
--ANOTHER HUNDRED THOUSAND COPIES!
OH MY **GOD!** THAT'S THE MARTIAN MANHUNTER!
INFINITIES

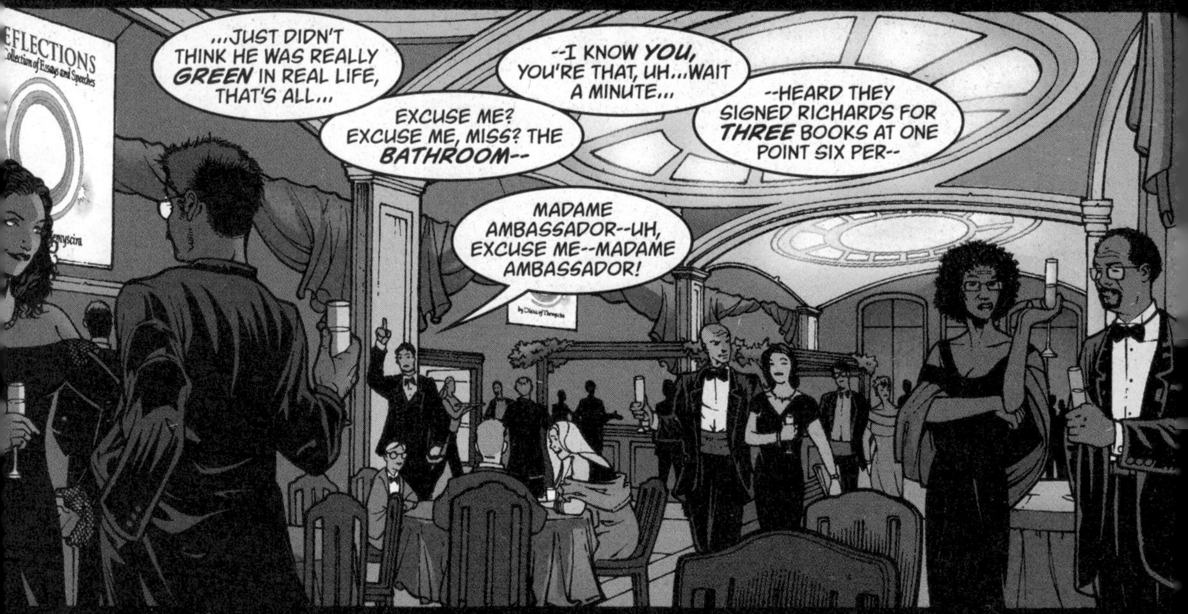
...JUST DIDN'T THINK HE WAS REALLY **GREEN** IN REAL LIFE, THAT'S ALL...
EXCUSE ME? EXCUSE ME, MISS? THE **BATHROOM--**
--I KNOW **YOU,** YOU'RE THAT, UH...WAIT A MINUTE...
--HEARD THEY SIGNED RICHARDS FOR **THREE** BOOKS AT ONE POINT SIX PER--
MADAME AMBASSADOR--UH, EXCUSE ME--MADAME AMBASSADOR!

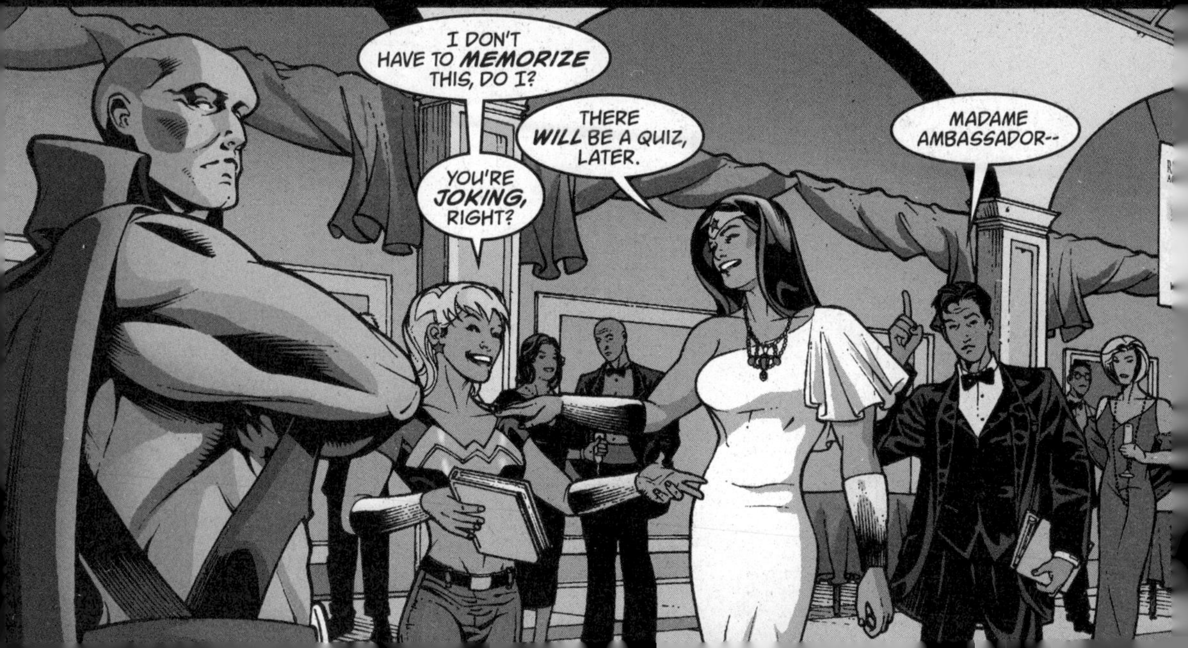
I DON'T HAVE TO **MEMORIZE** THIS, DO I?
THERE **WILL** BE A QUIZ, LATER.
YOU'RE **JOKING,** RIGHT?
MADAME AMBASSADOR--

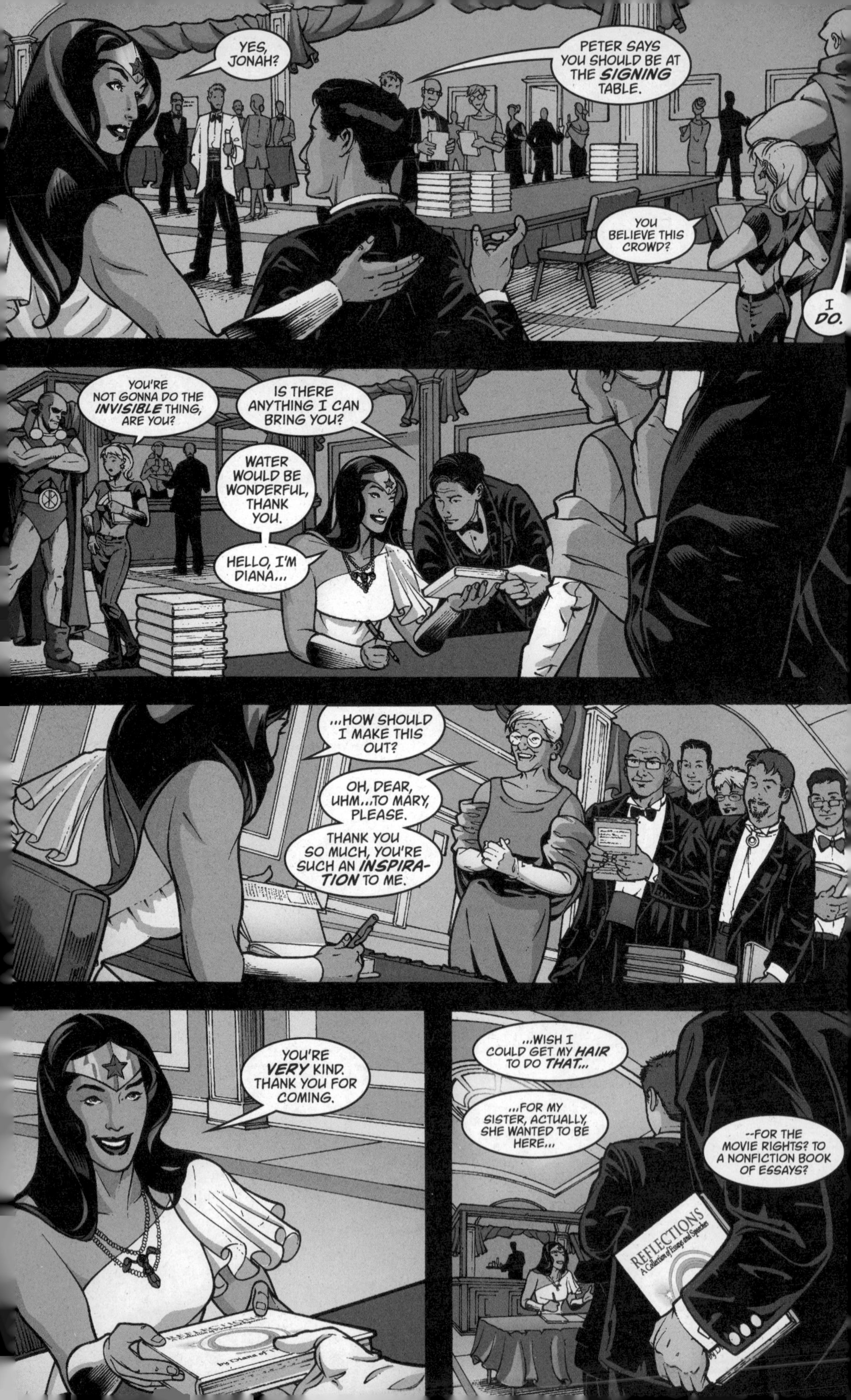
YES, JONAH?
PETER SAYS YOU SHOULD BE AT THE SIGNING TABLE.
YOU BELIEVE THIS CROWD?
I DO.
YOU'RE NOT GONNA DO THE INVISIBLE THING, ARE YOU?
IS THERE ANYTHING I CAN BRING YOU?
WATER WOULD BE WONDERFUL, THANK YOU.
HELLO, I'M DIANA...
...HOW SHOULD I MAKE THIS OUT?
OH, DEAR, UHM...TO MARY, PLEASE.
THANK YOU SO MUCH, YOU'RE SUCH AN INSPIRATION TO ME.
YOU'RE VERY KIND. THANK YOU FOR COMING.
...WISH I COULD GET MY HAIR TO DO THAT...
...FOR MY SISTER, ACTUALLY, SHE WANTED TO BE HERE...
--FOR THE MOVIE RIGHTS? TO A NONFICTION BOOK OF ESSAYS?
REFLECTIONS A Collection of Essays and Speeches

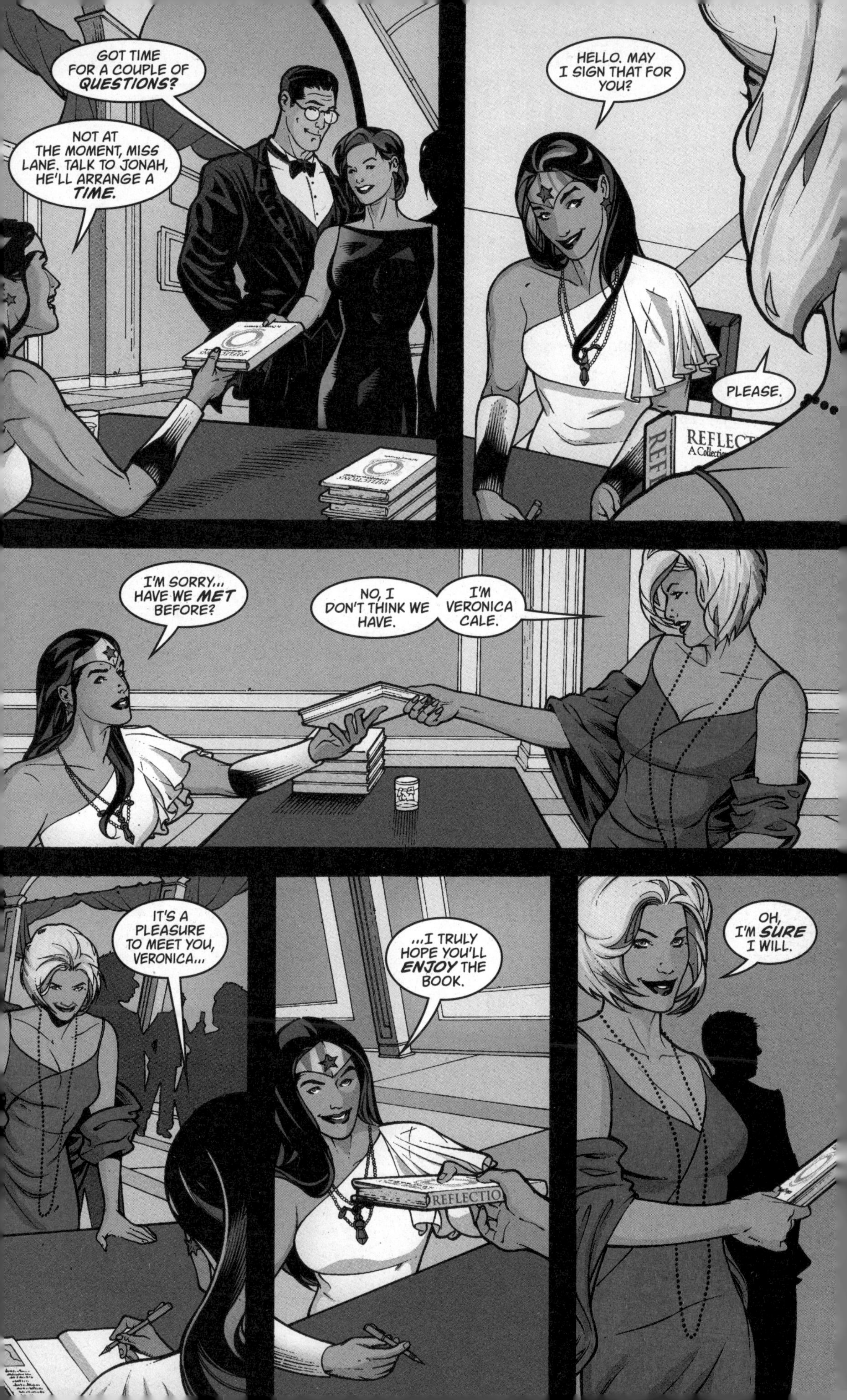
GOT TIME FOR A COUPLE OF QUESTIONS?
NOT AT THE MOMENT, MISS LANE. TALK TO JONAH, HE'LL ARRANGE A TIME.
HELLO. MAY I SIGN THAT FOR YOU?
PLEASE.
REFLECT
A Collection
I'M SORRY... HAVE WE MET BEFORE?
NO, I DON'T THINK WE HAVE.
I'M VERONICA CALE.
IT'S A PLEASURE TO MEET YOU, VERONICA...
...I TRULY HOPE YOU'LL ENJOY THE BOOK.
REFLECTIO
OH, I'M SURE I WILL.

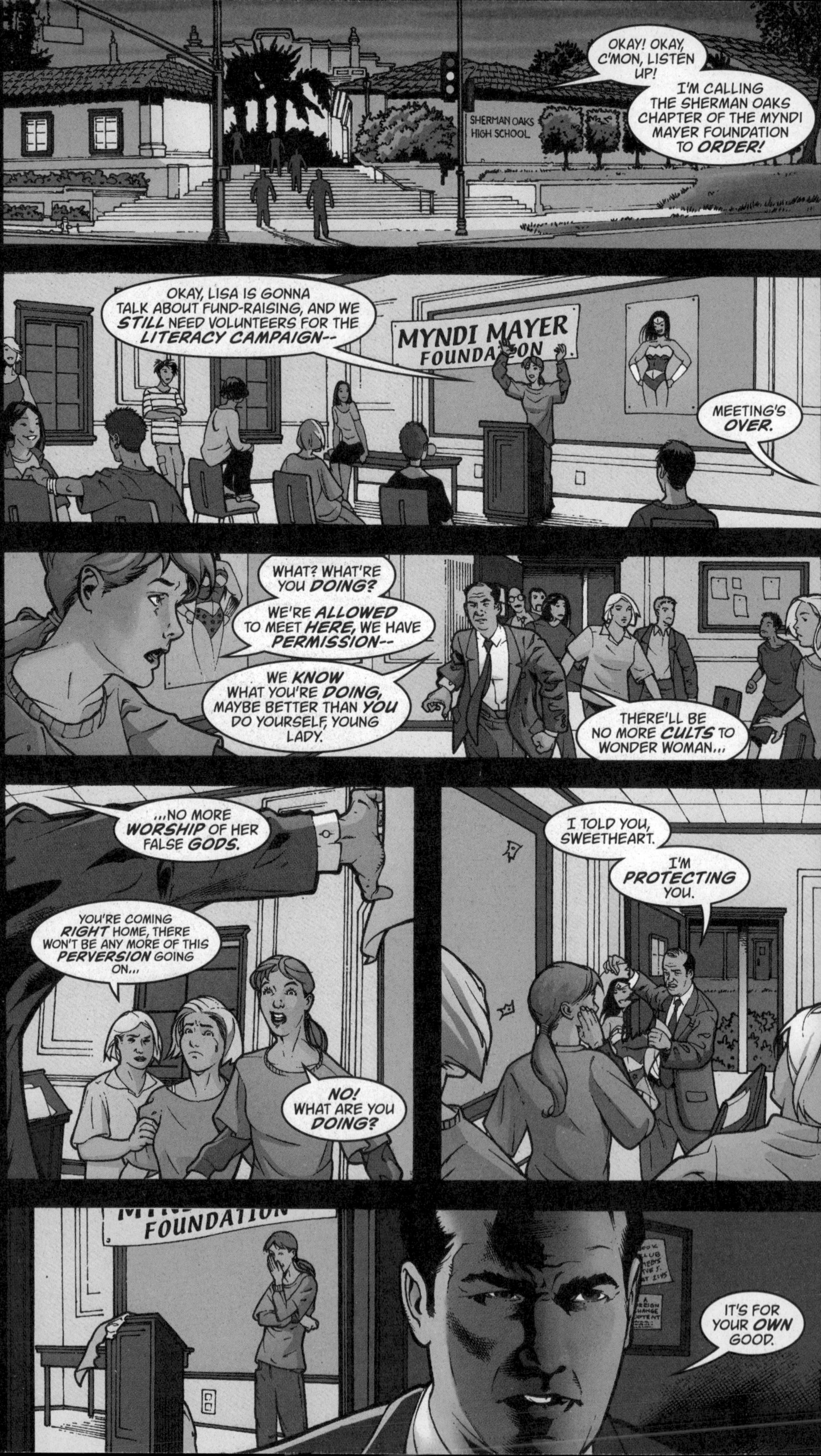

OKAY! OKAY, C'MON, LISTEN UP!
I'M CALLING THE SHERMAN OAKS CHAPTER OF THE MYNDI MAYER FOUNDATION TO ORDER!
SHERMAN OAKS HIGH SCHOOL
OKAY, LISA IS GONNA TALK ABOUT FUND-RAISING, AND WE STILL NEED VOLUNTEERS FOR THE LITERACY CAMPAIGN--
MYNDI MAYER FOUNDA
MEETING'S OVER.
WHAT? WHAT'RE YOU DOING?
WE'RE ALLOWED TO MEET HERE, WE HAVE PERMISSION--
WE KNOW WHAT YOU'RE DOING, MAYBE BETTER THAN YOU DO YOURSELF, YOUNG LADY.
THERE'LL BE NO MORE CULTS TO WONDER WOMAN...
...NO MORE WORSHIP OF HER FALSE GODS.
YOU'RE COMING RIGHT HOME, THERE WON'T BE ANY MORE OF THIS PERVERSION GOING ON...
NO! WHAT ARE YOU DOING?
I TOLD YOU, SWEETHEART.
I'M PROTECTING YOU.
FOUNDATION
IT'S FOR YOUR OWN GOOD.

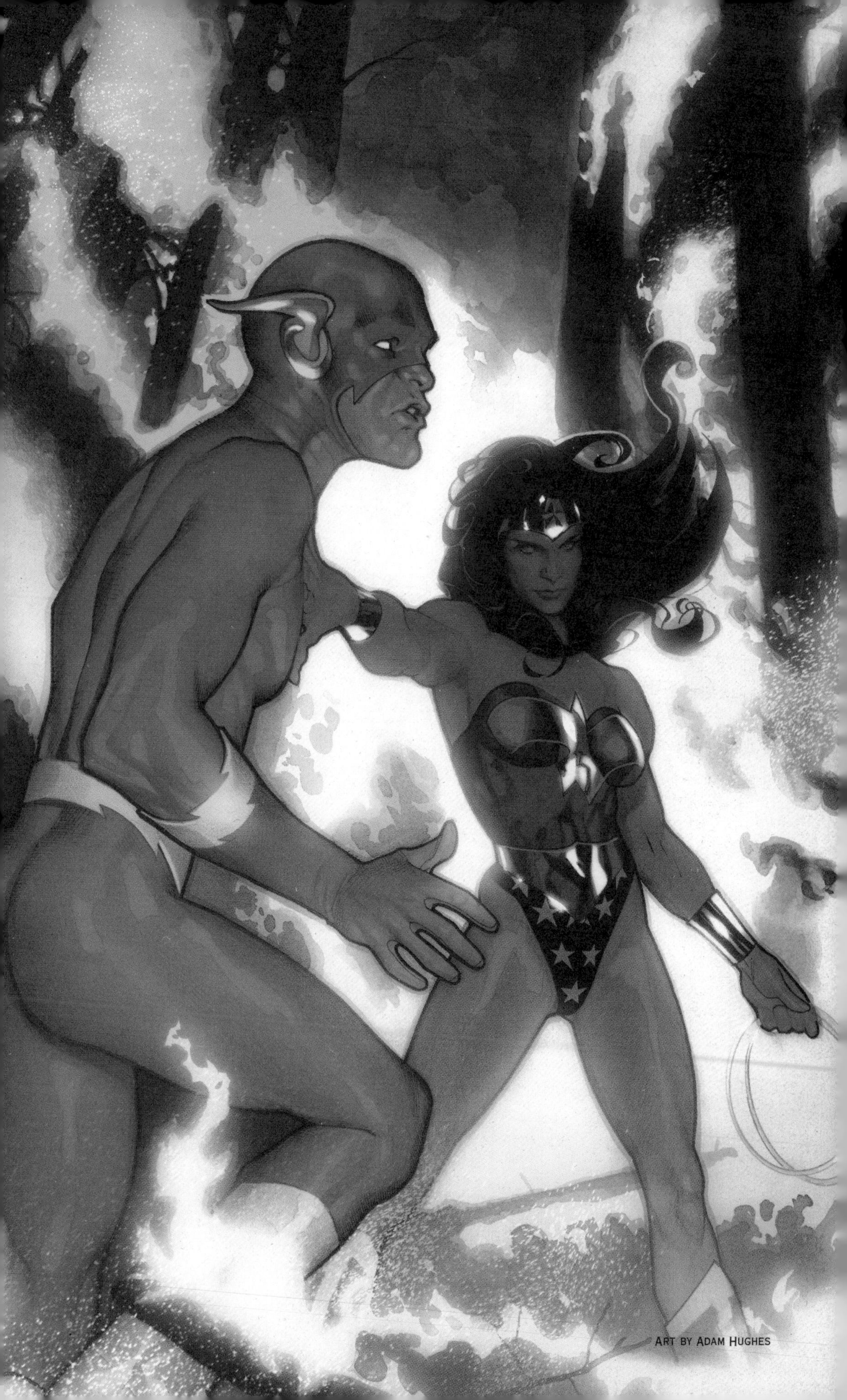

Art by Adam Hughes

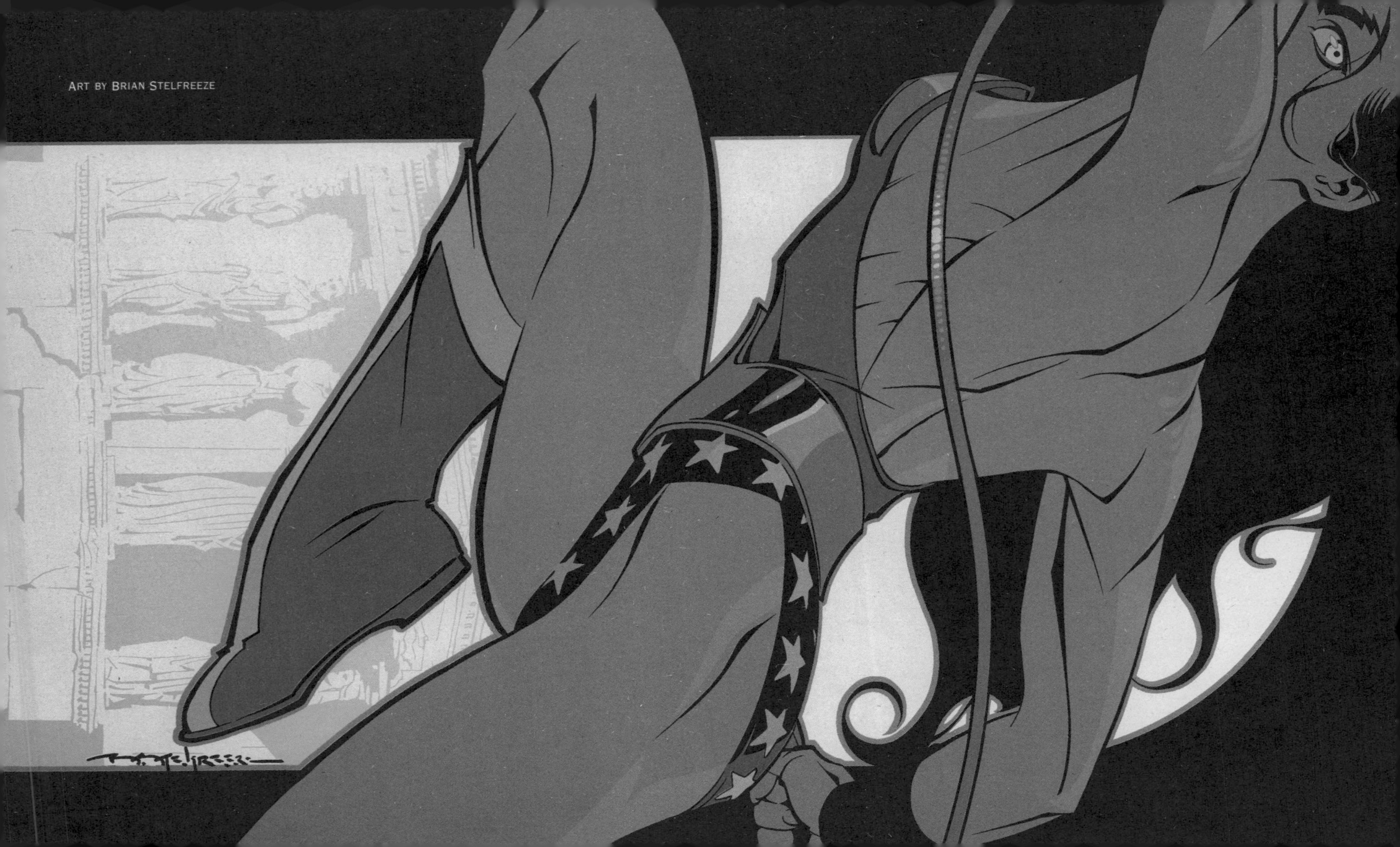

Art by Brian Stelfreeze

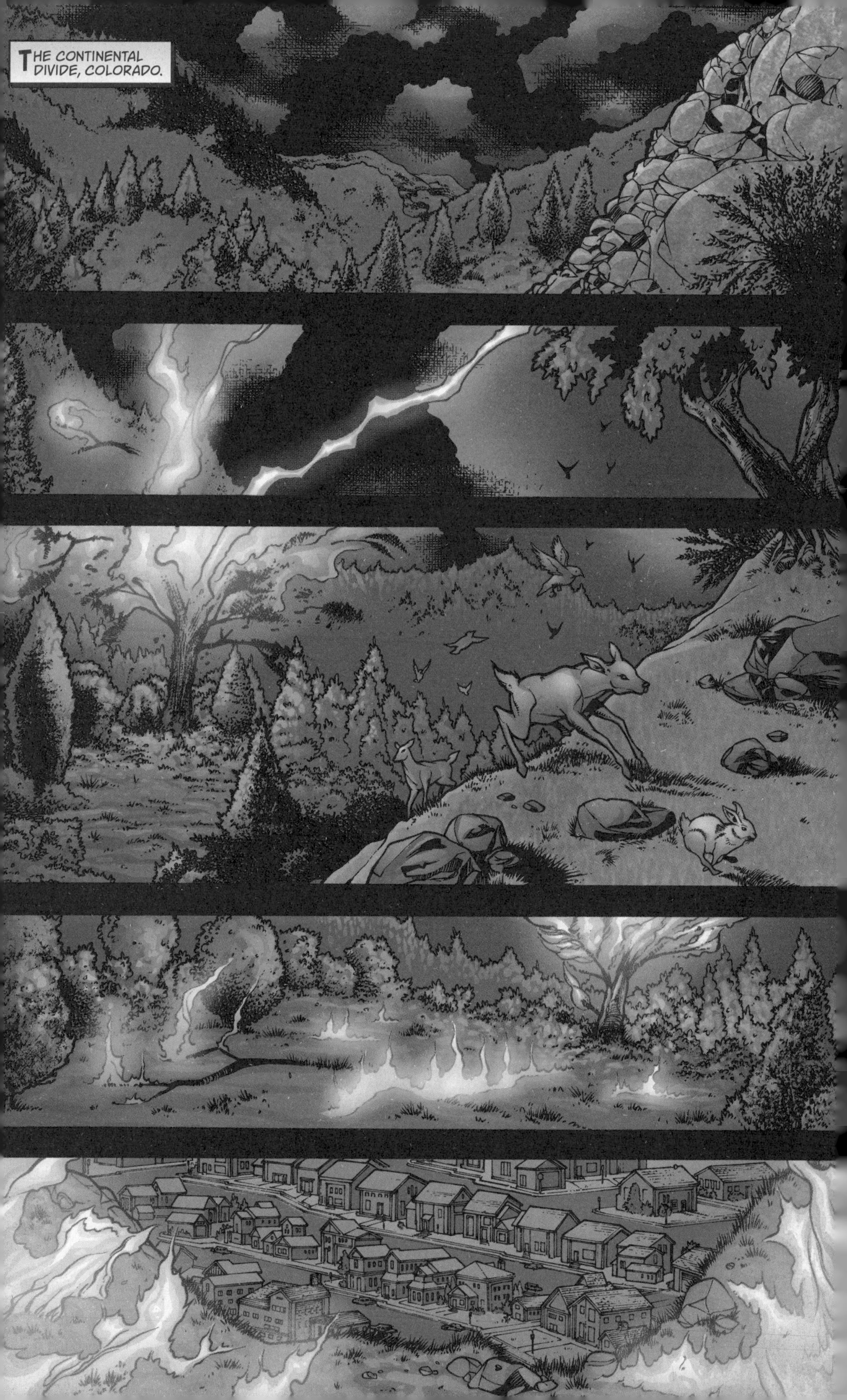
THE CONTINENTAL DIVIDE, COLORADO.

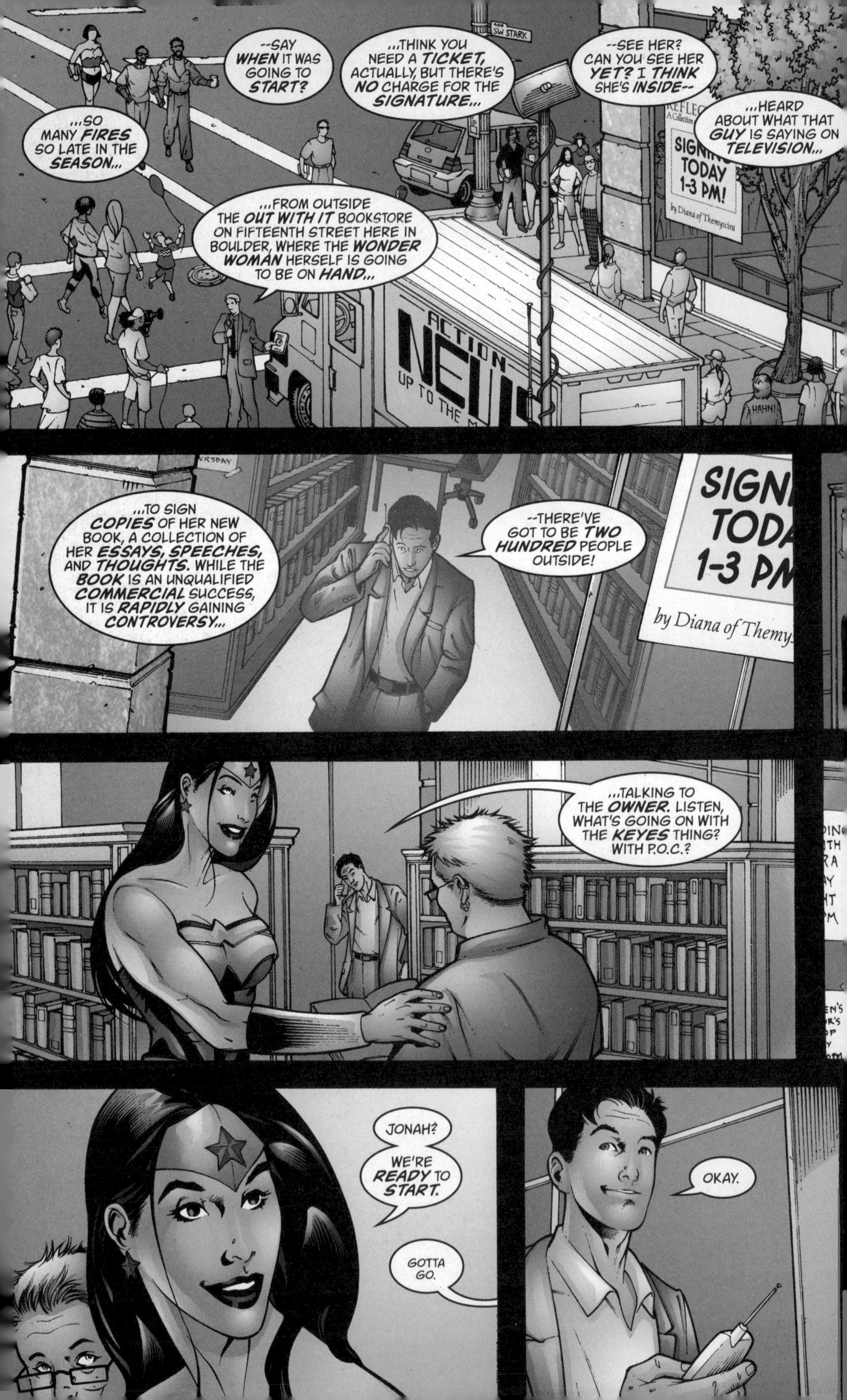
SW STARK
...SO MANY FIRES SO LATE IN THE SEASON...
--SAY WHEN IT WAS GOING TO START?
...THINK YOU NEED A TICKET, ACTUALLY, BUT THERE'S NO CHARGE FOR THE SIGNATURE...
--SEE HER? CAN YOU SEE HER YET? I THINK SHE'S INSIDE--
...HEARD ABOUT WHAT THAT GUY IS SAYING ON TELEVISION...
SIGNING TODAY 1-3 PM!
by Diana of Themyscira
...FROM OUTSIDE THE OUT WITH IT BOOKSTORE ON FIFTEENTH STREET HERE IN BOULDER, WHERE THE WONDER WOMAN HERSELF IS GOING TO BE ON HAND...
ACTION NEWS
HAHN!
...TO SIGN COPIES OF HER NEW BOOK, A COLLECTION OF HER ESSAYS, SPEECHES, AND THOUGHTS. WHILE THE BOOK IS AN UNQUALIFIED COMMERCIAL SUCCESS, IT IS RAPIDLY GAINING CONTROVERSY...
--THERE'VE GOT TO BE TWO HUNDRED PEOPLE OUTSIDE!
...TALKING TO THE OWNER. LISTEN, WHAT'S GOING ON WITH THE KEYES THING? WITH P.O.C.?
JONAH?
WE'RE READY TO START.
GOTTA GO.
OKAY.

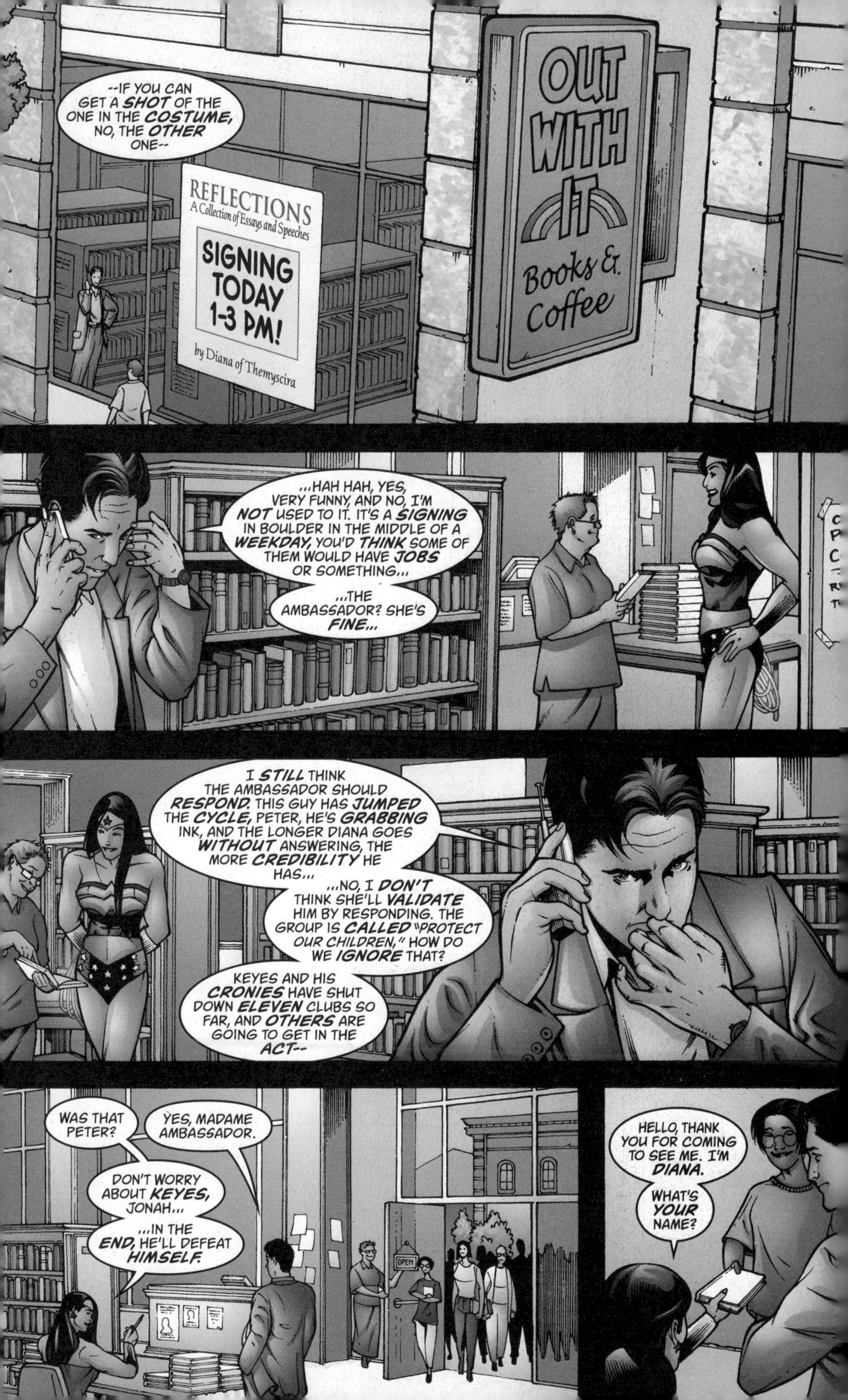
--IF YOU CAN GET A SHOT OF THE ONE IN THE COSTUME, NO, THE OTHER ONE--
REFLECTIONS
A Collection of Essays and Speeches
SIGNING TODAY 1-3 PM!
by Diana of Themyscira
OUT WITH IT
Books & Coffee
...HAH HAH, YES, VERY FUNNY, AND NO, I'M NOT USED TO IT. IT'S A SIGNING IN BOULDER IN THE MIDDLE OF A WEEKDAY, YOU'D THINK SOME OF THEM WOULD HAVE JOBS OR SOMETHING...
...THE AMBASSADOR? SHE'S FINE...
I STILL THINK THE AMBASSADOR SHOULD RESPOND. THIS GUY HAS JUMPED THE CYCLE, PETER, HE'S GRABBING INK, AND THE LONGER DIANA GOES WITHOUT ANSWERING, THE MORE CREDIBILITY HE HAS...
...NO, I DON'T THINK SHE'LL VALIDATE HIM BY RESPONDING. THE GROUP IS CALLED "PROTECT OUR CHILDREN," HOW DO WE IGNORE THAT?
KEYES AND HIS CRONIES HAVE SHUT DOWN ELEVEN CLUBS SO FAR, AND OTHERS ARE GOING TO GET IN THE ACT--
WAS THAT PETER?
YES, MADAME AMBASSADOR.
DON'T WORRY ABOUT KEYES, JONAH...
...IN THE END, HE'LL DEFEAT HIMSELF.
OPEN
HELLO, THANK YOU FOR COMING TO SEE ME. I'M DIANA.
WHAT'S YOUR NAME?

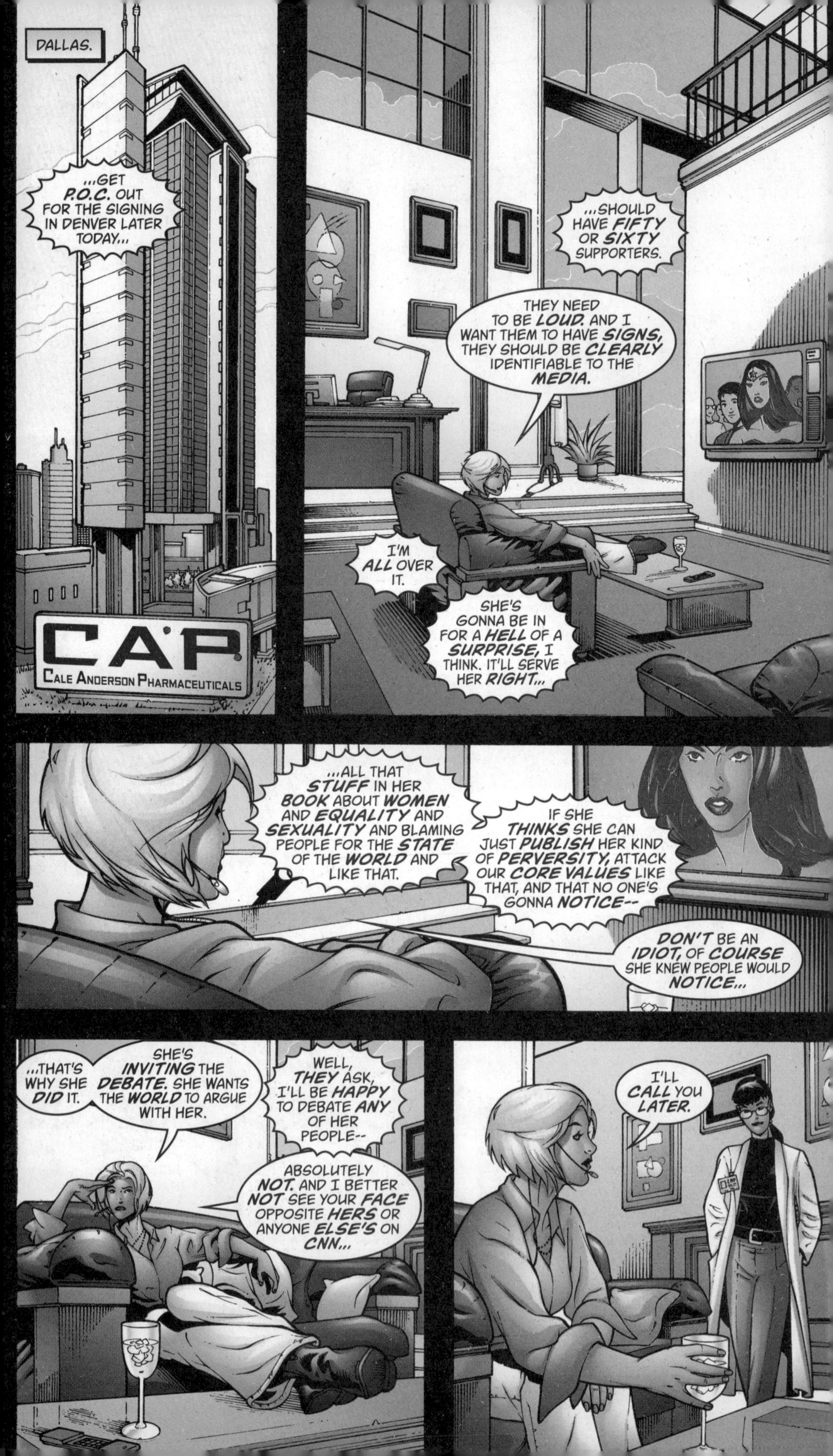
DALLAS.
...GET P.O.C. OUT FOR THE SIGNING IN DENVER LATER TODAY...
C.A.P.
CALE ANDERSON PHARMACEUTICALS
...SHOULD HAVE FIFTY OR SIXTY SUPPORTERS.
THEY NEED TO BE LOUD. AND I WANT THEM TO HAVE SIGNS, THEY SHOULD BE CLEARLY IDENTIFIABLE TO THE MEDIA.
I'M ALL OVER IT.
SHE'S GONNA BE IN FOR A HELL OF A SURPRISE, I THINK. IT'LL SERVE HER RIGHT...
...ALL THAT STUFF IN HER BOOK ABOUT WOMEN AND EQUALITY AND SEXUALITY AND BLAMING PEOPLE FOR THE STATE OF THE WORLD AND LIKE THAT.
IF SHE THINKS SHE CAN JUST PUBLISH HER KIND OF PERVERSITY, ATTACK OUR CORE VALUES LIKE THAT, AND THAT NO ONE'S GONNA NOTICE--
DON'T BE AN IDIOT, OF COURSE SHE KNEW PEOPLE WOULD NOTICE...
...THAT'S WHY SHE DID IT.
SHE'S INVITING THE DEBATE. SHE WANTS THE WORLD TO ARGUE WITH HER.
WELL, THEY ASK, I'LL BE HAPPY TO DEBATE ANY OF HER PEOPLE--
ABSOLUTELY NOT. AND I BETTER NOT SEE YOUR FACE OPPOSITE HERS OR ANYONE ELSE'S ON CNN...
I'LL CALL YOU LATER.

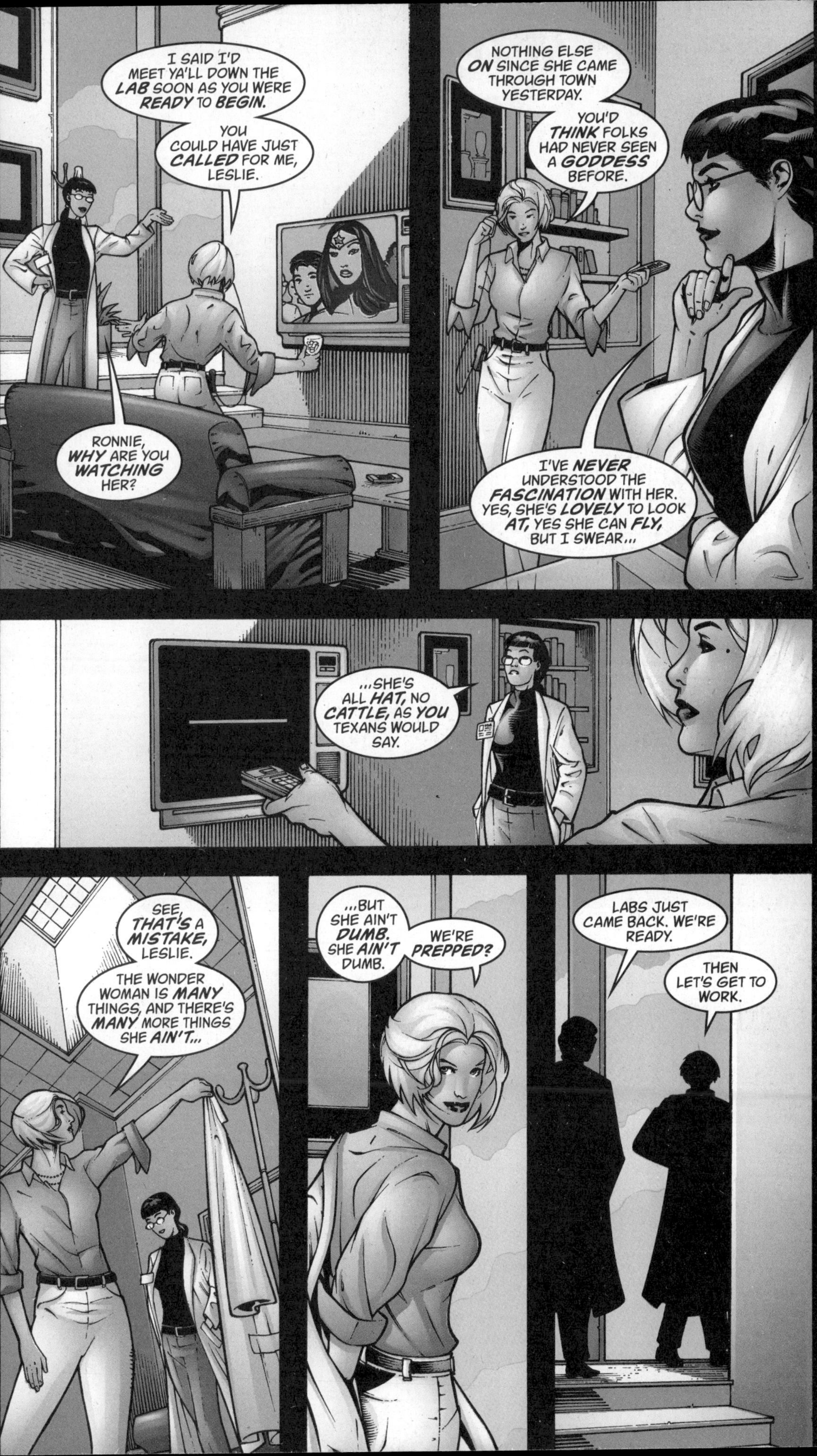
I SAID I'D MEET YA'LL DOWN THE LAB SOON AS YOU WERE READY TO BEGIN.
YOU COULD HAVE JUST CALLED FOR ME, LESLIE.
RONNIE, WHY ARE YOU WATCHING HER?
NOTHING ELSE ON SINCE SHE CAME THROUGH TOWN YESTERDAY.
YOU'D THINK FOLKS HAD NEVER SEEN A GODDESS BEFORE.
I'VE NEVER UNDERSTOOD THE FASCINATION WITH HER. YES, SHE'S LOVELY TO LOOK AT, YES SHE CAN FLY, BUT I SWEAR...
...SHE'S ALL HAT, NO CATTLE, AS YOU TEXANS WOULD SAY.
SEE, THAT'S A MISTAKE, LESLIE.
THE WONDER WOMAN IS MANY THINGS, AND THERE'S MANY MORE THINGS SHE AIN'T...
...BUT SHE AIN'T DUMB. SHE AIN'T DUMB.
WE'RE PREPPED?
LABS JUST CAME BACK. WE'RE READY.
THEN LET'S GET TO WORK.

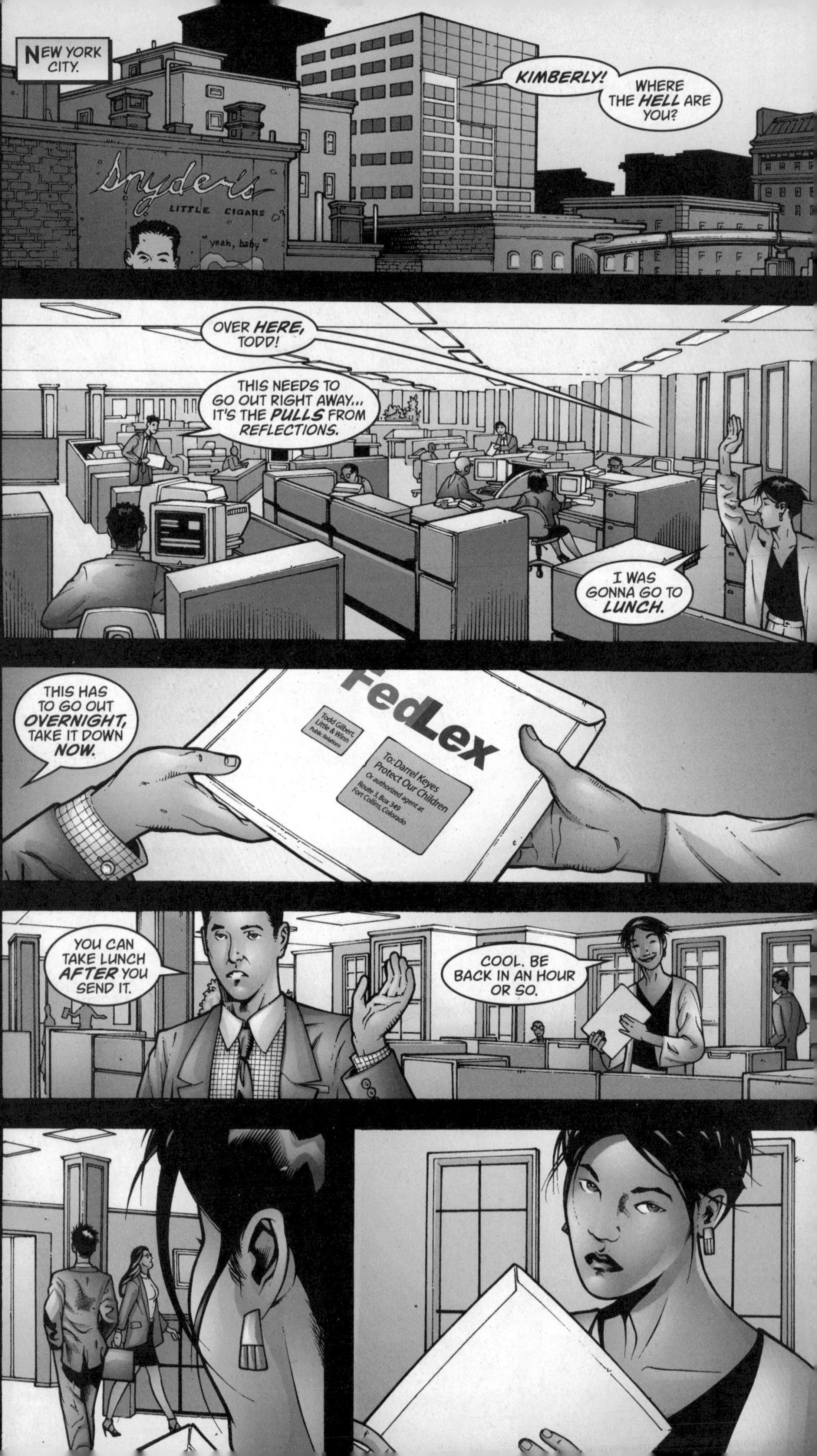
NEW YORK CITY.
snyder's LITTLE CIGARS
"yeah, baby"
KIMBERLY!
WHERE THE HELL ARE YOU?
OVER HERE, TODD!
THIS NEEDS TO GO OUT RIGHT AWAY... IT'S THE PULLS FROM REFLECTIONS.
I WAS GONNA GO TO LUNCH.
THIS HAS TO GO OUT OVERNIGHT, TAKE IT DOWN NOW.
FedLex
Todd Gilbert, Little & Winn Public Relations
To: Darrel Keyes Protect Our Children Or authorized agent at Route 3 Box 349 Fort Collins, Colorado
YOU CAN TAKE LUNCH AFTER YOU SEND IT.
COOL. BE BACK IN AN HOUR OR SO.

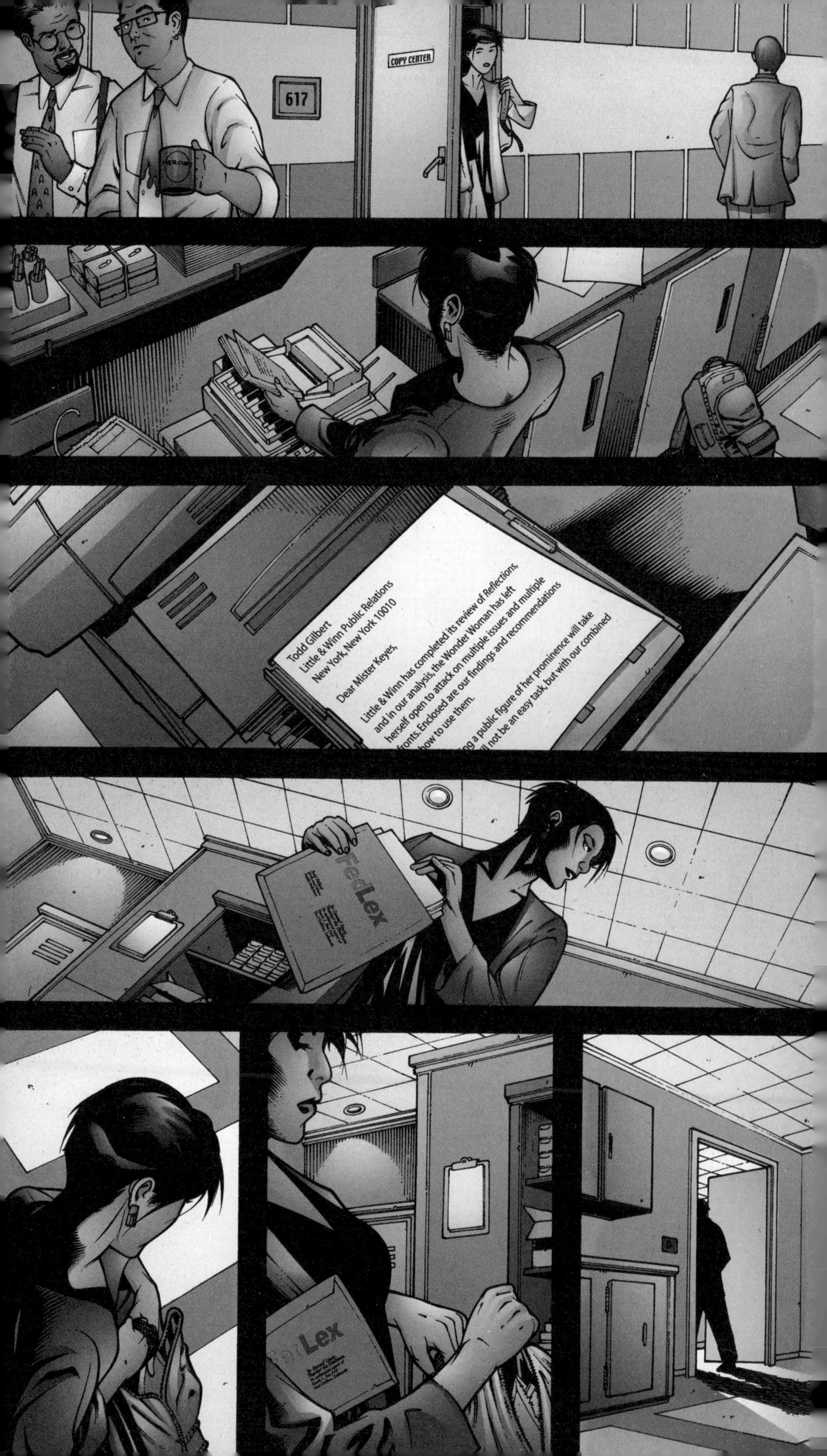
617
COPY CENTER
MERCURY
Todd Gilbert
Little & Winn Public Relations
New York, New York 10010
Dear Mister Keyes,
Little & Winn has completed its review of Reflections,
and in our analysis, the Wonder Woman has left
herself open to attack on multiple issues and multiple
fronts. Enclosed are our findings and recommendations
how to use them.
a public figure of her prominence will take
not be an easy task, but with our combined
FedLex
FedLex

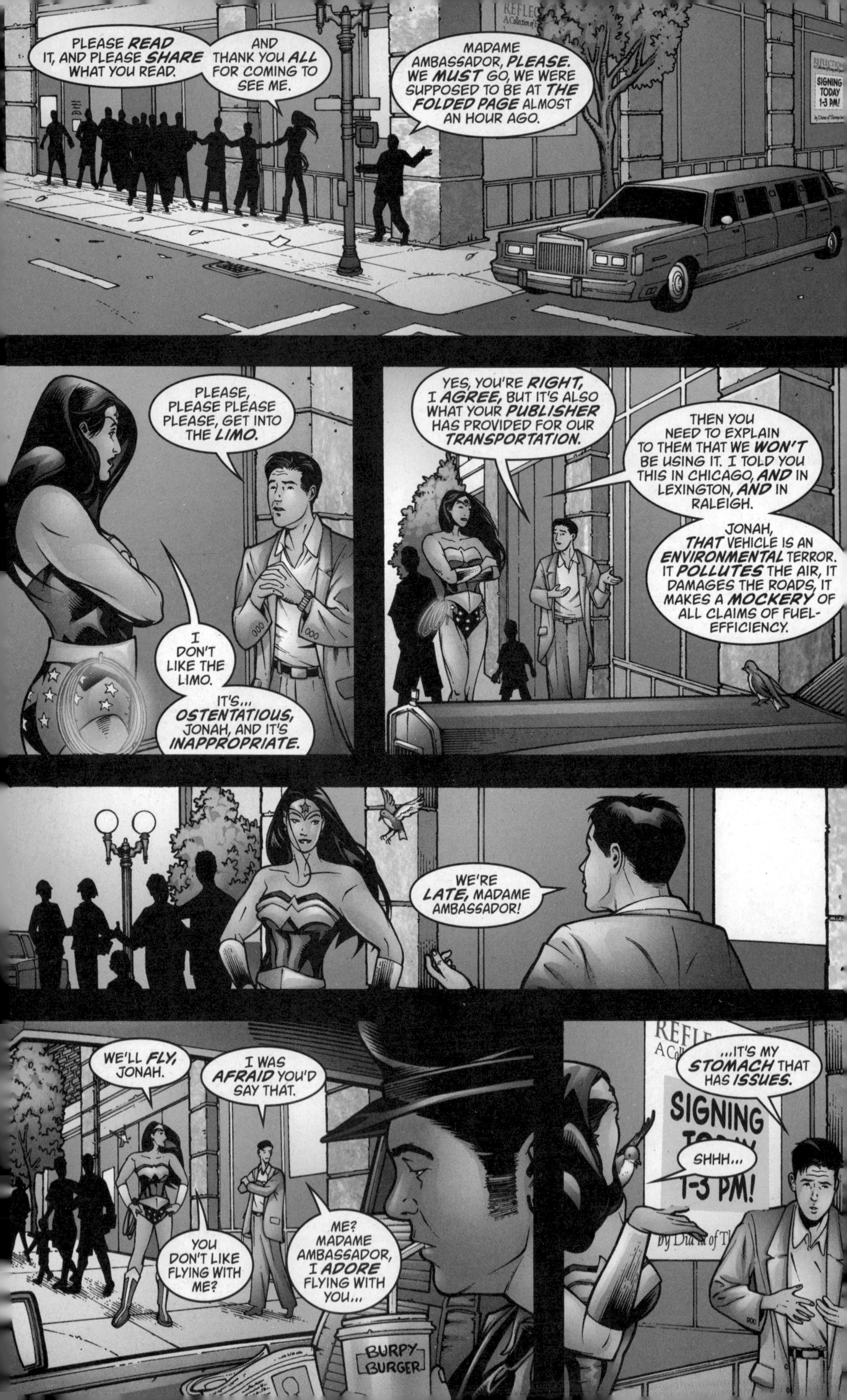

PLEASE READ IT, AND PLEASE SHARE WHAT YOU READ.
AND THANK YOU ALL FOR COMING TO SEE ME.
MADAME AMBASSADOR, PLEASE. WE MUST GO, WE WERE SUPPOSED TO BE AT THE FOLDED PAGE ALMOST AN HOUR AGO.
SIGNING TODAY 1-3 PM!
PLEASE, PLEASE PLEASE PLEASE, GET INTO THE LIMO.
I DON'T LIKE THE LIMO.
IT'S... OSTENTATIOUS, JONAH, AND IT'S INAPPROPRIATE.
YES, YOU'RE RIGHT, I AGREE, BUT IT'S ALSO WHAT YOUR PUBLISHER HAS PROVIDED FOR OUR TRANSPORTATION.
THEN YOU NEED TO EXPLAIN TO THEM THAT WE WON'T BE USING IT. I TOLD YOU THIS IN CHICAGO, AND IN LEXINGTON, AND IN RALEIGH.
JONAH, THAT VEHICLE IS AN ENVIRONMENTAL TERROR. IT POLLUTES THE AIR, IT DAMAGES THE ROADS, IT MAKES A MOCKERY OF ALL CLAIMS OF FUEL-EFFICIENCY.
WE'RE LATE, MADAME AMBASSADOR!
WE'LL FLY, JONAH.
I WAS AFRAID YOU'D SAY THAT.
YOU DON'T LIKE FLYING WITH ME?
ME? MADAME AMBASSADOR, I ADORE FLYING WITH YOU...
BURPY-BURGER
...IT'S MY STOMACH THAT HAS ISSUES.
SIGNING
1-3 PM!
SHHH...

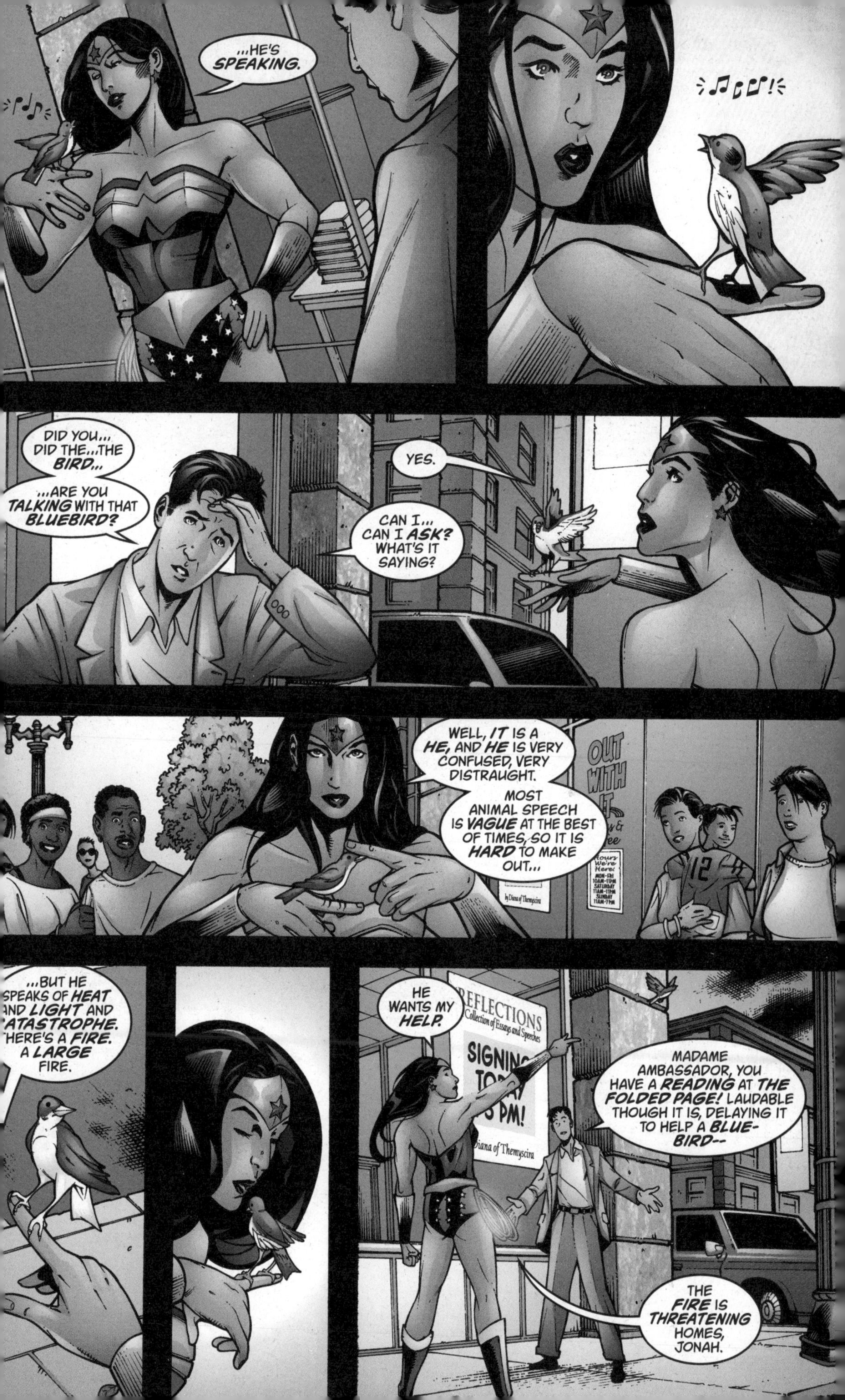
...HE'S SPEAKING.
DID YOU... DID THE...THE BIRD...
...ARE YOU TALKING WITH THAT BLUEBIRD?
YES.
CAN I... CAN I ASK? WHAT'S IT SAYING?
WELL, IT IS A HE, AND HE IS VERY CONFUSED, VERY DISTRAUGHT.
MOST ANIMAL SPEECH IS VAGUE AT THE BEST OF TIMES, SO IT IS HARD TO MAKE OUT...
OUT WITH IT
...BUT HE SPEAKS OF HEAT AND LIGHT AND ATASTROPHE. HERE'S A FIRE. A LARGE FIRE.
HE WANTS MY HELP.
REFLECTIONS
Collection of Essays and Speeches
Diana of Themyscira
MADAME AMBASSADOR, YOU HAVE A READING AT THE FOLDED PAGE! LAUDABLE THOUGH IT IS, DELAYING IT TO HELP A BLUE-BIRD--
THE FIRE IS THREATENING HOMES, JONAH.

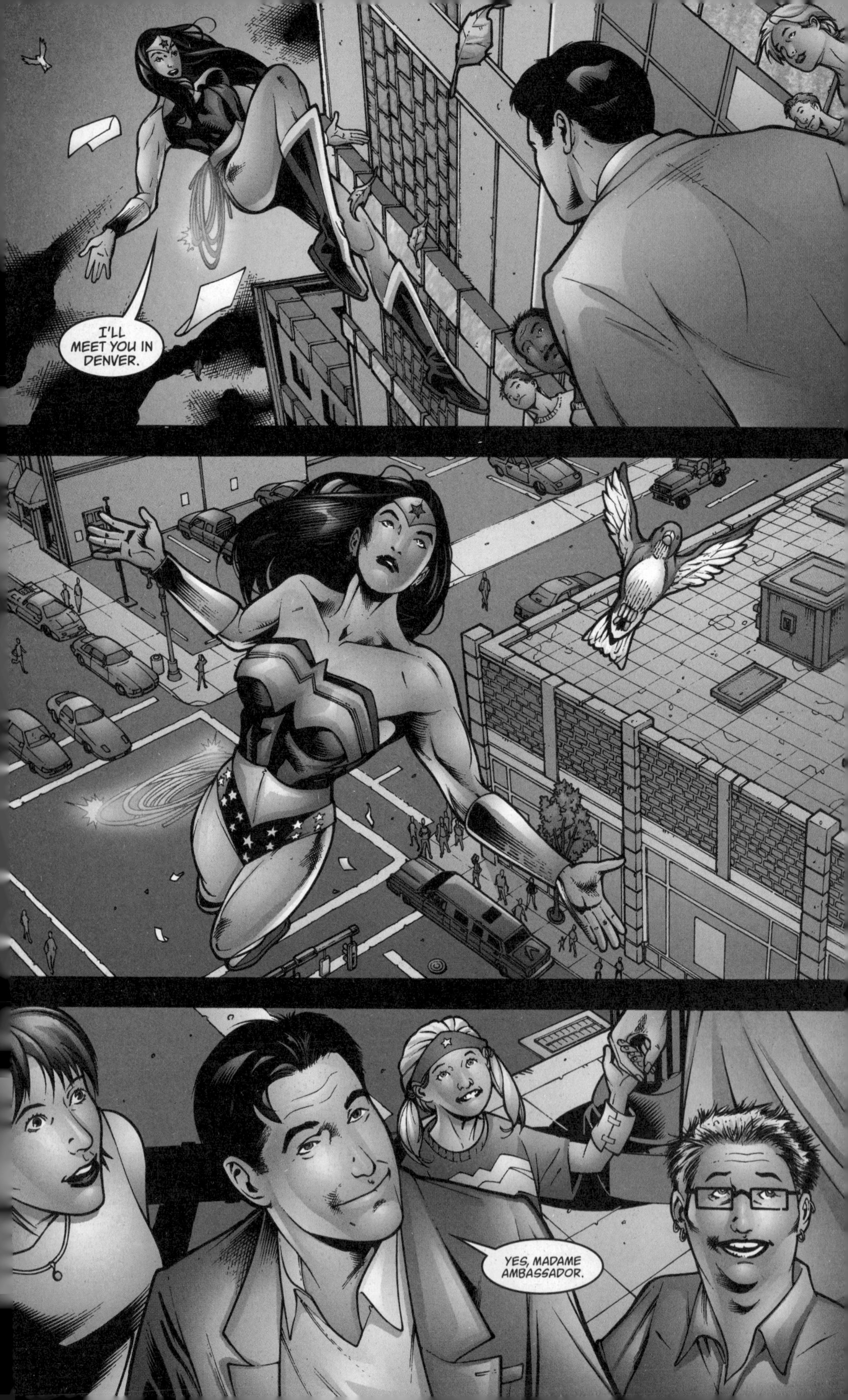

I'LL MEET YOU IN DENVER.
YES, MADAME AMBASSADOR.

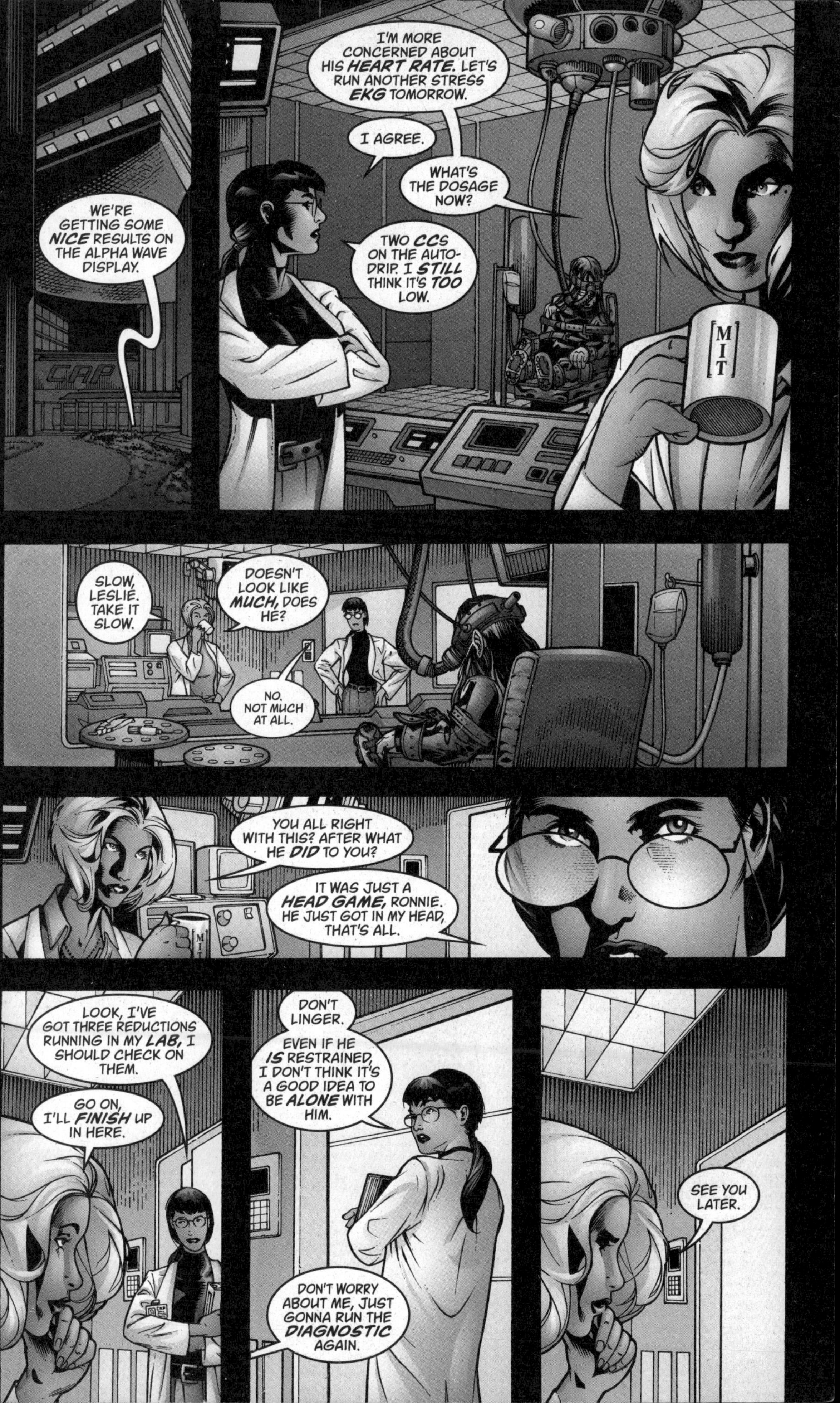

WE'RE GETTING SOME NICE RESULTS ON THE ALPHA WAVE DISPLAY.
I'M MORE CONCERNED ABOUT HIS HEART RATE. LET'S RUN ANOTHER STRESS EKG TOMORROW.
I AGREE.
WHAT'S THE DOSAGE NOW?
TWO CCS ON THE AUTO-DRIP. I STILL THINK IT'S TOO LOW.
MIT
SLOW, LESLIE. TAKE IT SLOW.
DOESN'T LOOK LIKE MUCH, DOES HE?
NO. NOT MUCH AT ALL.
YOU ALL RIGHT WITH THIS? AFTER WHAT HE DID TO YOU?
IT WAS JUST A HEAD GAME, RONNIE. HE JUST GOT IN MY HEAD, THAT'S ALL.
LOOK, I'VE GOT THREE REDUCTIONS RUNNING IN MY LAB, I SHOULD CHECK ON THEM.
GO ON, I'LL FINISH UP IN HERE.
DON'T LINGER.
EVEN IF HE IS RESTRAINED, I DON'T THINK IT'S A GOOD IDEA TO BE ALONE WITH HIM.
DON'T WORRY ABOUT ME, JUST GONNA RUN THE DIAGNOSTIC AGAIN.
SEE YOU LATER.

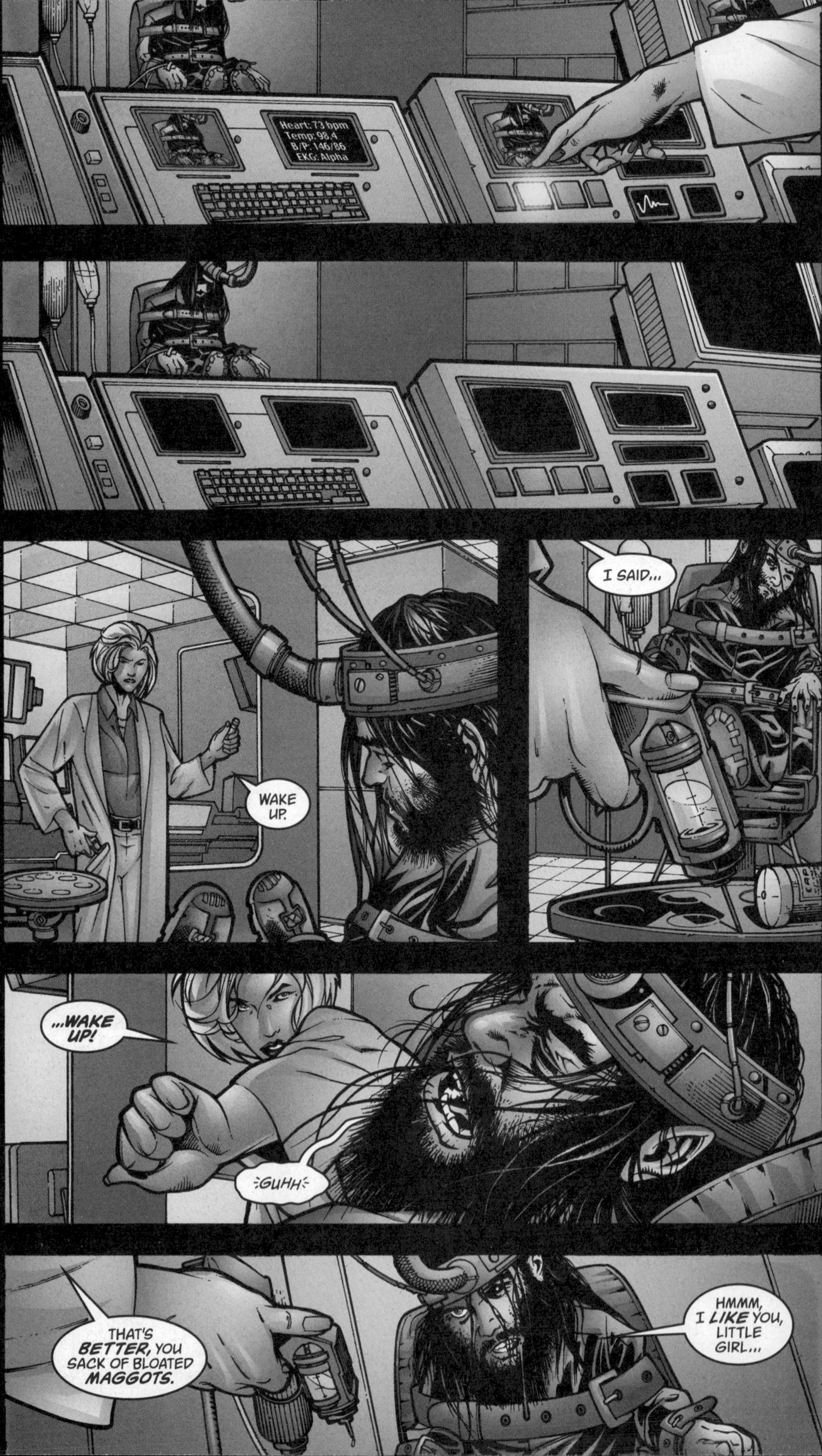
Heart: 73 bpm
Temp: 98.4
B/P: 146/86
EKG: Alpha
WAKE UP.
I SAID...
...WAKE UP!
GUHH
THAT'S BETTER, YOU SACK OF BLOATED MAGGOTS.
HMMM, I LIKE YOU, LITTLE GIRL...

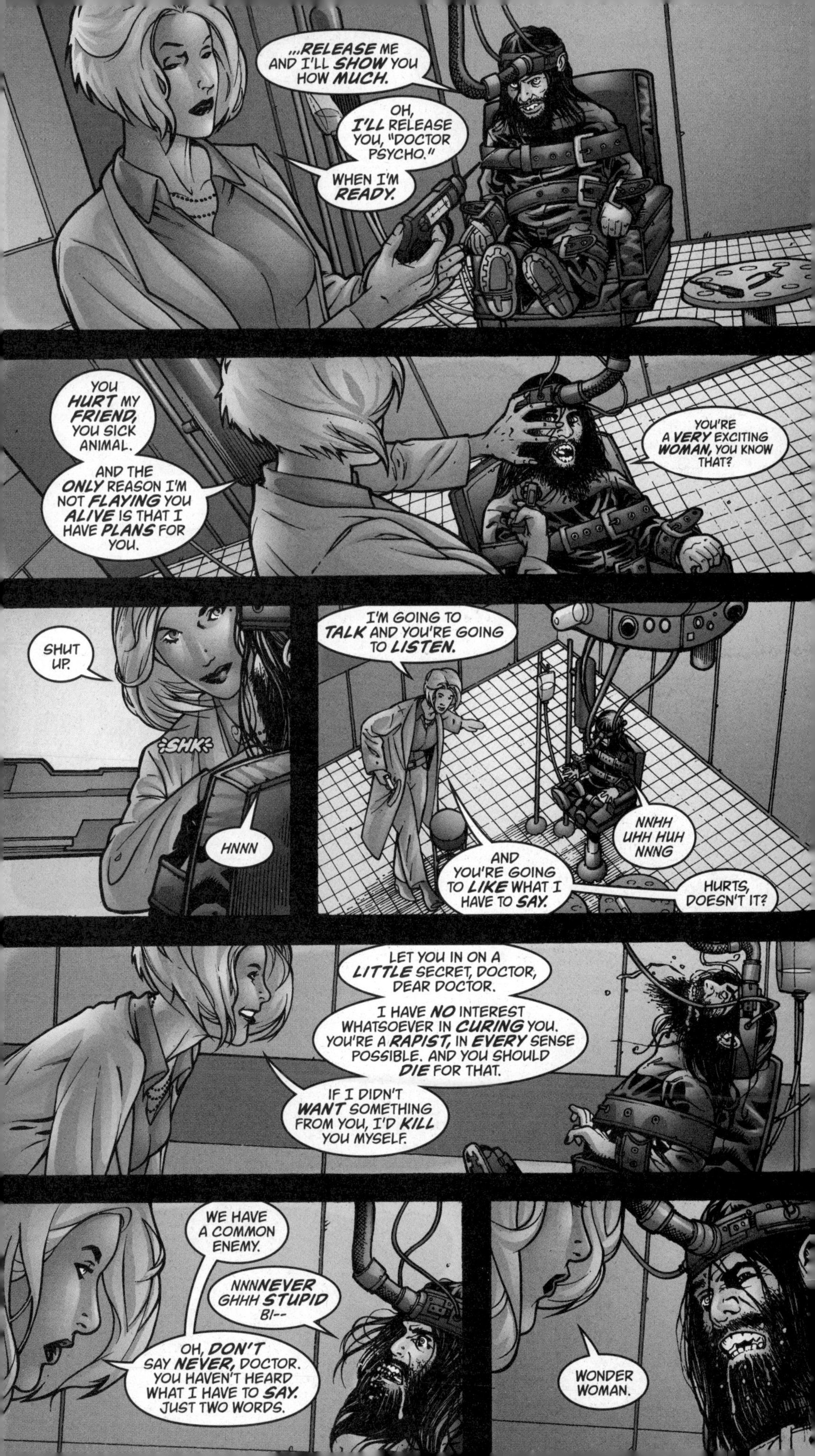

...RELEASE ME AND I'LL SHOW YOU HOW MUCH.
OH, I'LL RELEASE YOU, "DOCTOR PSYCHO."
WHEN I'M READY.
YOU HURT MY FRIEND, YOU SICK ANIMAL.
AND THE ONLY REASON I'M NOT FLAYING YOU ALIVE IS THAT I HAVE PLANS FOR YOU.
YOU'RE A VERY EXCITING WOMAN, YOU KNOW THAT?
SHUT UP.
SHK
HNNN
I'M GOING TO TALK AND YOU'RE GOING TO LISTEN.
NNHH UHH HUH NNNG
AND YOU'RE GOING TO LIKE WHAT I HAVE TO SAY.
HURTS, DOESN'T IT?
LET YOU IN ON A LITTLE SECRET, DOCTOR, DEAR DOCTOR.
I HAVE NO INTEREST WHATSOEVER IN CURING YOU. YOU'RE A RAPIST, IN EVERY SENSE POSSIBLE. AND YOU SHOULD DIE FOR THAT.
IF I DIDN'T WANT SOMETHING FROM YOU, I'D KILL YOU MYSELF.
WE HAVE A COMMON ENEMY.
NNNNEVER GHHH STUPID BI--
OH, DON'T SAY NEVER, DOCTOR. YOU HAVEN'T HEARD WHAT I HAVE TO SAY. JUST TWO WORDS.
WONDER WOMAN.

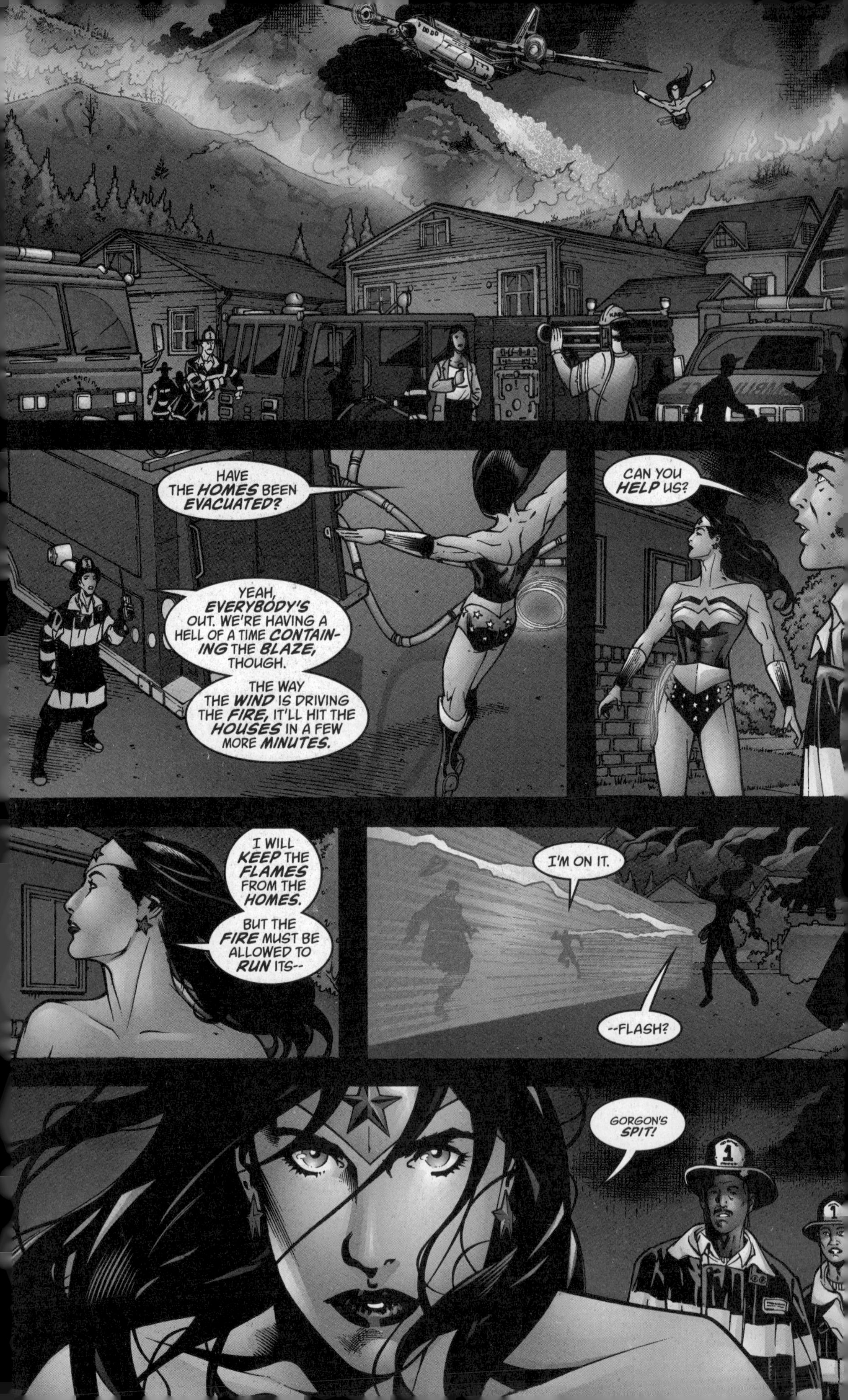
HAVE THE HOMES BEEN EVACUATED?
YEAH, EVERYBODY'S OUT. WE'RE HAVING A HELL OF A TIME CONTAIN-ING THE BLAZE, THOUGH.
THE WAY THE WIND IS DRIVING THE FIRE, IT'LL HIT THE HOUSES IN A FEW MORE MINUTES.
CAN YOU HELP US?
I WILL KEEP THE FLAMES FROM THE HOMES.
BUT THE FIRE MUST BE ALLOWED TO RUN ITS--
I'M ON IT.
--FLASH?
GORGON'S SPIT!

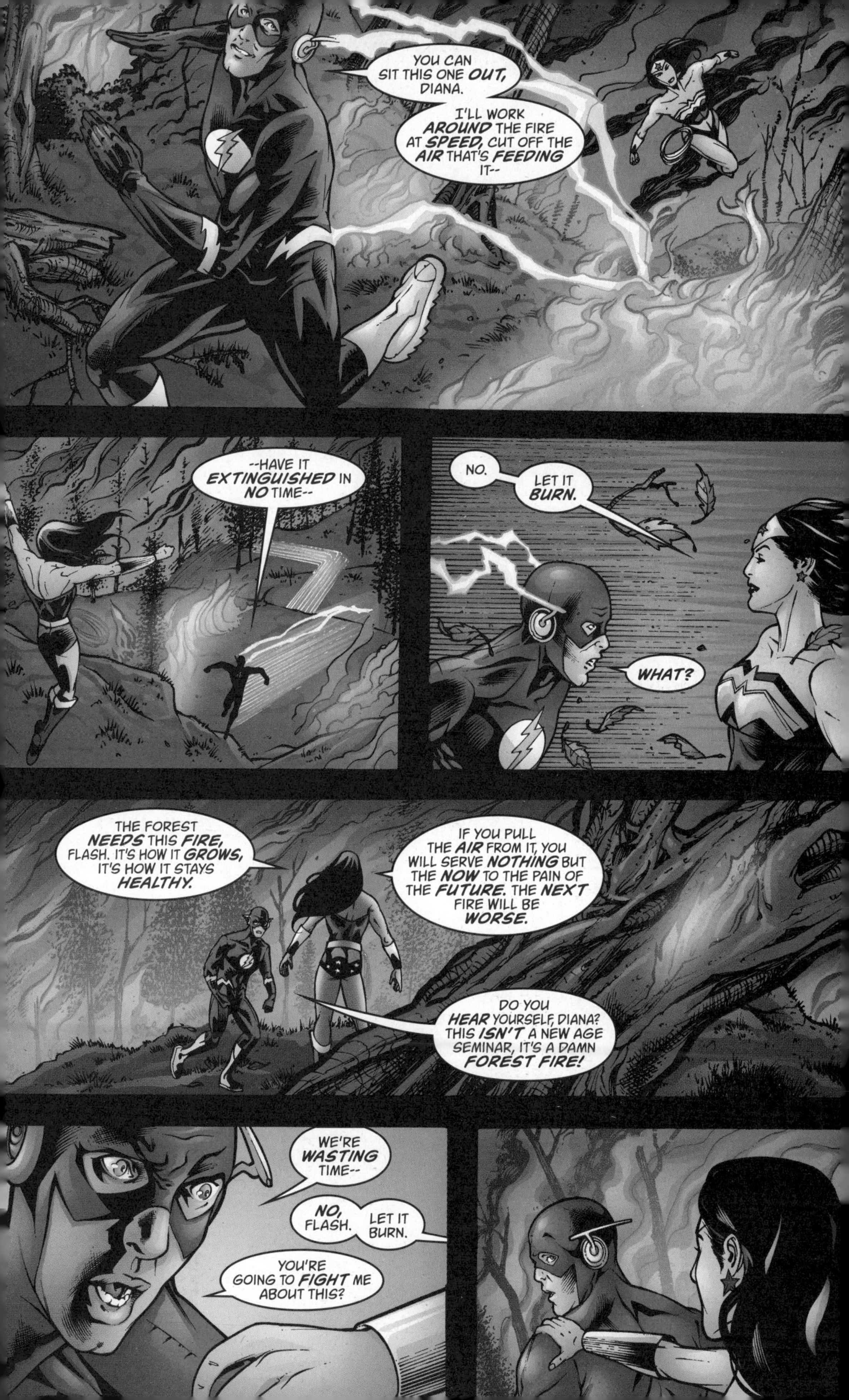
YOU CAN SIT THIS ONE OUT, DIANA.
I'LL WORK AROUND THE FIRE AT SPEED, CUT OFF THE AIR THAT'S FEEDING IT--
--HAVE IT EXTINGUISHED IN NO TIME--
NO.
LET IT BURN.
WHAT?
THE FOREST NEEDS THIS FIRE, FLASH. IT'S HOW IT GROWS, IT'S HOW IT STAYS HEALTHY.
IF YOU PULL THE AIR FROM IT, YOU WILL SERVE NOTHING BUT THE NOW TO THE PAIN OF THE FUTURE. THE NEXT FIRE WILL BE WORSE.
DO YOU HEAR YOURSELF, DIANA? THIS ISN'T A NEW AGE SEMINAR, IT'S A DAMN FOREST FIRE!
WE'RE WASTING TIME--
NO, FLASH.
LET IT BURN.
YOU'RE GOING TO FIGHT ME ABOUT THIS?

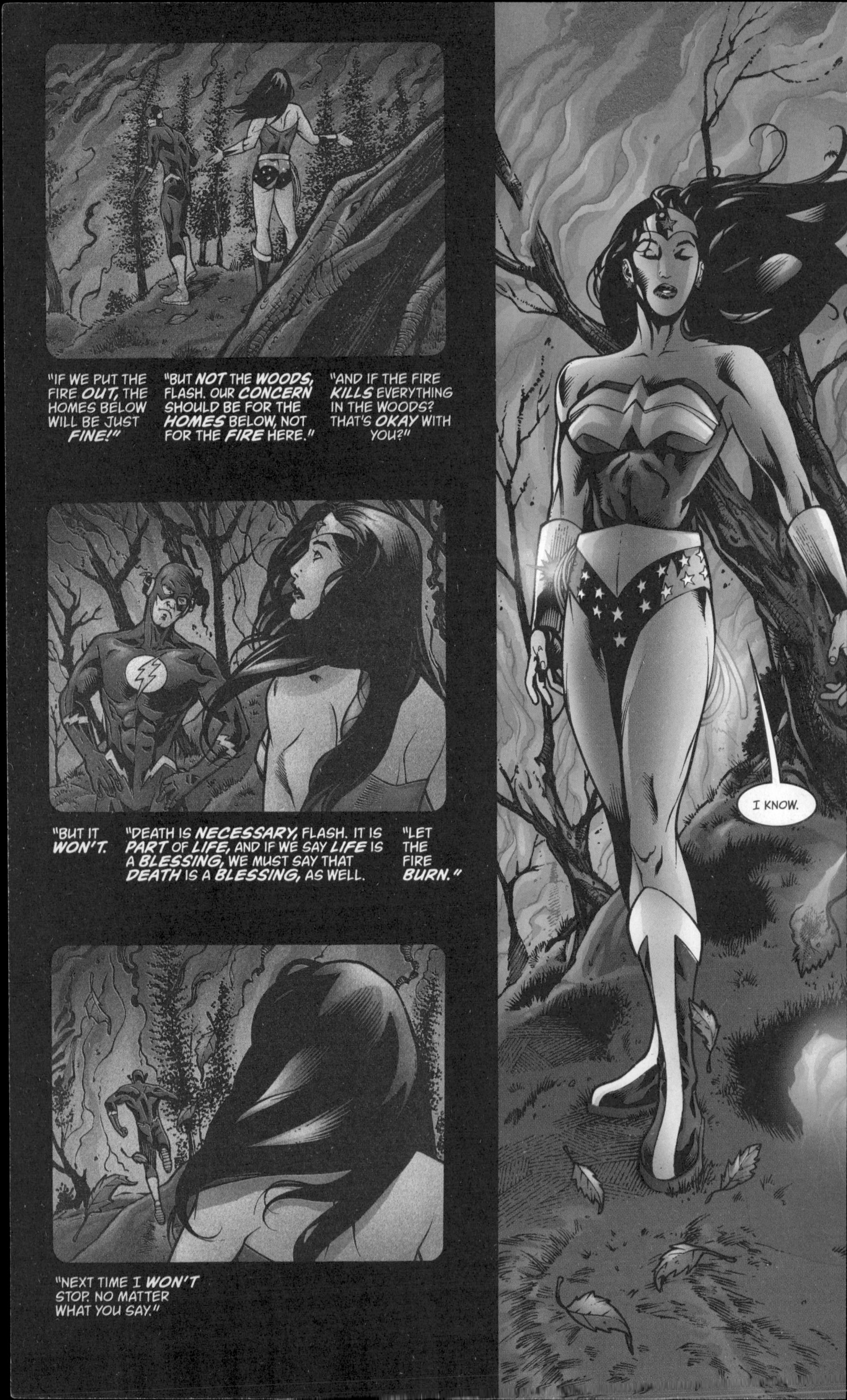
"IF WE PUT THE FIRE OUT, THE HOMES BELOW WILL BE JUST FINE!"
"BUT NOT THE WOODS, FLASH. OUR CONCERN SHOULD BE FOR THE HOMES BELOW, NOT FOR THE FIRE HERE."
"AND IF THE FIRE KILLS EVERYTHING IN THE WOODS? THAT'S OKAY WITH YOU?"
"BUT IT WON'T.
"DEATH IS NECESSARY, FLASH. IT IS PART OF LIFE, AND IF WE SAY LIFE IS A BLESSING, WE MUST SAY THAT DEATH IS A BLESSING, AS WELL.
"LET THE FIRE BURN."
"NEXT TIME I WON'T STOP. NO MATTER WHAT YOU SAY."
I KNOW.

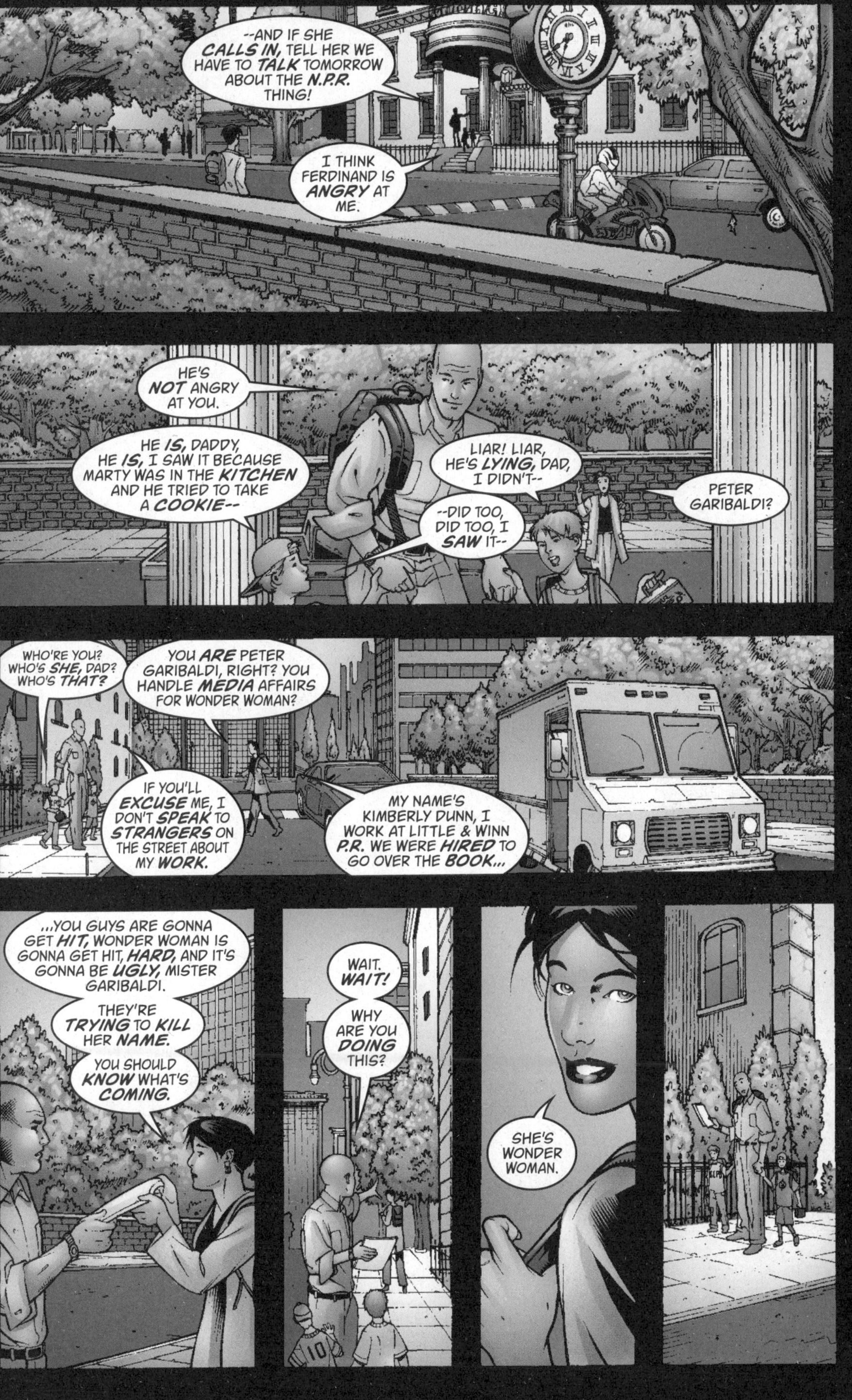
--AND IF SHE CALLS IN, TELL HER WE HAVE TO TALK TOMORROW ABOUT THE N.P.R. THING!
I THINK FERDINAND IS ANGRY AT ME.
HE'S NOT ANGRY AT YOU.
HE IS, DADDY, HE IS, I SAW IT BECAUSE MARTY WAS IN THE KITCHEN AND HE TRIED TO TAKE A COOKIE--
LIAR! LIAR, HE'S LYING, DAD, I DIDN'T--
--DID TOO, DID TOO, I SAW IT--
PETER GARIBALDI?
WHO'RE YOU? WHO'S SHE, DAD? WHO'S THAT?
YOU ARE PETER GARIBALDI, RIGHT? YOU HANDLE MEDIA AFFAIRS FOR WONDER WOMAN?
IF YOU'LL EXCUSE ME, I DON'T SPEAK TO STRANGERS ON THE STREET ABOUT MY WORK.
MY NAME'S KIMBERLY DUNN, I WORK AT LITTLE & WINN P.R. WE WERE HIRED TO GO OVER THE BOOK...
...YOU GUYS ARE GONNA GET HIT, WONDER WOMAN IS GONNA GET HIT, HARD, AND IT'S GONNA BE UGLY, MISTER GARIBALDI.
THEY'RE TRYING TO KILL HER NAME.
YOU SHOULD KNOW WHAT'S COMING.
WAIT. WAIT!
WHY ARE YOU DOING THIS?
SHE'S WONDER WOMAN.

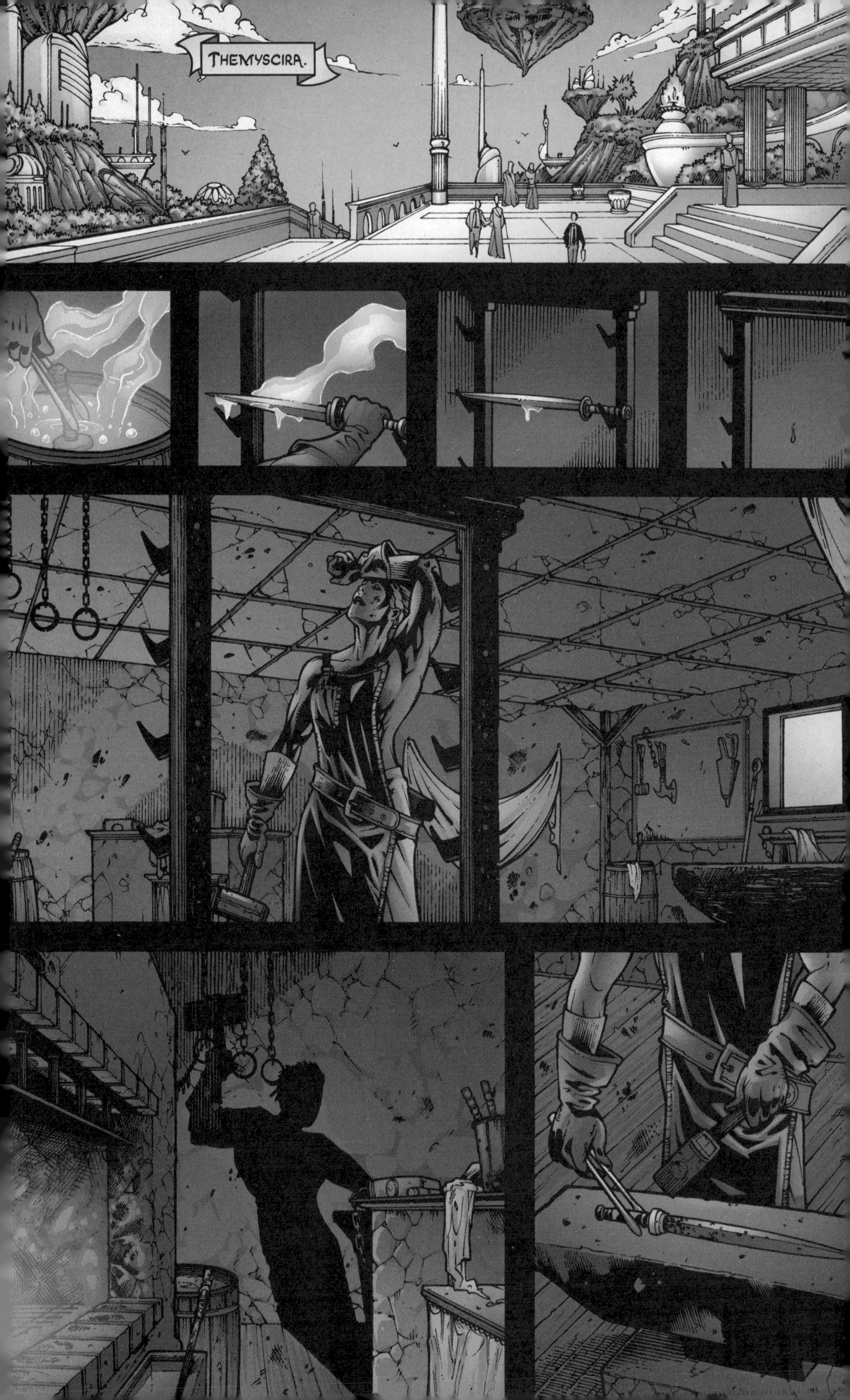
THEMYSCIRA.

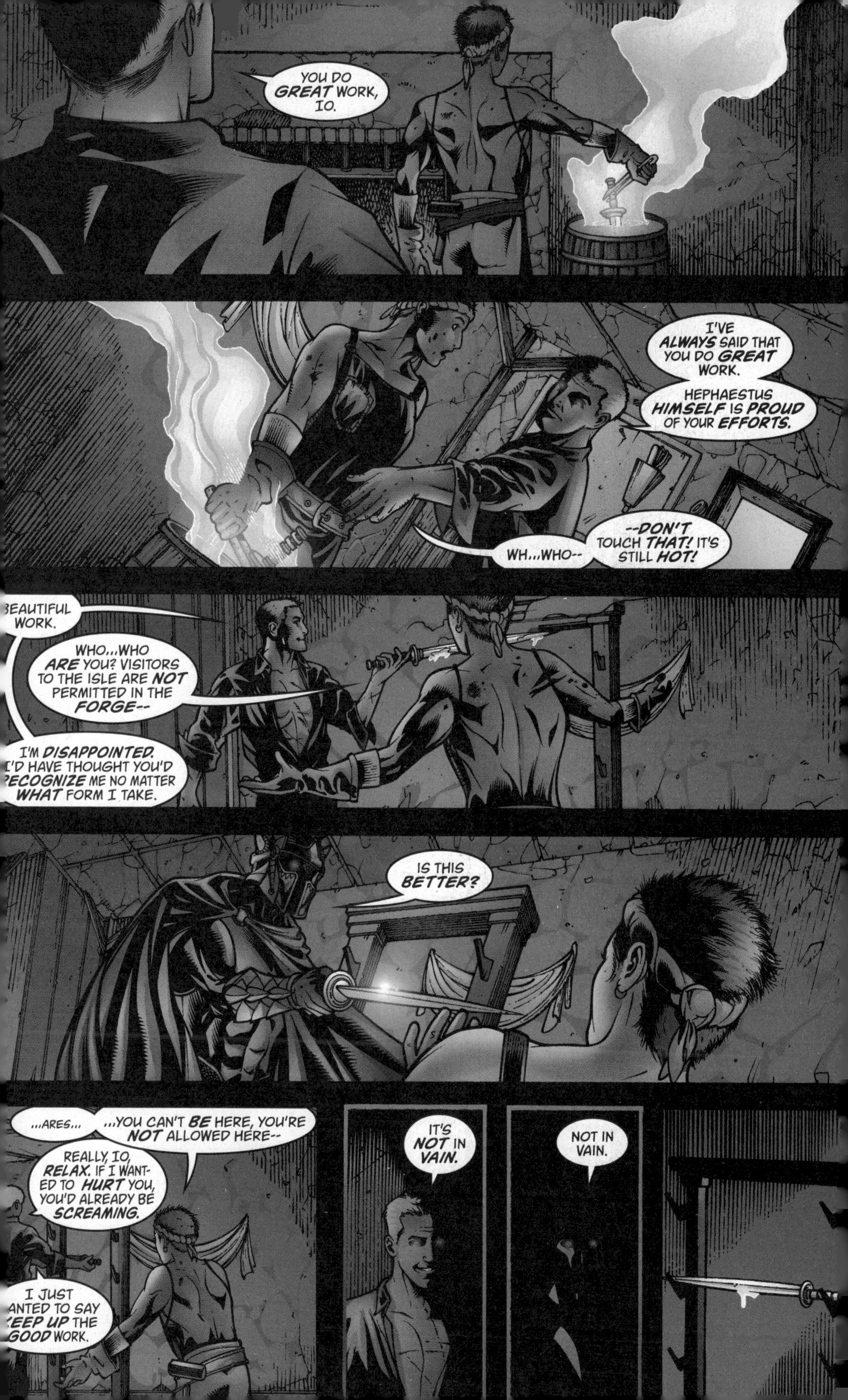
YOU DO GREAT WORK, IO.
I'VE ALWAYS SAID THAT YOU DO GREAT WORK.
HEPHAESTUS HIMSELF IS PROUD OF YOUR EFFORTS.
WH...WHO--
--DON'T TOUCH THAT! IT'S STILL HOT!
BEAUTIFUL WORK.
WHO...WHO ARE YOU? VISITORS TO THE ISLE ARE NOT PERMITTED IN THE FORGE--
I'M DISAPPOINTED. I'D HAVE THOUGHT YOU'D RECOGNIZE ME NO MATTER WHAT FORM I TAKE.
IS THIS BETTER?
...ARES...
...YOU CAN'T BE HERE, YOU'RE NOT ALLOWED HERE--
REALLY, IO, RELAX. IF I WANTED TO HURT YOU, YOU'D ALREADY BE SCREAMING.
I JUST WANTED TO SAY KEEP UP THE GOOD WORK.
IT'S NOT IN VAIN.
NOT IN VAIN.

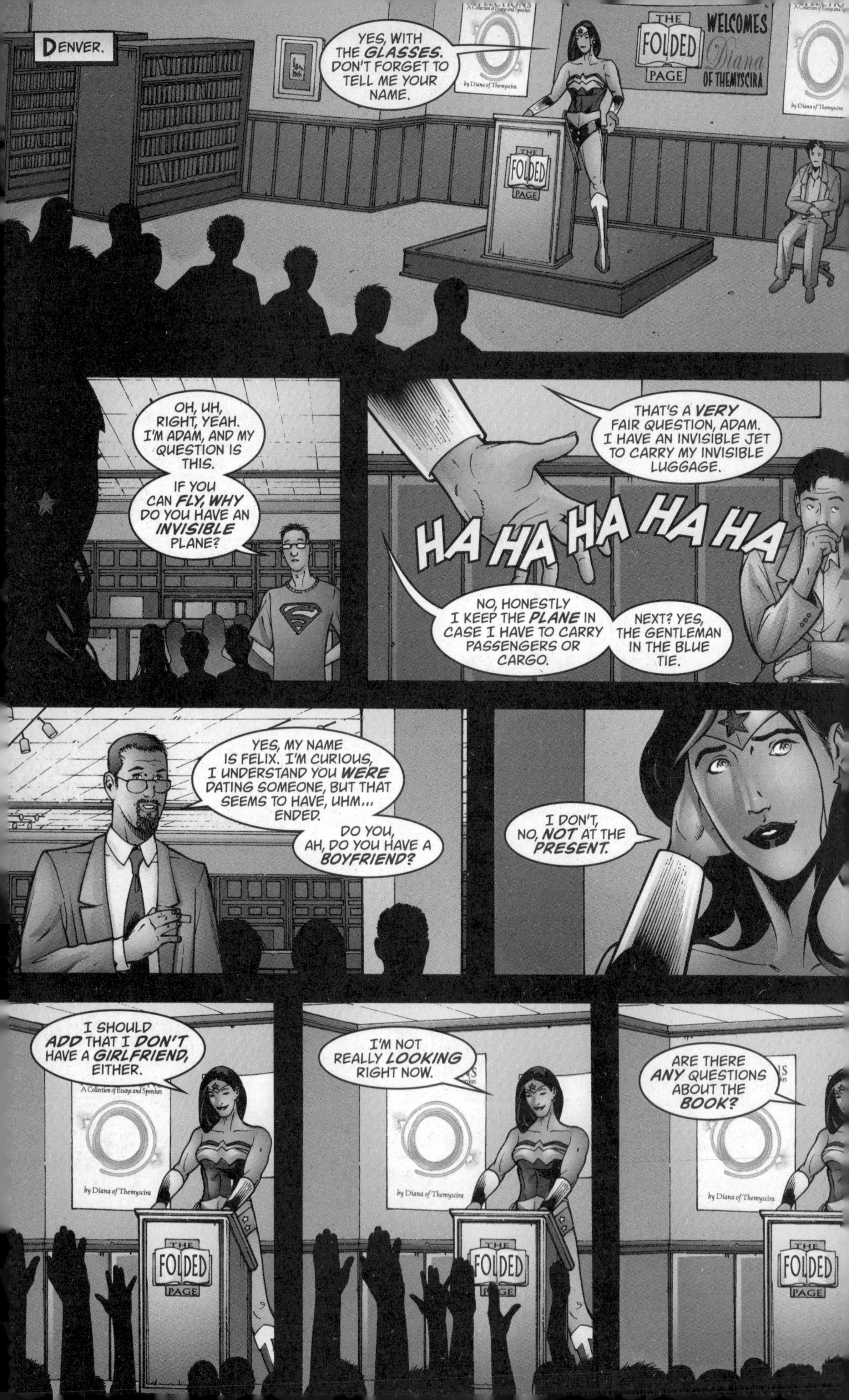
DENVER.
YES, WITH THE GLASSES. DON'T FORGET TO TELL ME YOUR NAME.
THE FOLDED PAGE WELCOMES Diana OF THEMYSCIRA
A Collection of Essays and Speeches
by Diana of Themyscira
OH, UH, RIGHT, YEAH. I'M ADAM, AND MY QUESTION IS THIS.
IF YOU CAN FLY, WHY DO YOU HAVE AN INVISIBLE PLANE?
THAT'S A VERY FAIR QUESTION, ADAM. I HAVE AN INVISIBLE JET TO CARRY MY INVISIBLE LUGGAGE.
HA HA HA HA HA HA
NO, HONESTLY I KEEP THE PLANE IN CASE I HAVE TO CARRY PASSENGERS OR CARGO.
NEXT? YES, THE GENTLEMAN IN THE BLUE TIE.
YES, MY NAME IS FELIX. I'M CURIOUS, I UNDERSTAND YOU WERE DATING SOMEONE, BUT THAT SEEMS TO HAVE, UHM... ENDED.
DO YOU, AH, DO YOU HAVE A BOYFRIEND?
I DON'T, NO, NOT AT THE PRESENT.
I SHOULD ADD THAT I DON'T HAVE A GIRLFRIEND, EITHER.
A Collection of Essays and Speeches
by Diana of Themyscira
THE FOLDED PAGE
I'M NOT REALLY LOOKING RIGHT NOW.
by Diana of Themyscira
ARE THERE ANY QUESTIONS ABOUT THE BOOK?
by Diana of Themyscira

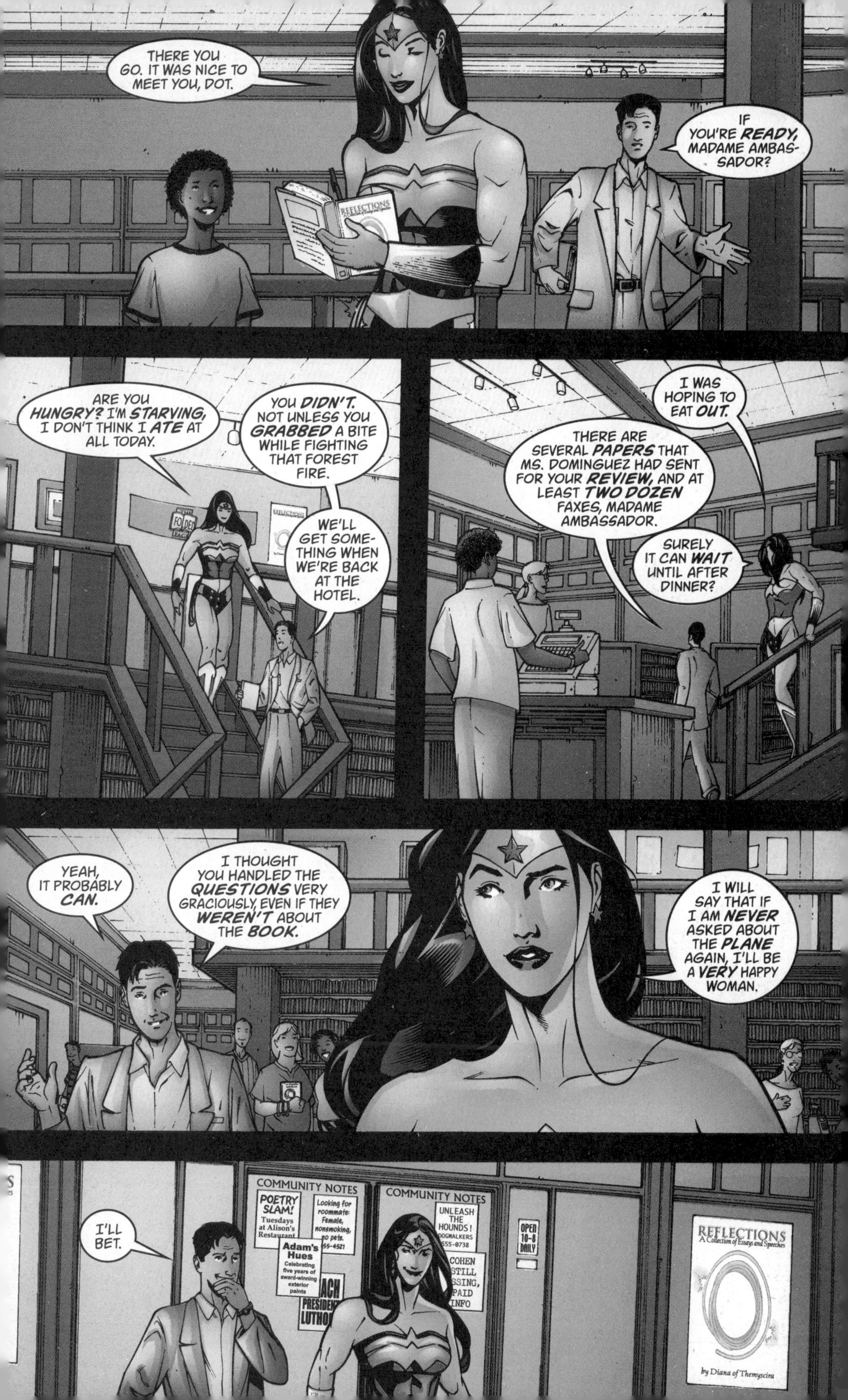
THERE YOU GO. IT WAS NICE TO MEET YOU, DOT.
REFLECTIONS A Collection of Essays and Speeches
IF YOU'RE READY, MADAME AMBASSADOR?
ARE YOU HUNGRY? I'M STARVING, I DON'T THINK I ATE AT ALL TODAY.
YOU DIDN'T. NOT UNLESS YOU GRABBED A BITE WHILE FIGHTING THAT FOREST FIRE.
WE'LL GET SOMETHING WHEN WE'RE BACK AT THE HOTEL.
I WAS HOPING TO EAT OUT.
THERE ARE SEVERAL PAPERS THAT MS. DOMINGUEZ HAD SENT FOR YOUR REVIEW, AND AT LEAST TWO DOZEN FAXES, MADAME AMBASSADOR.
SURELY IT CAN WAIT UNTIL AFTER DINNER?
YEAH, IT PROBABLY CAN.
I THOUGHT YOU HANDLED THE QUESTIONS VERY GRACIOUSLY, EVEN IF THEY WEREN'T ABOUT THE BOOK.
I WILL SAY THAT IF I AM NEVER ASKED ABOUT THE PLANE AGAIN, I'LL BE A VERY HAPPY WOMAN.
I'LL BET.
COMMUNITY NOTES
POETRY SLAM! Tuesdays at Alison's
Looking for roommate: Female, nonsmoking, no pets.
Adam's Hues Celebrating five years of award-winning exterior paints
COMMUNITY NOTES
UNLEASH THE HOUNDS! DOGWALKERS 555-0738
OPEN 10-8 DAILY
REFLECTIONS A Collection of Essays and Speeches
by Diana of Themyscira

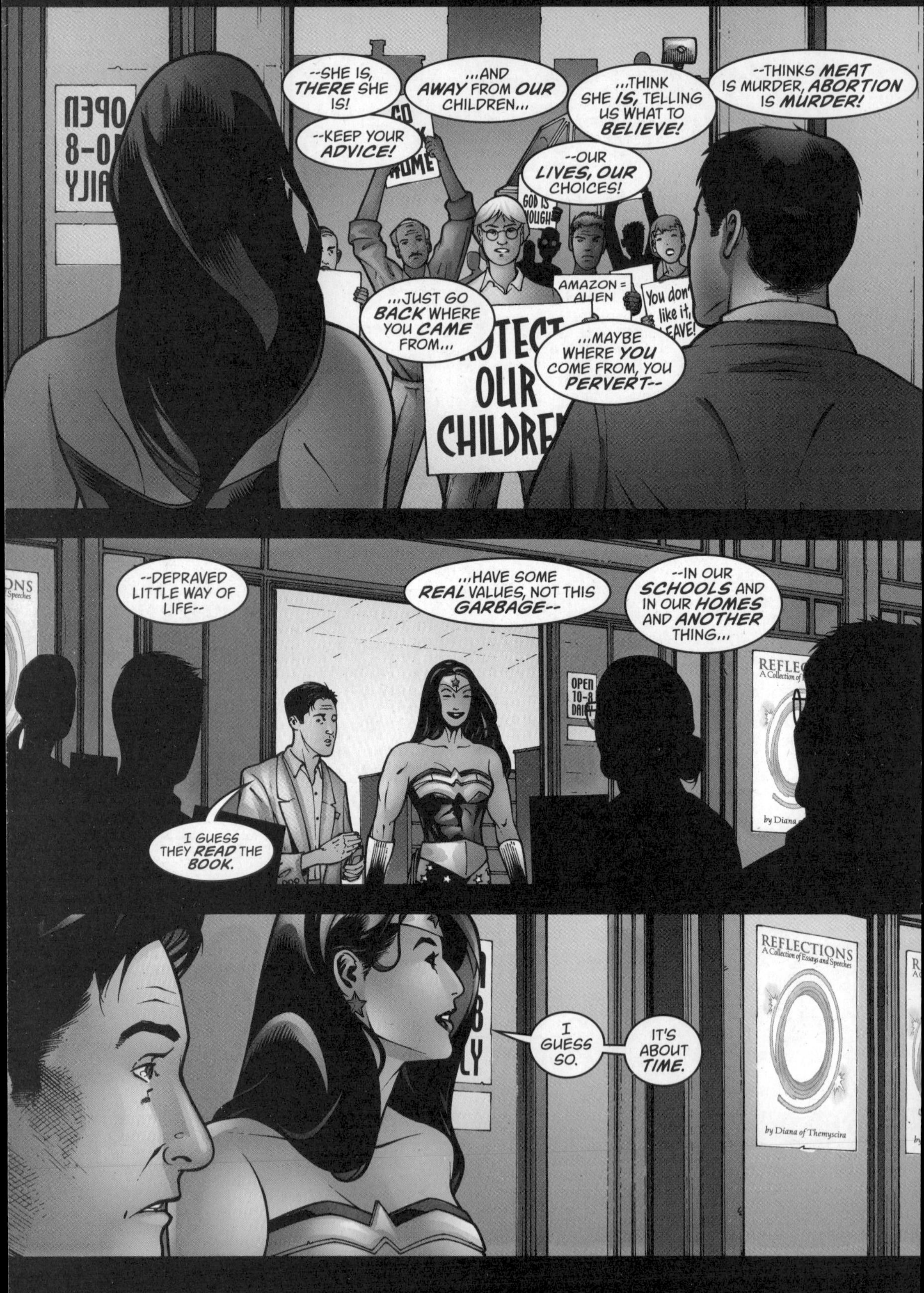
--SHE IS, THERE SHE IS!
...AND AWAY FROM OUR CHILDREN...
...THINK SHE IS, TELLING US WHAT TO BELIEVE!
--THINKS MEAT IS MURDER, ABORTION IS MURDER!
--KEEP YOUR ADVICE!
--OUR LIVES, OUR CHOICES!
...JUST GO BACK WHERE YOU CAME FROM...
...MAYBE WHERE YOU COME FROM, YOU PERVERT--
--DEPRAVED LITTLE WAY OF LIFE--
...HAVE SOME REAL VALUES, NOT THIS GARBAGE--
--IN OUR SCHOOLS AND IN OUR HOMES AND ANOTHER THING...
I GUESS THEY READ THE BOOK.
REFLECTIONS
A Collection of Essays and Speeches
by Diana of Themyscira
I GUESS SO.
IT'S ABOUT TIME.

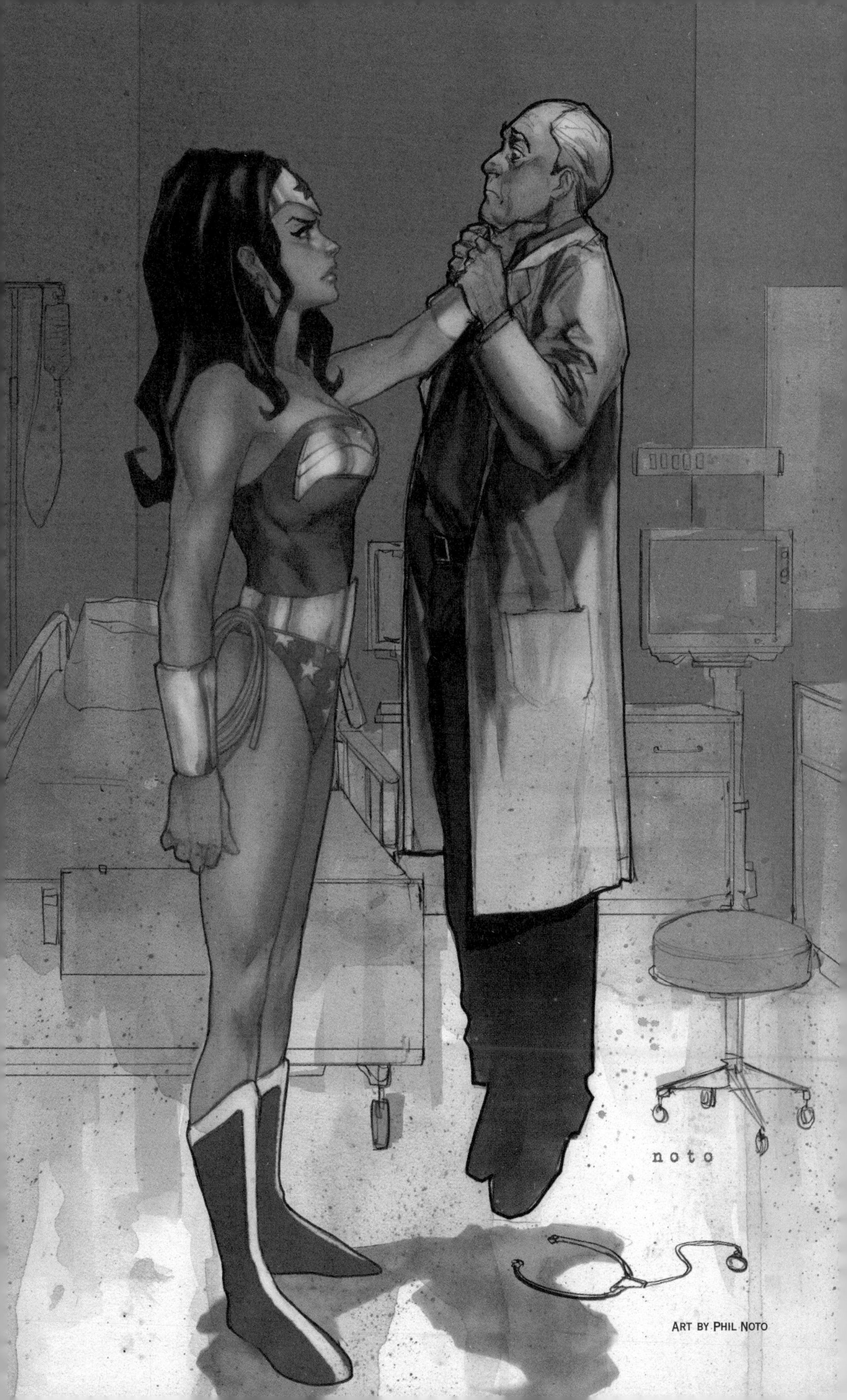
noto

ART BY PHIL NOTO

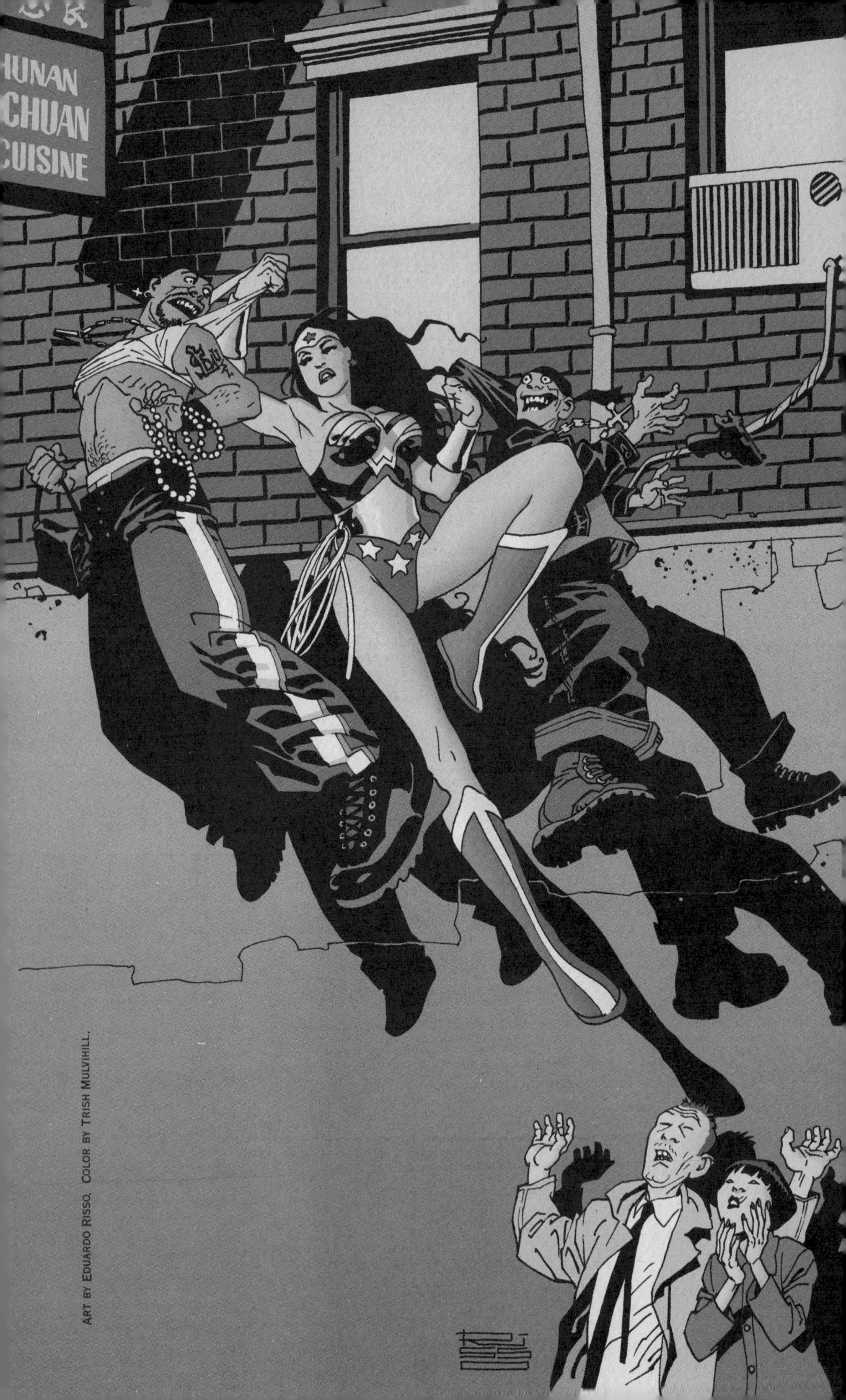
HUNAN
CHUAN
CUISINE

ART BY EDUARDO RISSO. COLOR BY TRISH MULVIHILL.

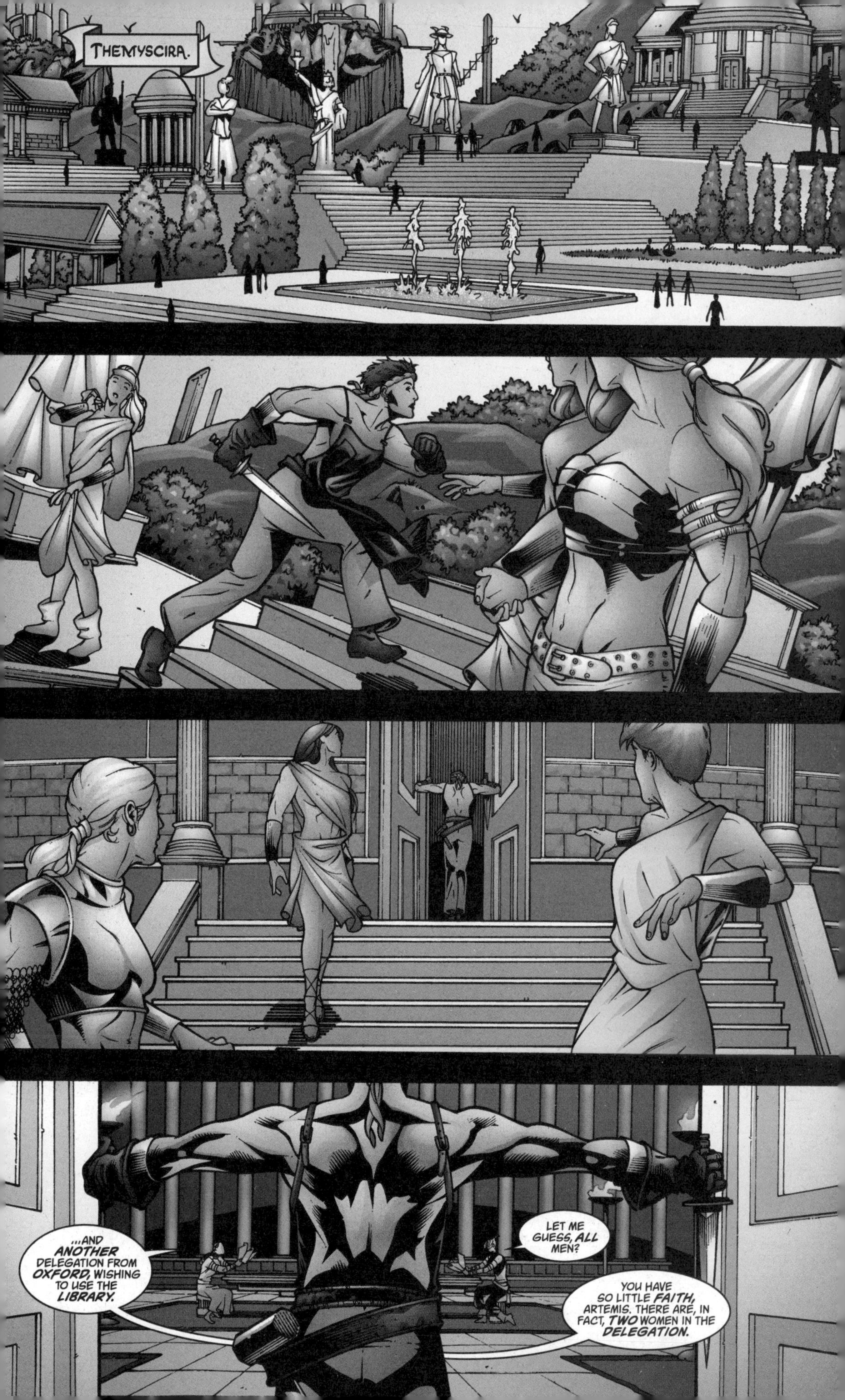
THEMYSCIRA.
...AND ANOTHER DELEGATION FROM OXFORD, WISHING TO USE THE LIBRARY.
LET ME GUESS, ALL MEN?
YOU HAVE SO LITTLE FAITH, ARTEMIS. THERE ARE, IN FACT, TWO WOMEN IN THE DELEGATION.

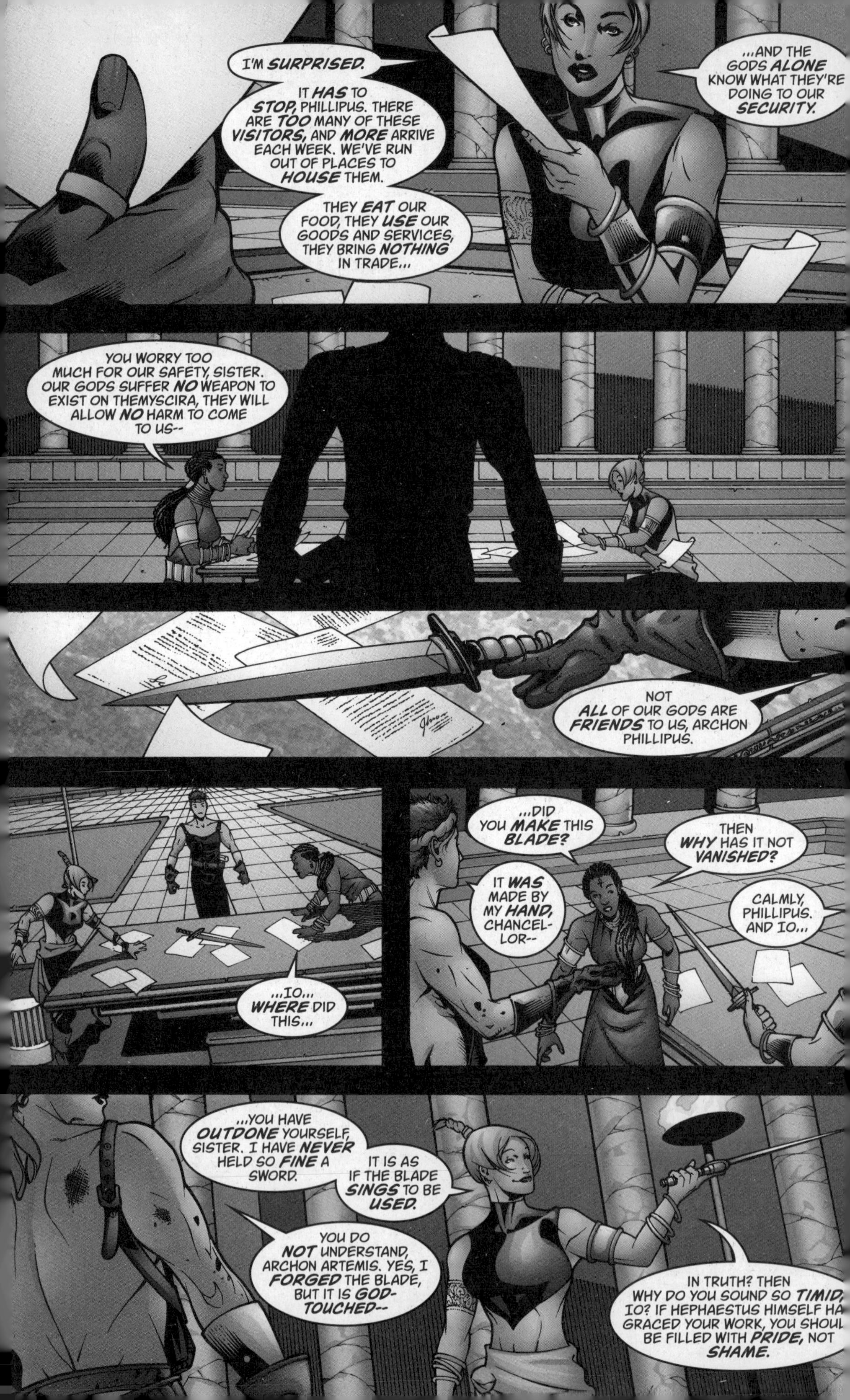

I'M SURPRISED.
IT HAS TO STOP, PHILLIPUS. THERE ARE TOO MANY OF THESE VISITORS, AND MORE ARRIVE EACH WEEK. WE'VE RUN OUT OF PLACES TO HOUSE THEM.
THEY EAT OUR FOOD, THEY USE OUR GOODS AND SERVICES, THEY BRING NOTHING IN TRADE...
...AND THE GODS ALONE KNOW WHAT THEY'RE DOING TO OUR SECURITY.
YOU WORRY TOO MUCH FOR OUR SAFETY, SISTER. OUR GODS SUFFER NO WEAPON TO EXIST ON THEMYSCIRA, THEY WILL ALLOW NO HARM TO COME TO US--
NOT ALL OF OUR GODS ARE FRIENDS TO US, ARCHON PHILLIPUS.
...IO... WHERE DID THIS...
...DID YOU MAKE THIS BLADE?
IT WAS MADE BY MY HAND, CHANCEL-LOR--
THEN WHY HAS IT NOT VANISHED?
CALMLY, PHILLIPUS. AND IO...
...YOU HAVE OUTDONE YOURSELF, SISTER. I HAVE NEVER HELD SO FINE A SWORD.
IT IS AS IF THE BLADE SINGS TO BE USED.
YOU DO NOT UNDERSTAND, ARCHON ARTEMIS. YES, I FORGED THE BLADE, BUT IT IS GOD-TOUCHED--
IN TRUTH? THEN WHY DO YOU SOUND SO TIMID, IO? IF HEPHAESTUS HIMSELF HA GRACED YOUR WORK, YOU SHOUL BE FILLED WITH PRIDE, NOT SHAME.

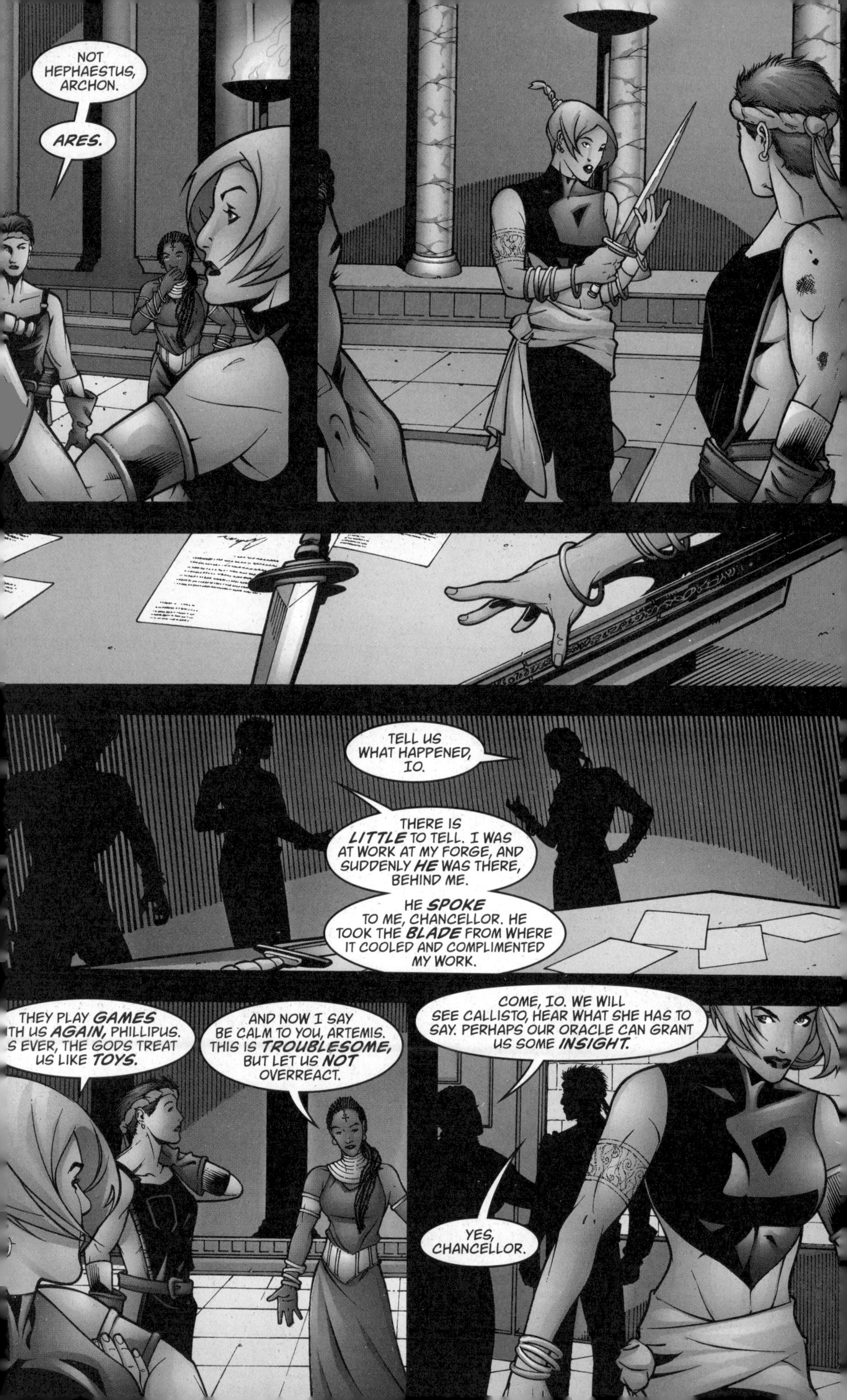
NOT HEPHAESTUS, ARCHON.
ARES.
TELL US WHAT HAPPENED, IO.
THERE IS LITTLE TO TELL. I WAS AT WORK AT MY FORGE, AND SUDDENLY HE WAS THERE, BEHIND ME.
HE SPOKE TO ME, CHANCELLOR. HE TOOK THE BLADE FROM WHERE IT COOLED AND COMPLIMENTED MY WORK.
THEY PLAY GAMES TH US AGAIN, PHILLIPUS. S EVER, THE GODS TREAT US LIKE TOYS.
AND NOW I SAY BE CALM TO YOU, ARTEMIS. THIS IS TROUBLESOME, BUT LET US NOT OVERREACT.
COME, IO. WE WILL SEE CALLISTO, HEAR WHAT SHE HAS TO SAY. PERHAPS OUR ORACLE CAN GRANT US SOME INSIGHT.
YES, CHANCELLOR.

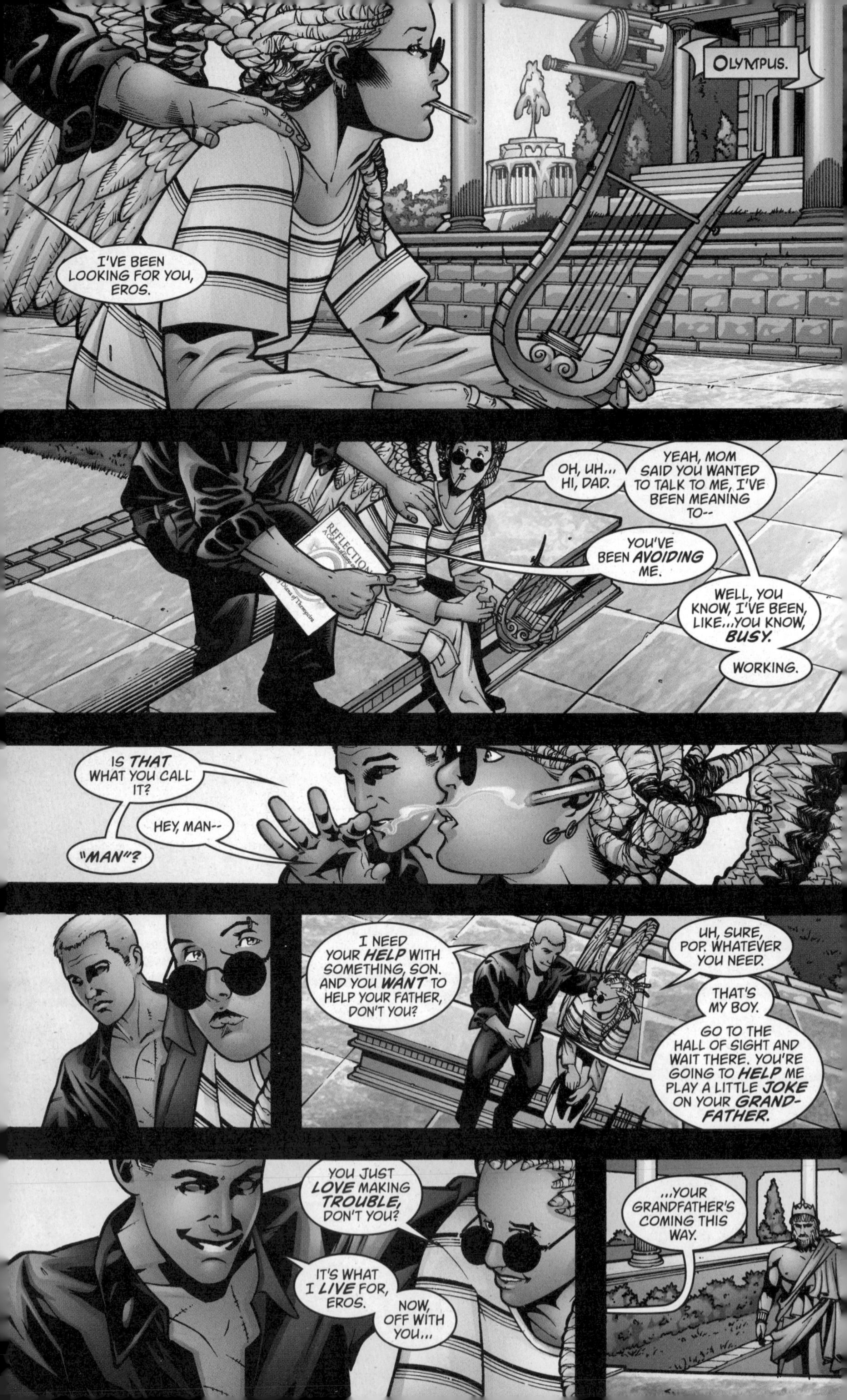

OLYMPUS.
I'VE BEEN LOOKING FOR YOU, EROS.
OH, UH... HI, DAD.
YEAH, MOM SAID YOU WANTED TO TALK TO ME, I'VE BEEN MEANING TO--
YOU'VE BEEN AVOIDING ME.
WELL, YOU KNOW, I'VE BEEN, LIKE...YOU KNOW, BUSY.
WORKING.
IS THAT WHAT YOU CALL IT?
HEY, MAN--
"MAN"?
I NEED YOUR HELP WITH SOMETHING, SON. AND YOU WANT TO HELP YOUR FATHER, DON'T YOU?
UH, SURE, POP. WHATEVER YOU NEED.
THAT'S MY BOY.
GO TO THE HALL OF SIGHT AND WAIT THERE. YOU'RE GOING TO HELP ME PLAY A LITTLE JOKE ON YOUR GRAND-FATHER.
YOU JUST LOVE MAKING TROUBLE, DON'T YOU?
IT'S WHAT I LIVE FOR, EROS.
NOW, OFF WITH YOU...
...YOUR GRANDFATHER'S COMING THIS WAY.

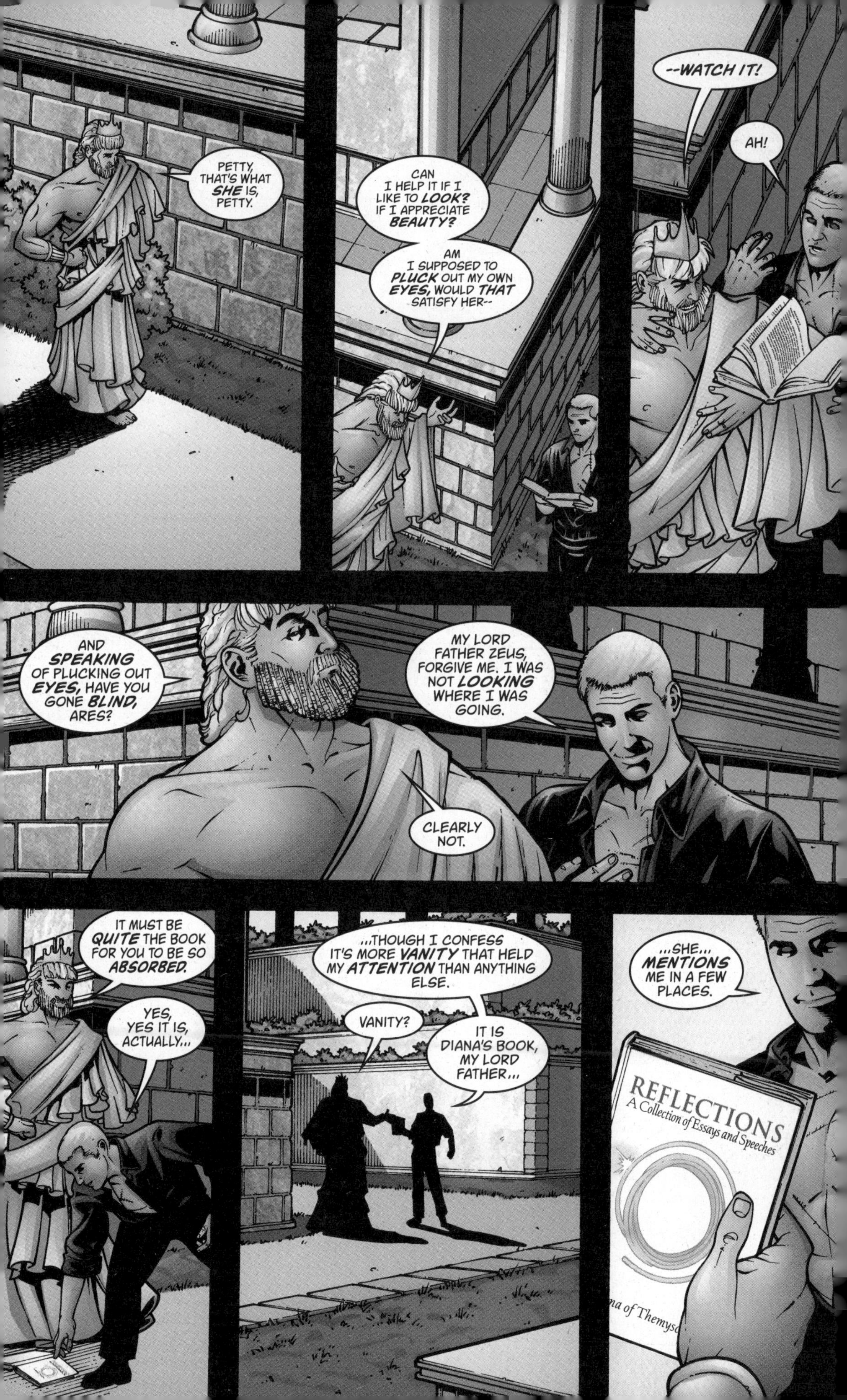
PETTY, THAT'S WHAT SHE IS, PETTY.
CAN I HELP IT IF I LIKE TO LOOK? IF I APPRECIATE BEAUTY?
AM I SUPPOSED TO PLUCK OUT MY OWN EYES, WOULD THAT SATISFY HER--
--WATCH IT!
AH!
AND SPEAKING OF PLUCKING OUT EYES, HAVE YOU GONE BLIND, ARES?
MY LORD FATHER ZEUS, FORGIVE ME. I WAS NOT LOOKING WHERE I WAS GOING.
CLEARLY NOT.
IT MUST BE QUITE THE BOOK FOR YOU TO BE SO ABSORBED.
YES, YES IT IS, ACTUALLY...
...THOUGH I CONFESS IT'S MORE VANITY THAT HELD MY ATTENTION THAN ANYTHING ELSE.
VANITY?
IT IS DIANA'S BOOK, MY LORD FATHER...
...SHE... MENTIONS ME IN A FEW PLACES.
REFLECTIONS
A Collection of Essays and Speeches
na of Themys

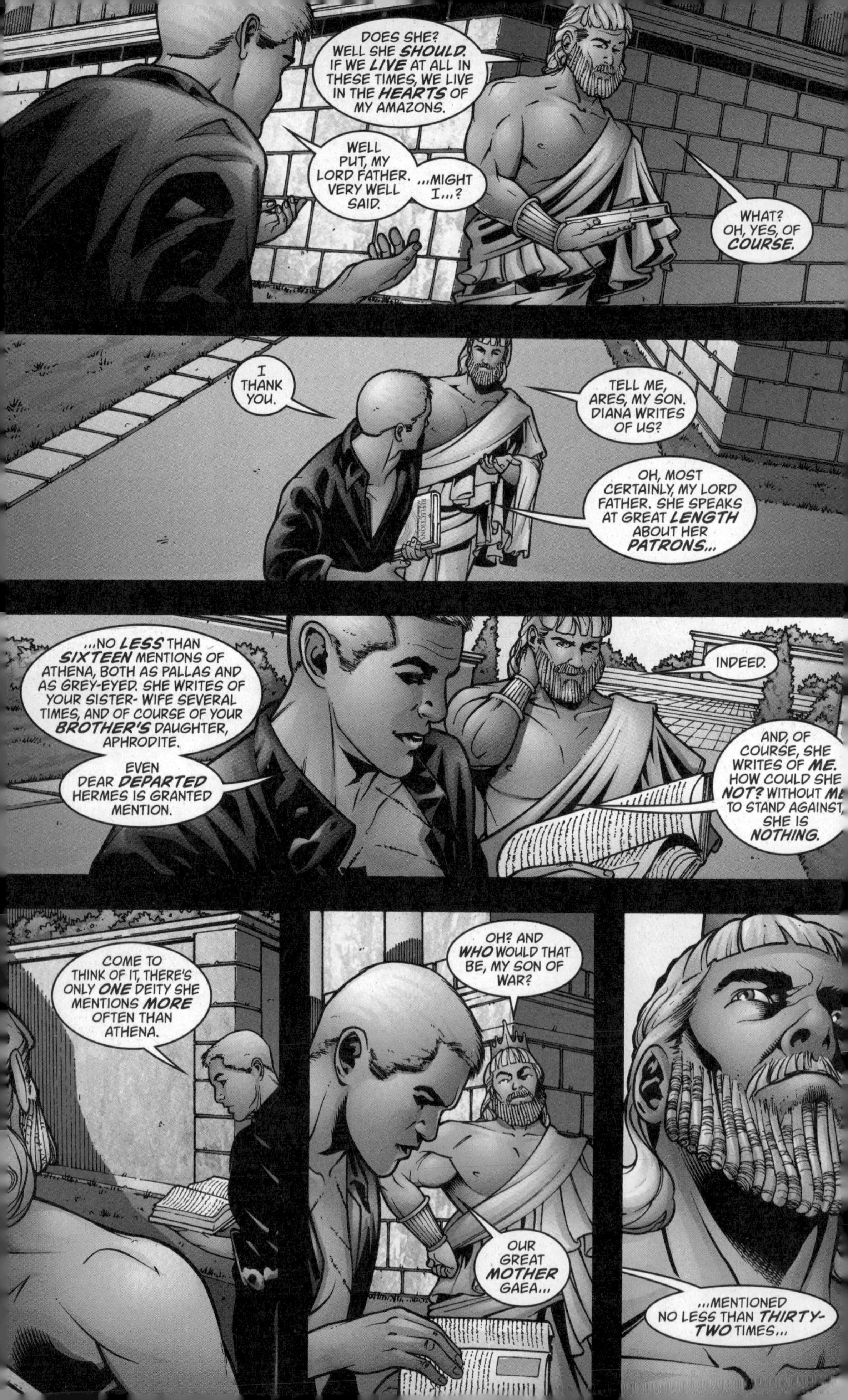
DOES SHE? WELL SHE SHOULD. IF WE LIVE AT ALL IN THESE TIMES, WE LIVE IN THE HEARTS OF MY AMAZONS.
WELL PUT, MY LORD FATHER. VERY WELL SAID.
...MIGHT I...?
WHAT? OH, YES, OF COURSE.
I THANK YOU.
TELL ME, ARES, MY SON. DIANA WRITES OF US?
OH, MOST CERTAINLY, MY LORD FATHER. SHE SPEAKS AT GREAT LENGTH ABOUT HER PATRONS...
REFLECTIONS
...NO LESS THAN SIXTEEN MENTIONS OF ATHENA, BOTH AS PALLAS AND AS GREY-EYED. SHE WRITES OF YOUR SISTER- WIFE SEVERAL TIMES, AND OF COURSE OF YOUR BROTHER'S DAUGHTER, APHRODITE.
EVEN DEAR DEPARTED HERMES IS GRANTED MENTION.
INDEED.
AND, OF COURSE, SHE WRITES OF ME. HOW COULD SHE NOT? WITHOUT ME TO STAND AGAINST, SHE IS NOTHING.
COME TO THINK OF IT, THERE'S ONLY ONE DEITY SHE MENTIONS MORE OFTEN THAN ATHENA.
OH? AND WHO WOULD THAT BE, MY SON OF WAR?
OUR GREAT MOTHER GAEA...
...MENTIONED NO LESS THAN THIRTY-TWO TIMES...

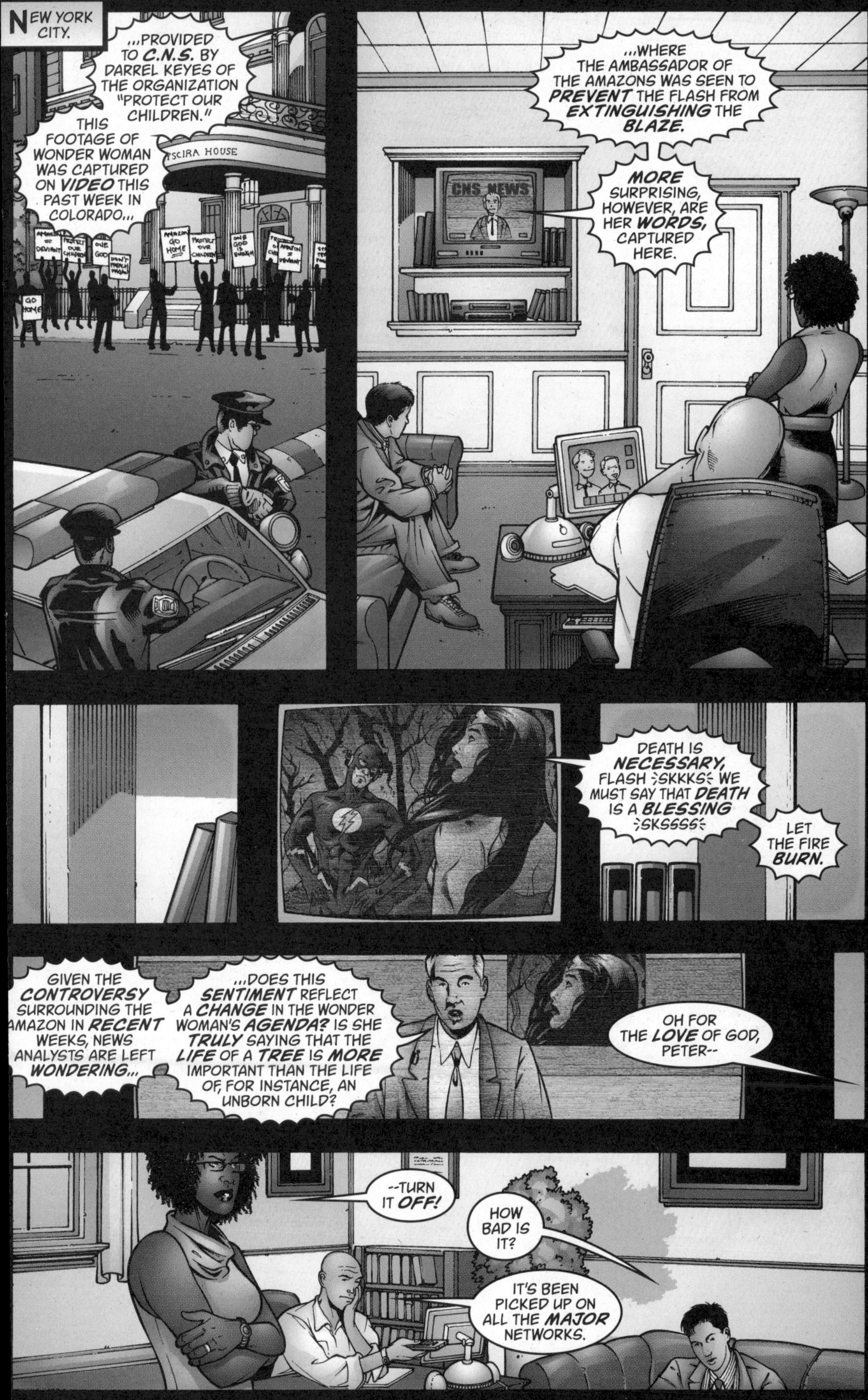
NEW YORK CITY.
...PROVIDED TO C.N.S. BY DARREL KEYES OF THE ORGANIZATION "PROTECT OUR CHILDREN."
THIS FOOTAGE OF WONDER WOMAN WAS CAPTURED ON VIDEO THIS PAST WEEK IN COLORADO...
SCIRA HOUSE
AMAZON GO HOME
PROTECT OUR CHILDREN
ONE GOD IS ENOUGH
AMAZON = DEVIANT
ONE GOD
GO HOME
...WHERE THE AMBASSADOR OF THE AMAZONS WAS SEEN TO PREVENT THE FLASH FROM EXTINGUISHING THE BLAZE.
CNS NEWS
MORE SURPRISING, HOWEVER, ARE HER WORDS, CAPTURED HERE.
DEATH IS NECESSARY, FLASH ⁝SKKKS⁝ WE MUST SAY THAT DEATH IS A BLESSING ⁝SKSSSS⁝
LET THE FIRE BURN.
GIVEN THE CONTROVERSY SURROUNDING THE AMAZON IN RECENT WEEKS, NEWS ANALYSTS ARE LEFT WONDERING...
...DOES THIS SENTIMENT REFLECT A CHANGE IN THE WONDER WOMAN'S AGENDA? IS SHE TRULY SAYING THAT THE LIFE OF A TREE IS MORE IMPORTANT THAN THE LIFE OF, FOR INSTANCE, AN UNBORN CHILD?
OH FOR THE LOVE OF GOD, PETER--
--TURN IT OFF!
HOW BAD IS IT?
IT'S BEEN PICKED UP ON ALL THE MAJOR NETWORKS.

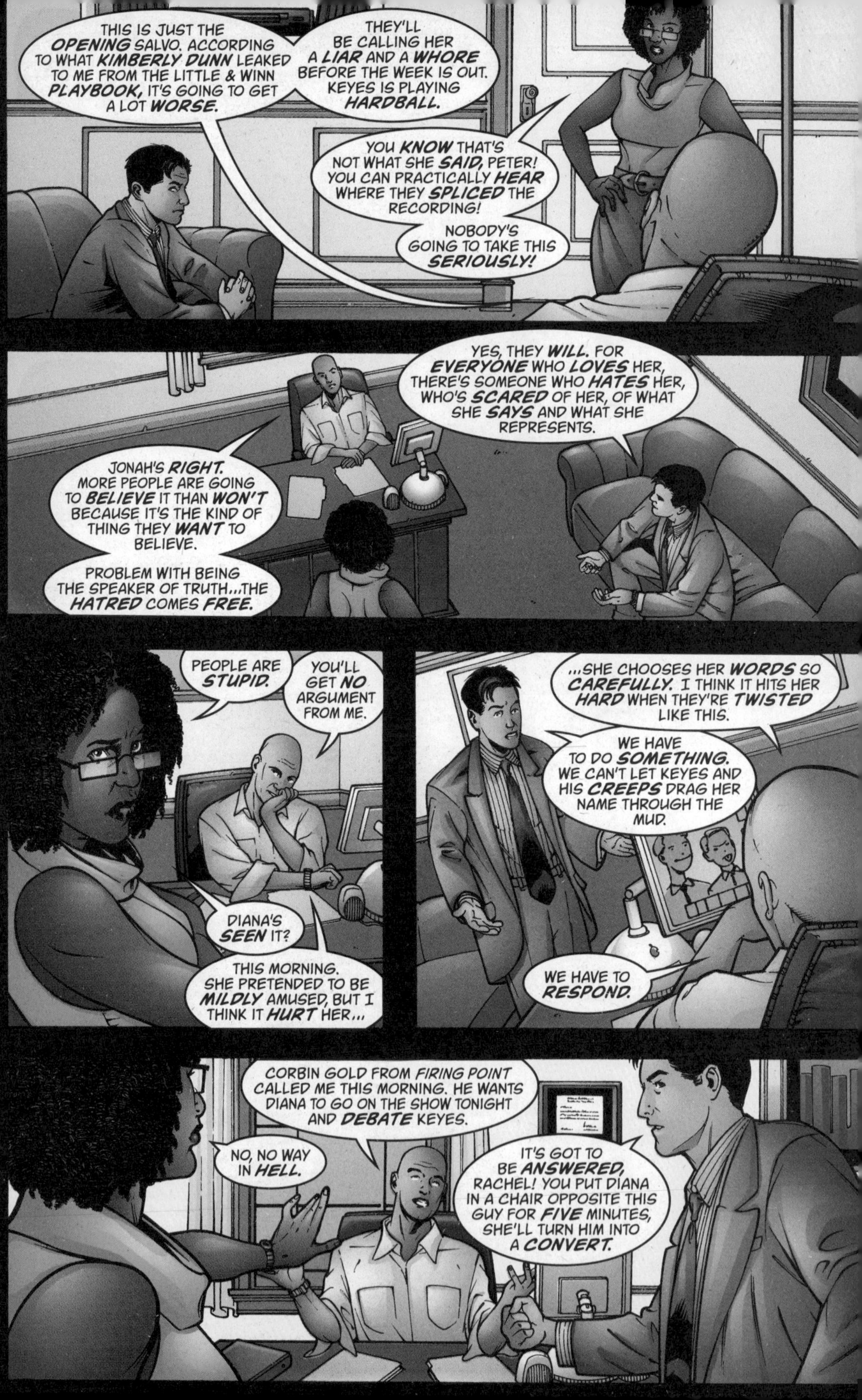
THIS IS JUST THE OPENING SALVO. ACCORDING TO WHAT KIMBERLY DUNN LEAKED TO ME FROM THE LITTLE & WINN PLAYBOOK, IT'S GOING TO GET A LOT WORSE.
THEY'LL BE CALLING HER A LIAR AND A WHORE BEFORE THE WEEK IS OUT. KEYES IS PLAYING HARDBALL.
YOU KNOW THAT'S NOT WHAT SHE SAID, PETER! YOU CAN PRACTICALLY HEAR WHERE THEY SPLICED THE RECORDING!
NOBODY'S GOING TO TAKE THIS SERIOUSLY!
YES, THEY WILL. FOR EVERYONE WHO LOVES HER, THERE'S SOMEONE WHO HATES HER, WHO'S SCARED OF HER, OF WHAT SHE SAYS AND WHAT SHE REPRESENTS.
JONAH'S RIGHT. MORE PEOPLE ARE GOING TO BELIEVE IT THAN WON'T BECAUSE IT'S THE KIND OF THING THEY WANT TO BELIEVE.
PROBLEM WITH BEING THE SPEAKER OF TRUTH...THE HATRED COMES FREE.
PEOPLE ARE STUPID.
YOU'LL GET NO ARGUMENT FROM ME.
DIANA'S SEEN IT?
THIS MORNING. SHE PRETENDED TO BE MILDLY AMUSED, BUT I THINK IT HURT HER...
...SHE CHOOSES HER WORDS SO CAREFULLY. I THINK IT HITS HER HARD WHEN THEY'RE TWISTED LIKE THIS.
WE HAVE TO DO SOMETHING. WE CAN'T LET KEYES AND HIS CREEPS DRAG HER NAME THROUGH THE MUD.
WE HAVE TO RESPOND.
CORBIN GOLD FROM FIRING POINT CALLED ME THIS MORNING. HE WANTS DIANA TO GO ON THE SHOW TONIGHT AND DEBATE KEYES.
NO, NO WAY IN HELL.
IT'S GOT TO BE ANSWERED, RACHEL! YOU PUT DIANA IN A CHAIR OPPOSITE THIS GUY FOR FIVE MINUTES, SHE'LL TURN HIM INTO A CONVERT.

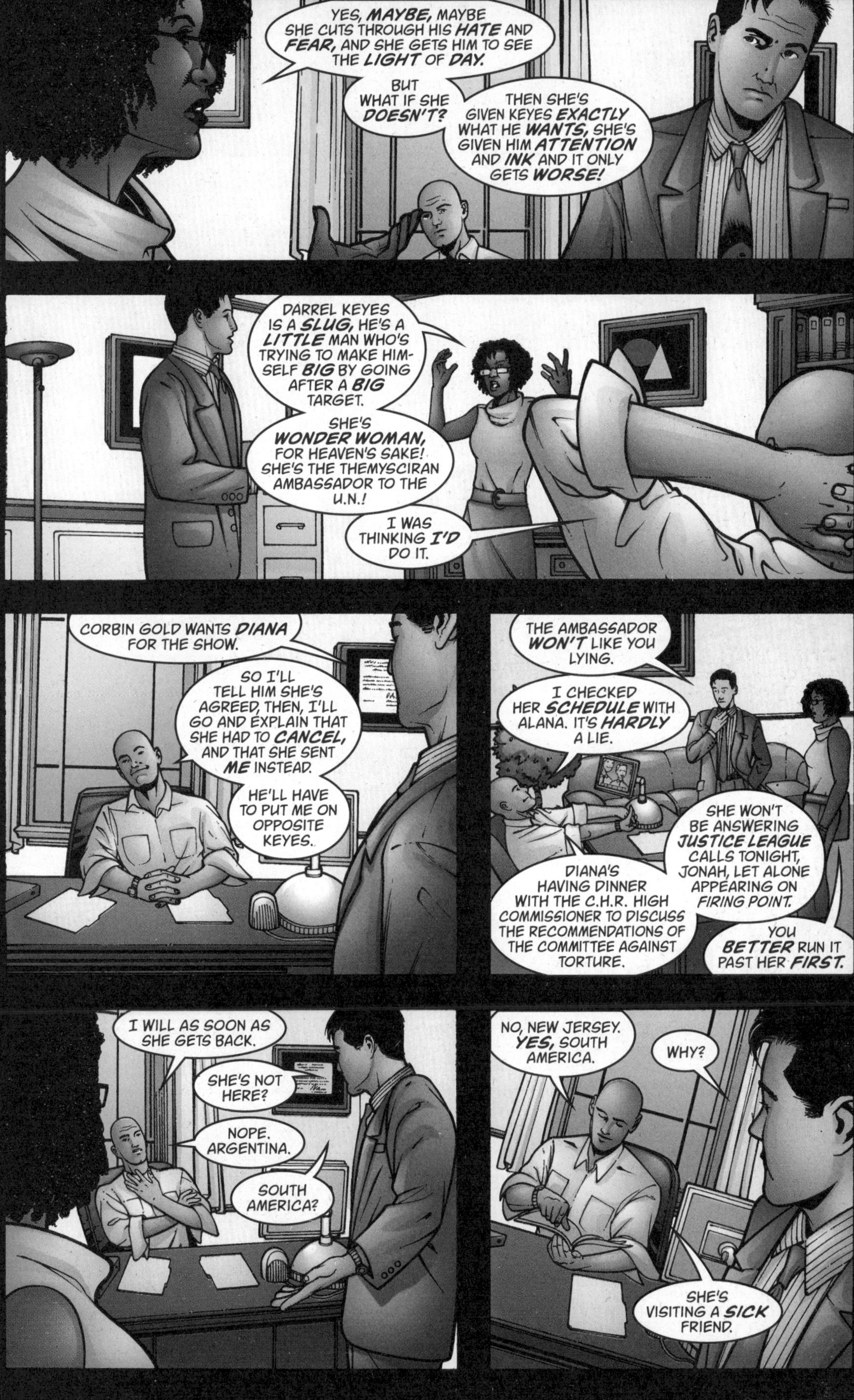
YES, MAYBE, MAYBE SHE CUTS THROUGH HIS HATE AND FEAR, AND SHE GETS HIM TO SEE THE LIGHT OF DAY.
BUT WHAT IF SHE DOESN'T?
THEN SHE'S GIVEN KEYES EXACTLY WHAT HE WANTS, SHE'S GIVEN HIM ATTENTION AND INK AND IT ONLY GETS WORSE!
DARREL KEYES IS A SLUG, HE'S A LITTLE MAN WHO'S TRYING TO MAKE HIMSELF BIG BY GOING AFTER A BIG TARGET.
SHE'S WONDER WOMAN, FOR HEAVEN'S SAKE! SHE'S THE THEMYSCIRAN AMBASSADOR TO THE U.N.!
I WAS THINKING I'D DO IT.
CORBIN GOLD WANTS DIANA FOR THE SHOW.
SO I'LL TELL HIM SHE'S AGREED, THEN, I'LL GO AND EXPLAIN THAT SHE HAD TO CANCEL, AND THAT SHE SENT ME INSTEAD.
HE'LL HAVE TO PUT ME ON OPPOSITE KEYES.
THE AMBASSADOR WON'T LIKE YOU LYING.
I CHECKED HER SCHEDULE WITH ALANA. IT'S HARDLY A LIE.
DIANA'S HAVING DINNER WITH THE C.H.R. HIGH COMMISSIONER TO DISCUSS THE RECOMMENDATIONS OF THE COMMITTEE AGAINST TORTURE.
SHE WON'T BE ANSWERING JUSTICE LEAGUE CALLS TONIGHT, JONAH, LET ALONE APPEARING ON FIRING POINT.
YOU BETTER RUN IT PAST HER FIRST.
I WILL AS SOON AS SHE GETS BACK.
SHE'S NOT HERE?
NOPE. ARGENTINA.
SOUTH AMERICA?
NO, NEW JERSEY. YES, SOUTH AMERICA.
WHY?
SHE'S VISITING A SICK FRIEND.

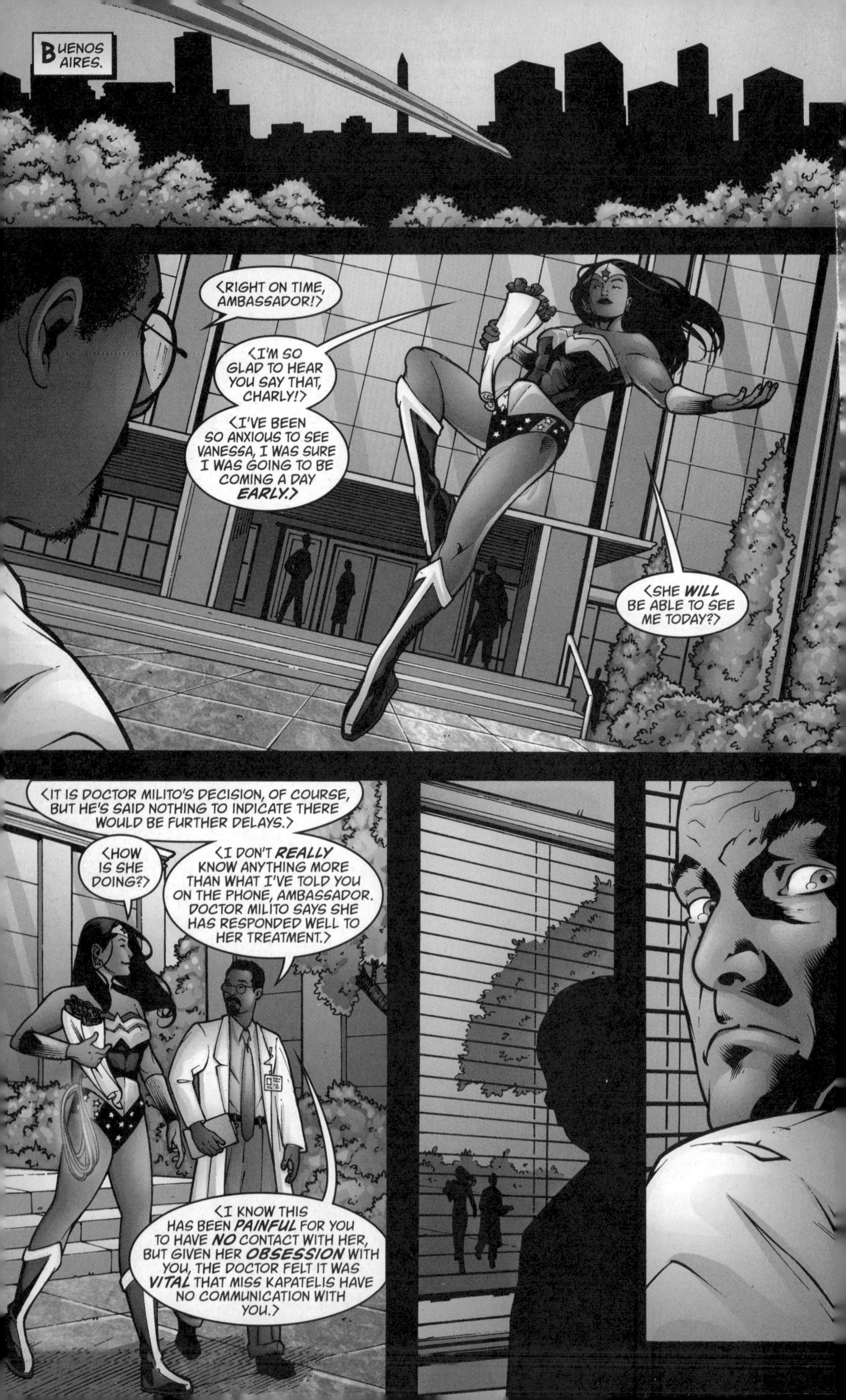
BUENOS AIRES.
<RIGHT ON TIME, AMBASSADOR!>
<I'M SO GLAD TO HEAR YOU SAY THAT, CHARLY!>
<I'VE BEEN SO ANXIOUS TO SEE VANESSA, I WAS SURE I WAS GOING TO BE COMING A DAY EARLY.>
<SHE WILL BE ABLE TO SEE ME TODAY?>
<IT IS DOCTOR MILITO'S DECISION, OF COURSE, BUT HE'S SAID NOTHING TO INDICATE THERE WOULD BE FURTHER DELAYS.>
<HOW IS SHE DOING?>
<I DON'T REALLY KNOW ANYTHING MORE THAN WHAT I'VE TOLD YOU ON THE PHONE, AMBASSADOR. DOCTOR MILITO SAYS SHE HAS RESPONDED WELL TO HER TREATMENT.>
<I KNOW THIS HAS BEEN PAINFUL FOR YOU TO HAVE NO CONTACT WITH HER, BUT GIVEN HER OBSESSION WITH YOU, THE DOCTOR FELT IT WAS VITAL THAT MISS KAPATELIS HAVE NO COMMUNICATION WITH YOU.>

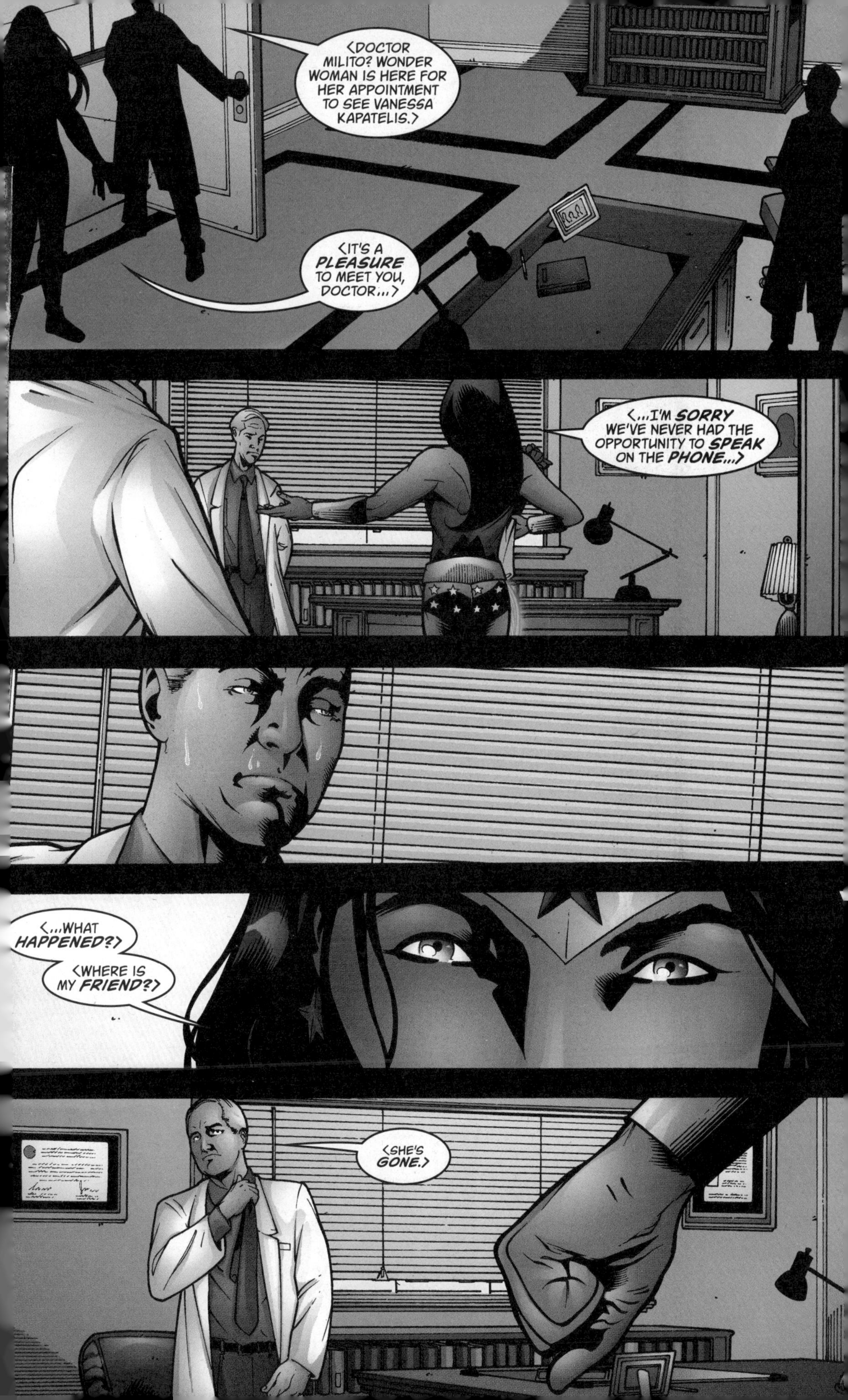

<DOCTOR MILITO? WONDER WOMAN IS HERE FOR HER APPOINTMENT TO SEE VANESSA KAPATELIS.>
<IT'S A PLEASURE TO MEET YOU, DOCTOR...>
<...I'M SORRY WE'VE NEVER HAD THE OPPORTUNITY TO SPEAK ON THE PHONE...>
<...WHAT HAPPENED?>
<WHERE IS MY FRIEND?>
<SHE'S GONE.>

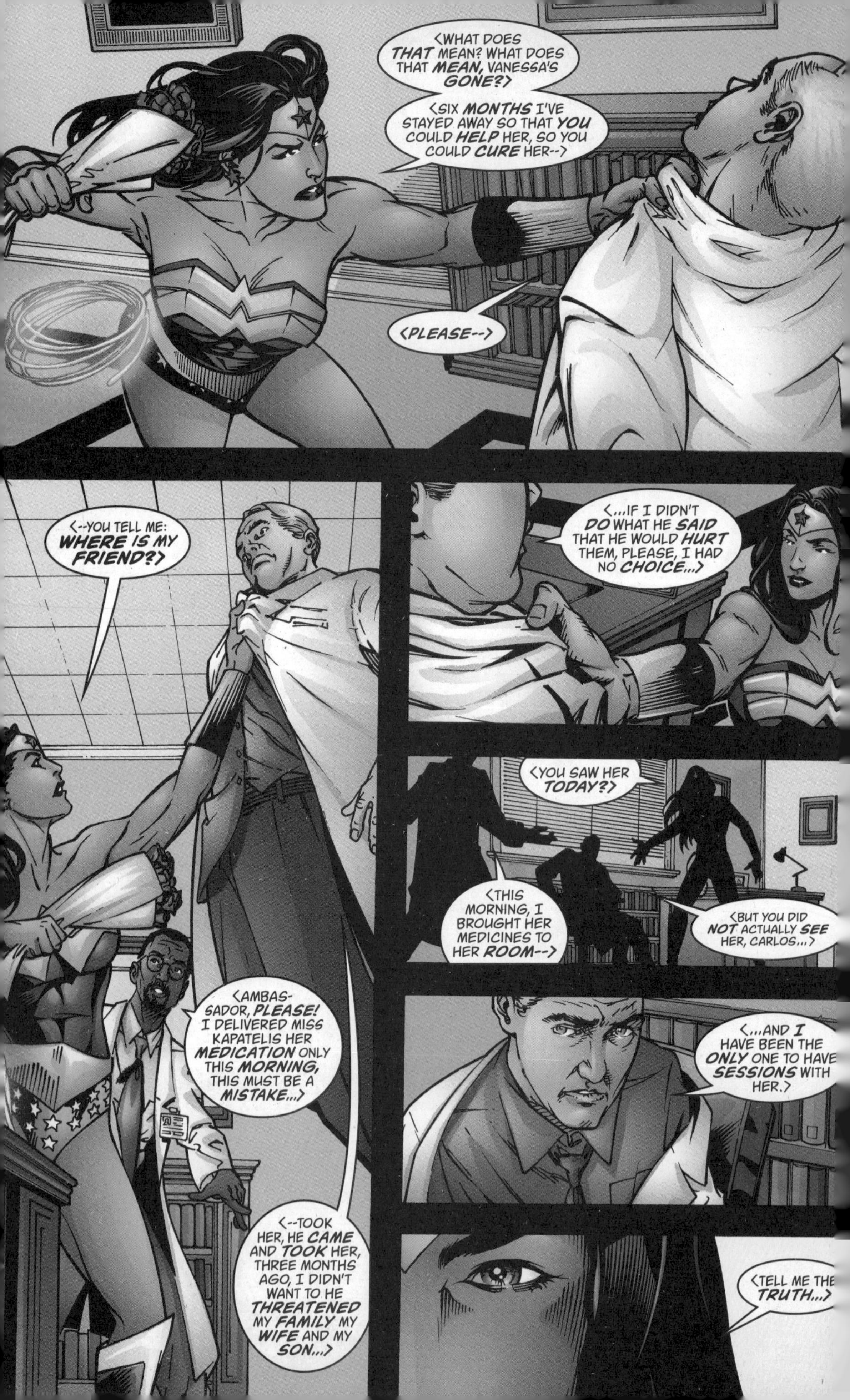
<WHAT DOES THAT MEAN? WHAT DOES THAT MEAN, VANESSA'S GONE?>
<SIX MONTHS I'VE STAYED AWAY SO THAT YOU COULD HELP HER, SO YOU COULD CURE HER-->
<PLEASE-->
<--YOU TELL ME: WHERE IS MY FRIEND?>
<AMBASSADOR, PLEASE! I DELIVERED MISS KAPATELIS HER MEDICATION ONLY THIS MORNING, THIS MUST BE A MISTAKE...>
<--TOOK HER, HE CAME AND TOOK HER, THREE MONTHS AGO, I DIDN'T WANT TO HE THREATENED MY FAMILY MY WIFE AND MY SON...>
<...IF I DIDN'T DO WHAT HE SAID THAT HE WOULD HURT THEM, PLEASE, I HAD NO CHOICE...>
<YOU SAW HER TODAY?>
<THIS MORNING, I BROUGHT HER MEDICINES TO HER ROOM-->
<BUT YOU DID NOT ACTUALLY SEE HER, CARLOS...>
<...AND I HAVE BEEN THE ONLY ONE TO HAVE SESSIONS WITH HER.>
<TELL ME THE TRUTH...>

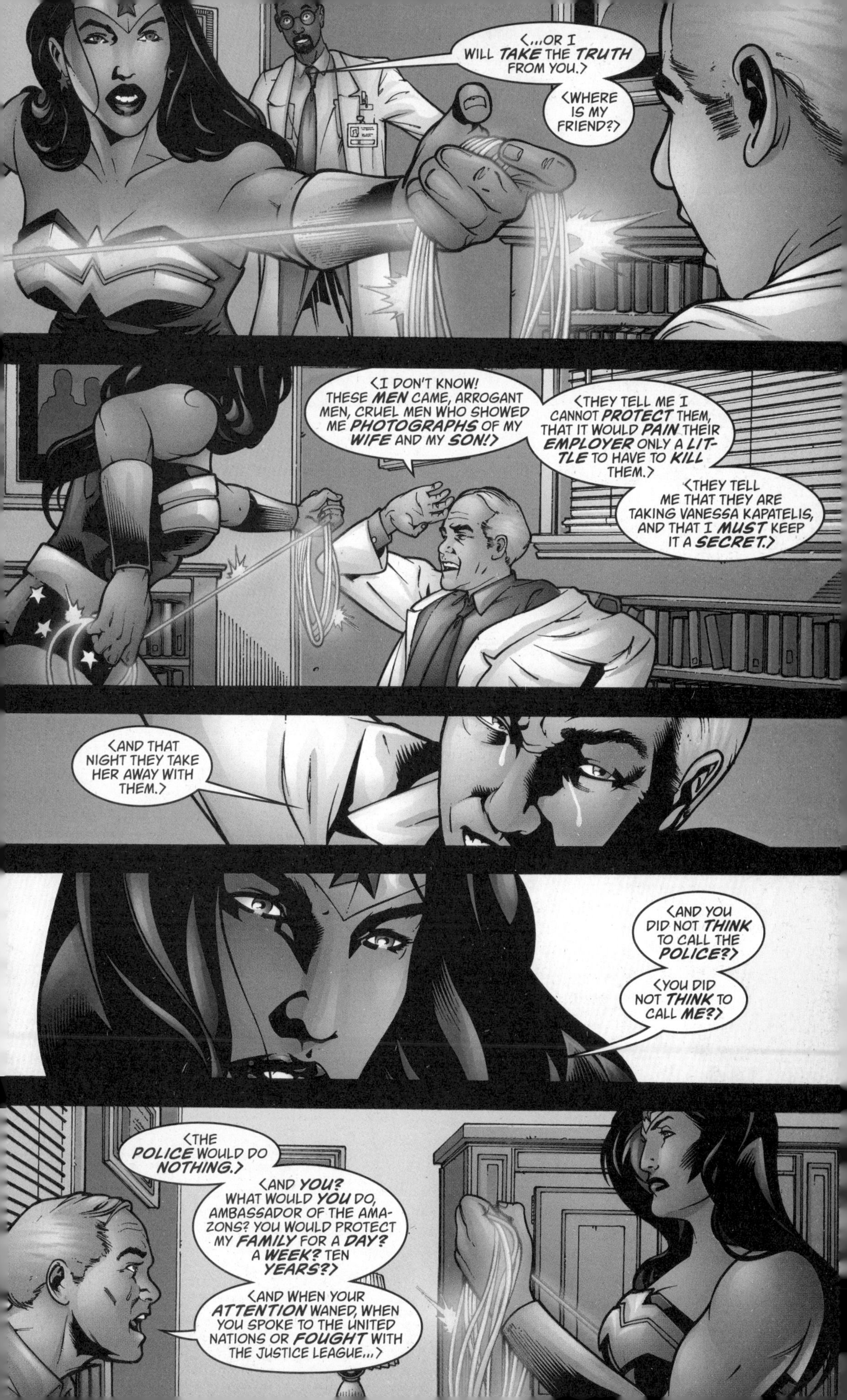

<...OR I WILL TAKE THE TRUTH FROM YOU.>
<WHERE IS MY FRIEND?>
<I DON'T KNOW! THESE MEN CAME, ARROGANT MEN, CRUEL MEN WHO SHOWED ME PHOTOGRAPHS OF MY WIFE AND MY SON!>
<THEY TELL ME I CANNOT PROTECT THEM, THAT IT WOULD PAIN THEIR EMPLOYER ONLY A LITTLE TO HAVE TO KILL THEM.>
<THEY TELL ME THAT THEY ARE TAKING VANESSA KAPATELIS, AND THAT I MUST KEEP IT A SECRET.>
<AND THAT NIGHT THEY TAKE HER AWAY WITH THEM.>
<AND YOU DID NOT THINK TO CALL THE POLICE?>
<YOU DID NOT THINK TO CALL ME?>
<THE POLICE WOULD DO NOTHING.>
<AND YOU? WHAT WOULD YOU DO, AMBASSADOR OF THE AMAZONS? YOU WOULD PROTECT MY FAMILY FOR A DAY? A WEEK? TEN YEARS?>
<AND WHEN YOUR ATTENTION WANED, WHEN YOU SPOKE TO THE UNITED NATIONS OR FOUGHT WITH THE JUSTICE LEAGUE...>

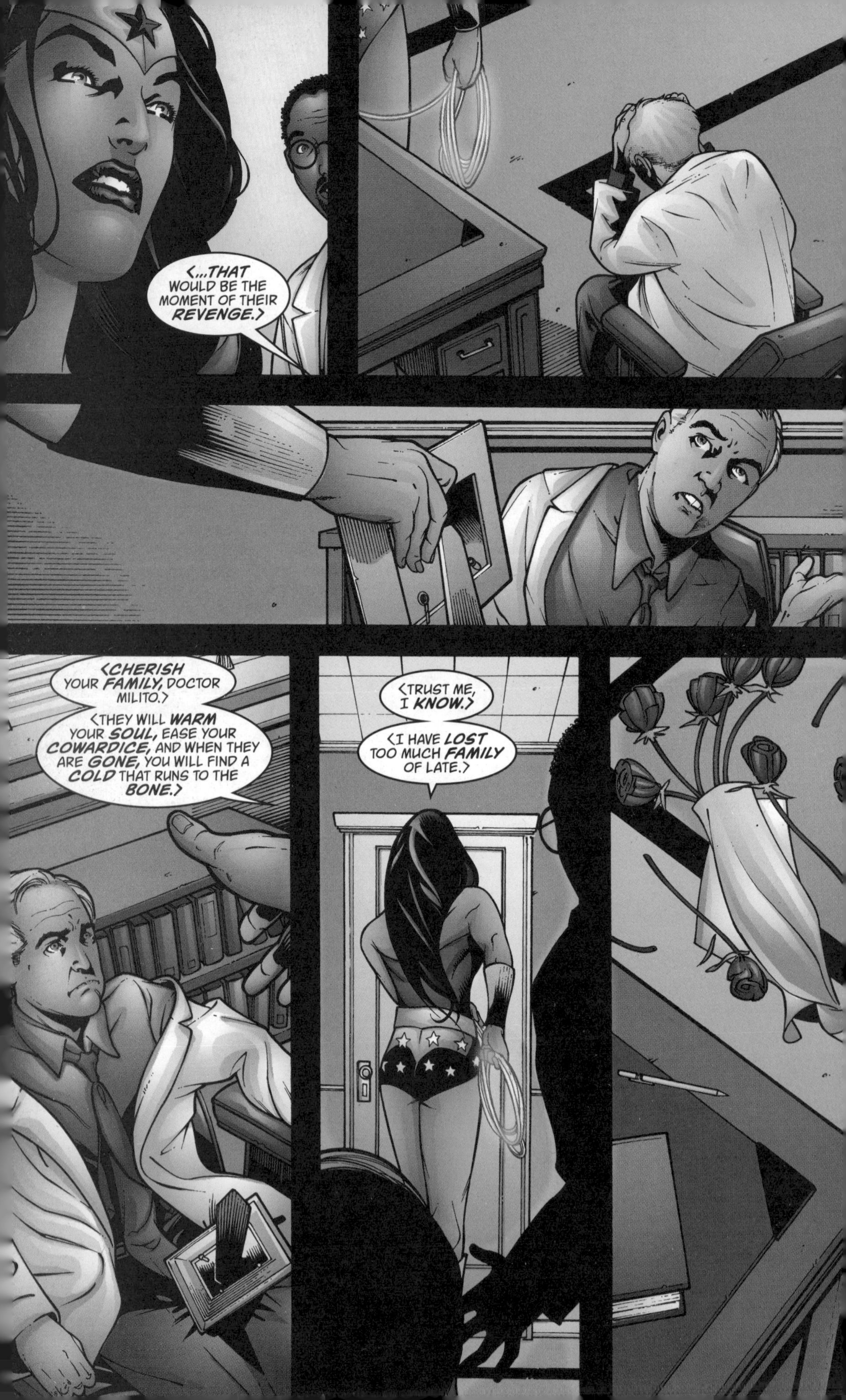

<...THAT WOULD BE THE MOMENT OF THEIR REVENGE.>
<CHERISH YOUR FAMILY, DOCTOR MILITO.>
<THEY WILL WARM YOUR SOUL, EASE YOUR COWARDICE, AND WHEN THEY ARE GONE, YOU WILL FIND A COLD THAT RUNS TO THE BONE.>
<TRUST ME, I KNOW.>
<I HAVE LOST TOO MUCH FAMILY OF LATE.>

...AMBASSADOR EXTENDS HER *REGRETS*, BUT UNFORTUNATELY SHE HAD A *PREVIOUS* ENGAGEMENT.

I *KNEW* SHE'D *CHICKEN* OUT.

THE AMBASSADOR FELT HER DINNER WITH THE HIGH COMMISSIONER ON HUMAN RIGHTS WAS *MORE* PRESSING THAN THE SHOW, I'M AFRAID.

SHE ASKED ME TO SEND HER REGARDS, AND HER REGRETS.

SHE CAN HAVE THE REGRETS *LATER*, WHEN THE SHOW'S *OVER*.

GUESS WE'LL HAVE TO WAIT AND SEE.

FIFTEEN SECONDS!

KEEP IT *CIVIL*, BOYS.

HEATED, BUT *CIVIL*.

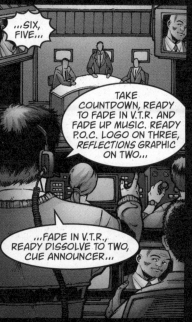

...SIX, FIVE....

TAKE COUNTDOWN, READY TO FADE IN V.T.R. AND FADE UP MUSIC. READY P.O.C. LOGO ON THREE, REFLECTIONS GRAPHIC ON TWO...

...FADE IN V.T.R., READY DISSOLVE TO TWO, CUE ANNOUNCER...

...DISSOLVE TO TWO, FADE DOWN MUSIC, CUE ANNOUNCER...

FIRING POINT, WITH *CORBIN GOLD!*

FIRING POINT
with
Corbin Gold

SHE'S LIVED AMONG US FOR NEARLY A DECADE, BUT WHAT DO WE REALLY KNOW ABOUT THE WONDER WOMAN?

REFLECTIONS
A Collection of Essays and Speeches

by Diana of Themyscira

WITH THE PUBLICATION OF HER BOOK, *REFLECTIONS*, DIANA OF THEMYSCIRA HAS GIVEN THE WORLD A *GLIMPSE* OF HER THINKING, HER PHILOSOPHY, AND HER *RELIGION*...

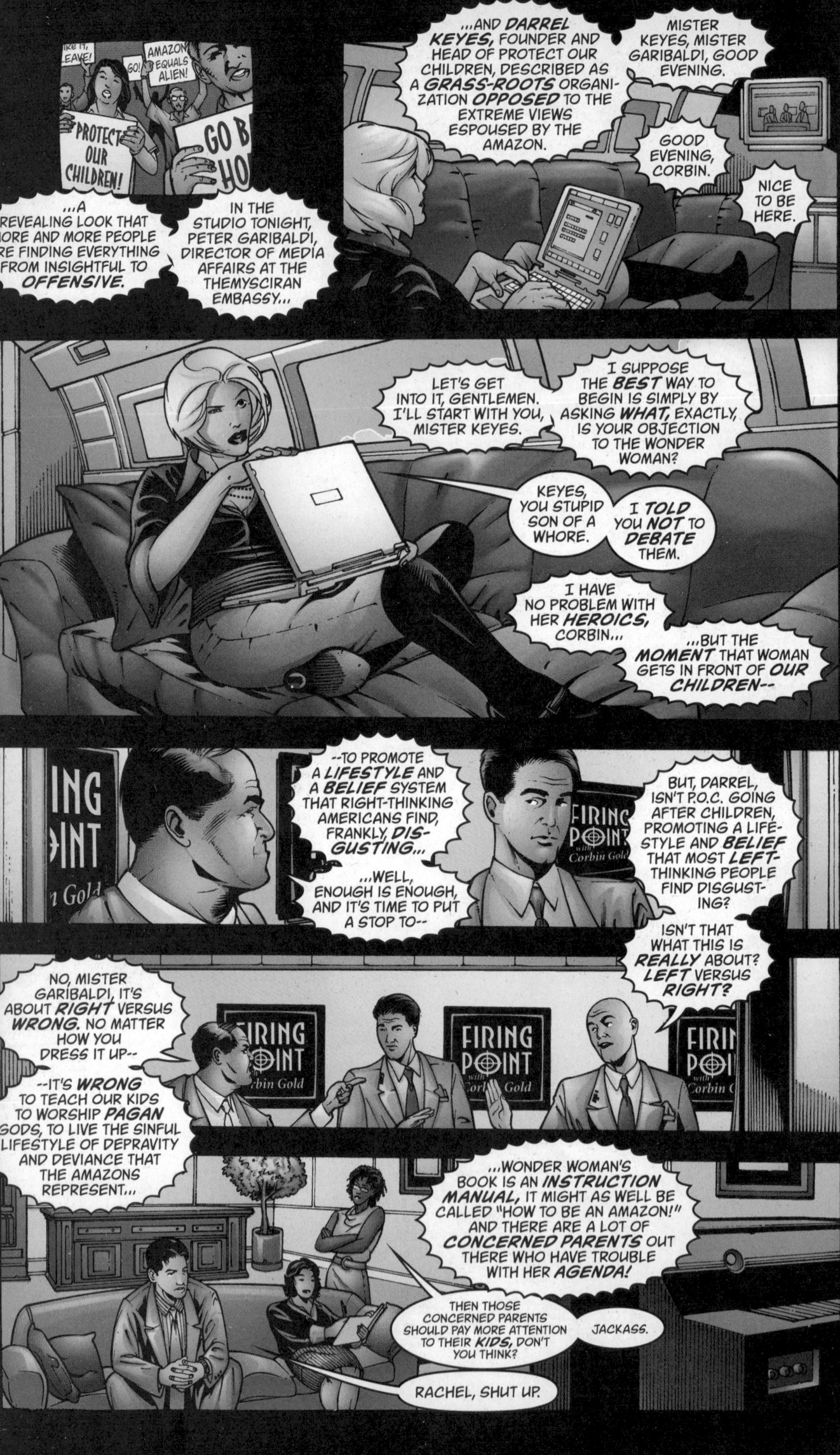
GO!
AMAZON EQUALS ALIEN!
PROTECT OUR CHILDREN!
...A REVEALING LOOK THAT MORE AND MORE PEOPLE ARE FINDING EVERYTHING FROM INSIGHTFUL TO OFFENSIVE.
IN THE STUDIO TONIGHT, PETER GARIBALDI, DIRECTOR OF MEDIA AFFAIRS AT THE THEMYSCIRAN EMBASSY...
...AND DARREL KEYES, FOUNDER AND HEAD OF PROTECT OUR CHILDREN, DESCRIBED AS A GRASS-ROOTS ORGANIZATION OPPOSED TO THE EXTREME VIEWS ESPOUSED BY THE AMAZON.
MISTER KEYES, MISTER GARIBALDI, GOOD EVENING.
GOOD EVENING, CORBIN.
NICE TO BE HERE.
LET'S GET INTO IT, GENTLEMEN. I'LL START WITH YOU, MISTER KEYES.
I SUPPOSE THE BEST WAY TO BEGIN IS SIMPLY BY ASKING WHAT, EXACTLY, IS YOUR OBJECTION TO THE WONDER WOMAN?
KEYES, YOU STUPID SON OF A WHORE.
I TOLD YOU NOT TO DEBATE THEM.
I HAVE NO PROBLEM WITH HER HEROICS, CORBIN...
...BUT THE MOMENT THAT WOMAN GETS IN FRONT OF OUR CHILDREN--
--TO PROMOTE A LIFESTYLE AND A BELIEF SYSTEM THAT RIGHT-THINKING AMERICANS FIND, FRANKLY, DISGUSTING...
...WELL, ENOUGH IS ENOUGH, AND IT'S TIME TO PUT A STOP TO--
FIRING POINT with Corbin Gold
BUT, DARREL, ISN'T P.O.C. GOING AFTER CHILDREN, PROMOTING A LIFESTYLE AND BELIEF THAT MOST LEFT-THINKING PEOPLE FIND DISGUSTING?
ISN'T THAT WHAT THIS IS REALLY ABOUT? LEFT VERSUS RIGHT?
NO, MISTER GARIBALDI, IT'S ABOUT RIGHT VERSUS WRONG. NO MATTER HOW YOU DRESS IT UP--
--IT'S WRONG TO TEACH OUR KIDS TO WORSHIP PAGAN GODS, TO LIVE THE SINFUL LIFESTYLE OF DEPRAVITY AND DEVIANCE THAT THE AMAZONS REPRESENT...
...WONDER WOMAN'S BOOK IS AN INSTRUCTION MANUAL, IT MIGHT AS WELL BE CALLED "HOW TO BE AN AMAZON!" AND THERE ARE A LOT OF CONCERNED PARENTS OUT THERE WHO HAVE TROUBLE WITH HER AGENDA!
THEN THOSE CONCERNED PARENTS SHOULD PAY MORE ATTENTION TO THEIR KIDS, DON'T YOU THINK?
JACKASS.
RACHEL, SHUT UP.

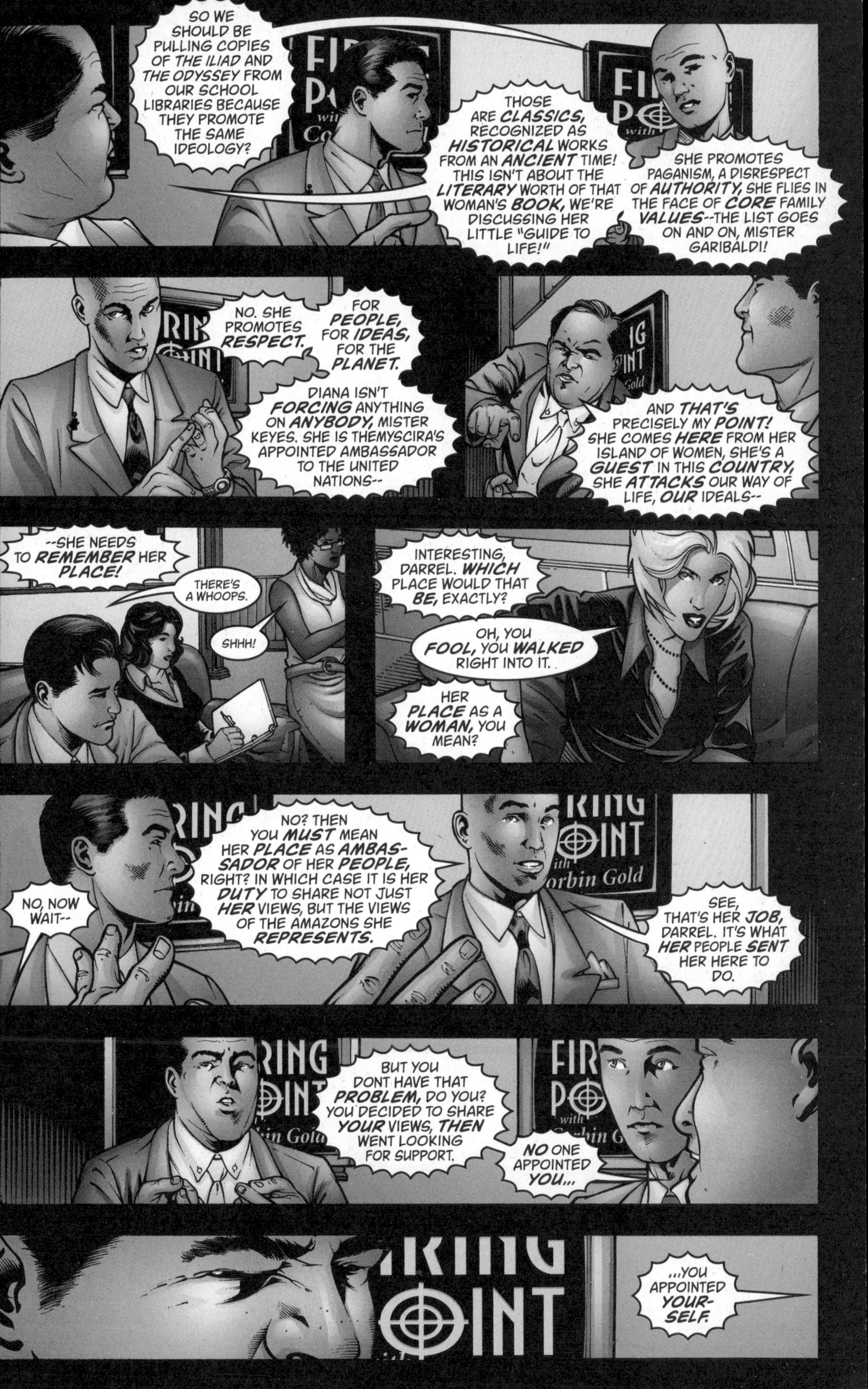

FIRING POINT with Corbin Gold
SO WE SHOULD BE PULLING COPIES OF THE ILIAD AND THE ODYSSEY FROM OUR SCHOOL LIBRARIES BECAUSE THEY PROMOTE THE SAME IDEOLOGY?
THOSE ARE CLASSICS, RECOGNIZED AS HISTORICAL WORKS FROM AN ANCIENT TIME! THIS ISN'T ABOUT THE LITERARY WORTH OF THAT WOMAN'S BOOK, WE'RE DISCUSSING HER LITTLE "GUIDE TO LIFE!"
SHE PROMOTES PAGANISM, A DISRESPECT OF AUTHORITY, SHE FLIES IN THE FACE OF CORE FAMILY VALUES--THE LIST GOES ON AND ON, MISTER GARIBALDI!
NO. SHE PROMOTES RESPECT.
FOR PEOPLE, FOR IDEAS, FOR THE PLANET.
DIANA ISN'T FORCING ANYTHING ON ANYBODY, MISTER KEYES. SHE IS THEMYSCIRA'S APPOINTED AMBASSADOR TO THE UNITED NATIONS--
AND THAT'S PRECISELY MY POINT! SHE COMES HERE FROM HER ISLAND OF WOMEN, SHE'S A GUEST IN THIS COUNTRY, SHE ATTACKS OUR WAY OF LIFE, OUR IDEALS--
--SHE NEEDS TO REMEMBER HER PLACE!
THERE'S A WHOOPS.
SHHH!
INTERESTING, DARREL. WHICH PLACE WOULD THAT BE, EXACTLY?
OH, YOU FOOL, YOU WALKED RIGHT INTO IT.
HER PLACE AS A WOMAN, YOU MEAN?
NO? THEN YOU MUST MEAN HER PLACE AS AMBASSADOR OF HER PEOPLE, RIGHT? IN WHICH CASE IT IS HER DUTY TO SHARE NOT JUST HER VIEWS, BUT THE VIEWS OF THE AMAZONS SHE REPRESENTS.
NO, NOW WAIT--
SEE, THAT'S HER JOB, DARREL. IT'S WHAT HER PEOPLE SENT HER HERE TO DO.
BUT YOU DONT HAVE THAT PROBLEM, DO YOU? YOU DECIDED TO SHARE YOUR VIEWS, THEN WENT LOOKING FOR SUPPORT.
NO ONE APPOINTED YOU...
...YOU APPOINTED YOURSELF.

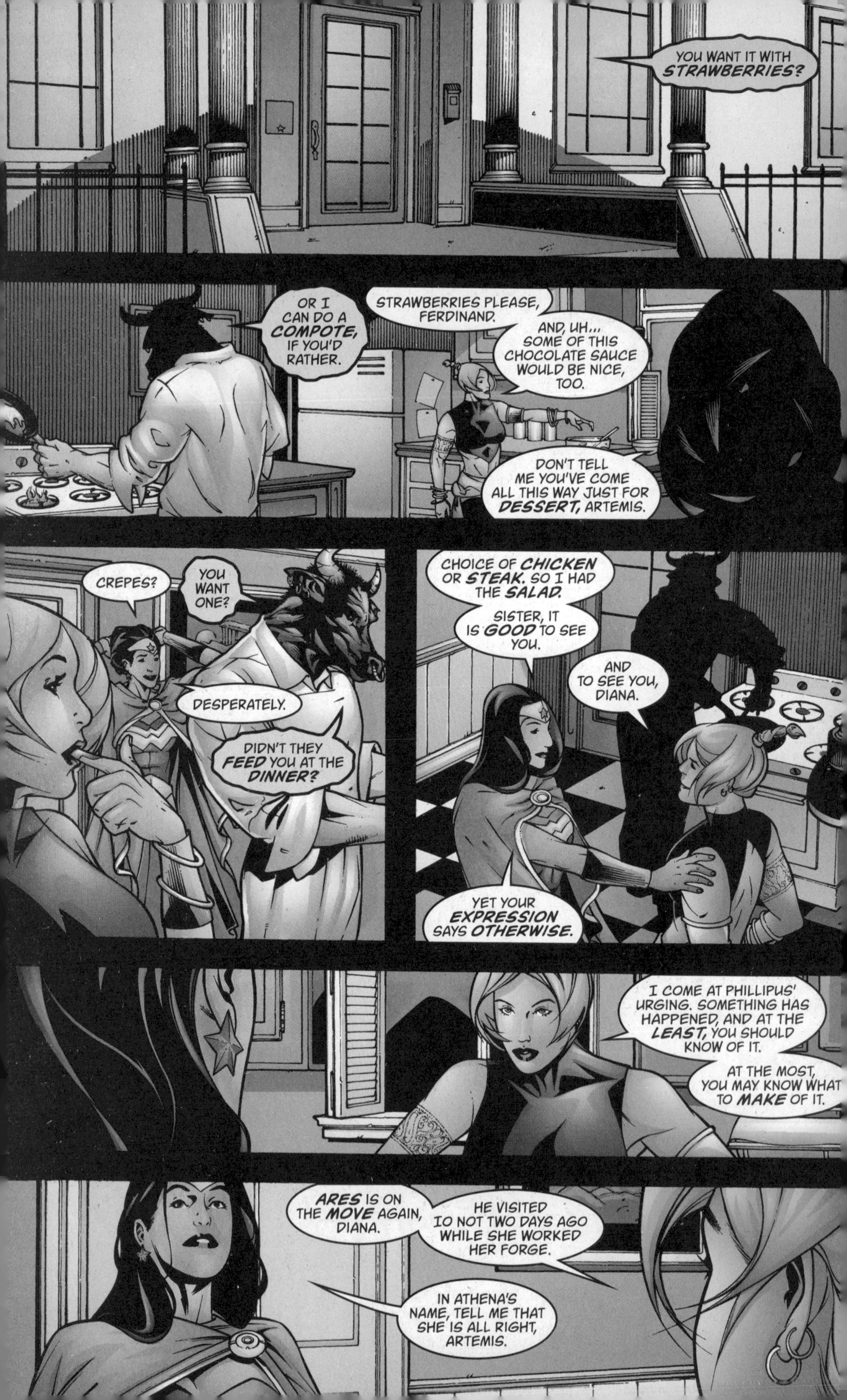
YOU WANT IT WITH STRAWBERRIES?
OR I CAN DO A COMPOTE, IF YOU'D RATHER.
STRAWBERRIES PLEASE, FERDINAND.
AND, UH... SOME OF THIS CHOCOLATE SAUCE WOULD BE NICE, TOO.
DON'T TELL ME YOU'VE COME ALL THIS WAY JUST FOR DESSERT, ARTEMIS.
CREPES?
YOU WANT ONE?
DESPERATELY.
DIDN'T THEY FEED YOU AT THE DINNER?
CHOICE OF CHICKEN OR STEAK. SO I HAD THE SALAD.
SISTER, IT IS GOOD TO SEE YOU.
AND TO SEE YOU, DIANA.
YET YOUR EXPRESSION SAYS OTHERWISE.
I COME AT PHILLIPUS' URGING. SOMETHING HAS HAPPENED, AND AT THE LEAST, YOU SHOULD KNOW OF IT.
AT THE MOST, YOU MAY KNOW WHAT TO MAKE OF IT.
ARES IS ON THE MOVE AGAIN, DIANA.
HE VISITED IO NOT TWO DAYS AGO WHILE SHE WORKED HER FORGE.
IN ATHENA'S NAME, TELL ME THAT SHE IS ALL RIGHT, ARTEMIS.

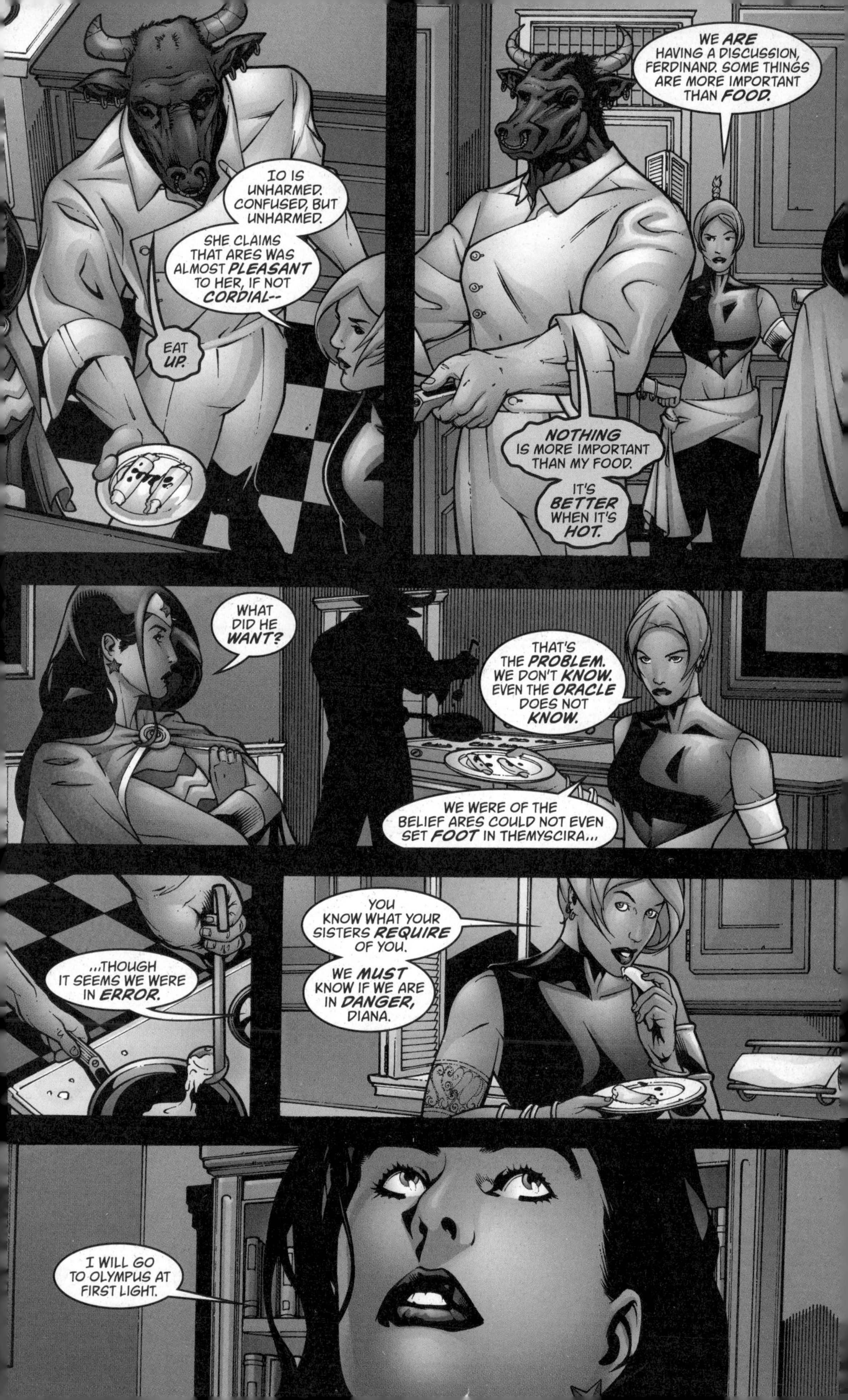
IO IS UNHARMED. CONFUSED, BUT UNHARMED.
SHE CLAIMS THAT ARES WAS ALMOST PLEASANT TO HER, IF NOT CORDIAL--
EAT UP.
WE ARE HAVING A DISCUSSION, FERDINAND. SOME THINGS ARE MORE IMPORTANT THAN FOOD.
NOTHING IS MORE IMPORTANT THAN MY FOOD.
IT'S BETTER WHEN IT'S HOT.
WHAT DID HE WANT?
THAT'S THE PROBLEM. WE DON'T KNOW. EVEN THE ORACLE DOES NOT KNOW.
WE WERE OF THE BELIEF ARES COULD NOT EVEN SET FOOT IN THEMYSCIRA...
...THOUGH IT SEEMS WE WERE IN ERROR.
YOU KNOW WHAT YOUR SISTERS REQUIRE OF YOU.
WE MUST KNOW IF WE ARE IN DANGER, DIANA.
I WILL GO TO OLYMPUS AT FIRST LIGHT.

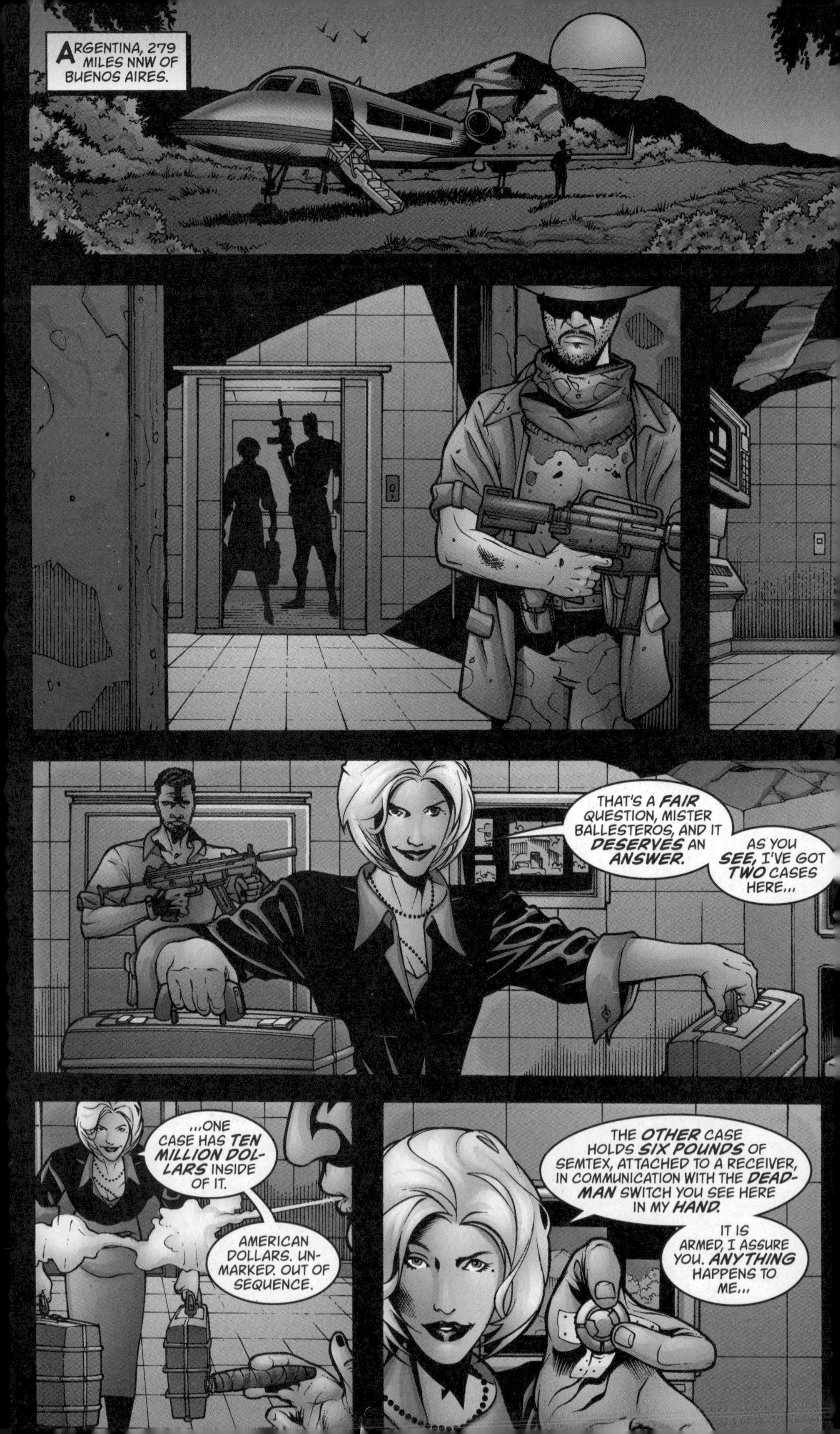
ARGENTINA, 279 MILES NNW OF BUENOS AIRES.
THAT'S A FAIR QUESTION, MISTER BALLESTEROS, AND IT DESERVES AN ANSWER.
AS YOU SEE, I'VE GOT TWO CASES HERE...
...ONE CASE HAS TEN MILLION DOLLARS INSIDE OF IT.
AMERICAN DOLLARS. UNMARKED. OUT OF SEQUENCE.
THE OTHER CASE HOLDS SIX POUNDS OF SEMTEX, ATTACHED TO A RECEIVER, IN COMMUNICATION WITH THE DEAD-MAN SWITCH YOU SEE HERE IN MY HAND.
IT IS ARMED, I ASSURE YOU. ANYTHING HAPPENS TO ME...

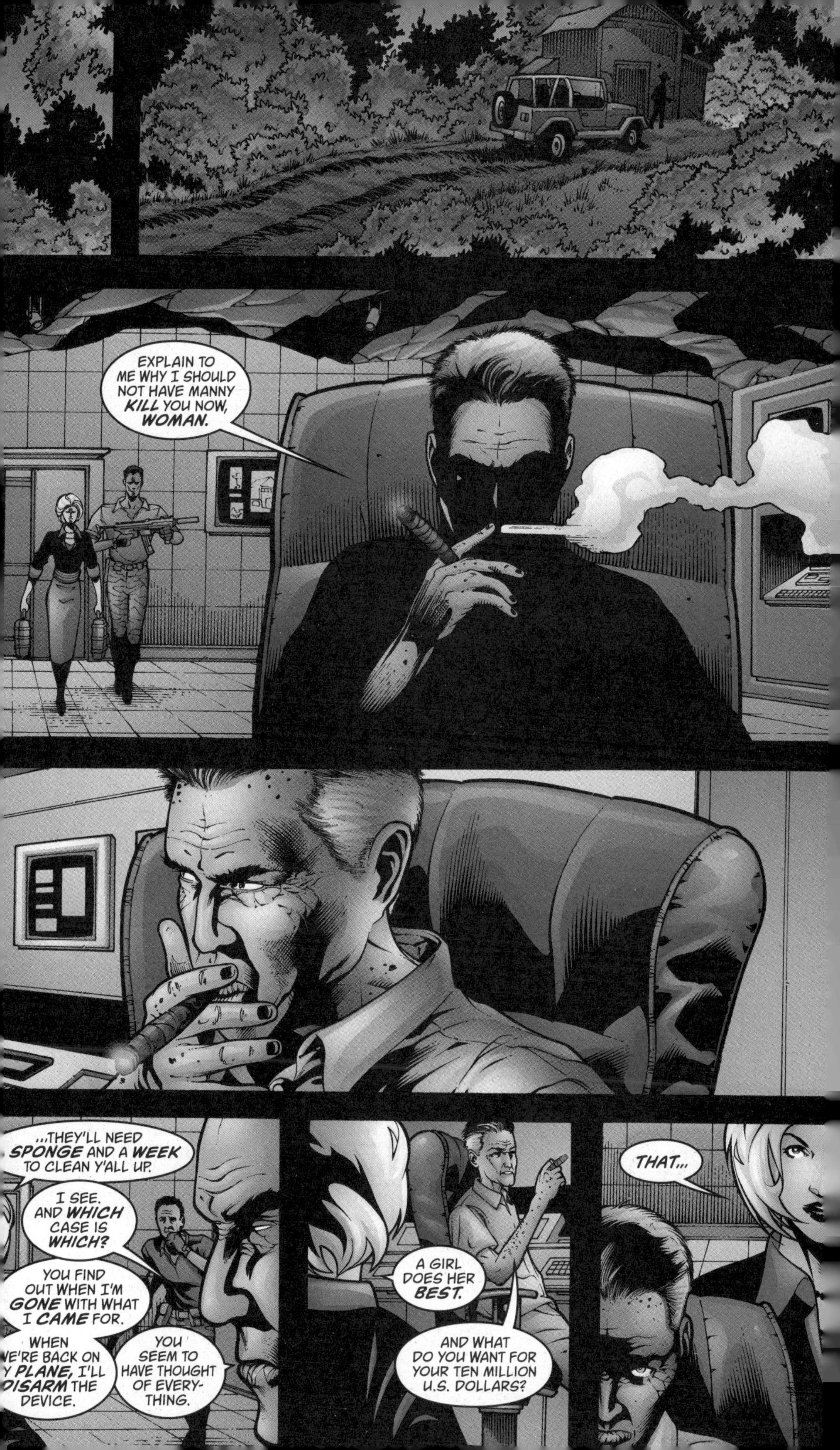
EXPLAIN TO ME WHY I SHOULD NOT HAVE MANNY KILL YOU NOW, WOMAN.
...THEY'LL NEED SPONGE AND A WEEK TO CLEAN Y'ALL UP.
I SEE. AND WHICH CASE IS WHICH?
YOU FIND OUT WHEN I'M GONE WITH WHAT I CAME FOR.
WHEN VE'RE BACK ON Y PLANE, I'LL DISARM THE DEVICE.
YOU SEEM TO HAVE THOUGHT OF EVERYTHING.
A GIRL DOES HER BEST.
AND WHAT DO YOU WANT FOR YOUR TEN MILLION U.S. DOLLARS?
THAT...

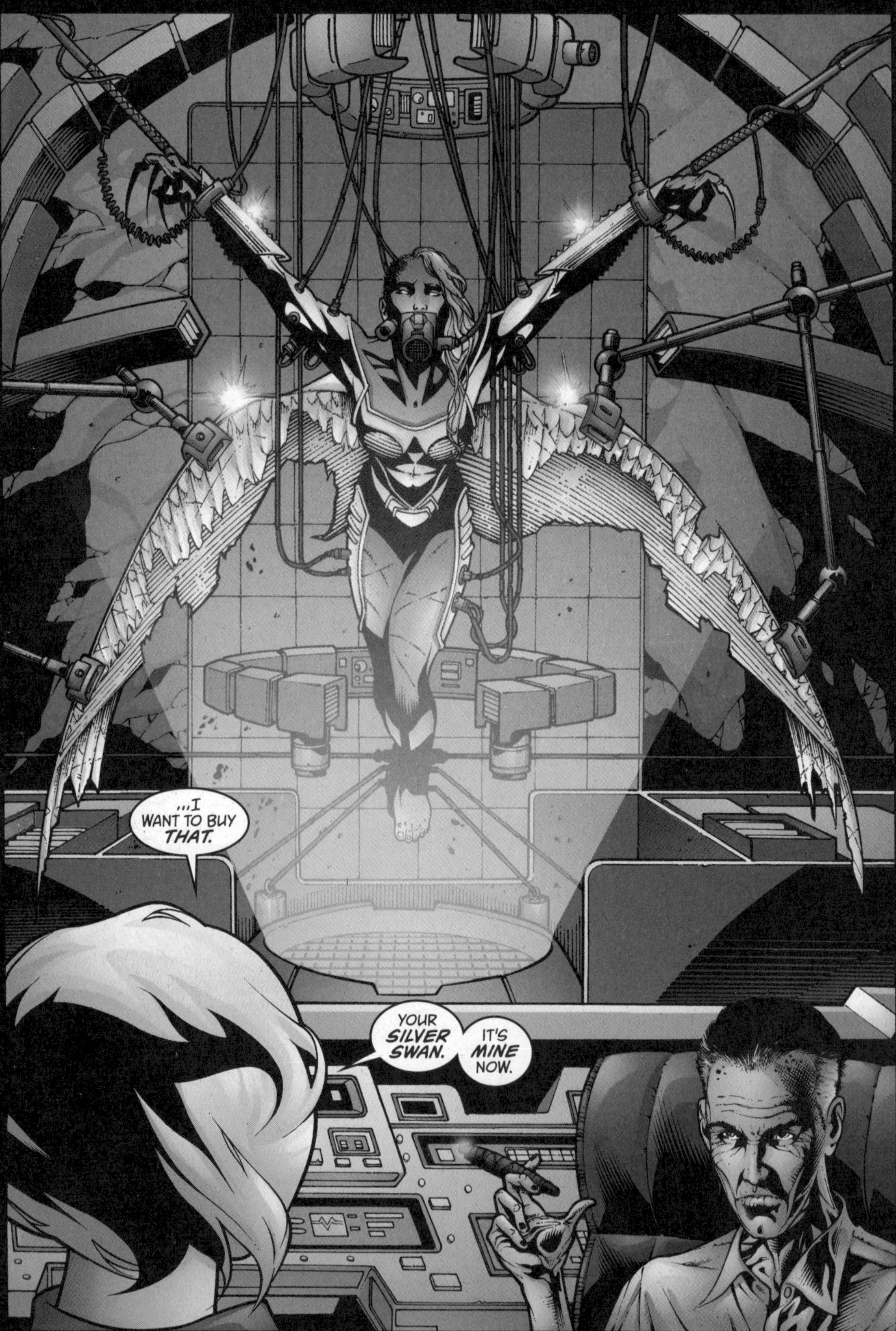
...I WANT TO BUY *THAT.*
YOUR *SILVER SWAN.*
IT'S *MINE* NOW.

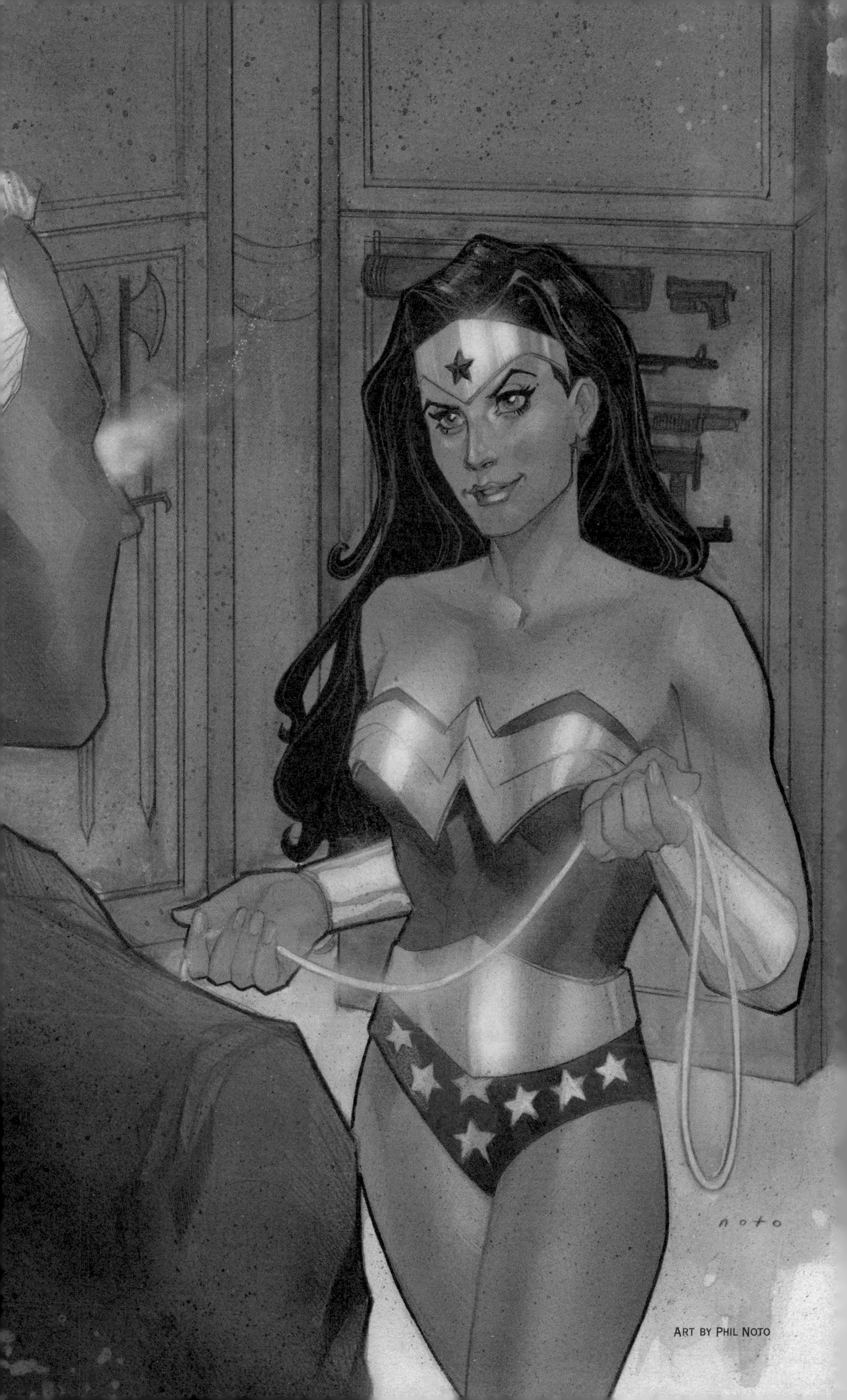
noto

Art by Phil Noto

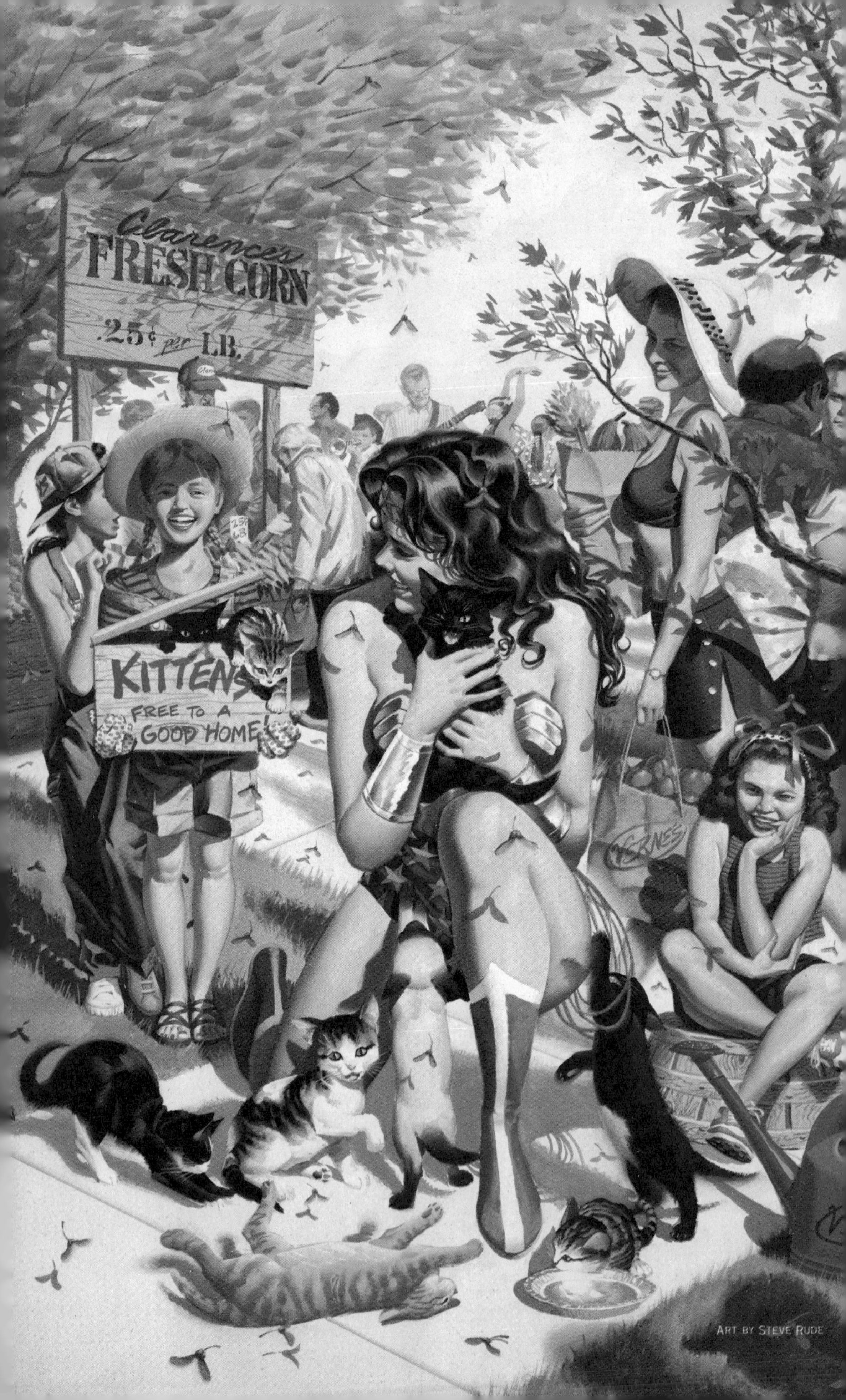
Clarence's
FRESH CORN
.25¢ per LB.
KITTENS
FREE TO A
GOOD HOME!
ART BY STEVE RUDE

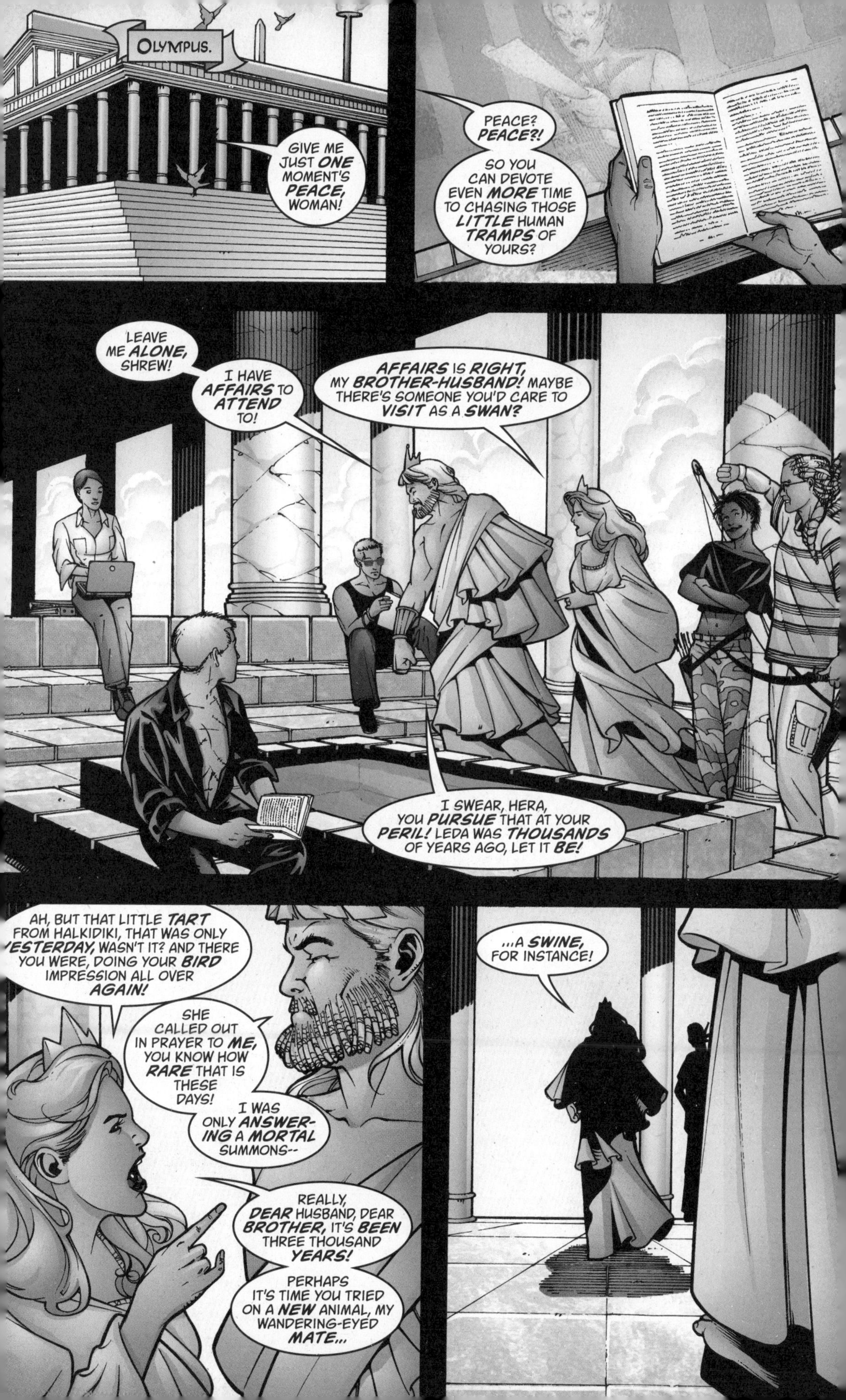
OLYMPUS.
GIVE ME JUST ONE MOMENT'S PEACE, WOMAN!
PEACE? PEACE?!
SO YOU CAN DEVOTE EVEN MORE TIME TO CHASING THOSE LITTLE HUMAN TRAMPS OF YOURS?
LEAVE ME ALONE, SHREW!
I HAVE AFFAIRS TO ATTEND TO!
AFFAIRS IS RIGHT, MY BROTHER-HUSBAND! MAYBE THERE'S SOMEONE YOU'D CARE TO VISIT AS A SWAN?
I SWEAR, HERA, YOU PURSUE THAT AT YOUR PERIL! LEDA WAS THOUSANDS OF YEARS AGO, LET IT BE!
AH, BUT THAT LITTLE TART FROM HALKIDIKI, THAT WAS ONLY YESTERDAY, WASN'T IT? AND THERE YOU WERE, DOING YOUR BIRD IMPRESSION ALL OVER AGAIN!
SHE CALLED OUT IN PRAYER TO ME, YOU KNOW HOW RARE THESE IS THESE DAYS!
I WAS ONLY ANSWERING A MORTAL SUMMONS--
REALLY, DEAR HUSBAND, DEAR BROTHER, IT'S BEEN THREE THOUSAND YEARS!
PERHAPS IT'S TIME YOU TRIED ON A NEW ANIMAL, MY WANDERING-EYED MATE...
...A SWINE, FOR INSTANCE!

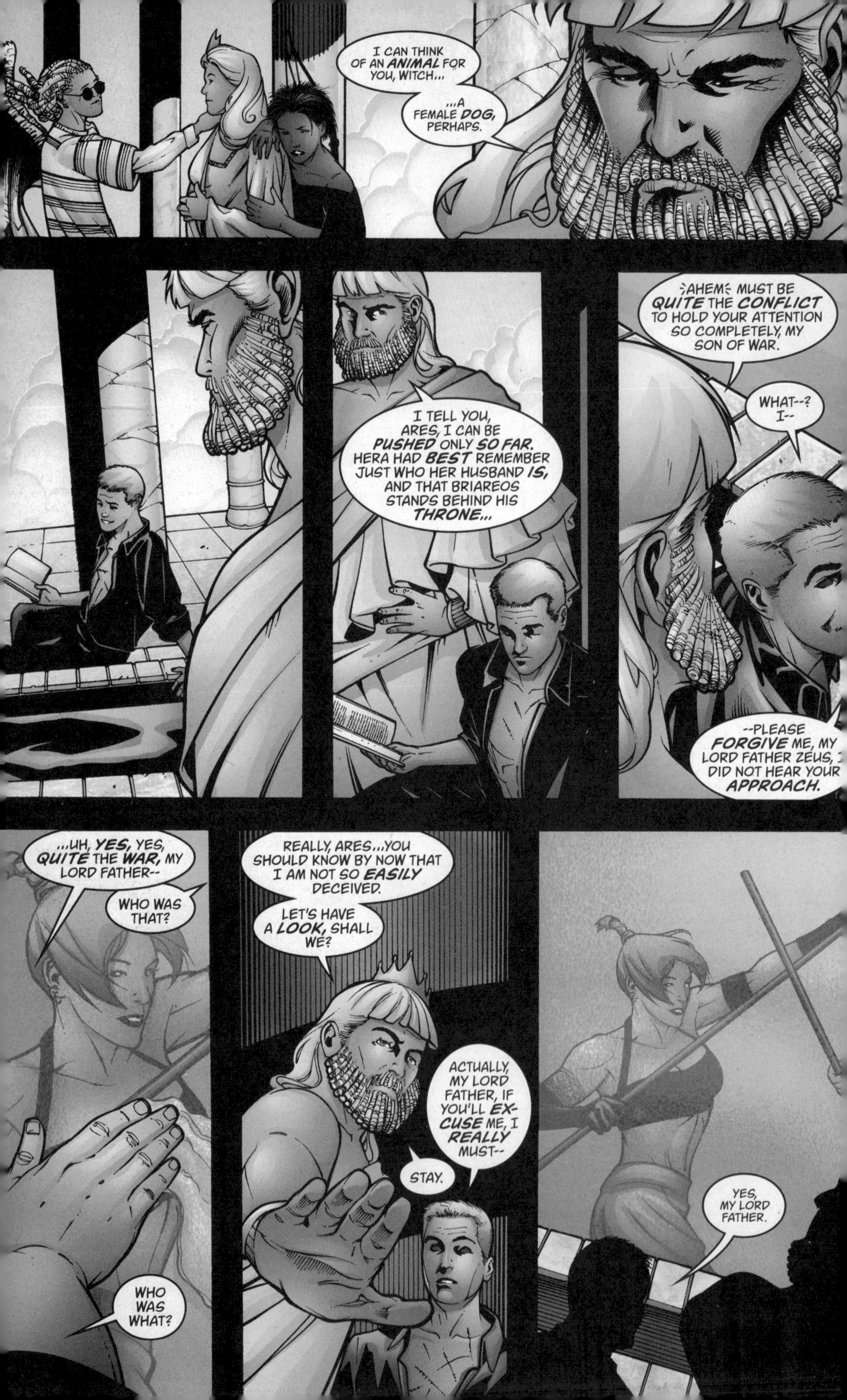
I CAN THINK OF AN ANIMAL FOR YOU, WITCH...
...A FEMALE DOG, PERHAPS.
I TELL YOU, ARES, I CAN BE PUSHED ONLY SO FAR. HERA HAD BEST REMEMBER JUST WHO HER HUSBAND IS, AND THAT BRIAREOS STANDS BEHIND HIS THRONE...
AHEM MUST BE QUITE THE CONFLICT TO HOLD YOUR ATTENTION SO COMPLETELY, MY SON OF WAR.
WHAT--? I--
--PLEASE FORGIVE ME, MY LORD FATHER ZEUS, I DID NOT HEAR YOUR APPROACH.
...UH, YES, YES, QUITE THE WAR, MY LORD FATHER--
WHO WAS THAT?
WHO WAS WHAT?
REALLY, ARES...YOU SHOULD KNOW BY NOW THAT I AM NOT SO EASILY DECEIVED.
LET'S HAVE A LOOK, SHALL WE?
ACTUALLY, MY LORD FATHER, IF YOU'LL EXCUSE ME, I REALLY MUST--
STAY.
YES, MY LORD FATHER.

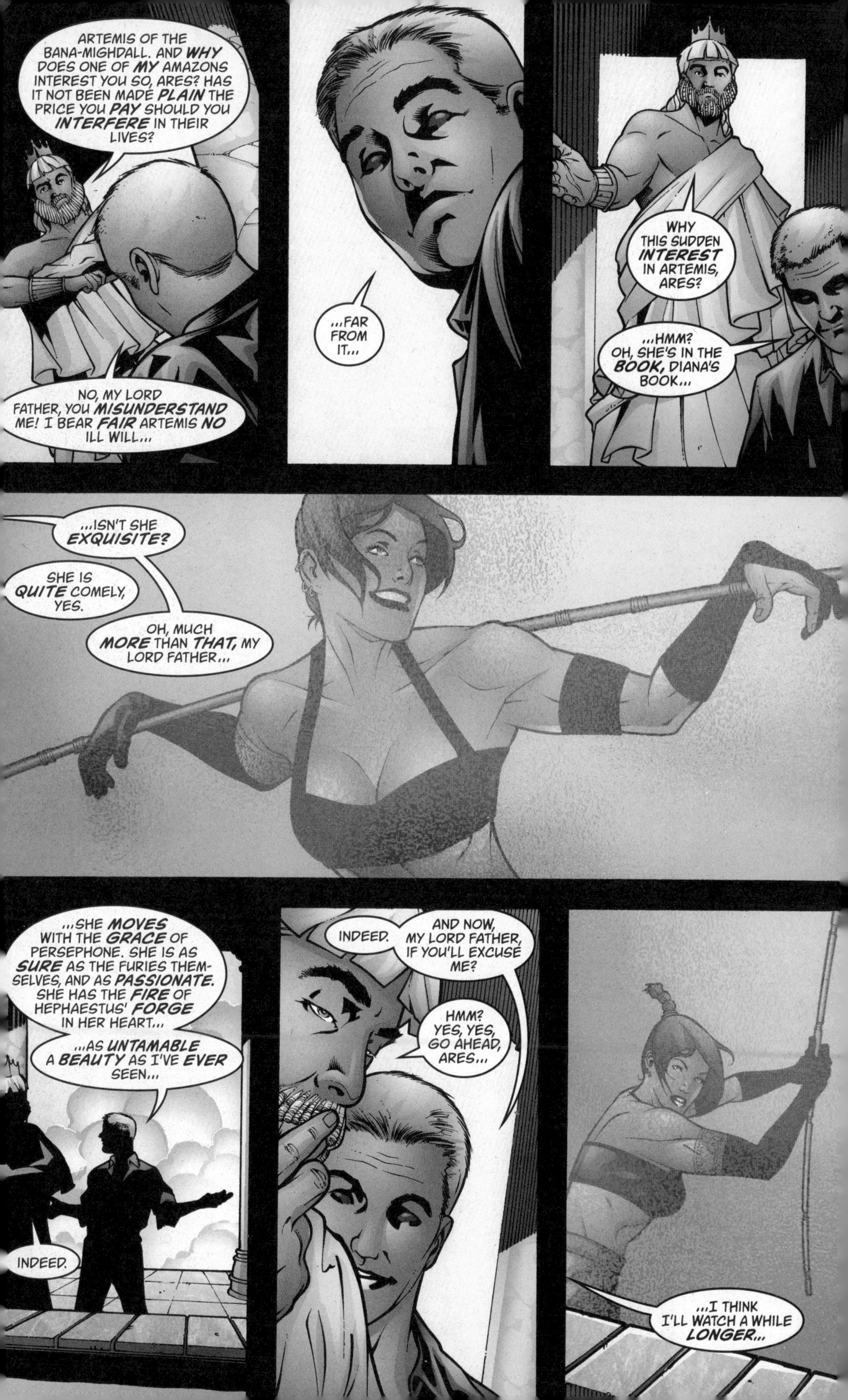
ARTEMIS OF THE BANA-MIGHDALL. AND WHY DOES ONE OF MY AMAZONS INTEREST YOU SO, ARES? HAS IT NOT BEEN MADE PLAIN THE PRICE YOU PAY SHOULD YOU INTERFERE IN THEIR LIVES?
NO, MY LORD FATHER, YOU MISUNDERSTAND ME! I BEAR FAIR ARTEMIS NO ILL WILL...
...FAR FROM IT...
WHY THIS SUDDEN INTEREST IN ARTEMIS, ARES?
...HMM? OH, SHE'S IN THE BOOK, DIANA'S BOOK...
...ISN'T SHE EXQUISITE?
SHE IS QUITE COMELY, YES.
OH, MUCH MORE THAN THAT, MY LORD FATHER...
...SHE MOVES WITH THE GRACE OF PERSEPHONE. SHE IS AS SURE AS THE FURIES THEMSELVES, AND AS PASSIONATE. SHE HAS THE FIRE OF HEPHAESTUS' FORGE IN HER HEART...
...AS UNTAMABLE A BEAUTY AS I'VE EVER SEEN...
INDEED.
INDEED.
AND NOW, MY LORD FATHER, IF YOU'LL EXCUSE ME?
HMM? YES, YES, GO AHEAD, ARES...
...I THINK I'LL WATCH A WHILE LONGER...

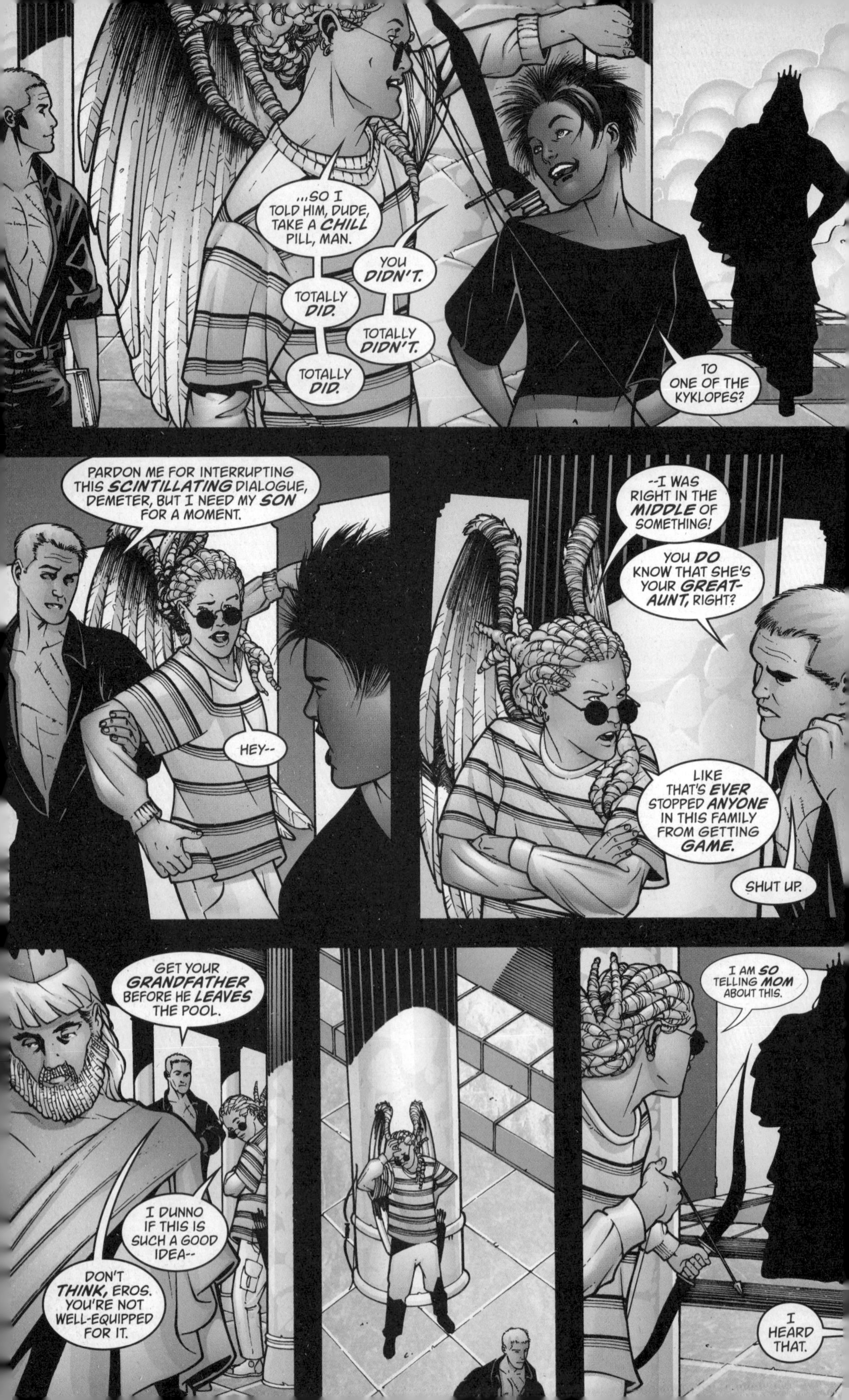

...SO I TOLD HIM, DUDE, TAKE A CHILL PILL, MAN.
YOU DIDN'T.
TOTALLY DID.
TOTALLY DIDN'T.
TOTALLY DID.
TO ONE OF THE KYKLOPES?
PARDON ME FOR INTERRUPTING THIS SCINTILLATING DIALOGUE, DEMETER, BUT I NEED MY SON FOR A MOMENT.
HEY--
--I WAS RIGHT IN THE MIDDLE OF SOMETHING!
YOU DO KNOW THAT SHE'S YOUR GREAT-AUNT, RIGHT?
LIKE THAT'S EVER STOPPED ANYONE IN THIS FAMILY FROM GETTING GAME.
SHUT UP.
GET YOUR GRANDFATHER BEFORE HE LEAVES THE POOL.
I DUNNO IF THIS IS SUCH A GOOD IDEA--
DON'T THINK, EROS. YOU'RE NOT WELL-EQUIPPED FOR IT.
I AM SO TELLING MOM ABOUT THIS.
I HEARD THAT.

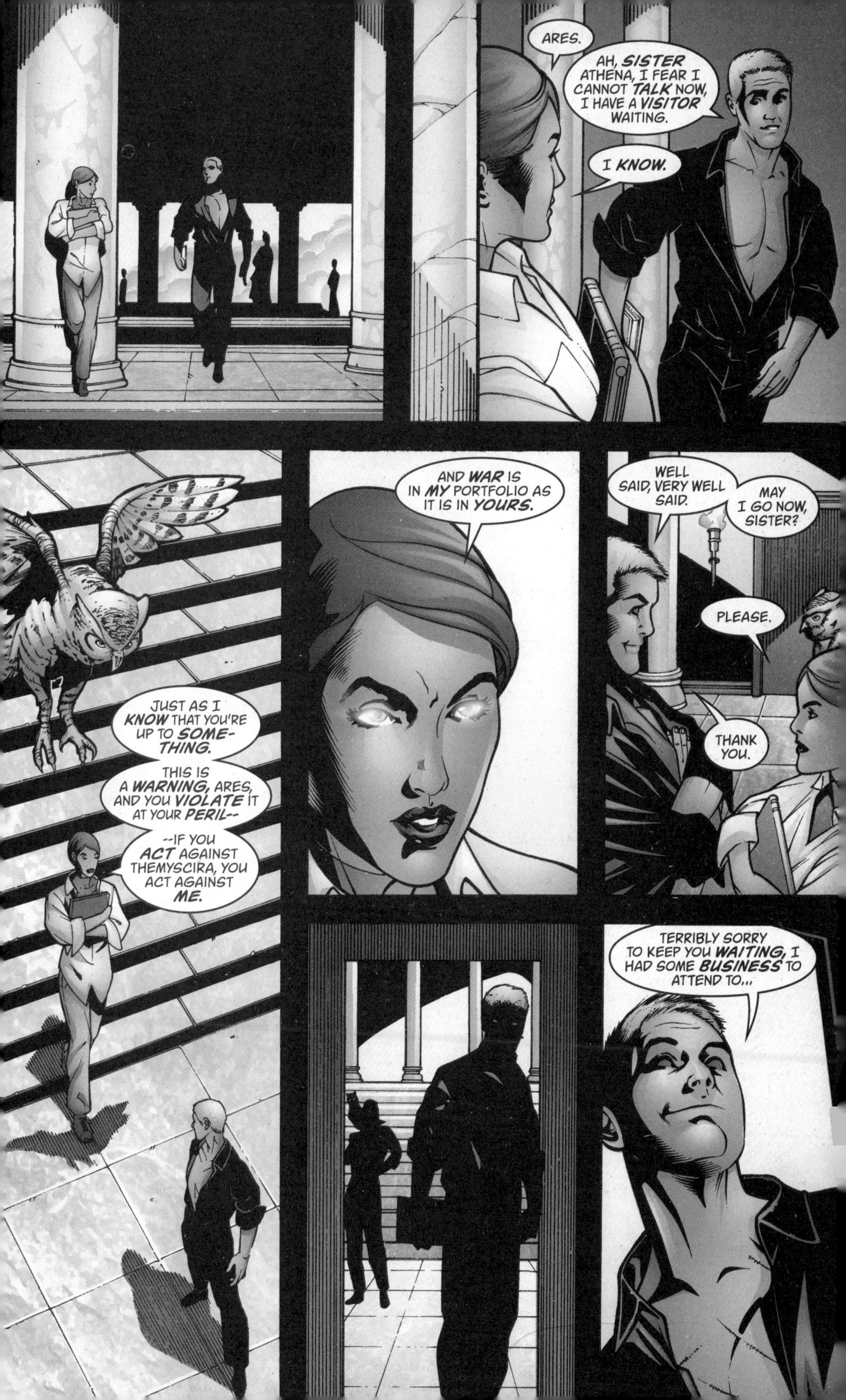
ARES.
AH, SISTER ATHENA, I FEAR I CANNOT TALK NOW, I HAVE A VISITOR WAITING.
I KNOW.
JUST AS I KNOW THAT YOU'RE UP TO SOME-THING.
THIS IS A WARNING, ARES, AND YOU VIOLATE IT AT YOUR PERIL--
--IF YOU ACT AGAINST THEMYSCIRA, YOU ACT AGAINST ME.
AND WAR IS IN MY PORTFOLIO AS IT IS IN YOURS.
WELL SAID, VERY WELL SAID.
MAY I GO NOW, SISTER?
PLEASE.
THANK YOU.
TERRIBLY SORRY TO KEEP YOU WAITING, I HAD SOME BUSINESS TO ATTEND TO...

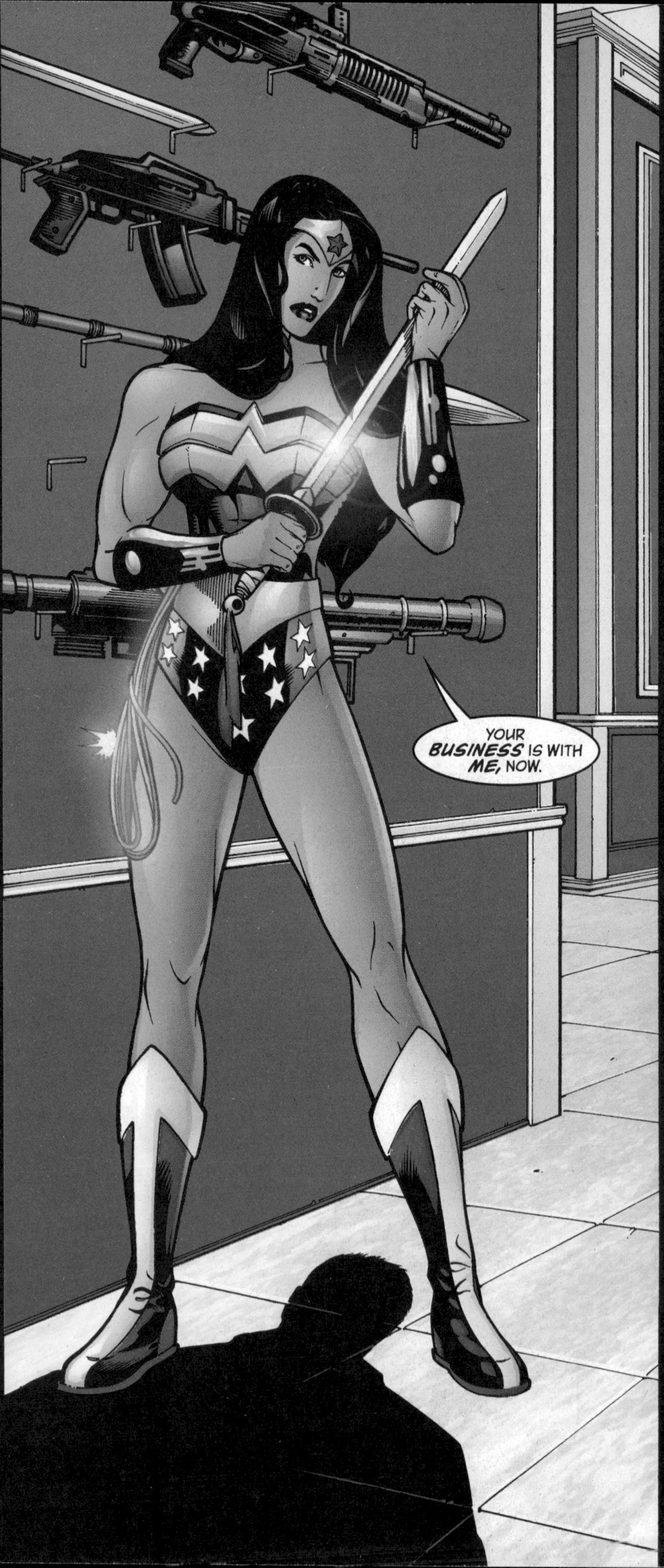
YOUR BUSINESS IS WITH ME, NOW.

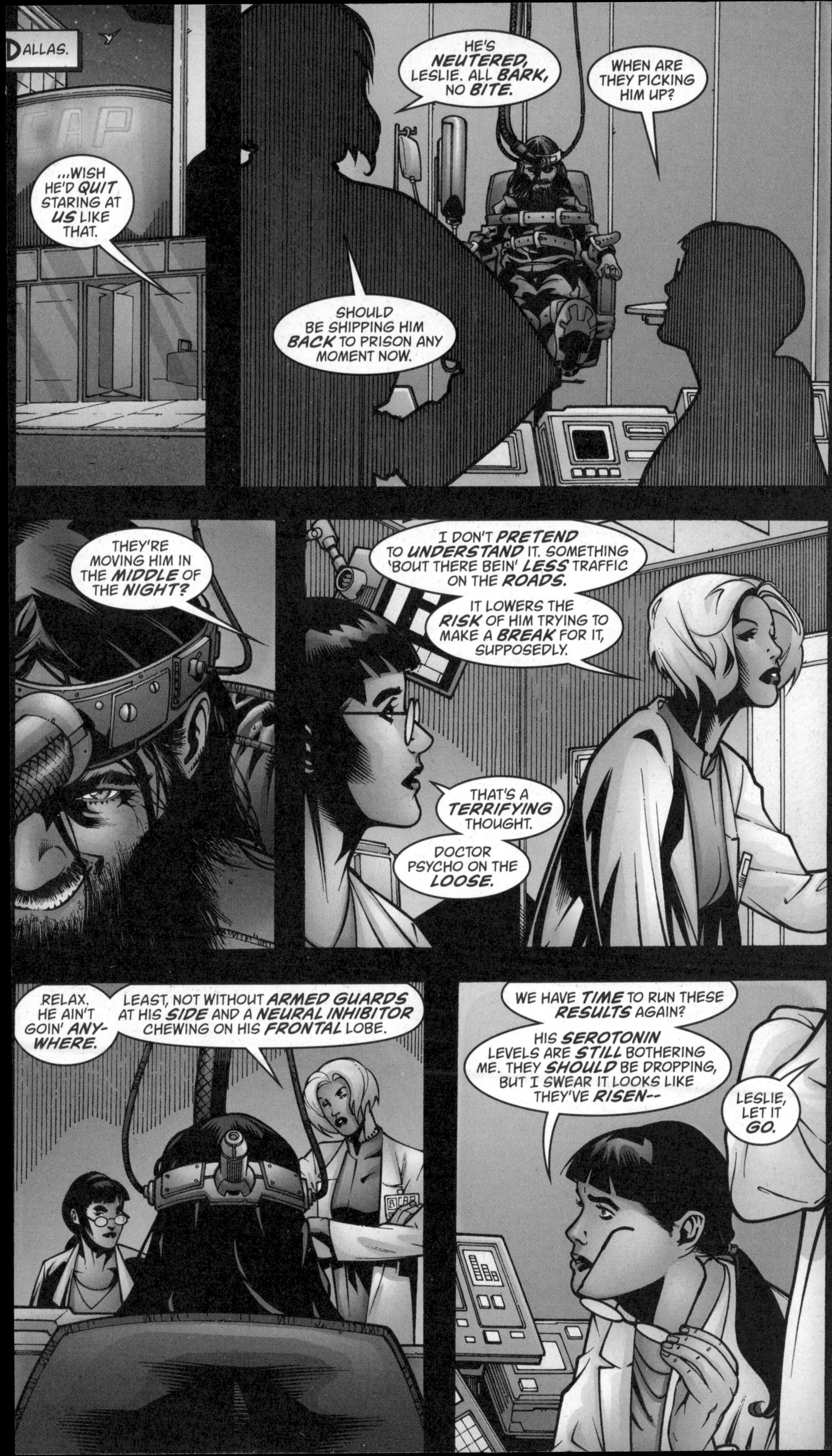
DALLAS.
...WISH HE'D QUIT STARING AT US LIKE THAT.
HE'S NEUTERED, LESLIE. ALL BARK, NO BITE.
SHOULD BE SHIPPING HIM BACK TO PRISON ANY MOMENT NOW.
WHEN ARE THEY PICKING HIM UP?
THEY'RE MOVING HIM IN THE MIDDLE OF THE NIGHT?
I DON'T PRETEND TO UNDERSTAND IT. SOMETHING 'BOUT THERE BEIN' LESS TRAFFIC ON THE ROADS.
IT LOWERS THE RISK OF HIM TRYING TO MAKE A BREAK FOR IT, SUPPOSEDLY.
THAT'S A TERRIFYING THOUGHT.
DOCTOR PSYCHO ON THE LOOSE.
RELAX. HE AIN'T GOIN' ANYWHERE.
LEAST, NOT WITHOUT ARMED GUARDS AT HIS SIDE AND A NEURAL INHIBITOR CHEWING ON HIS FRONTAL LOBE.
WE HAVE TIME TO RUN THESE RESULTS AGAIN?
HIS SEROTONIN LEVELS ARE STILL BOTHERING ME. THEY SHOULD BE DROPPING, BUT I SWEAR IT LOOKS LIKE THEY'VE RISEN--
LESLIE, LET IT GO.

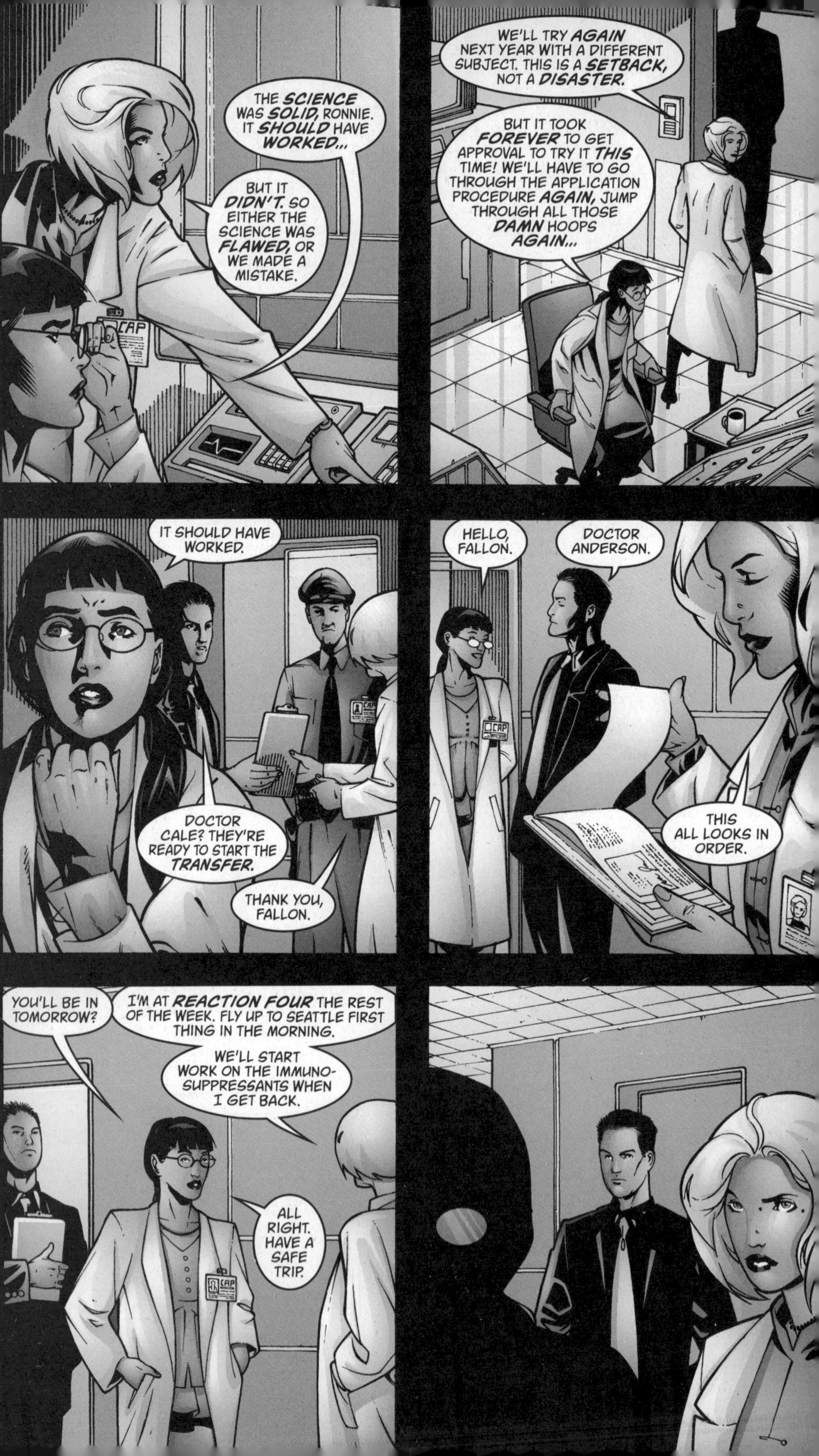
THE SCIENCE WAS SOLID, RONNIE. IT SHOULD HAVE WORKED...
BUT IT DIDN'T. SO EITHER THE SCIENCE WAS FLAWED, OR WE MADE A MISTAKE.
WE'LL TRY AGAIN NEXT YEAR WITH A DIFFERENT SUBJECT. THIS IS A SETBACK, NOT A DISASTER.
BUT IT TOOK FOREVER TO GET APPROVAL TO TRY IT THIS TIME! WE'LL HAVE TO GO THROUGH THE APPLICATION PROCEDURE AGAIN, JUMP THROUGH ALL THOSE DAMN HOOPS AGAIN...
IT SHOULD HAVE WORKED.
DOCTOR CALE? THEY'RE READY TO START THE TRANSFER.
THANK YOU, FALLON.
HELLO, FALLON.
DOCTOR ANDERSON.
THIS ALL LOOKS IN ORDER.
YOU'LL BE IN TOMORROW?
I'M AT REACTION FOUR THE REST OF THE WEEK. FLY UP TO SEATTLE FIRST THING IN THE MORNING.
WE'LL START WORK ON THE IMMUNO-SUPPRESSANTS WHEN I GET BACK.
ALL RIGHT. HAVE A SAFE TRIP.

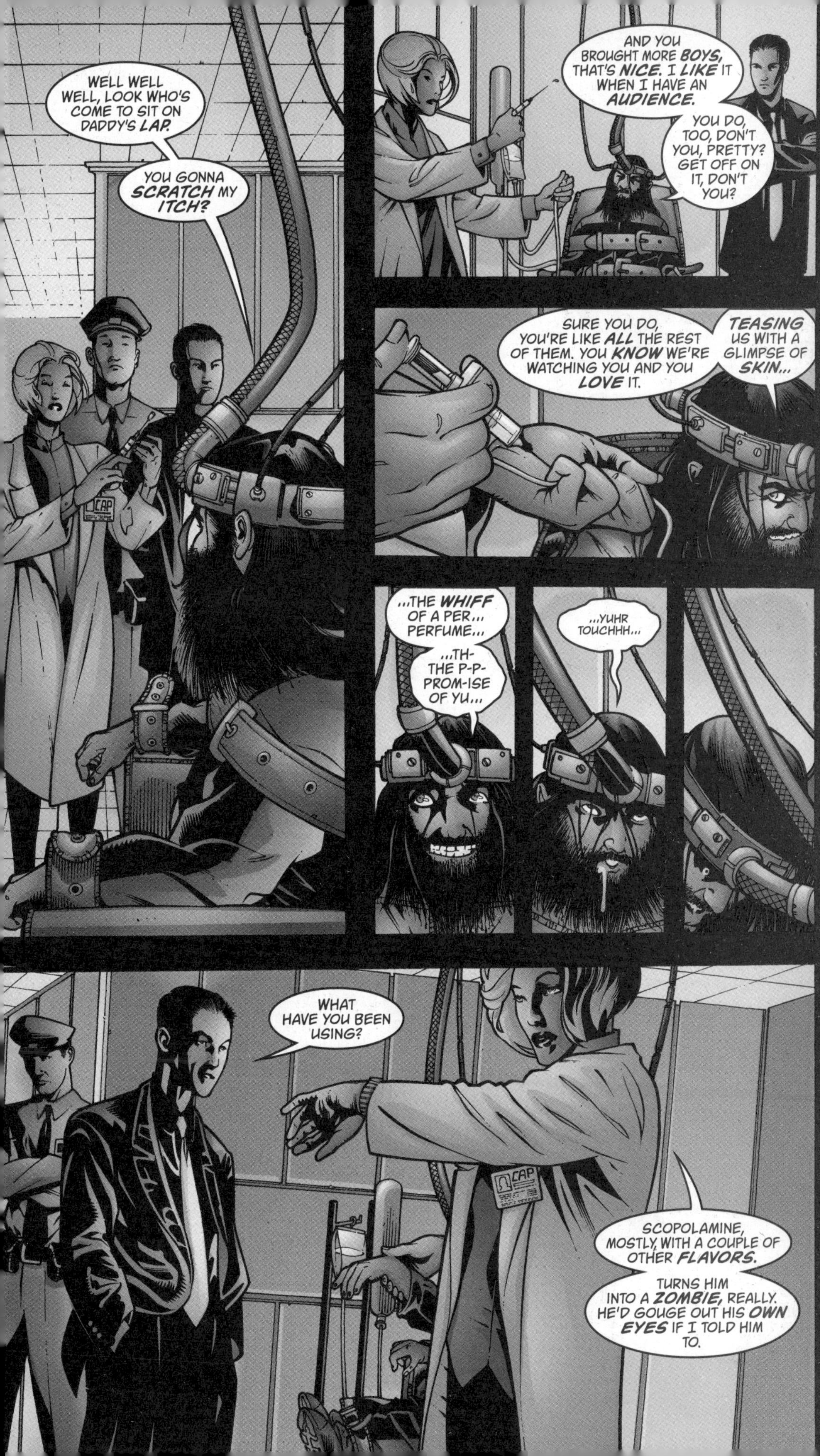
WELL WELL WELL, LOOK WHO'S COME TO SIT ON DADDY'S LAP.
YOU GONNA SCRATCH MY ITCH?
AND YOU BROUGHT MORE BOYS, THAT'S NICE. I LIKE IT WHEN I HAVE AN AUDIENCE.
YOU DO, TOO, DON'T YOU, PRETTY? GET OFF ON IT, DON'T YOU?
SURE YOU DO, YOU'RE LIKE ALL THE REST OF THEM. YOU KNOW WE'RE WATCHING YOU AND YOU LOVE IT.
TEASING US WITH A GLIMPSE OF SKIN...
...THE WHIFF OF A PER... PERFUME...
...TH-THE P-P-PROM-ISE OF YU...
...YUHR TOUCHHH...
WHAT HAVE YOU BEEN USING?
SCOPOLAMINE, MOSTLY, WITH A COUPLE OF OTHER FLAVORS.
TURNS HIM INTO A ZOMBIE, REALLY. HE'D GOUGE OUT HIS OWN EYES IF I TOLD HIM TO.

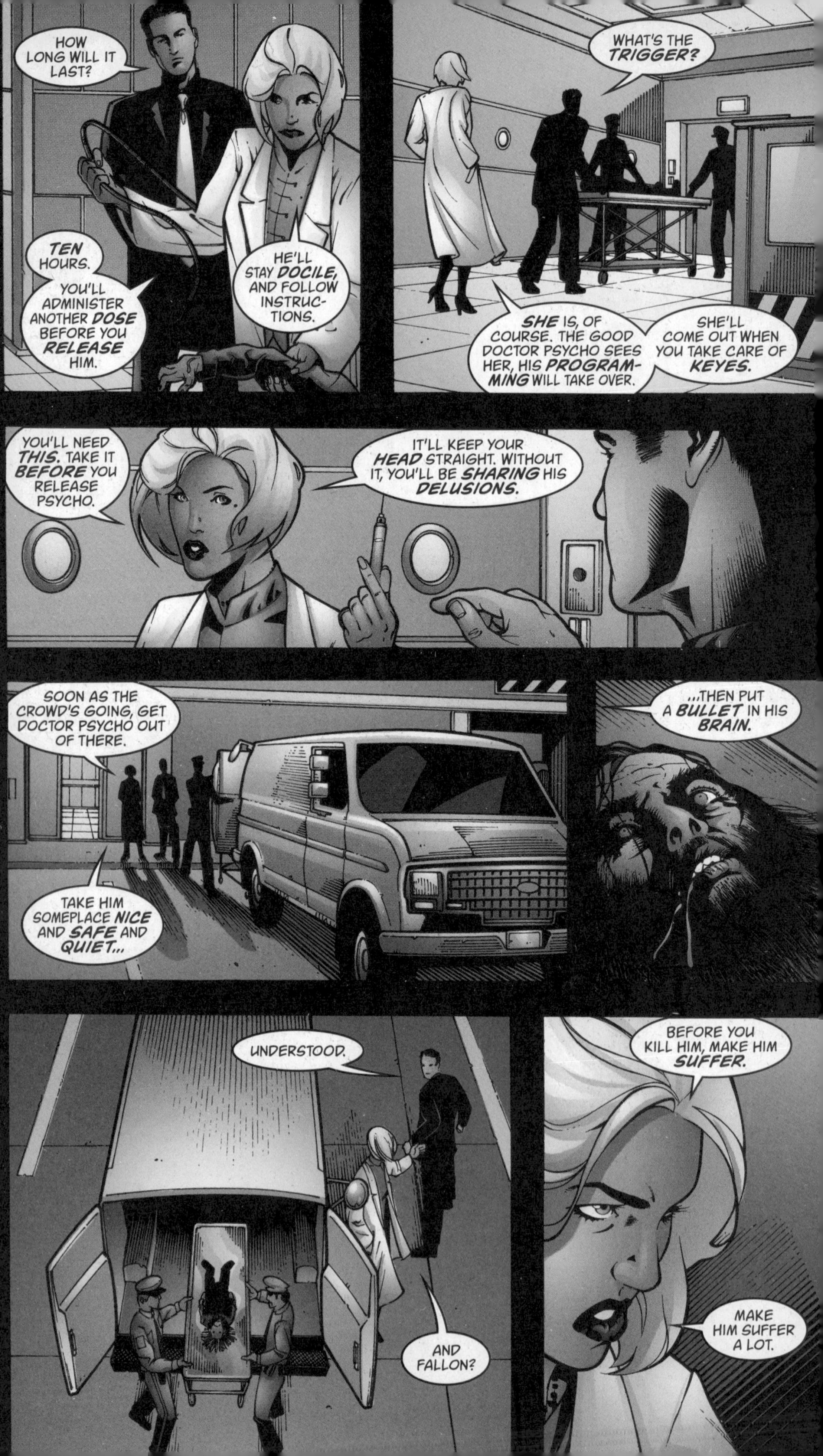
HOW LONG WILL IT LAST?
TEN HOURS.
YOU'LL ADMINISTER ANOTHER DOSE BEFORE YOU RELEASE HIM.
HE'LL STAY DOCILE, AND FOLLOW INSTRUC-TIONS.
WHAT'S THE TRIGGER?
SHE IS, OF COURSE. THE GOOD DOCTOR PSYCHO SEES HER, HIS PROGRAM-MING WILL TAKE OVER.
SHE'LL COME OUT WHEN YOU TAKE CARE OF KEYES.
YOU'LL NEED THIS. TAKE IT BEFORE YOU RELEASE PSYCHO.
IT'LL KEEP YOUR HEAD STRAIGHT. WITHOUT IT, YOU'LL BE SHARING HIS DELUSIONS.
SOON AS THE CROWD'S GOING, GET DOCTOR PSYCHO OUT OF THERE.
TAKE HIM SOMEPLACE NICE AND SAFE AND QUIET...
...THEN PUT A BULLET IN HIS BRAIN.
UNDERSTOOD.
AND FALLON?
BEFORE YOU KILL HIM, MAKE HIM SUFFER.
MAKE HIM SUFFER A LOT.

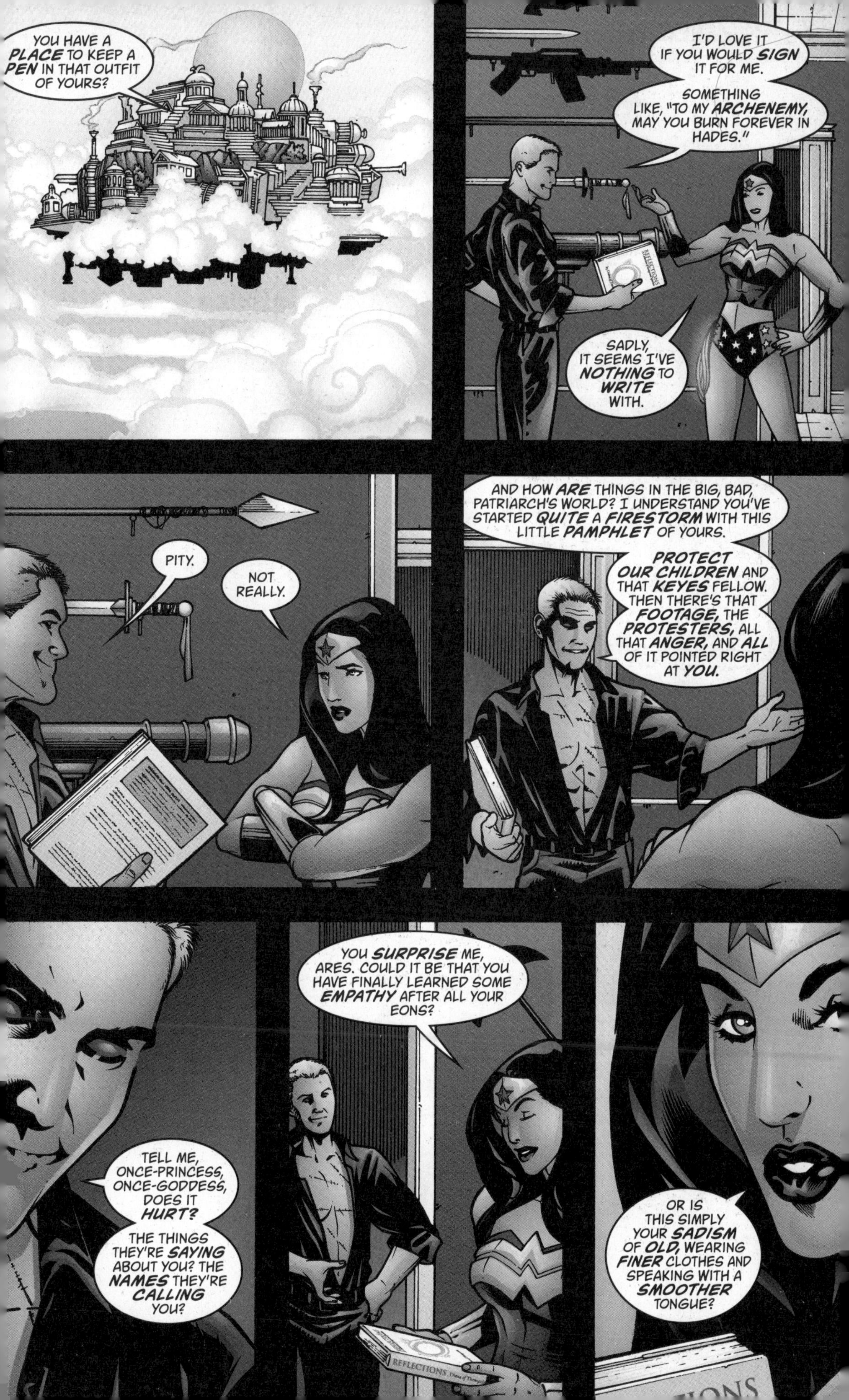
YOU HAVE A PLACE TO KEEP A PEN IN THAT OUTFIT OF YOURS?
I'D LOVE IT IF YOU WOULD SIGN IT FOR ME.
SOMETHING LIKE, "TO MY ARCHENEMY, MAY YOU BURN FOREVER IN HADES."
SADLY, IT SEEMS I'VE NOTHING TO WRITE WITH.
PITY.
NOT REALLY.
AND HOW ARE THINGS IN THE BIG, BAD, PATRIARCH'S WORLD? I UNDERSTAND YOU'VE STARTED QUITE A FIRESTORM WITH THIS LITTLE PAMPHLET OF YOURS.
PROTECT OUR CHILDREN AND THAT KEYES FELLOW. THEN THERE'S THAT FOOTAGE, THE PROTESTERS, ALL THAT ANGER, AND ALL OF IT POINTED RIGHT AT YOU.
TELL ME, ONCE-PRINCESS, ONCE-GODDESS, DOES IT HURT?
THE THINGS THEY'RE SAYING ABOUT YOU? THE NAMES THEY'RE CALLING YOU?
YOU SURPRISE ME, ARES. COULD IT BE THAT YOU HAVE FINALLY LEARNED SOME EMPATHY AFTER ALL YOUR EONS?
REFLECTIONS
OR IS THIS SIMPLY YOUR SADISM OF OLD, WEARING FINER CLOTHES AND SPEAKING WITH A SMOOTHER TONGUE?

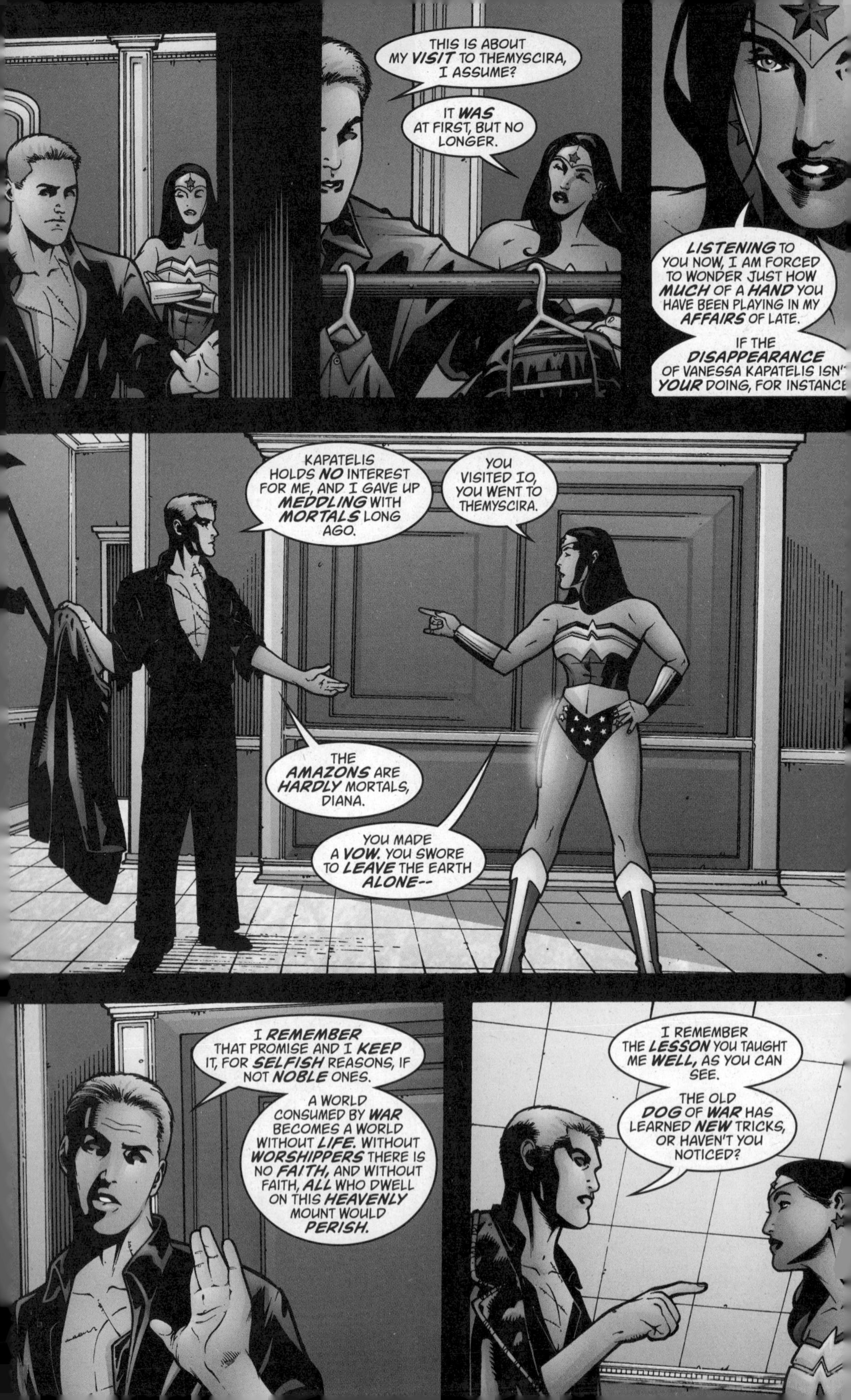
THIS IS ABOUT MY VISIT TO THEMYSCIRA, I ASSUME?
IT WAS AT FIRST, BUT NO LONGER.
LISTENING TO YOU NOW, I AM FORCED TO WONDER JUST HOW MUCH OF A HAND YOU HAVE BEEN PLAYING IN MY AFFAIRS OF LATE.
IF THE DISAPPEARANCE OF VANESSA KAPATELIS ISN'T YOUR DOING, FOR INSTANCE
KAPATELIS HOLDS NO INTEREST FOR ME, AND I GAVE UP MEDDLING WITH MORTALS LONG AGO.
YOU VISITED IO, YOU WENT TO THEMYSCIRA.
THE AMAZONS ARE HARDLY MORTALS, DIANA.
YOU MADE A VOW. YOU SWORE TO LEAVE THE EARTH ALONE--
I REMEMBER THAT PROMISE AND I KEEP IT, FOR SELFISH REASONS, IF NOT NOBLE ONES.
A WORLD CONSUMED BY WAR BECOMES A WORLD WITHOUT LIFE. WITHOUT WORSHIPPERS THERE IS NO FAITH, AND WITHOUT FAITH, ALL WHO DWELL ON THIS HEAVENLY MOUNT WOULD PERISH.
I REMEMBER THE LESSON YOU TAUGHT ME WELL, AS YOU CAN SEE.
THE OLD DOG OF WAR HAS LEARNED NEW TRICKS, OR HAVEN'T YOU NOTICED?

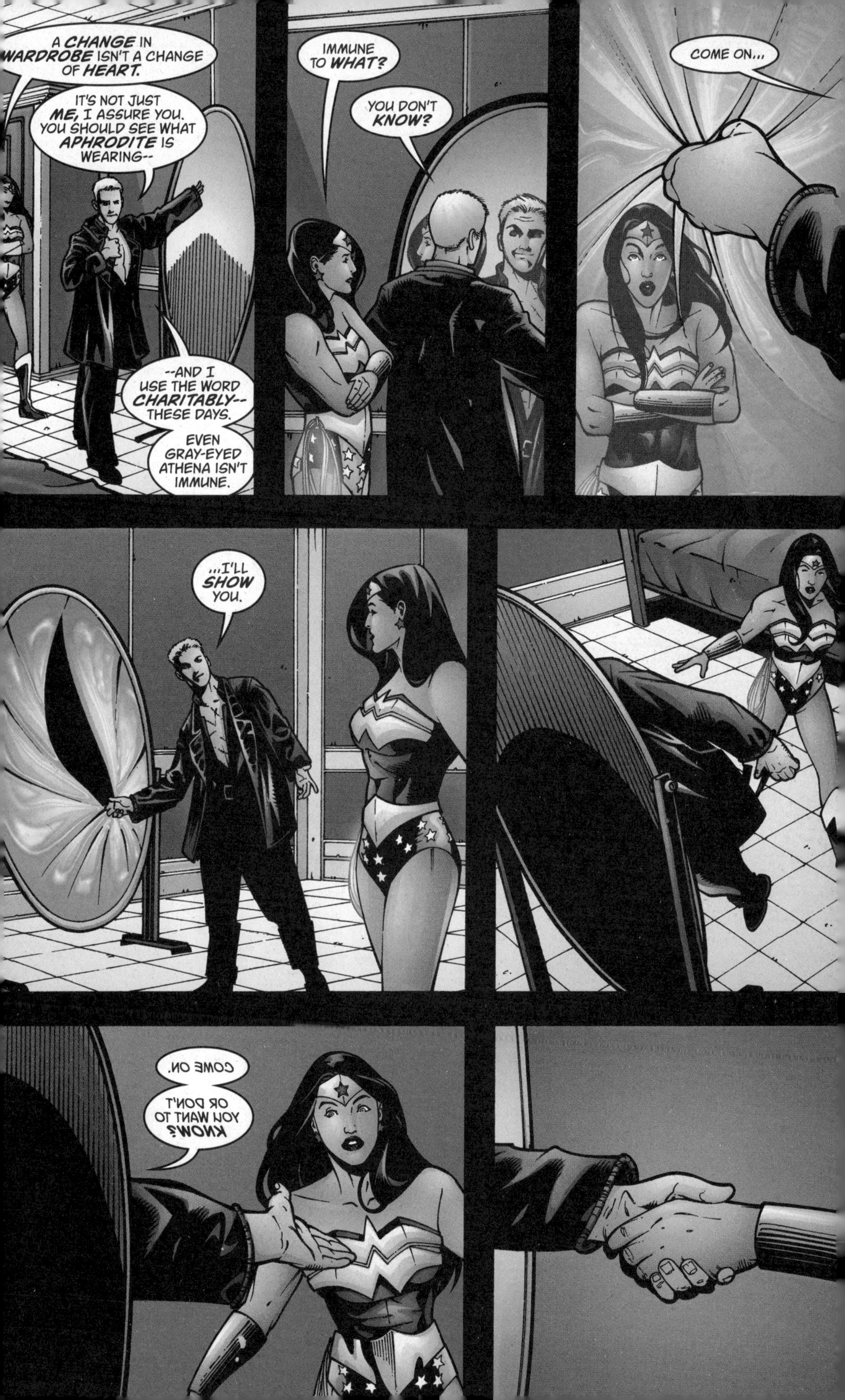
A CHANGE IN WARDROBE ISN'T A CHANGE OF HEART.
IT'S NOT JUST ME, I ASSURE YOU. YOU SHOULD SEE WHAT APHRODITE IS WEARING--
--AND I USE THE WORD CHARITABLY-- THESE DAYS.
EVEN GRAY-EYED ATHENA ISN'T IMMUNE.
IMMUNE TO WHAT?
YOU DON'T KNOW?
COME ON...
...I'LL SHOW YOU.
COME ON.
OR DON'T YOU WANT TO KNOW?

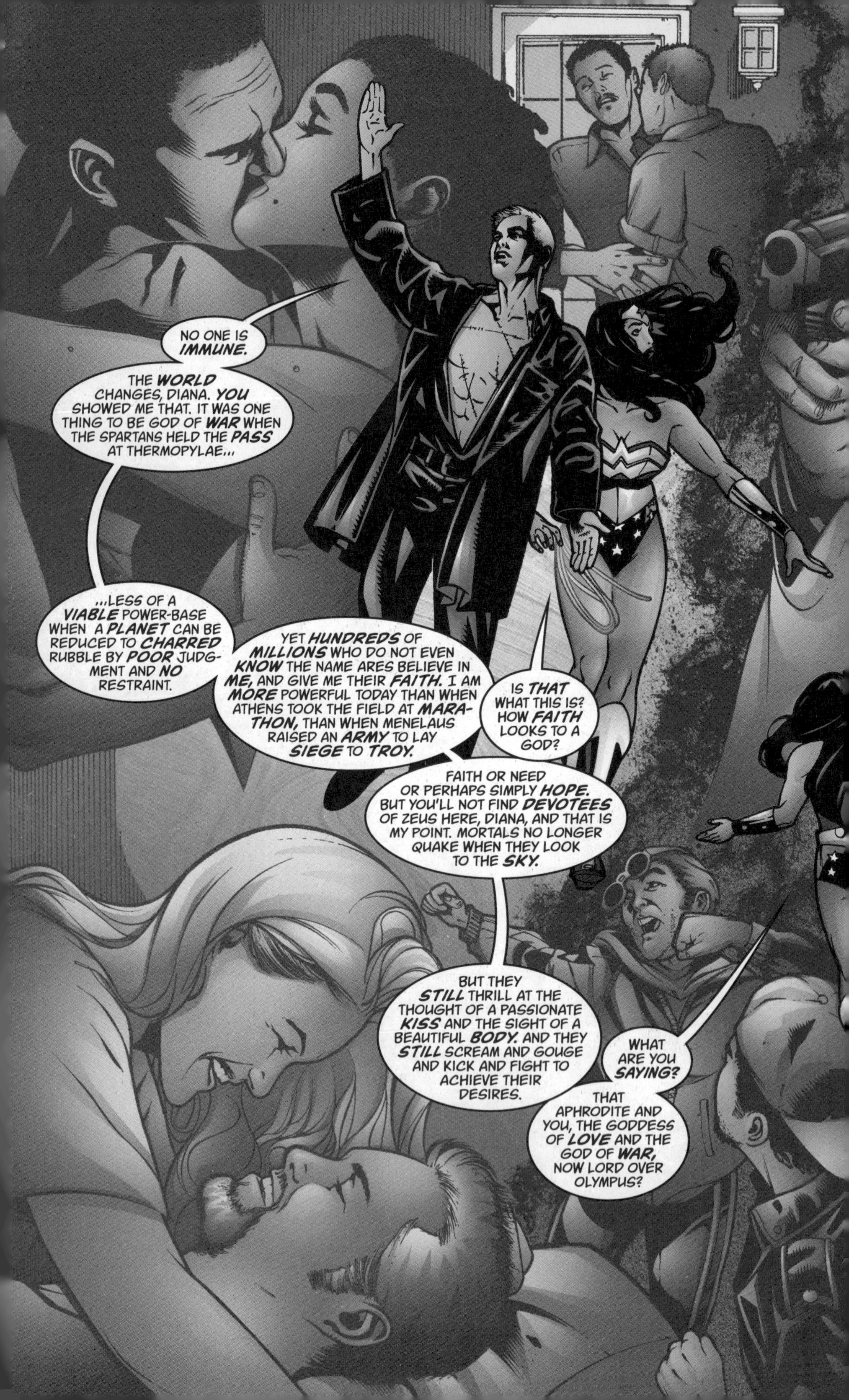
NO ONE IS IMMUNE.
THE WORLD CHANGES, DIANA. YOU SHOWED ME THAT. IT WAS ONE THING TO BE GOD OF WAR WHEN THE SPARTANS HELD THE PASS AT THERMOPYLAE...
...LESS OF A VIABLE POWER-BASE WHEN A PLANET CAN BE REDUCED TO CHARRED RUBBLE BY POOR JUDG-MENT AND NO RESTRAINT.
YET HUNDREDS OF MILLIONS WHO DO NOT EVEN KNOW THE NAME ARES BELIEVE IN ME, AND GIVE ME THEIR FAITH. I AM MORE POWERFUL TODAY THAN WHEN ATHENS TOOK THE FIELD AT MARA-THON, THAN WHEN MENELAUS RAISED AN ARMY TO LAY SIEGE TO TROY.
IS THAT WHAT THIS IS? HOW FAITH LOOKS TO A GOD?
FAITH OR NEED OR PERHAPS SIMPLY HOPE. BUT YOU'LL NOT FIND DEVOTEES OF ZEUS HERE, DIANA, AND THAT IS MY POINT. MORTALS NO LONGER QUAKE WHEN THEY LOOK TO THE SKY.
BUT THEY STILL THRILL AT THE THOUGHT OF A PASSIONATE KISS AND THE SIGHT OF A BEAUTIFUL BODY. AND THEY STILL SCREAM AND GOUGE AND KICK AND FIGHT TO ACHIEVE THEIR DESIRES.
WHAT ARE YOU SAYING?
THAT APHRODITE AND YOU, THE GODDESS OF LOVE AND THE GOD OF WAR, NOW LORD OVER OLYMPUS?

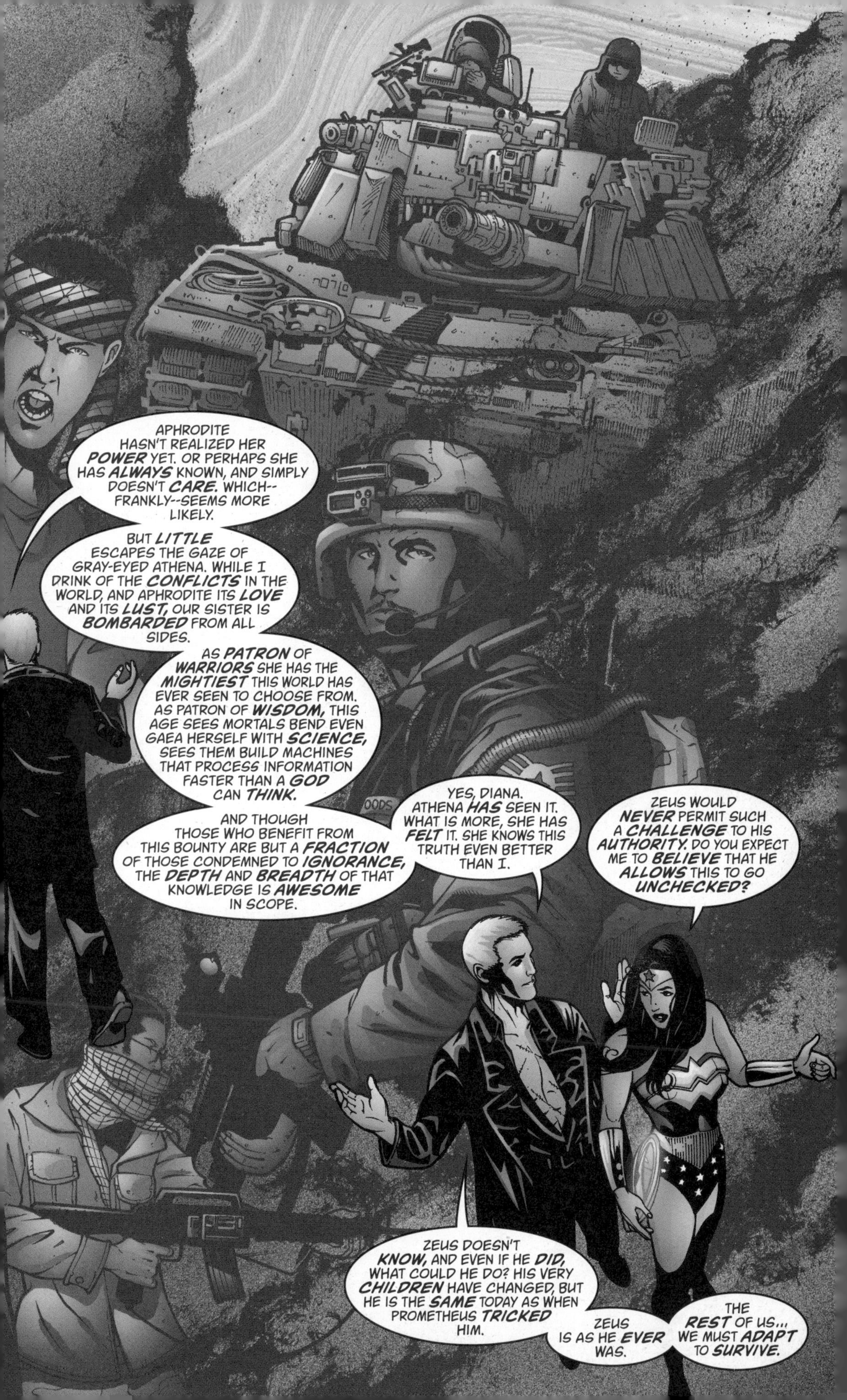

APHRODITE HASN'T REALIZED HER POWER YET. OR PERHAPS SHE HAS ALWAYS KNOWN, AND SIMPLY DOESN'T CARE. WHICH--FRANKLY--SEEMS MORE LIKELY.
BUT LITTLE ESCAPES THE GAZE OF GRAY-EYED ATHENA. WHILE I DRINK OF THE CONFLICTS IN THE WORLD, AND APHRODITE ITS LOVE AND ITS LUST, OUR SISTER IS BOMBARDED FROM ALL SIDES.
AS PATRON OF WARRIORS SHE HAS THE MIGHTIEST THIS WORLD HAS EVER SEEN TO CHOOSE FROM. AS PATRON OF WISDOM, THIS AGE SEES MORTALS BEND EVEN GAEA HERSELF WITH SCIENCE, SEES THEM BUILD MACHINES THAT PROCESS INFORMATION FASTER THAN A GOD CAN THINK.
AND THOUGH THOSE WHO BENEFIT FROM THIS BOUNTY ARE BUT A FRACTION OF THOSE CONDEMNED TO IGNORANCE, THE DEPTH AND BREADTH OF THAT KNOWLEDGE IS AWESOME IN SCOPE.
YES, DIANA. ATHENA HAS SEEN IT. WHAT IS MORE, SHE HAS FELT IT. SHE KNOWS THIS TRUTH EVEN BETTER THAN I.
ZEUS WOULD NEVER PERMIT SUCH A CHALLENGE TO HIS AUTHORITY. DO YOU EXPECT ME TO BELIEVE THAT HE ALLOWS THIS TO GO UNCHECKED?
ZEUS DOESN'T KNOW, AND EVEN IF HE DID, WHAT COULD HE DO? HIS VERY CHILDREN HAVE CHANGED, BUT HE IS THE SAME TODAY AS WHEN PROMETHEUS TRICKED HIM.
ZEUS IS AS HE EVER WAS.
THE REST OF US... WE MUST ADAPT TO SURVIVE.

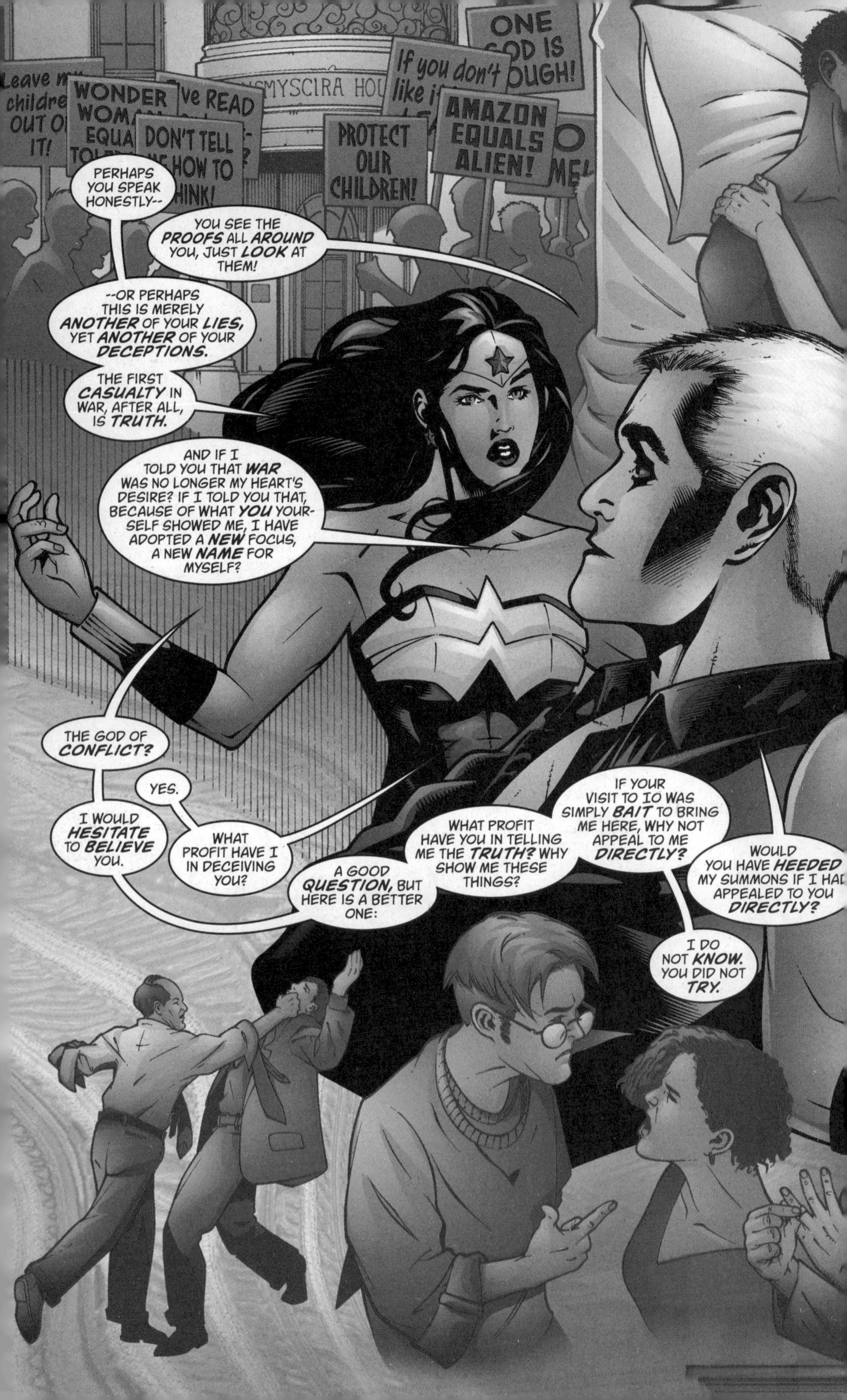
PROTECT OUR CHILDREN!
AMAZON EQUALS ALIEN!
PERHAPS YOU SPEAK HONESTLY--
YOU SEE THE PROOFS ALL AROUND YOU, JUST LOOK AT THEM!
--OR PERHAPS THIS IS MERELY ANOTHER OF YOUR LIES, YET ANOTHER OF YOUR DECEPTIONS.
THE FIRST CASUALTY IN WAR, AFTER ALL, IS TRUTH.
AND IF I TOLD YOU THAT WAR WAS NO LONGER MY HEART'S DESIRE? IF I TOLD YOU THAT, BECAUSE OF WHAT YOU YOURSELF SHOWED ME, I HAVE ADOPTED A NEW FOCUS, A NEW NAME FOR MYSELF?
THE GOD OF CONFLICT?
YES.
I WOULD HESITATE TO BELIEVE YOU.
WHAT PROFIT HAVE I IN DECEIVING YOU?
A GOOD QUESTION, BUT HERE IS A BETTER ONE:
WHAT PROFIT HAVE YOU IN TELLING ME THE TRUTH? WHY SHOW ME THESE THINGS?
IF YOUR VISIT TO IO WAS SIMPLY BAIT TO BRING ME HERE, WHY NOT APPEAL TO ME DIRECTLY?
WOULD YOU HAVE HEEDED MY SUMMONS IF I HAD APPEALED TO YOU DIRECTLY?
I DO NOT KNOW. YOU DID NOT TRY.

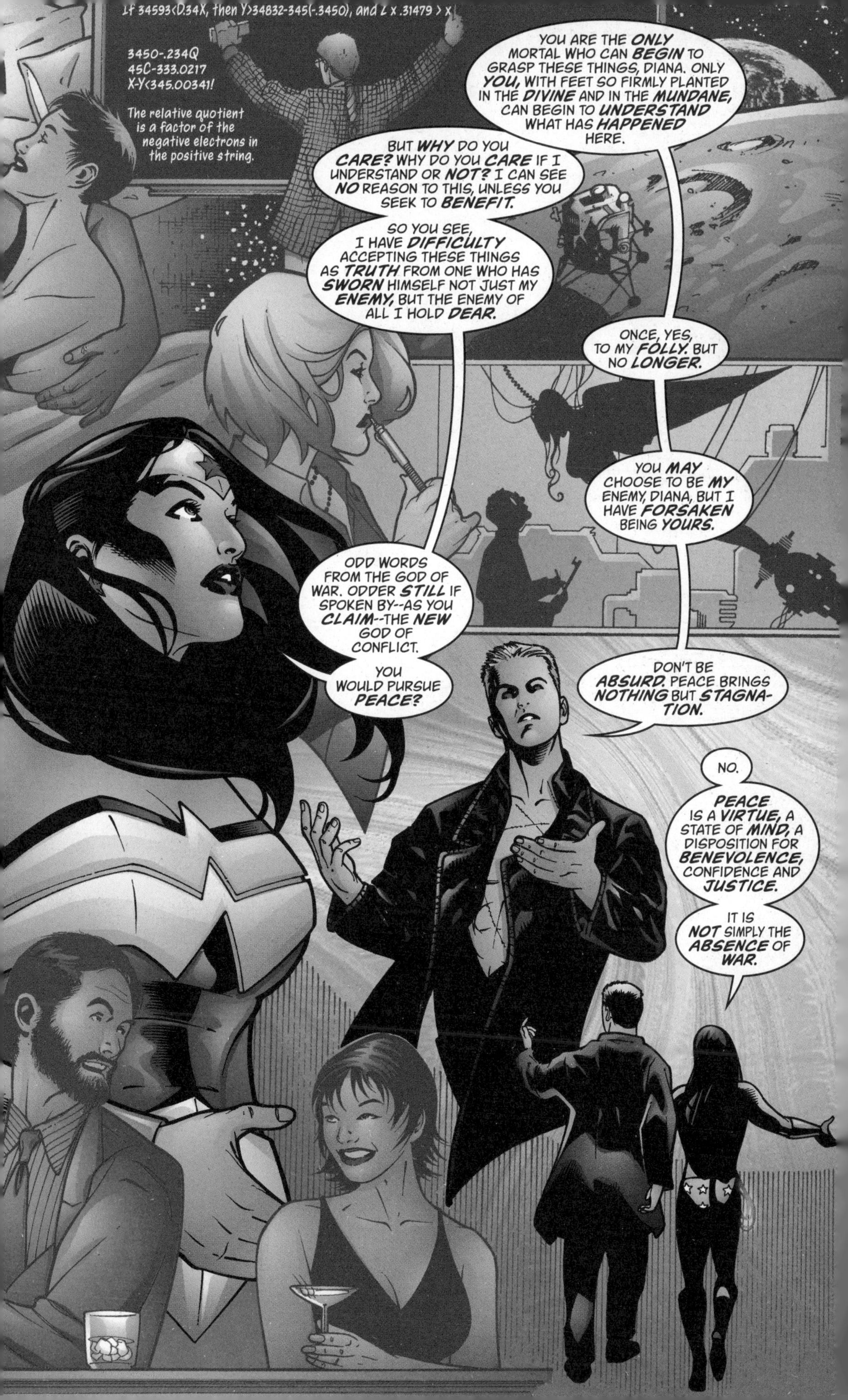
If 34593<D.34X, then Y>34832-345(-.3450), and ∠ x .31479 > x
3450-.234Q
45C-333.0217
X-Y<345.00341!
The relative quotient is a factor of the negative electrons in the positive string.
YOU ARE THE ONLY MORTAL WHO CAN BEGIN TO GRASP THESE THINGS, DIANA. ONLY YOU, WITH FEET SO FIRMLY PLANTED IN THE DIVINE AND IN THE MUNDANE, CAN BEGIN TO UNDERSTAND WHAT HAS HAPPENED HERE.
BUT WHY DO YOU CARE? WHY DO YOU CARE IF I UNDERSTAND OR NOT? I CAN SEE NO REASON TO THIS, UNLESS YOU SEEK TO BENEFIT.
SO YOU SEE, I HAVE DIFFICULTY ACCEPTING THESE THINGS AS TRUTH FROM ONE WHO HAS SWORN HIMSELF NOT JUST MY ENEMY, BUT THE ENEMY OF ALL I HOLD DEAR.
ONCE, YES, TO MY FOLLY. BUT NO LONGER.
YOU MAY CHOOSE TO BE MY ENEMY, DIANA, BUT I HAVE FORSAKEN BEING YOURS.
ODD WORDS FROM THE GOD OF WAR. ODDER STILL IF SPOKEN BY--AS YOU CLAIM--THE NEW GOD OF CONFLICT.
YOU WOULD PURSUE PEACE?
DON'T BE ABSURD. PEACE BRINGS NOTHING BUT STAGNATION.
NO.
PEACE IS A VIRTUE, A STATE OF MIND, A DISPOSITION FOR BENEVOLENCE, CONFIDENCE AND JUSTICE.
IT IS NOT SIMPLY THE ABSENCE OF WAR.

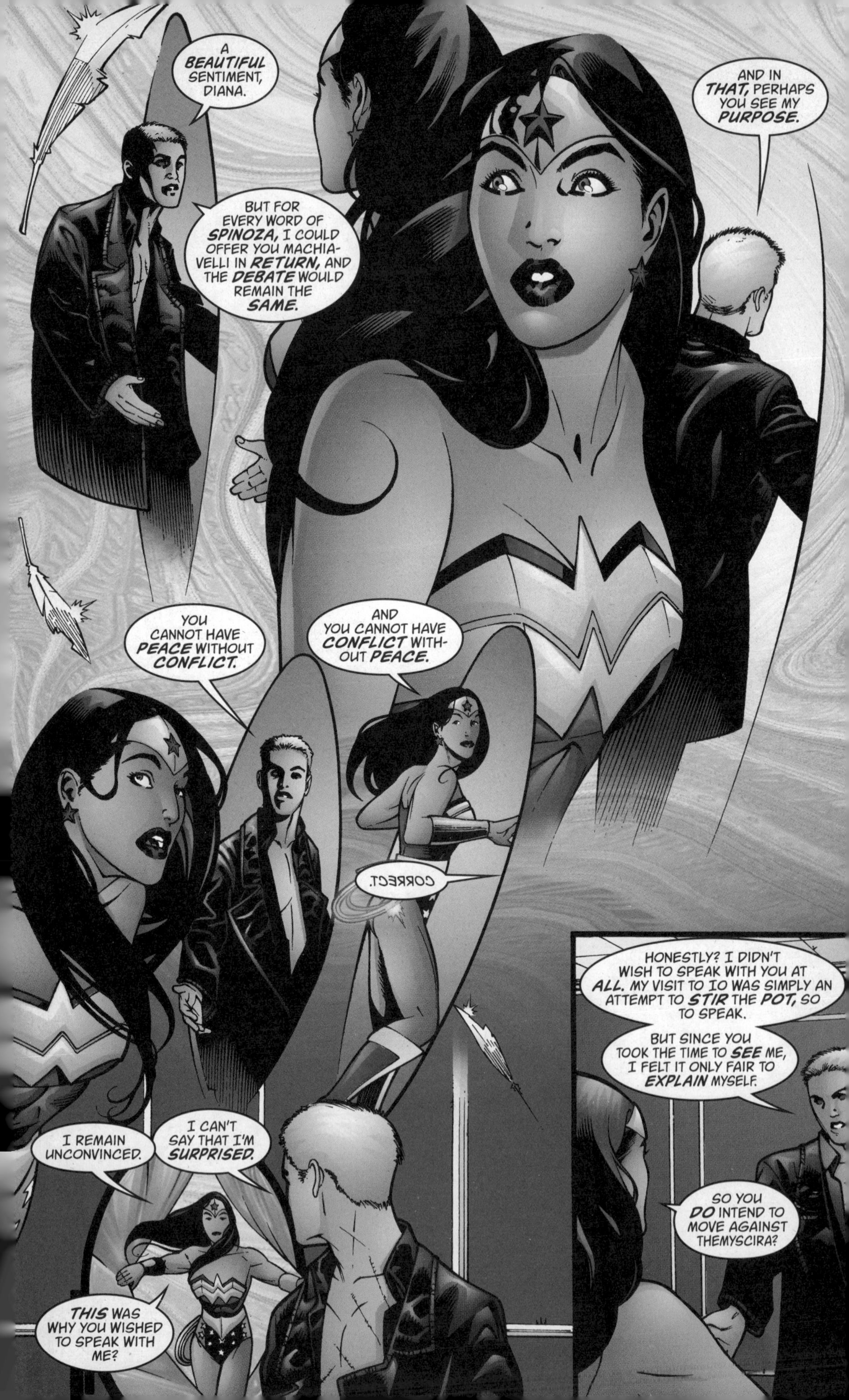
A BEAUTIFUL SENTIMENT, DIANA.
BUT FOR EVERY WORD OF SPINOZA, I COULD OFFER YOU MACHIAVELLI IN RETURN, AND THE DEBATE WOULD REMAIN THE SAME.
AND IN THAT, PERHAPS YOU SEE MY PURPOSE.
YOU CANNOT HAVE PEACE WITHOUT CONFLICT.
AND YOU CANNOT HAVE CONFLICT WITHOUT PEACE.
CORRECT.
I REMAIN UNCONVINCED.
I CAN'T SAY THAT I'M SURPRISED.
THIS WAS WHY YOU WISHED TO SPEAK WITH ME?
HONESTLY? I DIDN'T WISH TO SPEAK WITH YOU AT ALL. MY VISIT TO IO WAS SIMPLY AN ATTEMPT TO STIR THE POT, SO TO SPEAK.
BUT SINCE YOU TOOK THE TIME TO SEE ME, I FELT IT ONLY FAIR TO EXPLAIN MYSELF.
SO YOU DO INTEND TO MOVE AGAINST THEMYSCIRA?

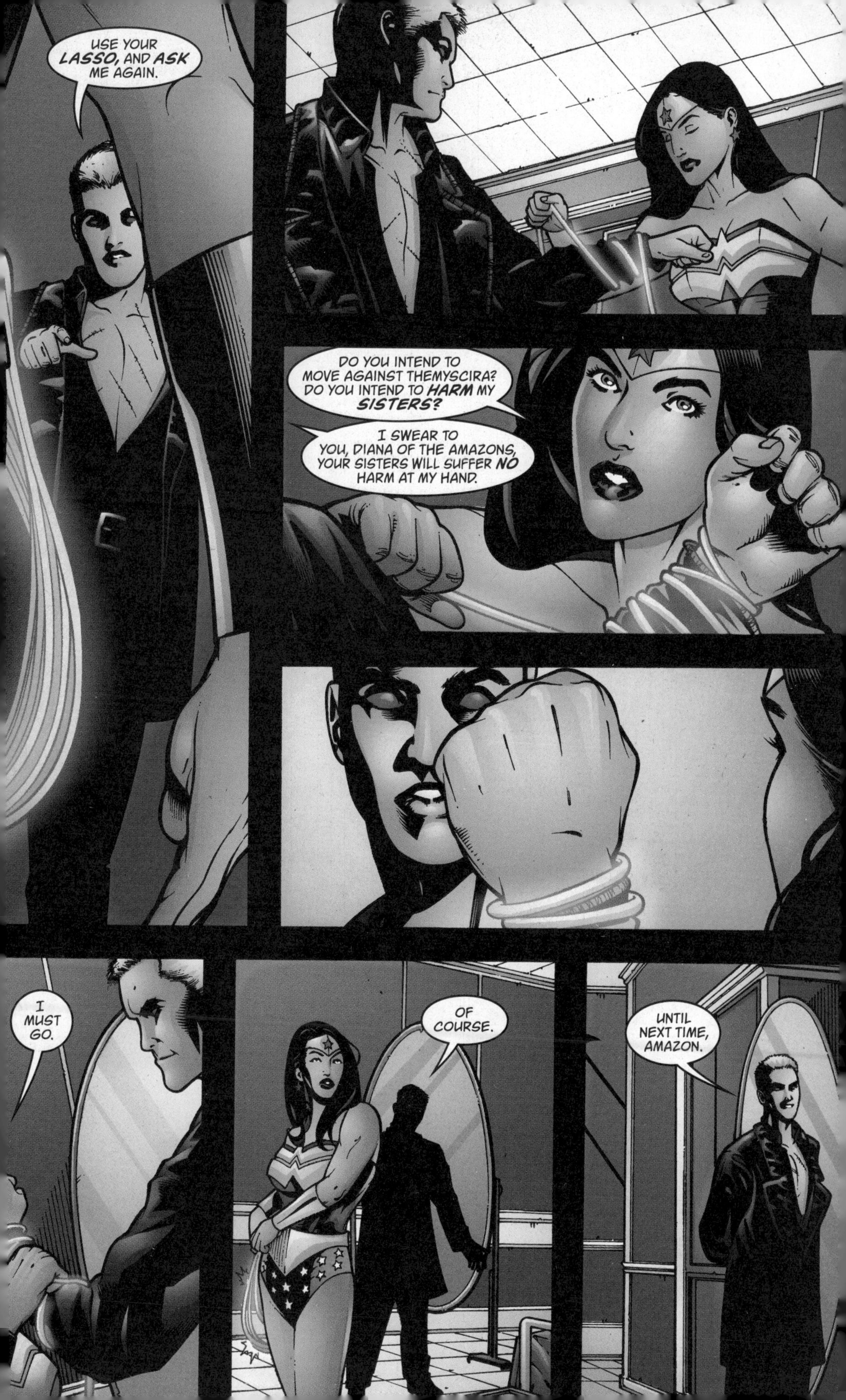
USE YOUR LASSO, AND ASK ME AGAIN.
DO YOU INTEND TO MOVE AGAINST THEMYSCIRA? DO YOU INTEND TO HARM MY SISTERS?
I SWEAR TO YOU, DIANA OF THE AMAZONS, YOUR SISTERS WILL SUFFER NO HARM AT MY HAND.
I MUST GO.
OF COURSE.
UNTIL NEXT TIME, AMAZON.

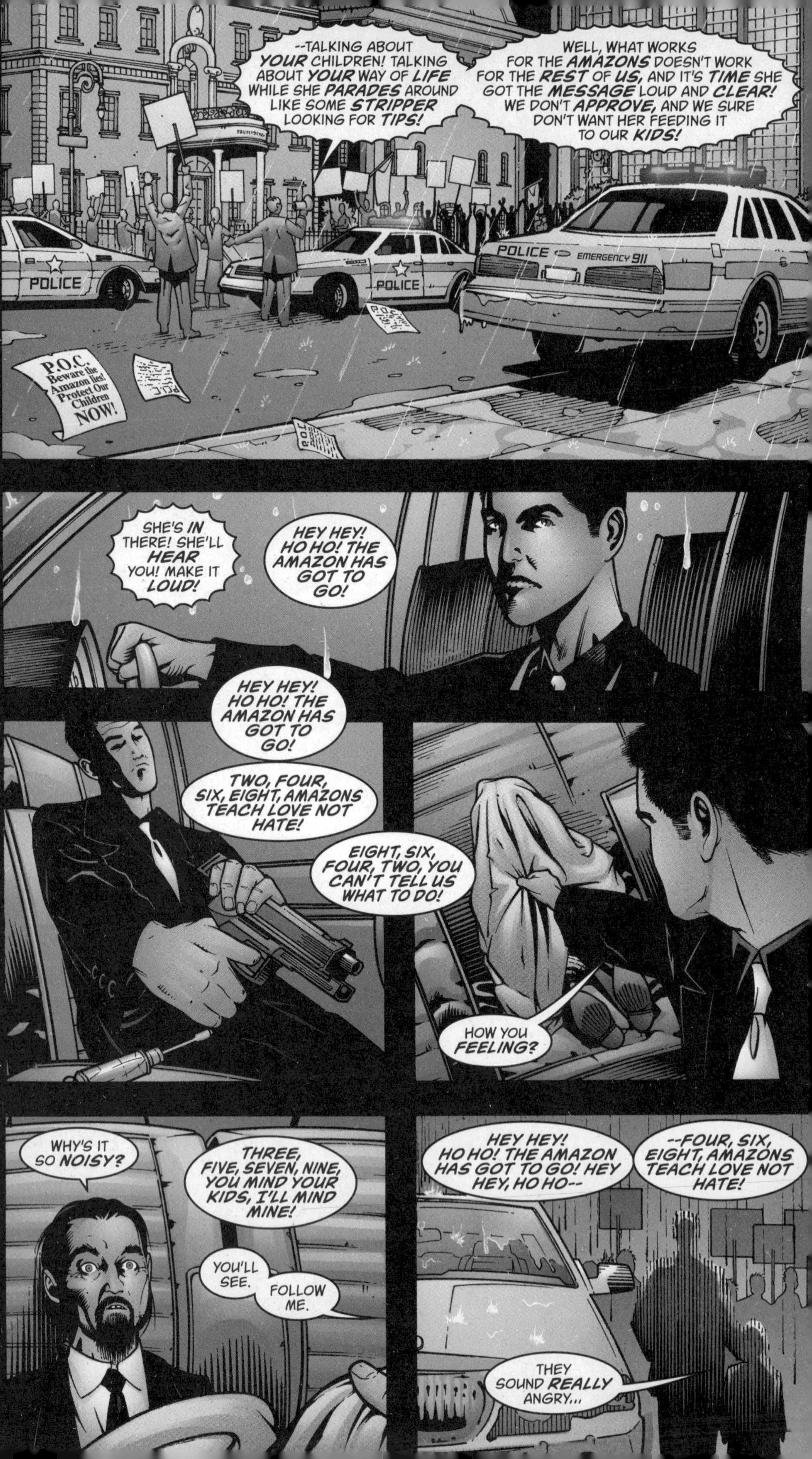
--TALKING ABOUT YOUR CHILDREN! TALKING ABOUT YOUR WAY OF LIFE WHILE SHE PARADES AROUND LIKE SOME STRIPPER LOOKING FOR TIPS!
WELL, WHAT WORKS FOR THE AMAZONS DOESN'T WORK FOR THE REST OF US, AND IT'S TIME SHE GOT THE MESSAGE LOUD AND CLEAR! WE DON'T APPROVE, AND WE SURE DON'T WANT HER FEEDING IT TO OUR KIDS!
POLICE
POLICE
POLICE
EMERGENCY 911
P.O.C. Beware the Amazon lies! Protect Our Children NOW!
SHE'S IN THERE! SHE'LL HEAR YOU! MAKE IT LOUD!
HEY HEY! HO HO! THE AMAZON HAS GOT TO GO!
HEY HEY! HO HO! THE AMAZON HAS GOT TO GO!
TWO, FOUR, SIX, EIGHT, AMAZONS TEACH LOVE NOT HATE!
EIGHT, SIX, FOUR, TWO, YOU CAN'T TELL US WHAT TO DO!
HOW YOU FEELING?
WHY'S IT SO NOISY?
THREE, FIVE, SEVEN, NINE, YOU MIND YOUR KIDS, I'LL MIND MINE!
YOU'LL SEE.
FOLLOW ME.
HEY HEY! HO HO! THE AMAZON HAS GOT TO GO! HEY HEY, HO HO--
--FOUR, SIX, EIGHT, AMAZONS TEACH LOVE NOT HATE!
THEY SOUND REALLY ANGRY...

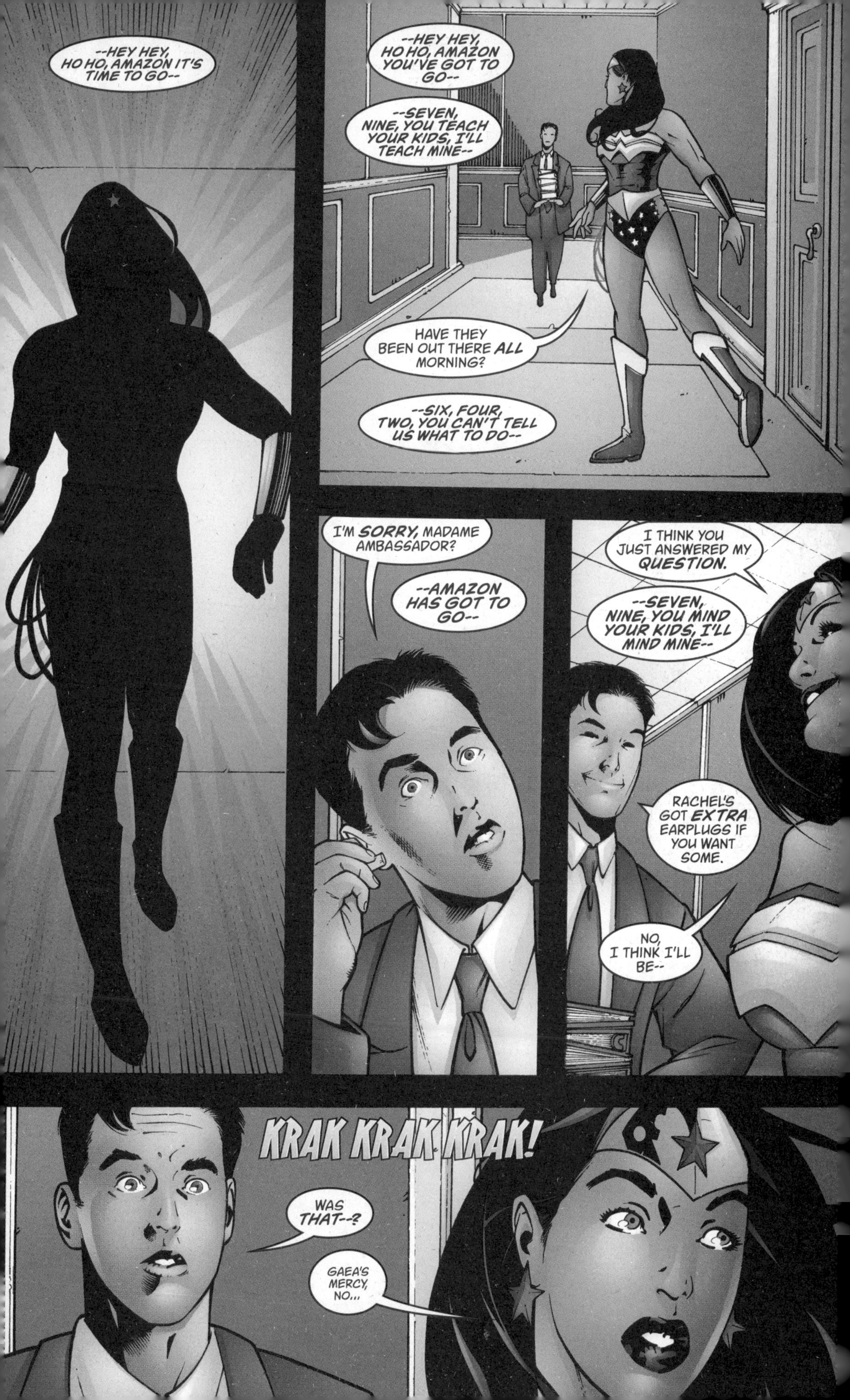
--HEY HEY, HO HO, AMAZON IT'S TIME TO GO--
--HEY HEY, HO HO, AMAZON YOU'VE GOT TO GO--
--SEVEN, NINE, YOU TEACH YOUR KIDS, I'LL TEACH MINE--
HAVE THEY BEEN OUT THERE ALL MORNING?
--SIX, FOUR, TWO, YOU CAN'T TELL US WHAT TO DO--
I'M SORRY, MADAME AMBASSADOR?
--AMAZON HAS GOT TO GO--
I THINK YOU JUST ANSWERED MY QUESTION.
--SEVEN, NINE, YOU MIND YOUR KIDS, I'LL MIND MINE--
RACHEL'S GOT EXTRA EARPLUGS IF YOU WANT SOME.
NO, I THINK I'LL BE--
KRAK KRAK KRAK!
WAS THAT--?
GAEA'S MERCY, NO...

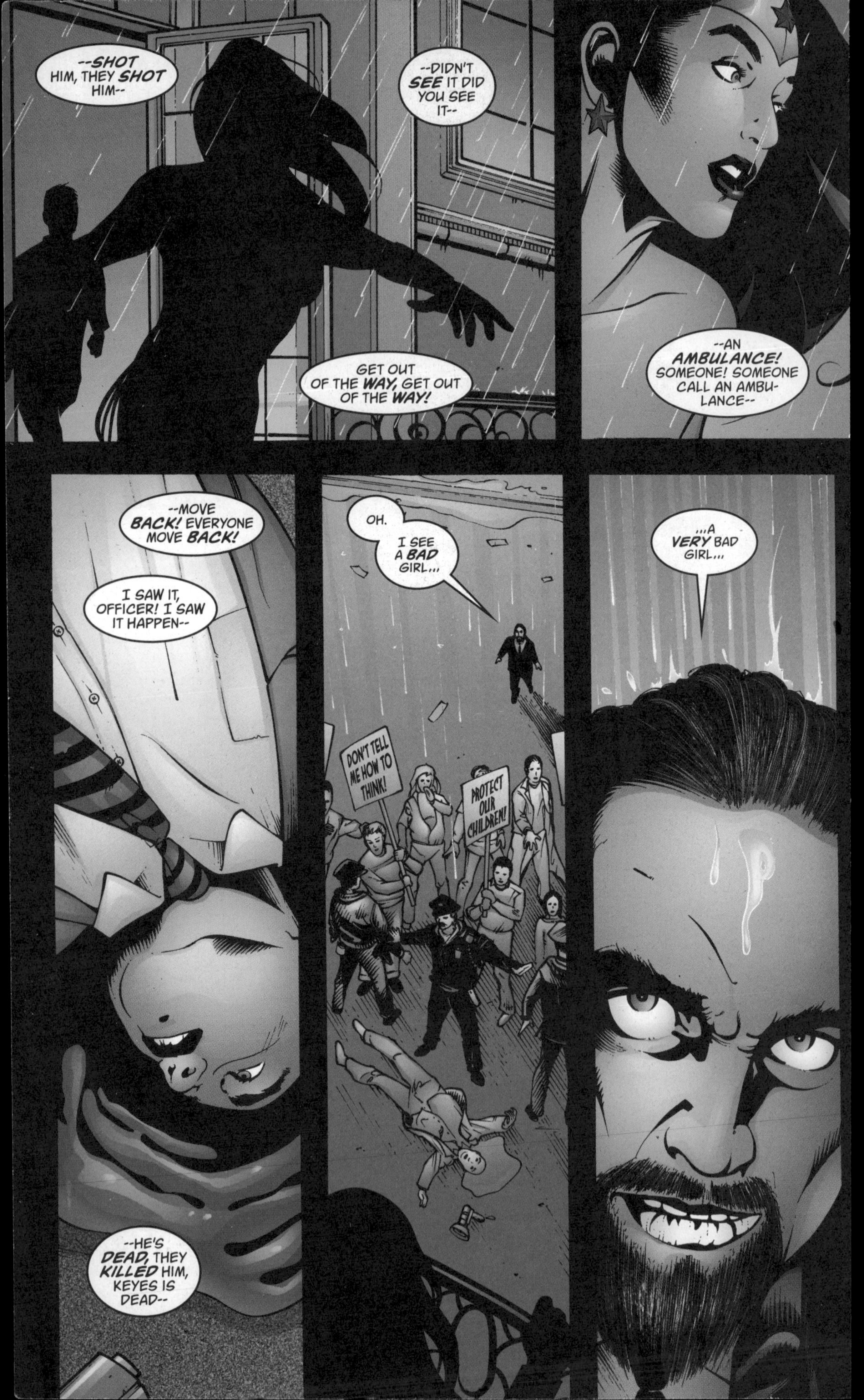
--SHOT HIM, THEY SHOT HIM--
--DIDN'T SEE IT DID YOU SEE IT--
GET OUT OF THE WAY, GET OUT OF THE WAY!
--AN AMBULANCE! SOMEONE! SOMEONE CALL AN AMBULANCE--
--MOVE BACK! EVERYONE MOVE BACK!
I SAW IT, OFFICER! I SAW IT HAPPEN--
--HE'S DEAD, THEY KILLED HIM, KEYES IS DEAD--
OH.
I SEE A BAD GIRL...
DON'T TELL ME HOW TO THINK!
PROTECT OUR CHILDREN!
...A VERY BAD GIRL...

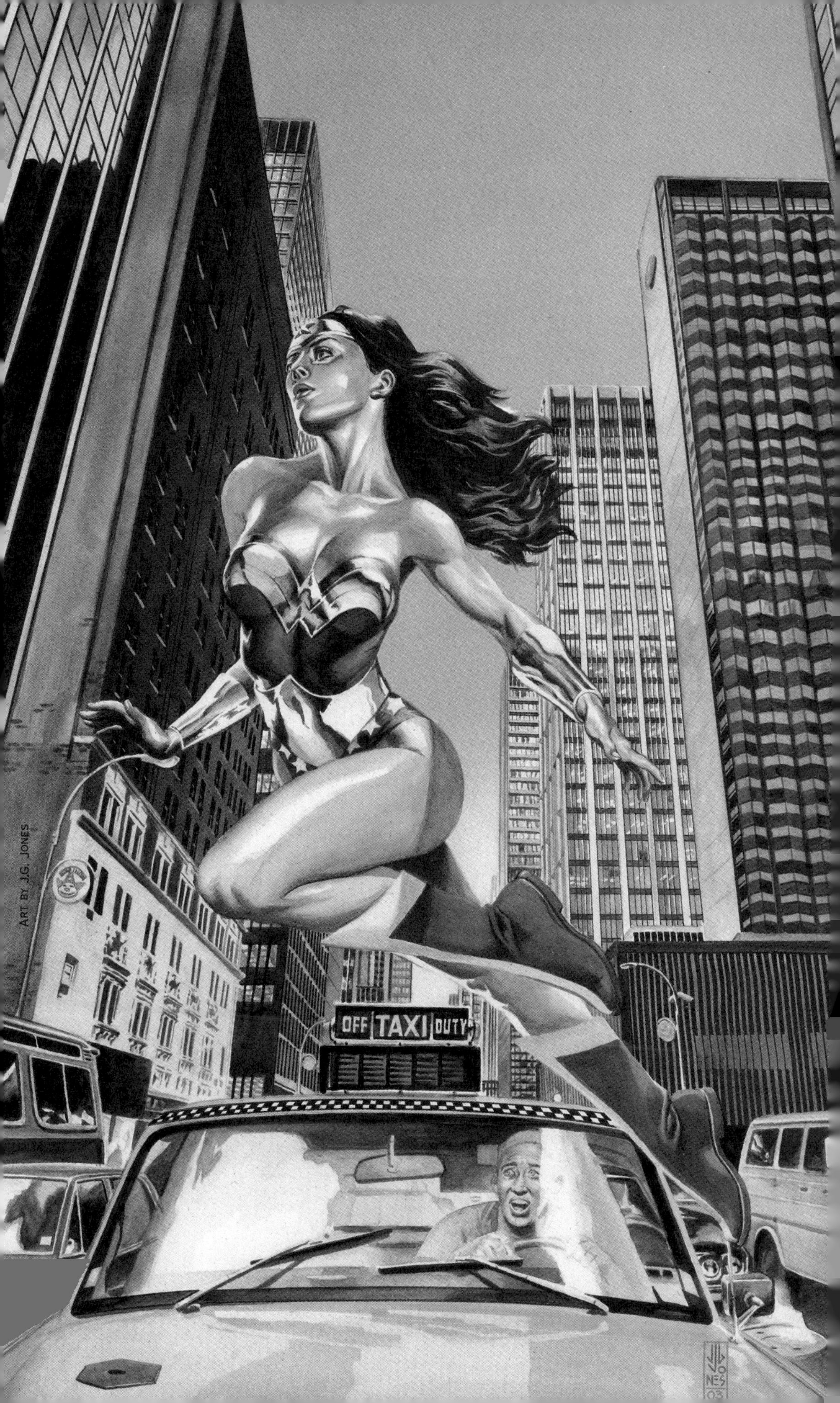
OFF TAXI DUTY
ART BY J.G. JONES

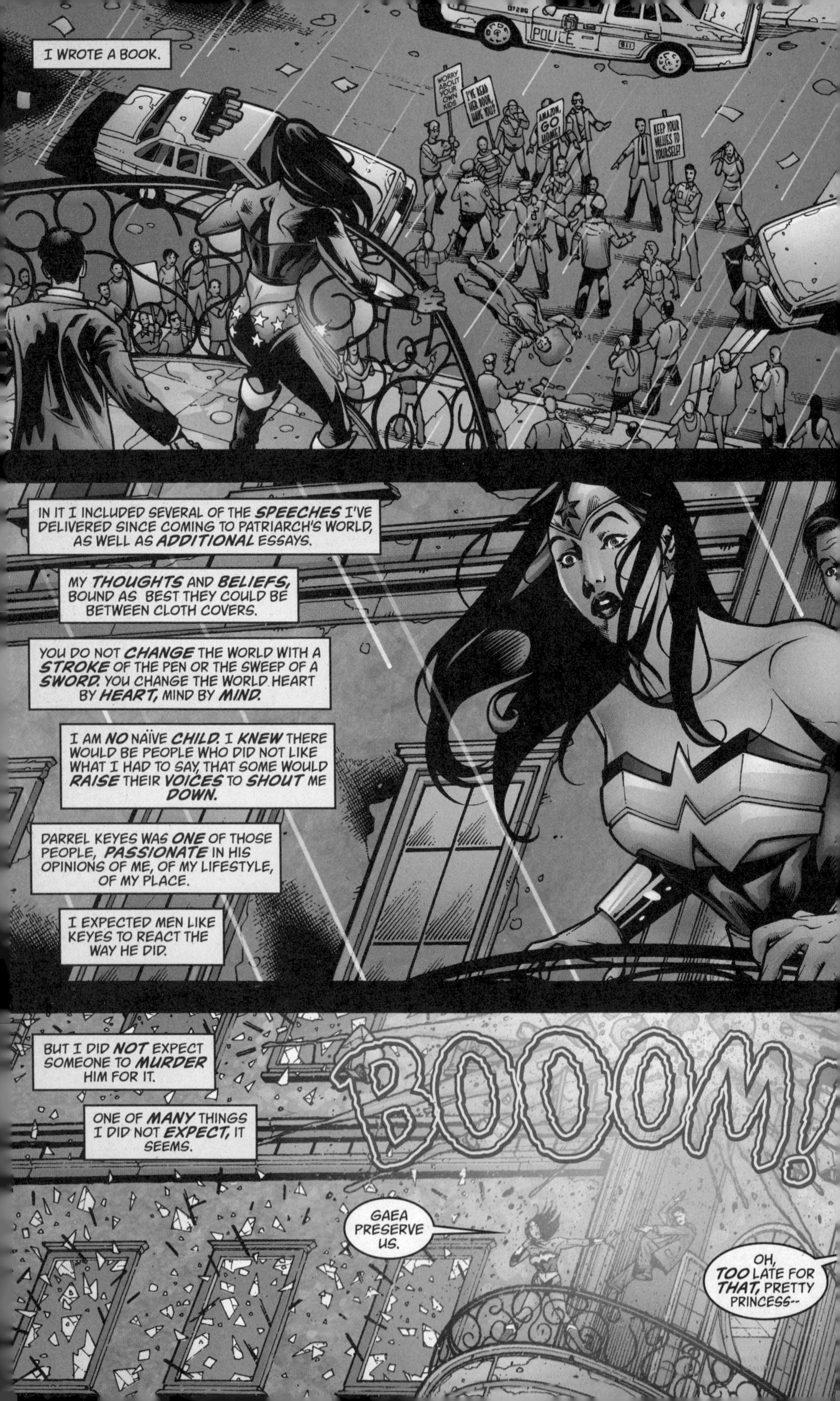

I WROTE A BOOK.
WORRY ABOUT YOUR OWN KIDS
I'VE READ HER BOOK, HAVE YOU?
AMAZON, GO HOME!
KEEP YOUR VALUES TO YOURSELF!
POLICE
IN IT I INCLUDED SEVERAL OF THE SPEECHES I'VE DELIVERED SINCE COMING TO PATRIARCH'S WORLD, AS WELL AS ADDITIONAL ESSAYS.
MY THOUGHTS AND BELIEFS, BOUND AS BEST THEY COULD BE BETWEEN CLOTH COVERS.
YOU DO NOT CHANGE THE WORLD WITH A STROKE OF THE PEN OR THE SWEEP OF A SWORD. YOU CHANGE THE WORLD HEART BY HEART, MIND BY MIND.
I AM NO NAÏVE CHILD. I KNEW THERE WOULD BE PEOPLE WHO DID NOT LIKE WHAT I HAD TO SAY, THAT SOME WOULD RAISE THEIR VOICES TO SHOUT ME DOWN.
DARREL KEYES WAS ONE OF THOSE PEOPLE, PASSIONATE IN HIS OPINIONS OF ME, OF MY LIFESTYLE, OF MY PLACE.
I EXPECTED MEN LIKE KEYES TO REACT THE WAY HE DID.
BUT I DID NOT EXPECT SOMEONE TO MURDER HIM FOR IT.
ONE OF MANY THINGS I DID NOT EXPECT, IT SEEMS.
BOOOOM!
GAEA PRESERVE US.
OH, TOO LATE FOR THAT, PRETTY PRINCESS--

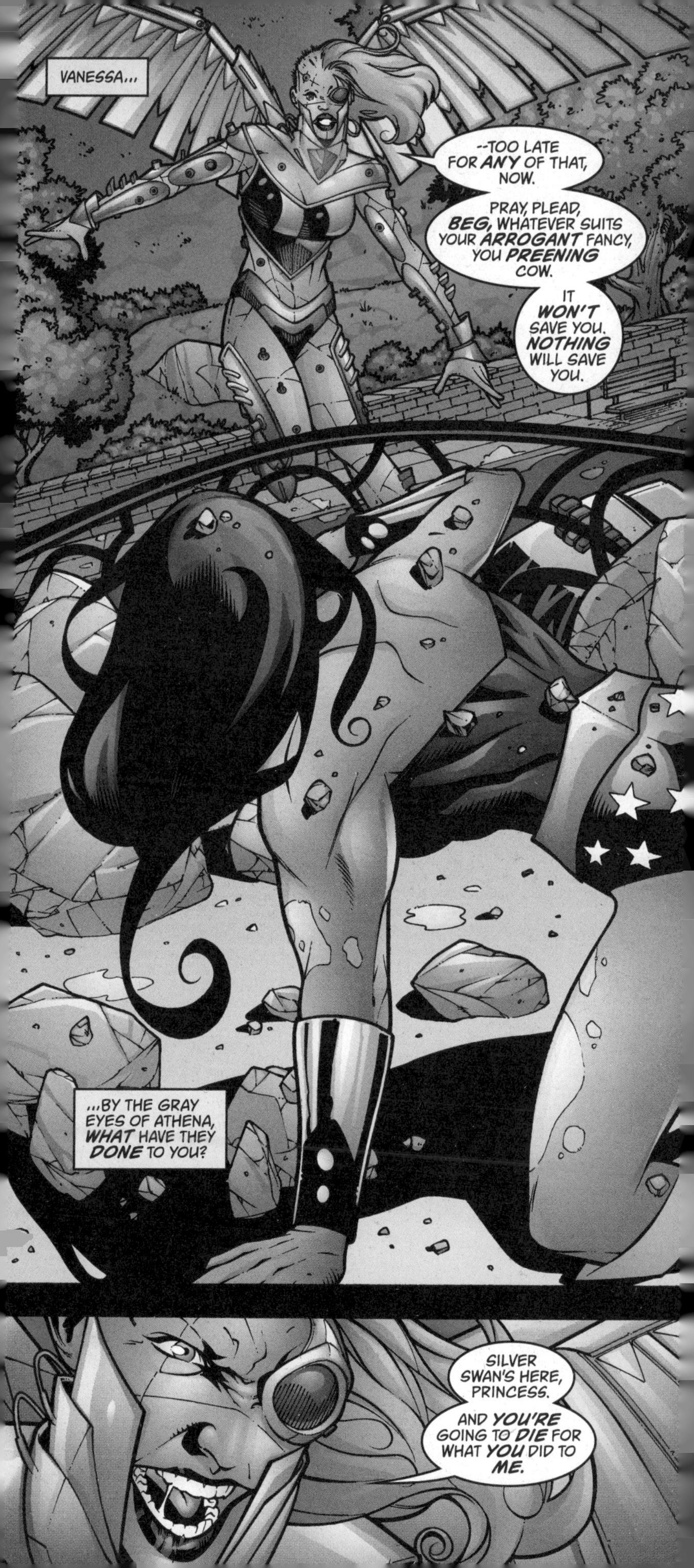
VANESSA...
--TOO LATE FOR ANY OF THAT, NOW.
PRAY, PLEAD, BEG, WHATEVER SUITS YOUR ARROGANT FANCY, YOU PREENING COW.
IT WON'T SAVE YOU. NOTHING WILL SAVE YOU.
...BY THE GRAY EYES OF ATHENA, WHAT HAVE THEY DONE TO YOU?
SILVER SWAN'S HERE, PRINCESS.
AND YOU'RE GOING TO DIE FOR WHAT YOU DID TO ME.

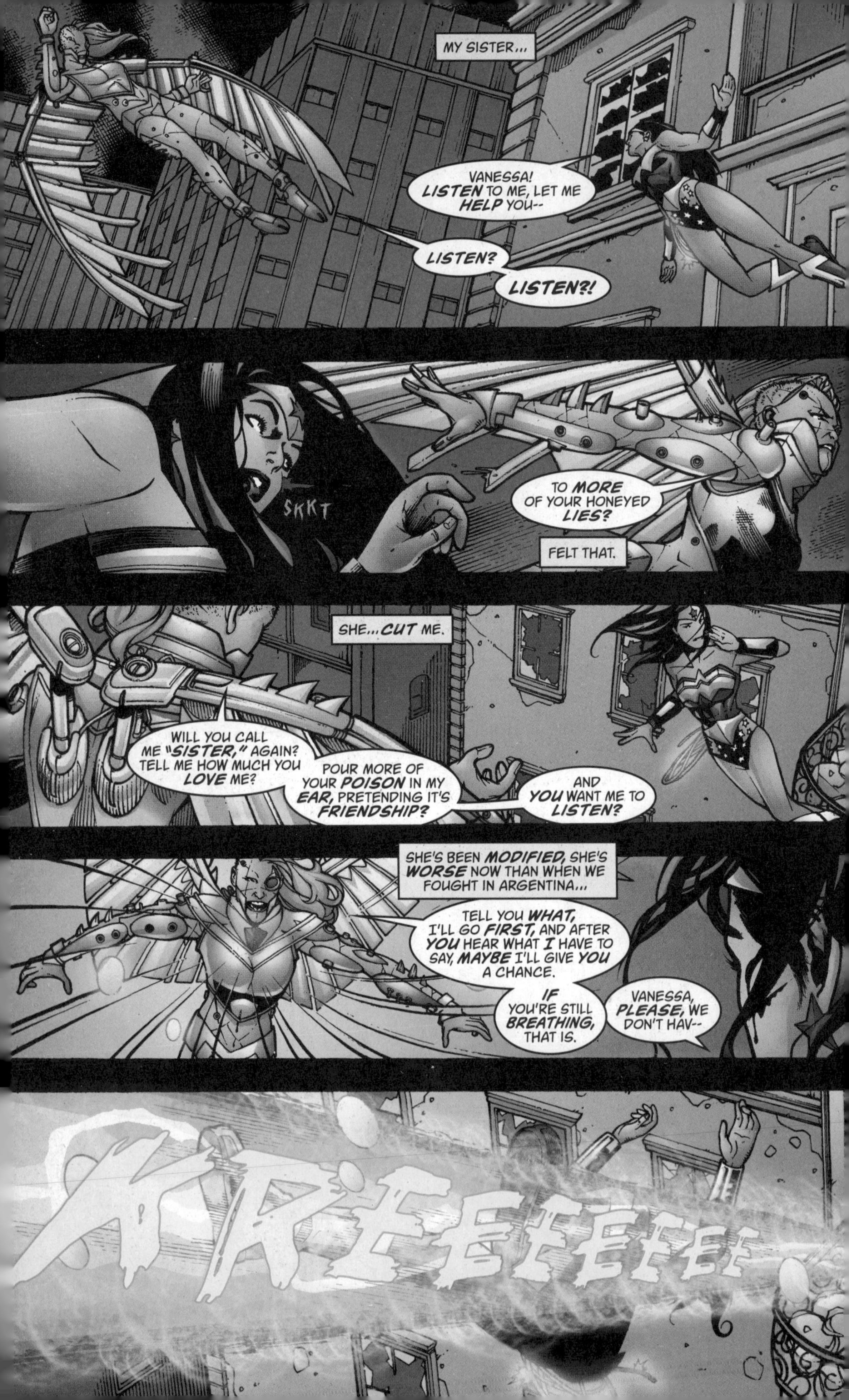
MY SISTER...
VANESSA! LISTEN TO ME, LET ME HELP YOU--
LISTEN?
LISTEN?!
SKKT
TO MORE OF YOUR HONEYED LIES?
FELT THAT.
SHE...CUT ME.
WILL YOU CALL ME "SISTER," AGAIN? TELL ME HOW MUCH YOU LOVE ME?
POUR MORE OF YOUR POISON IN MY EAR, PRETENDING IT'S FRIENDSHIP?
AND YOU WANT ME TO LISTEN?
SHE'S BEEN MODIFIED, SHE'S WORSE NOW THAN WHEN WE FOUGHT IN ARGENTINA...
TELL YOU WHAT, I'LL GO FIRST, AND AFTER YOU HEAR WHAT I HAVE TO SAY, MAYBE I'LL GIVE YOU A CHANCE.
IF YOU'RE STILL BREATHING, THAT IS.
VANESSA, PLEASE, WE DON'T HAV--
KREEEEEE

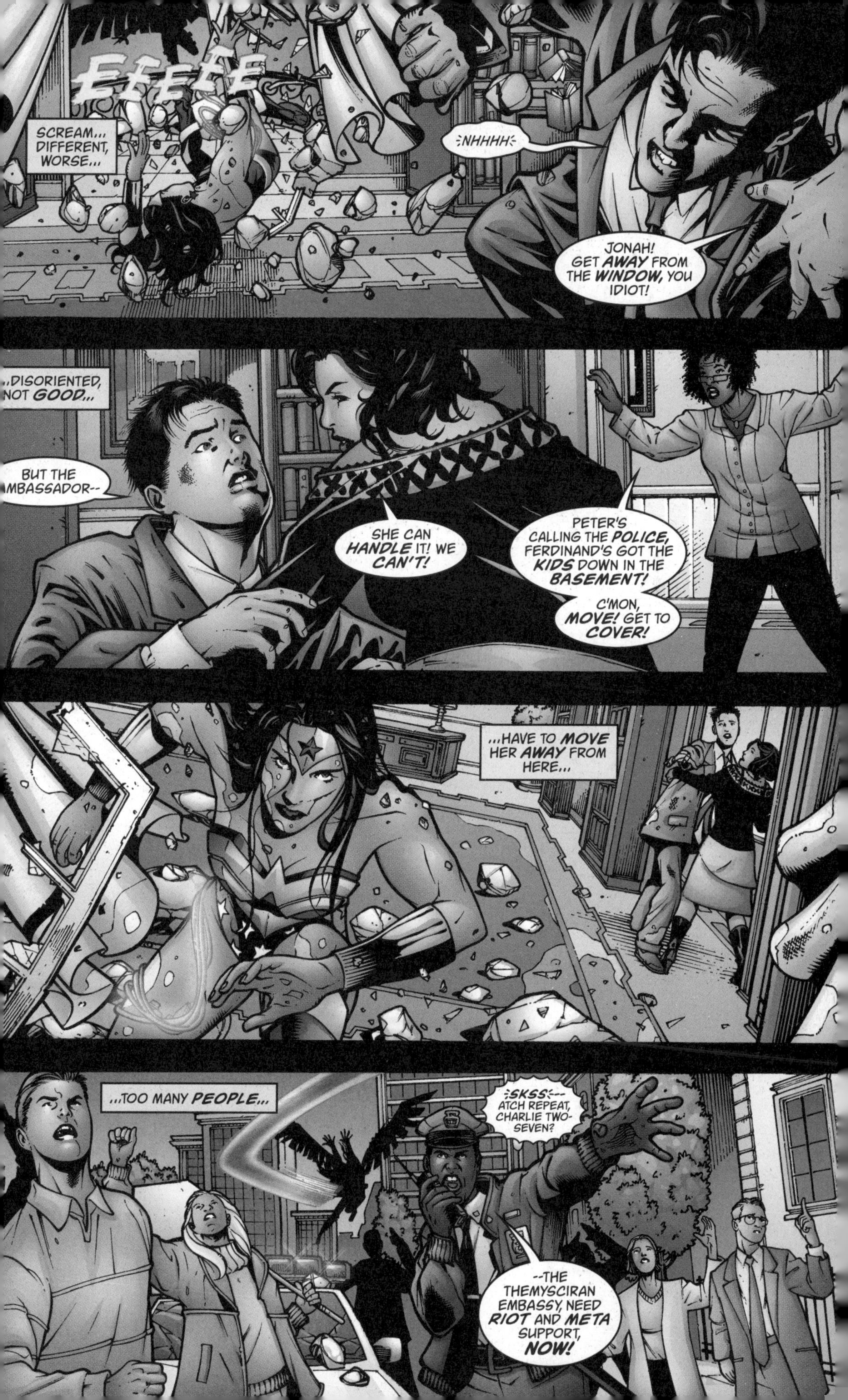
EEEEE
SCREAM... DIFFERENT, WORSE...
NHHHH
JONAH! GET AWAY FROM THE WINDOW, YOU IDIOT!
...DISORIENTED, NOT GOOD...
BUT THE AMBASSADOR--
SHE CAN HANDLE IT! WE CAN'T!
PETER'S CALLING THE POLICE, FERDINAND'S GOT THE KIDS DOWN IN THE BASEMENT!
C'MON, MOVE! GET TO COVER!
...HAVE TO MOVE HER AWAY FROM HERE...
...TOO MANY PEOPLE...
SKSS--- ATCH REPEAT, CHARLIE TWO-SEVEN?
--THE THEMYSCIRAN EMBASSY, NEED RIOT AND META SUPPORT, NOW!

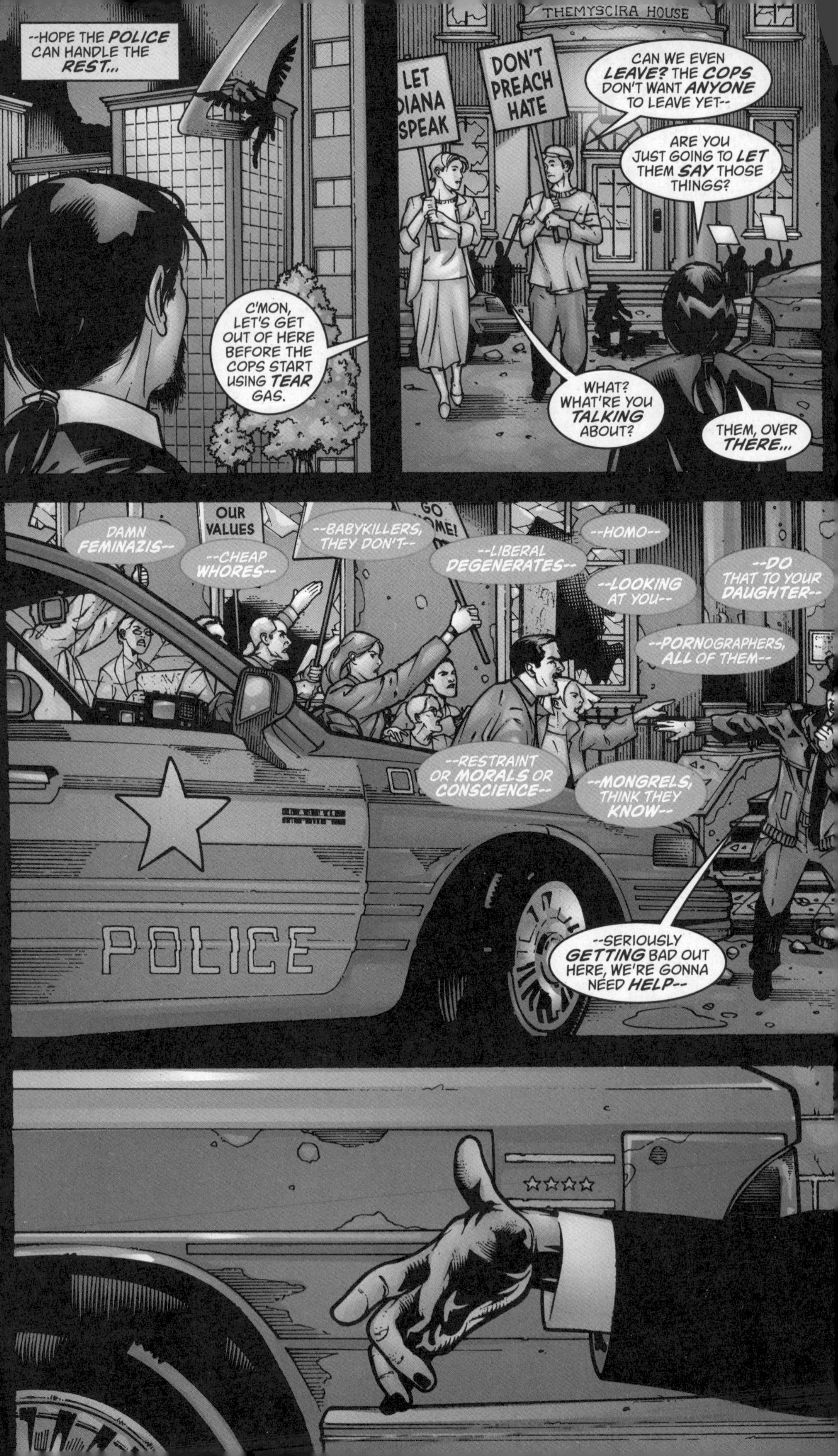

--HOPE THE POLICE CAN HANDLE THE REST...
C'MON, LET'S GET OUT OF HERE BEFORE THE COPS START USING TEAR GAS.
THEMYSCIRA HOUSE
LET DIANA SPEAK
DON'T PREACH HATE
CAN WE EVEN LEAVE? THE COPS DON'T WANT ANYONE TO LEAVE YET--
ARE YOU JUST GOING TO LET THEM SAY THOSE THINGS?
WHAT? WHAT'RE YOU TALKING ABOUT?
THEM, OVER THERE...
OUR VALUES
DAMN FEMINAZIS--
--CHEAP WHORES--
--BABYKILLERS, THEY DON'T--
--LIBERAL DEGENERATES--
--HOMO--
--LOOKING AT YOU--
--DO THAT TO YOUR DAUGHTER--
--PORNOGRAPHERS, ALL OF THEM--
--RESTRAINT OR MORALS OR CONSCIENCE--
--MONGRELS, THINK THEY KNOW--
POLICE
--SERIOUSLY GETTING BAD OUT HERE, WE'RE GONNA NEED HELP--

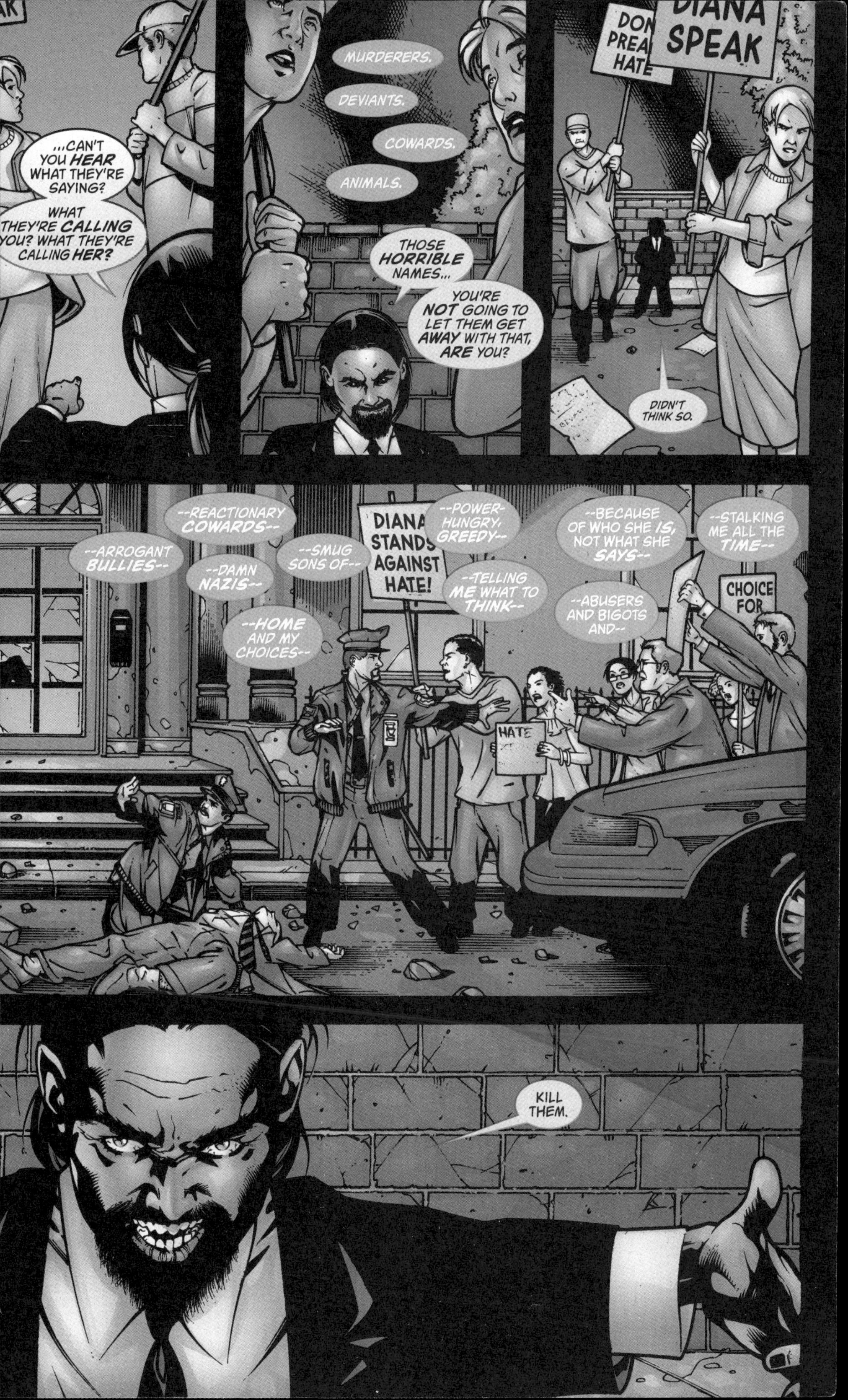
...CAN'T YOU HEAR WHAT THEY'RE SAYING?
WHAT THEY'RE CALLING YOU? WHAT THEY'RE CALLING HER?
MURDERERS.
DEVIANTS.
COWARDS.
ANIMALS.
THOSE HORRIBLE NAMES...
YOU'RE NOT GOING TO LET THEM GET AWAY WITH THAT, ARE YOU?
DIANA SPEAK
HATE
DIDN'T THINK SO.
--ARROGANT BULLIES--
--REACTIONARY COWARDS--
--DAMN NAZIS--
--SMUG SONS OF--
--HOME AND MY CHOICES--
DIANA STANDS AGAINST HATE!
--POWER-HUNGRY, GREEDY--
--TELLING ME WHAT TO THINK--
--BECAUSE OF WHO SHE IS, NOT WHAT SHE SAYS--
--ABUSERS AND BIGOTS AND--
--STALKING ME ALL THE TIME--
CHOICE FOR
HATE
KILL THEM.

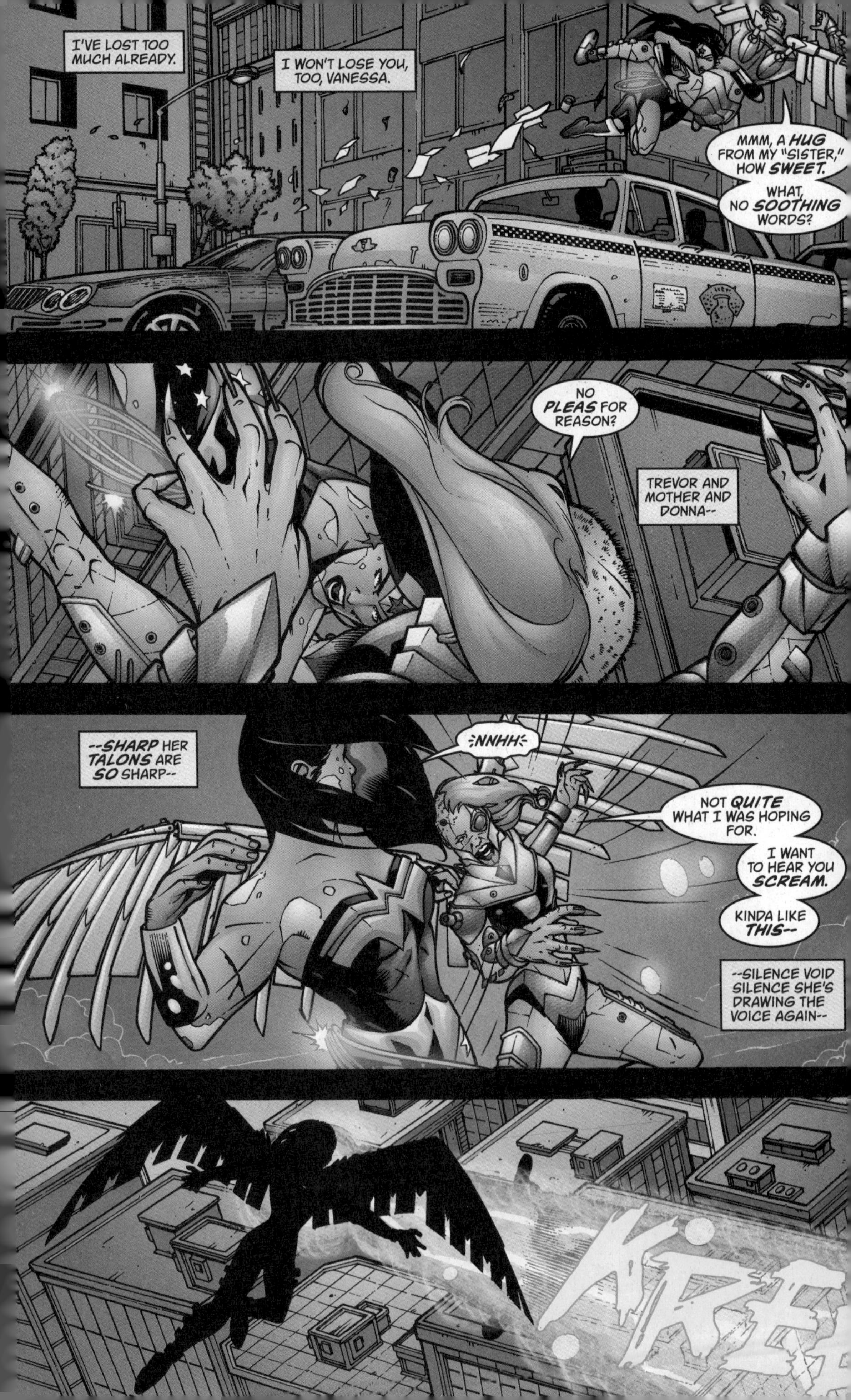

I'VE LOST TOO MUCH ALREADY.
I WON'T LOSE YOU, TOO, VANESSA.
MMM, A HUG FROM MY "SISTER," HOW SWEET.
WHAT, NO SOOTHING WORDS?
NO PLEAS FOR REASON?
TREVOR AND MOTHER AND DONNA--
--SHARP HER TALONS ARE SO SHARP--
NNHH
NOT QUITE WHAT I WAS HOPING FOR.
I WANT TO HEAR YOU SCREAM.
KINDA LIKE THIS--
--SILENCE VOID SILENCE SHE'S DRAWING THE VOICE AGAIN--

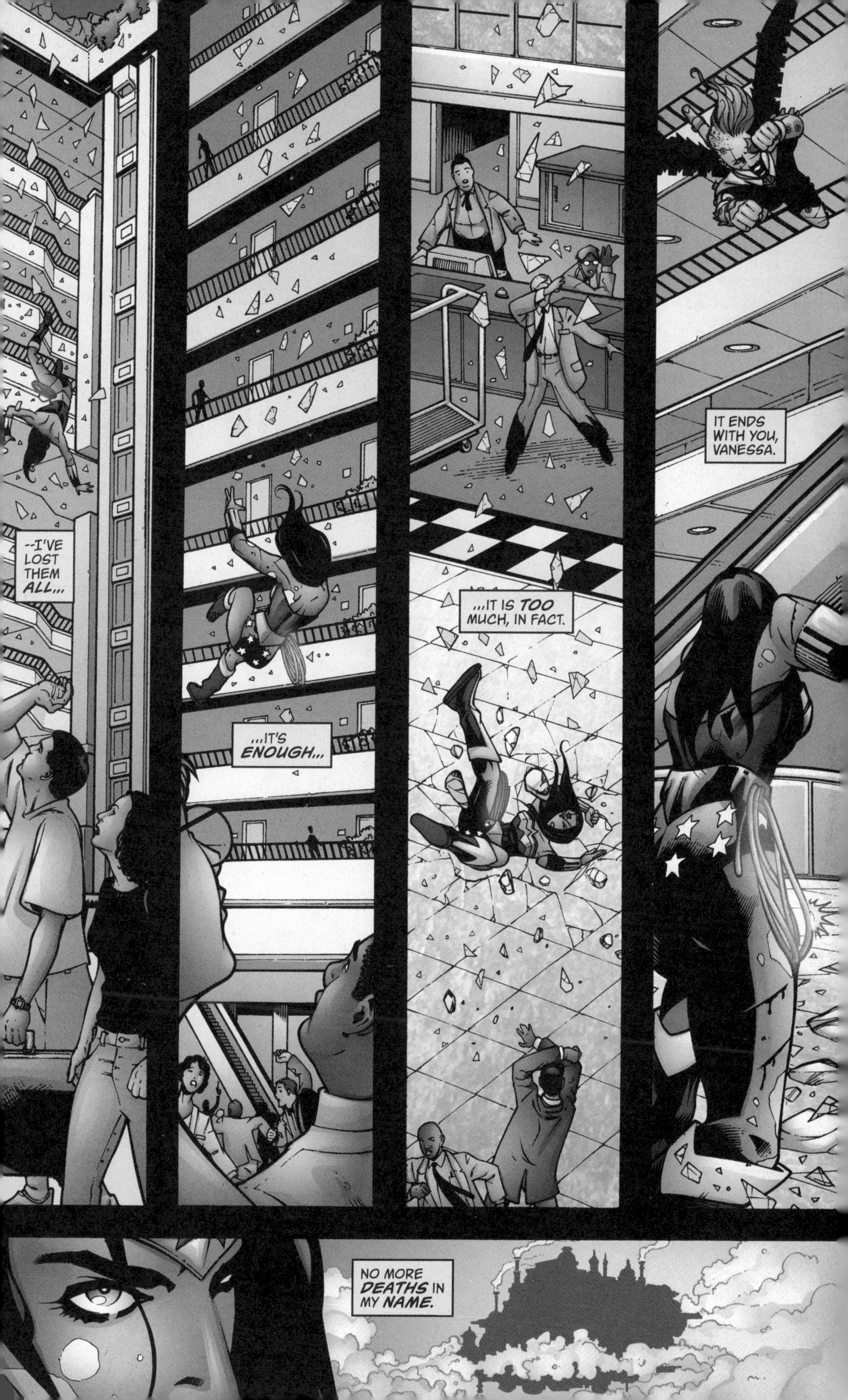
--I'VE LOST THEM ALL...
...IT'S ENOUGH...
...IT IS TOO MUCH, IN FACT.
IT ENDS WITH YOU, VANESSA.
NO MORE DEATHS IN MY NAME.

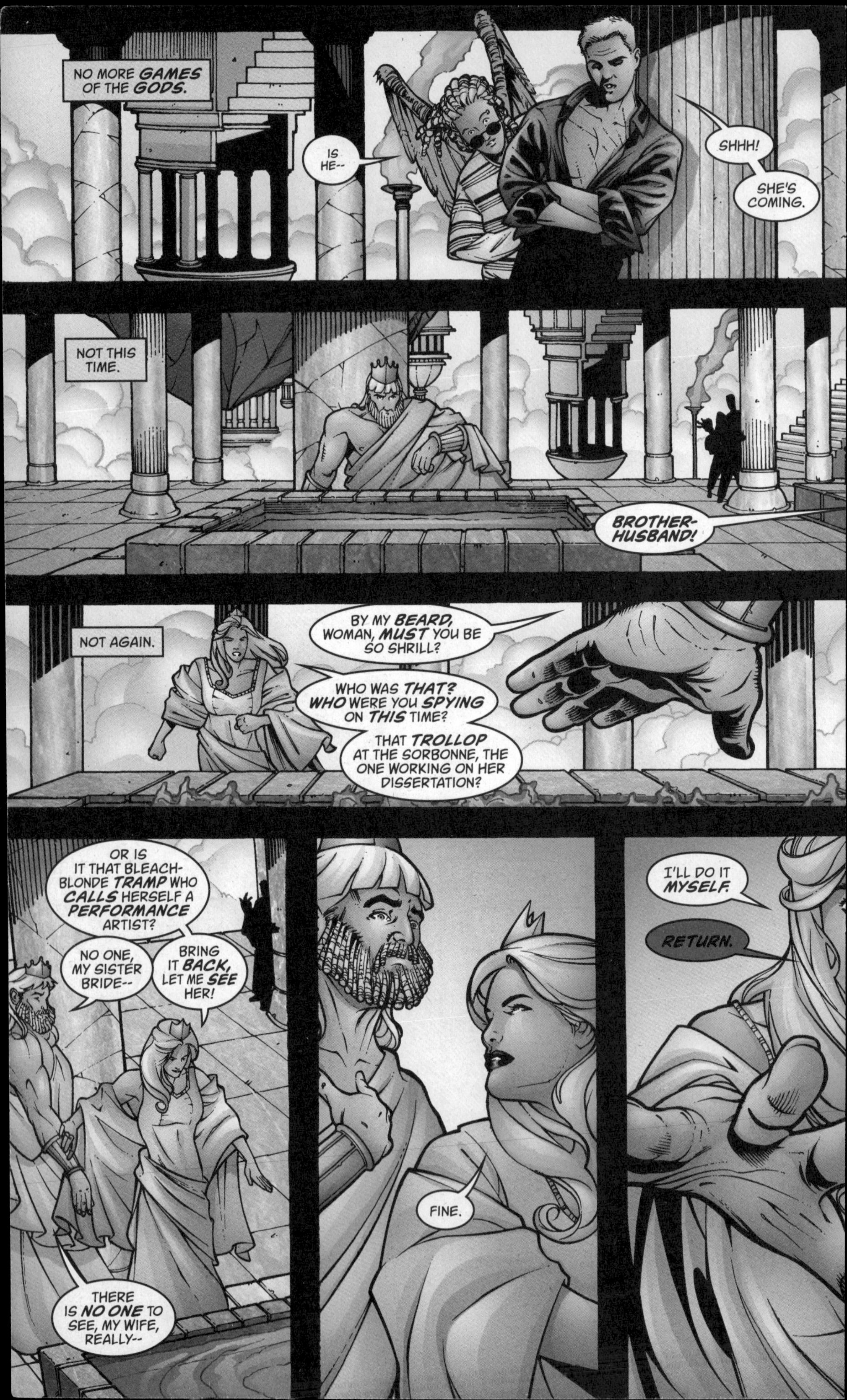
NO MORE GAMES OF THE GODS.
IS HE--
SHHH!
SHE'S COMING.
NOT THIS TIME.
BROTHER-HUSBAND!
NOT AGAIN.
BY MY BEARD, WOMAN, MUST YOU BE SO SHRILL?
WHO WAS THAT? WHO WERE YOU SPYING ON THIS TIME?
THAT TROLLOP AT THE SORBONNE, THE ONE WORKING ON HER DISSERTATION?
OR IS IT THAT BLEACH-BLONDE TRAMP WHO CALLS HERSELF A PERFORMANCE ARTIST?
NO ONE, MY SISTER BRIDE--
BRING IT BACK, LET ME SEE HER!
THERE IS NO ONE TO SEE, MY WIFE, REALLY--
FINE.
I'LL DO IT MYSELF.
RETURN.

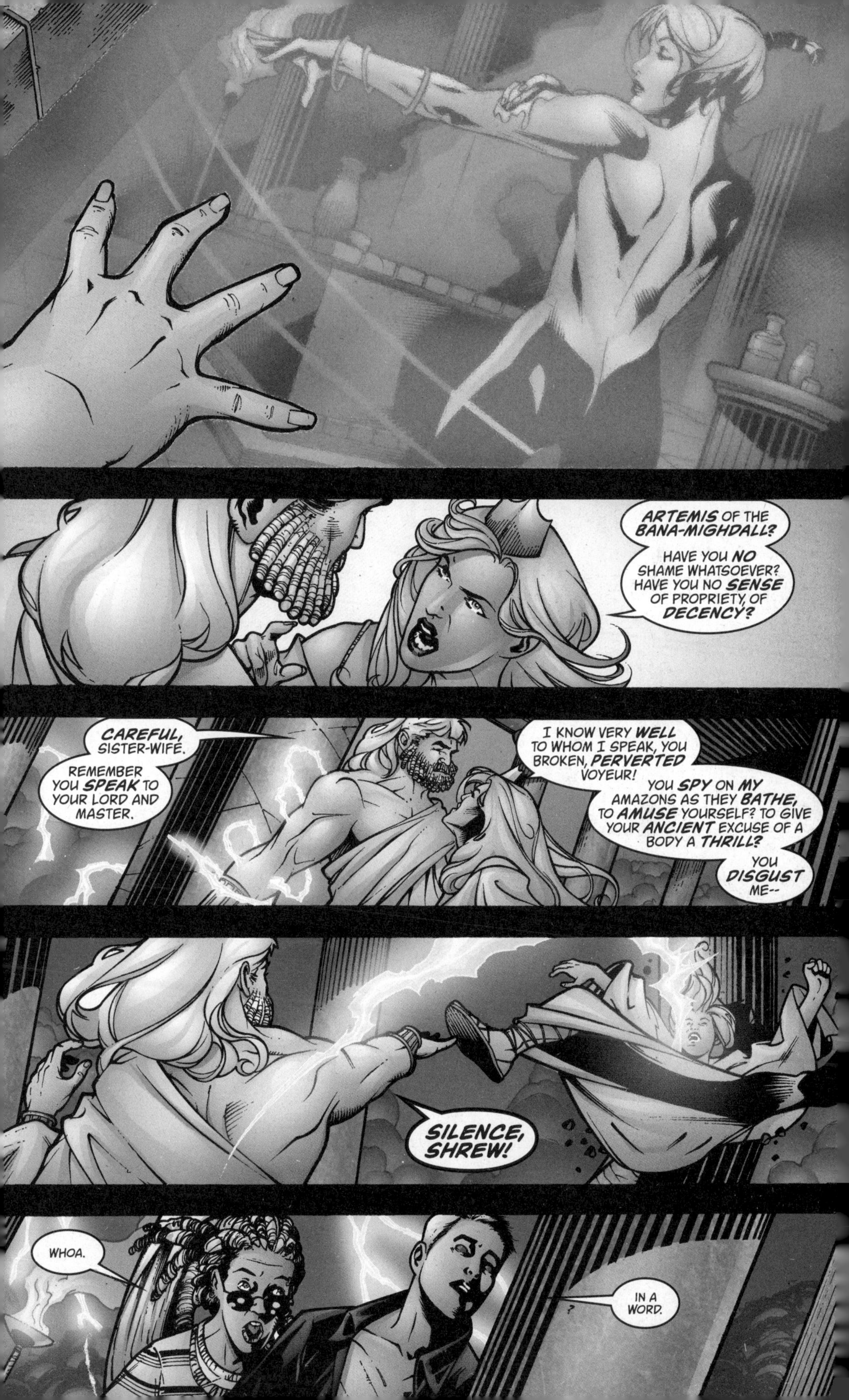
ARTEMIS OF THE BANA-MIGHDALL?
HAVE YOU NO SHAME WHATSOEVER? HAVE YOU NO SENSE OF PROPRIETY, OF DECENCY?
CAREFUL, SISTER-WIFE.
REMEMBER YOU SPEAK TO YOUR LORD AND MASTER.
I KNOW VERY WELL TO WHOM I SPEAK, YOU BROKEN, PERVERTED VOYEUR!
YOU SPY ON MY AMAZONS AS THEY BATHE, TO AMUSE YOURSELF? TO GIVE YOUR ANCIENT EXCUSE OF A BODY A THRILL?
YOU DISGUST ME--
SILENCE, SHREW!
WHOA.
?
IN A WORD.

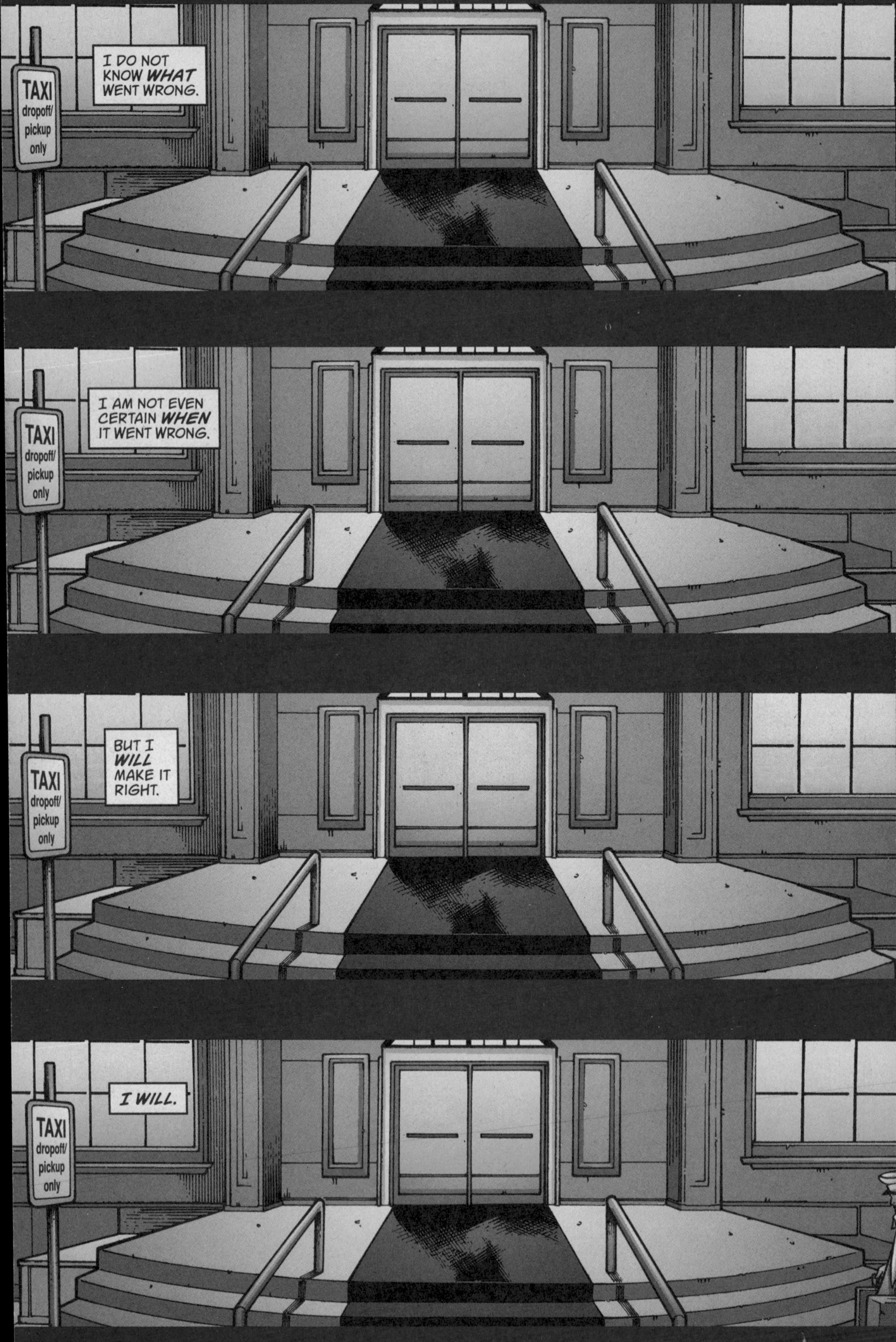
TAXI dropoff/ pickup only
I DO NOT KNOW *WHAT* WENT WRONG.
TAXI dropoff/ pickup only
I AM NOT EVEN CERTAIN *WHEN* IT WENT WRONG.
TAXI dropoff/ pickup only
BUT I *WILL* MAKE IT RIGHT.
TAXI dropoff/ pickup only
I WILL.

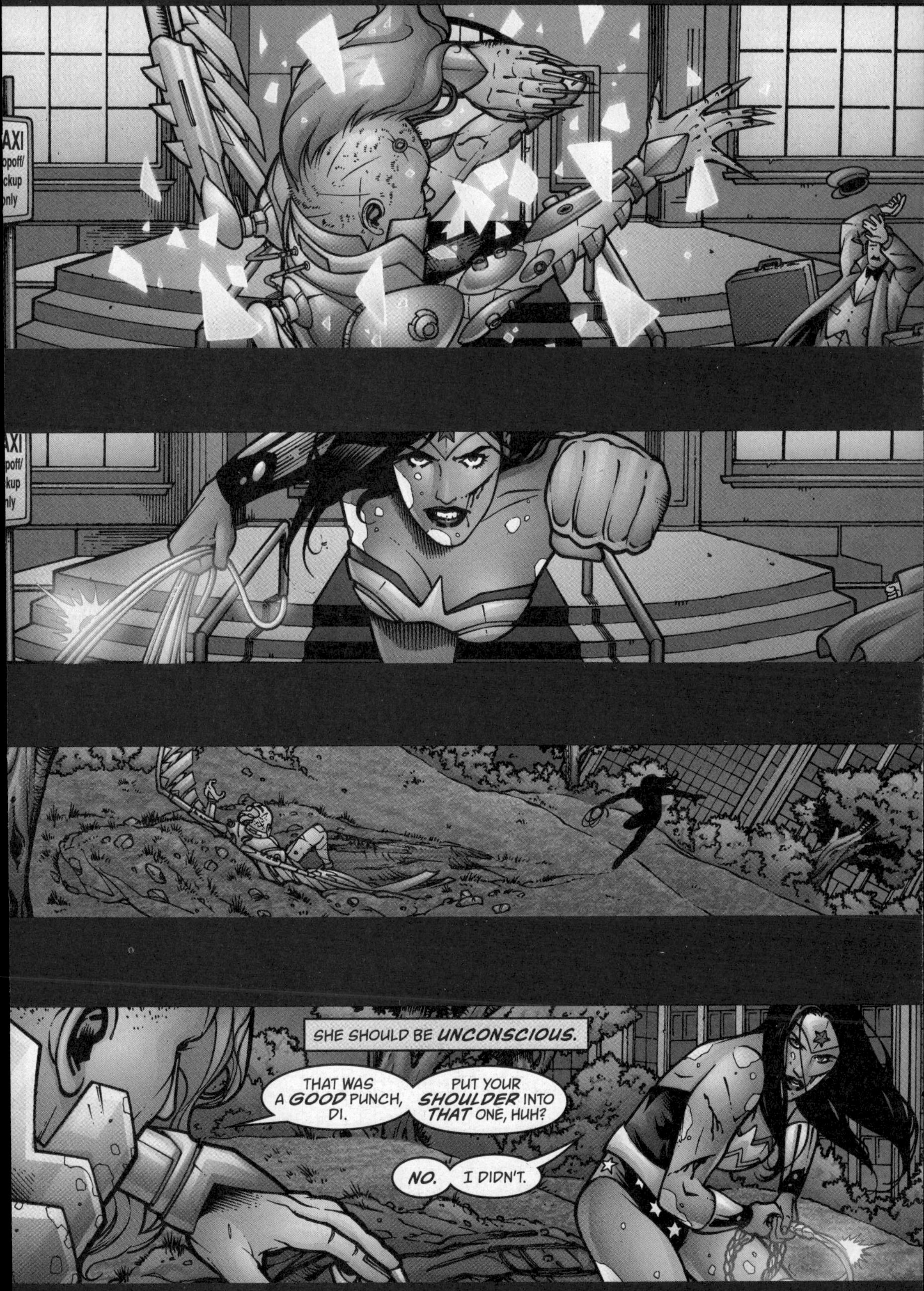
SHE SHOULD BE UNCONSCIOUS.
THAT WAS A GOOD PUNCH, DI.
PUT YOUR SHOULDER INTO THAT ONE, HUH?
NO.
I DIDN'T.

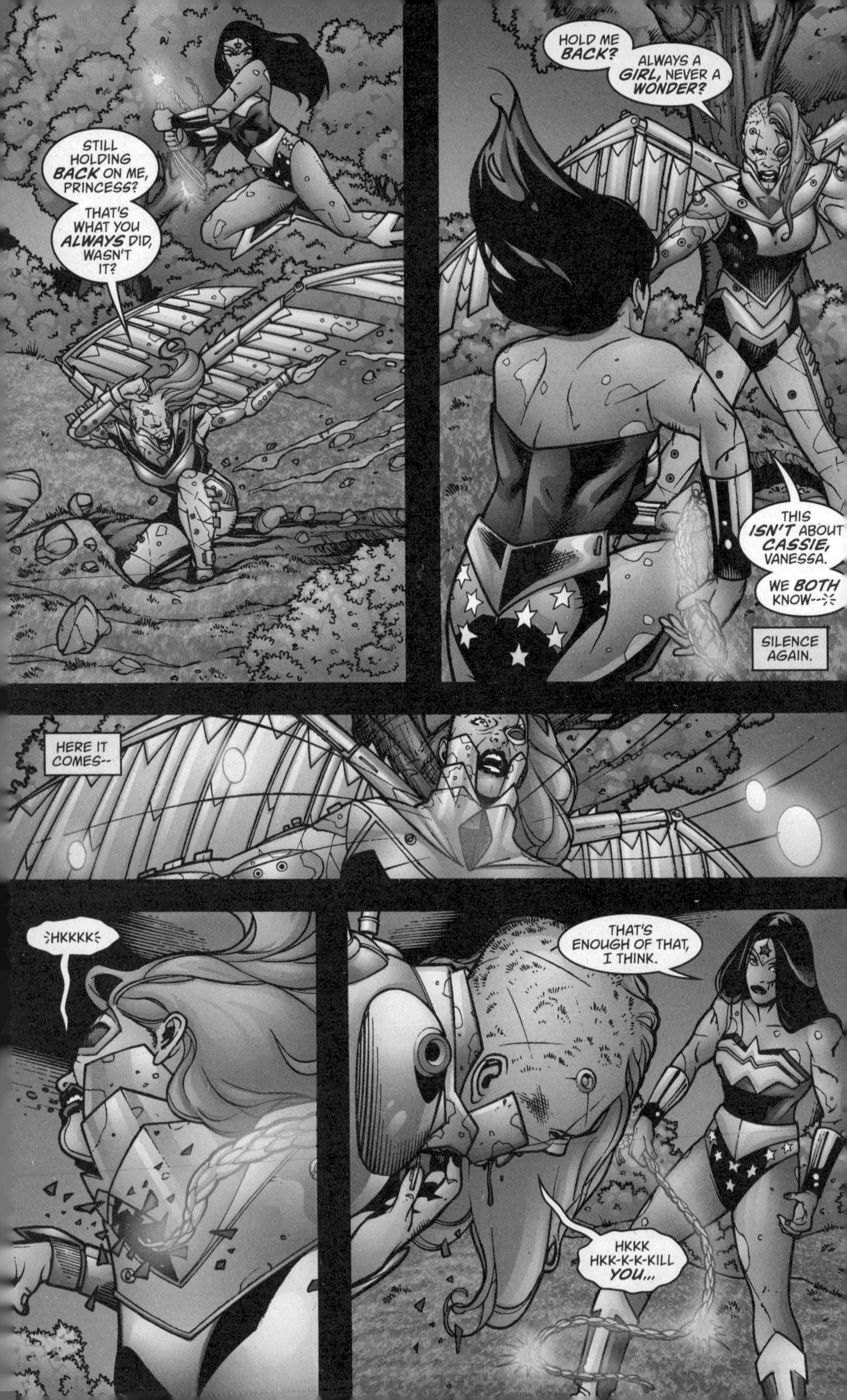
STILL HOLDING BACK ON ME, PRINCESS?
THAT'S WHAT YOU ALWAYS DID, WASN'T IT?
HOLD ME BACK?
ALWAYS A GIRL, NEVER A WONDER?
THIS ISN'T ABOUT CASSIE, VANESSA.
WE BOTH KNOW--
SILENCE AGAIN.
HERE IT COMES--
HKKKK
THAT'S ENOUGH OF THAT, I THINK.
HKKK HKK-K-K-KILL YOU...

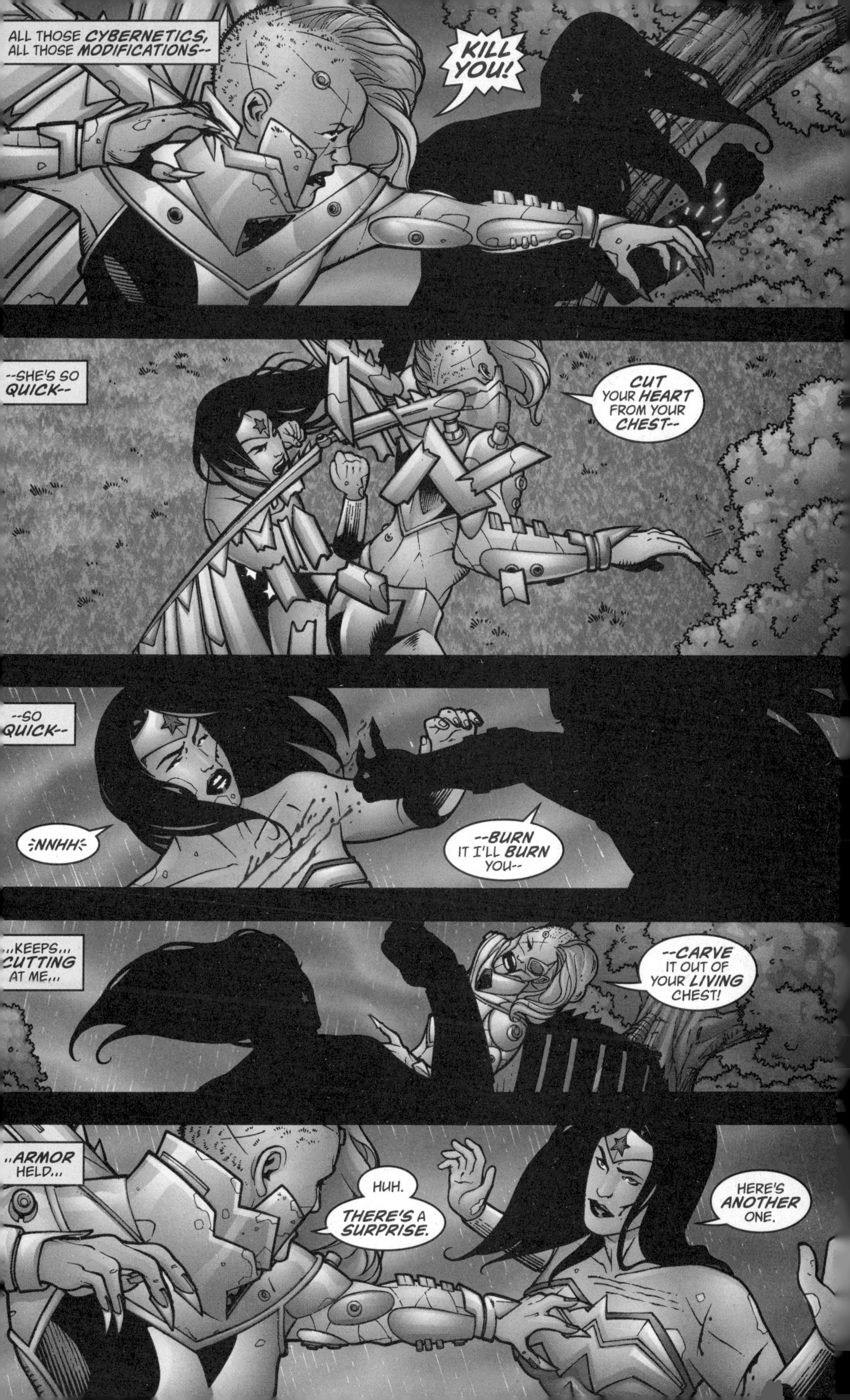
ALL THOSE CYBERNETICS, ALL THOSE MODIFICATIONS--
KILL YOU!
--SHE'S SO QUICK--
CUT YOUR HEART FROM YOUR CHEST--
--SO QUICK--
NNHH
--BURN IT I'LL BURN YOU--
...KEEPS... CUTTING AT ME...
--CARVE IT OUT OF YOUR LIVING CHEST!
...ARMOR HELD...
HUH. THERE'S A SURPRISE.
HERE'S ANOTHER ONE.

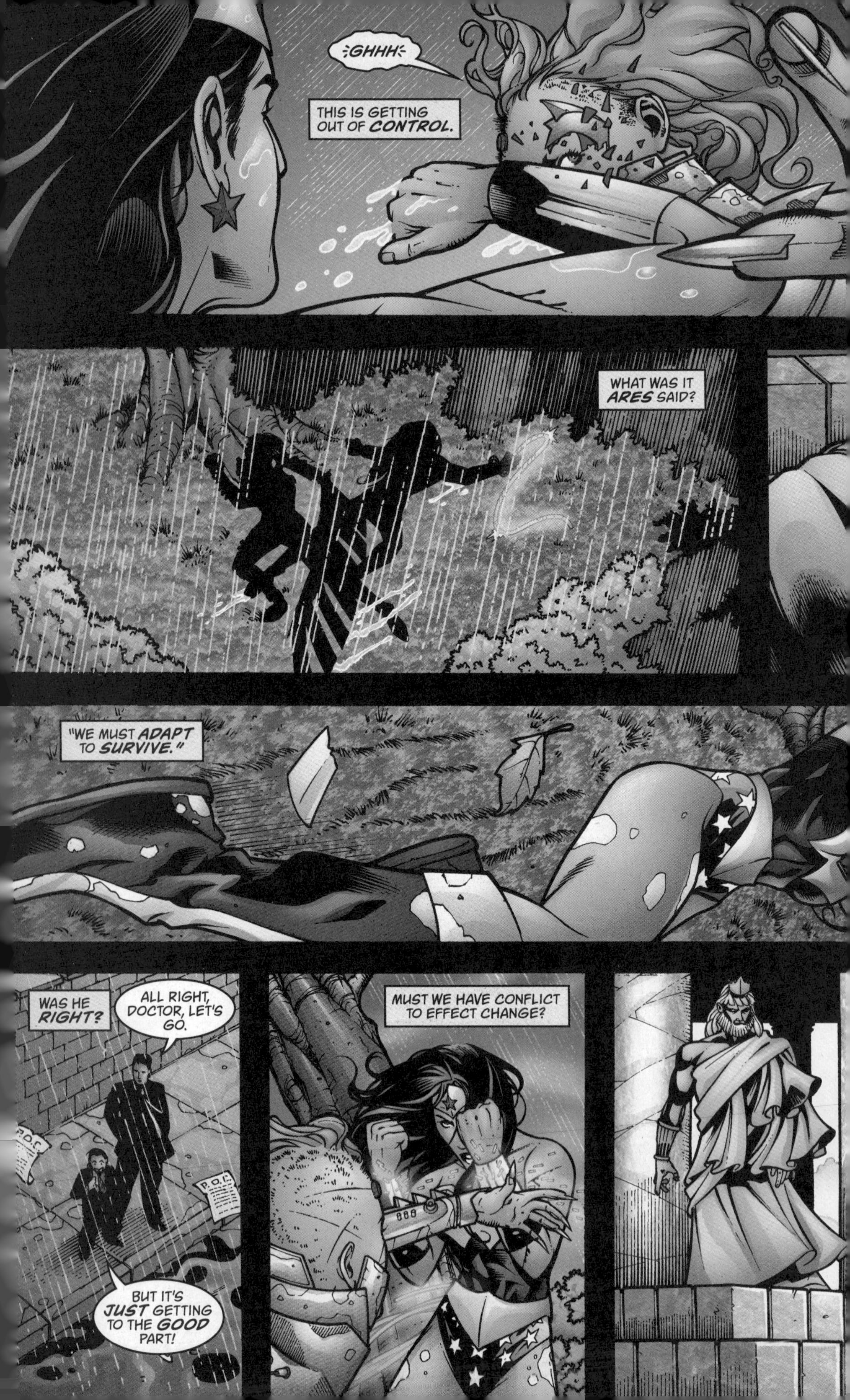
GHHH
THIS IS GETTING OUT OF CONTROL.
WHAT WAS IT ARES SAID?
"WE MUST ADAPT TO SURVIVE."
WAS HE RIGHT?
ALL RIGHT, DOCTOR, LET'S GO.
BUT IT'S JUST GETTING TO THE GOOD PART!
MUST WE HAVE CONFLICT TO EFFECT CHANGE?

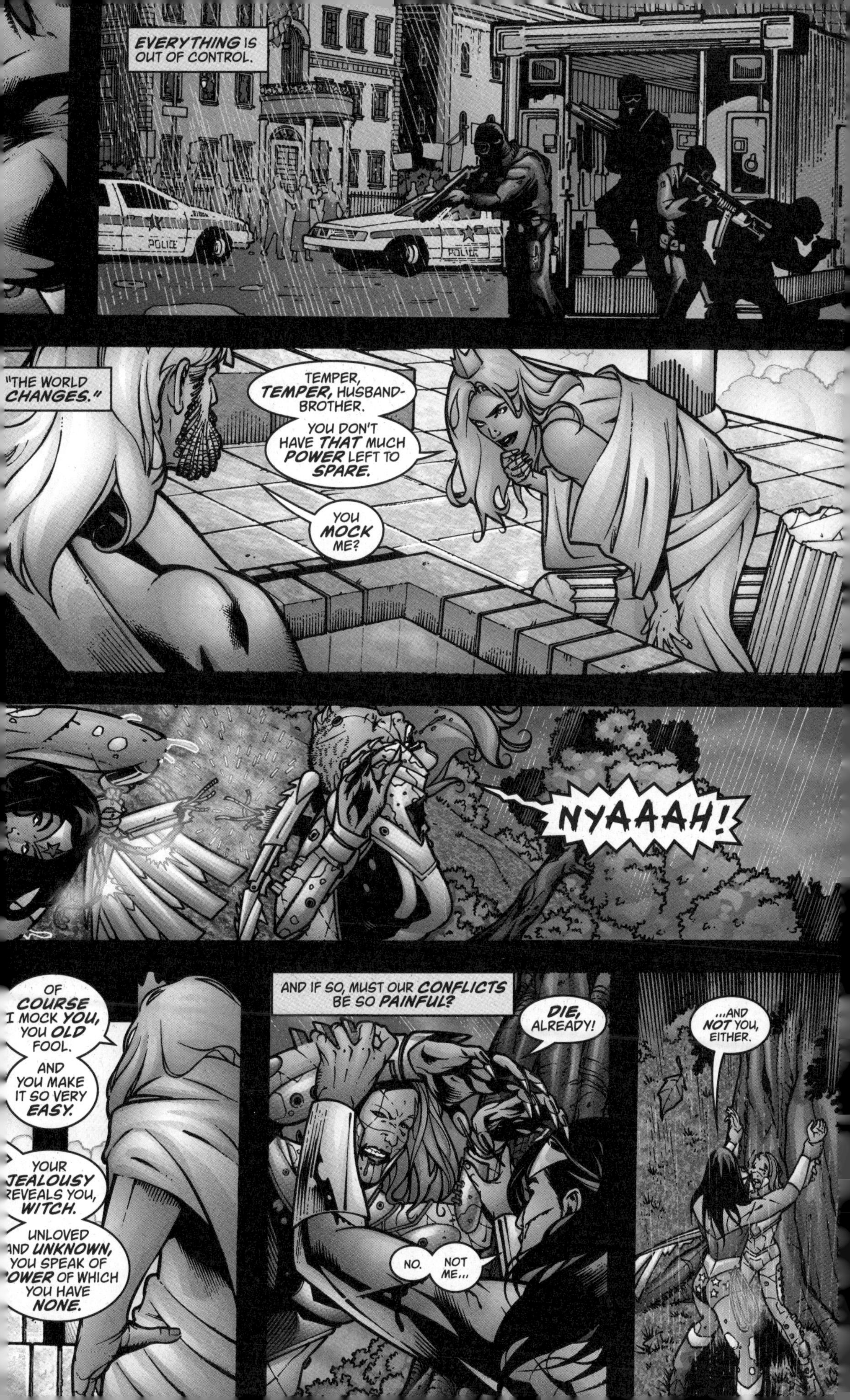
EVERYTHING IS OUT OF CONTROL.
POLICE
POLICE
"THE WORLD CHANGES."
TEMPER, TEMPER, HUSBAND-BROTHER.
YOU DON'T HAVE THAT MUCH POWER LEFT TO SPARE.
YOU MOCK ME?
NYAAAH!
OF COURSE I MOCK YOU, YOU OLD FOOL.
AND YOU MAKE IT SO VERY EASY.
YOUR JEALOUSY REVEALS YOU, WITCH.
UNLOVED AND UNKNOWN, YOU SPEAK OF POWER OF WHICH YOU HAVE NONE.
AND IF SO, MUST OUR CONFLICTS BE SO PAINFUL?
DIE, ALREADY!
NO.
NOT ME...
...AND NOT YOU, EITHER.

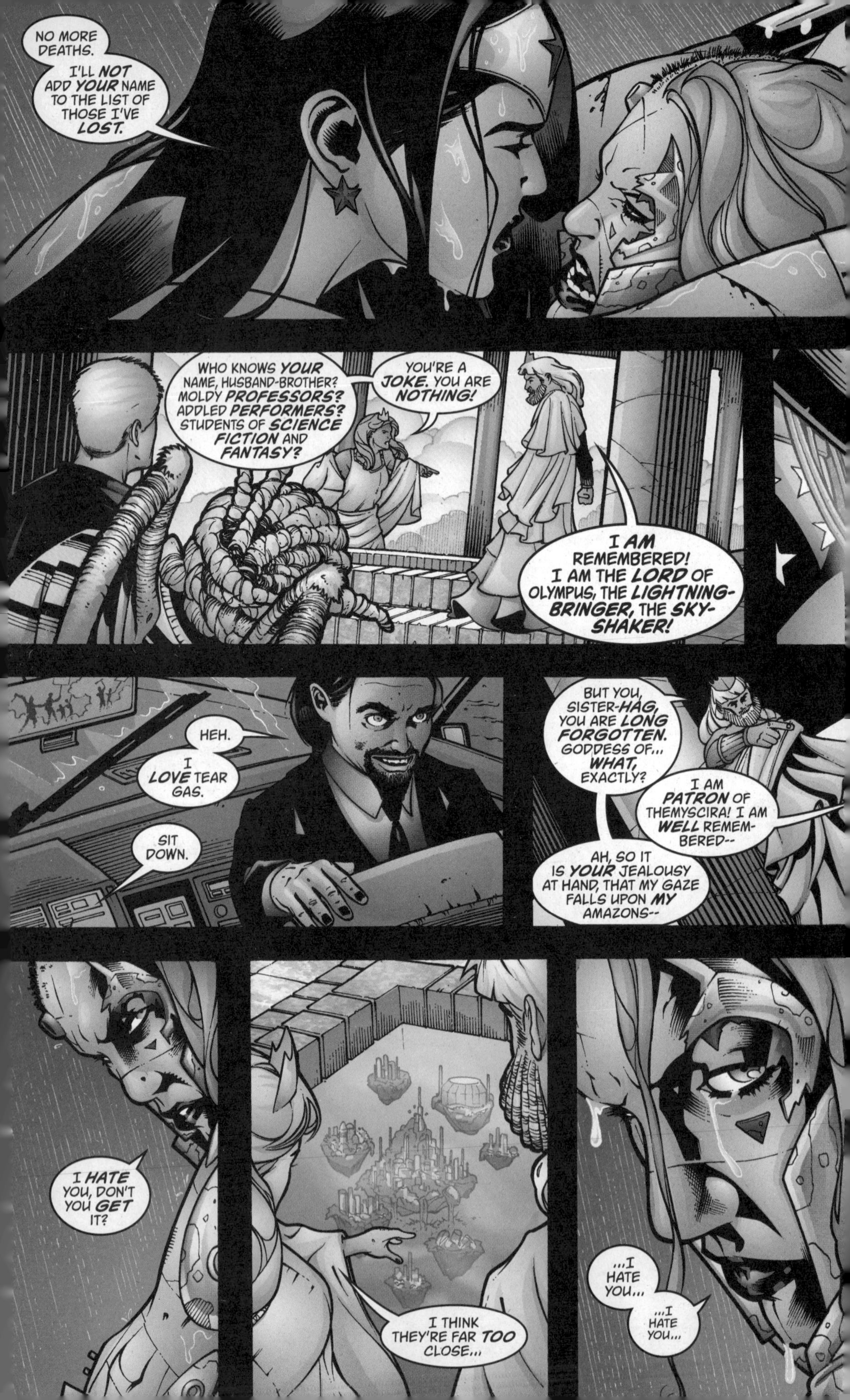
NO MORE DEATHS.
I'LL NOT ADD YOUR NAME TO THE LIST OF THOSE I'VE LOST.
WHO KNOWS YOUR NAME, HUSBAND-BROTHER? MOLDY PROFESSORS? ADDLED PERFORMERS? STUDENTS OF SCIENCE FICTION AND FANTASY?
YOU'RE A JOKE. YOU ARE NOTHING!
I AM REMEMBERED! I AM THE LORD OF OLYMPUS, THE LIGHTNING-BRINGER, THE SKY-SHAKER!
HEH.
I LOVE TEAR GAS.
SIT DOWN.
BUT YOU, SISTER-HAG, YOU ARE LONG FORGOTTEN. GODDESS OF... WHAT, EXACTLY?
I AM PATRON OF THEMYSCIRA! I AM WELL REMEMBERED--
AH, SO IT IS YOUR JEALOUSY AT HAND, THAT MY GAZE FALLS UPON MY AMAZONS--
I HATE YOU, DON'T YOU GET IT?
I THINK THEY'RE FAR TOO CLOSE...
...I HATE YOU...
...I HATE YOU...

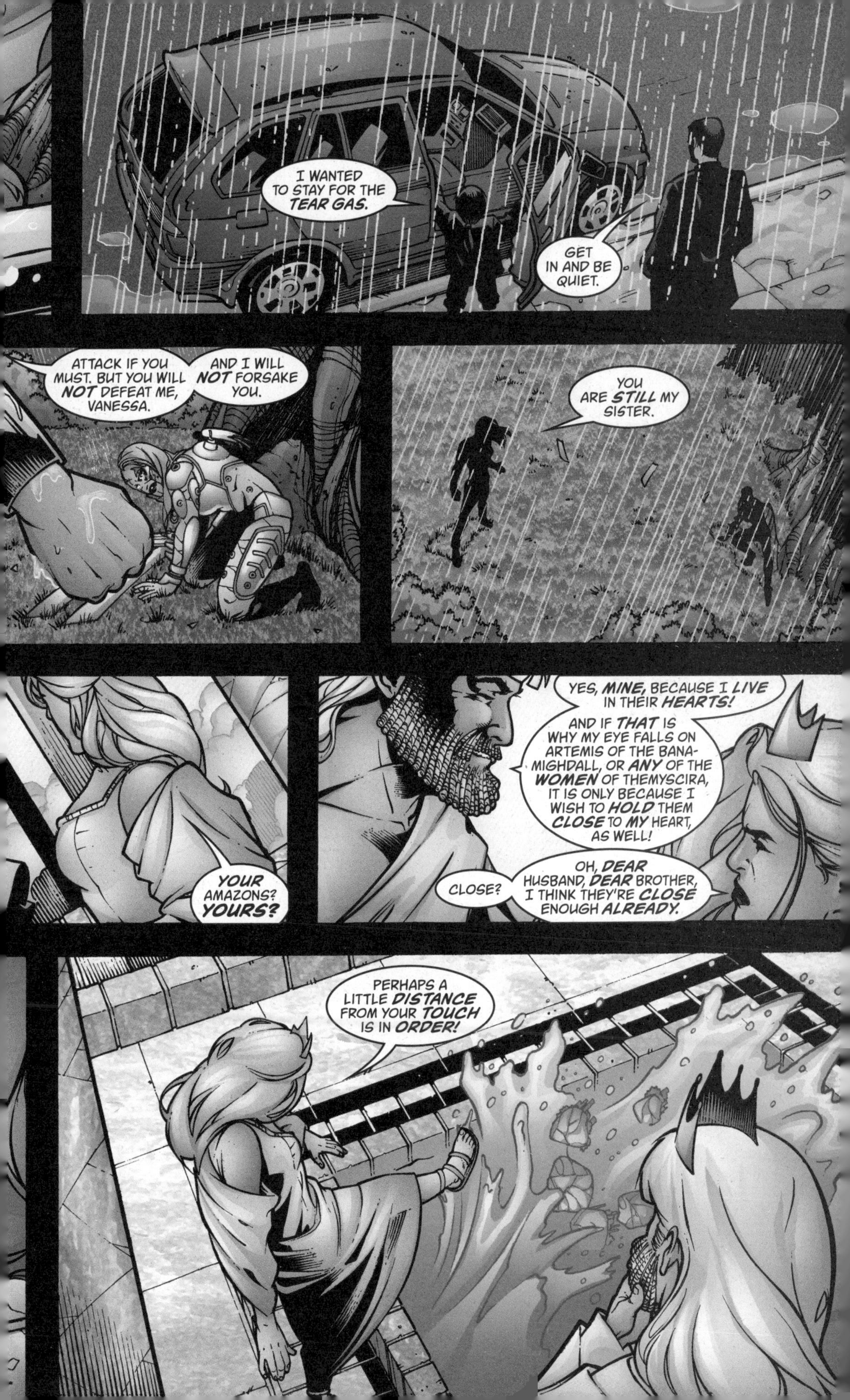

I WANTED TO STAY FOR THE TEAR GAS.
GET IN AND BE QUIET.
ATTACK IF YOU MUST. BUT YOU WILL NOT DEFEAT ME, VANESSA.
AND I WILL NOT FORSAKE YOU.
YOU ARE STILL MY SISTER.
YOUR AMAZONS? YOURS?
YES, MINE, BECAUSE I LIVE IN THEIR HEARTS!
AND IF THAT IS WHY MY EYE FALLS ON ARTEMIS OF THE BANA-MIGHDALL, OR ANY OF THE WOMEN OF THEMYSCIRA, IT IS ONLY BECAUSE I WISH TO HOLD THEM CLOSE TO MY HEART, AS WELL!
CLOSE?
OH, DEAR HUSBAND, DEAR BROTHER, I THINK THEY'RE CLOSE ENOUGH ALREADY.
PERHAPS A LITTLE DISTANCE FROM YOUR TOUCH IS IN ORDER!

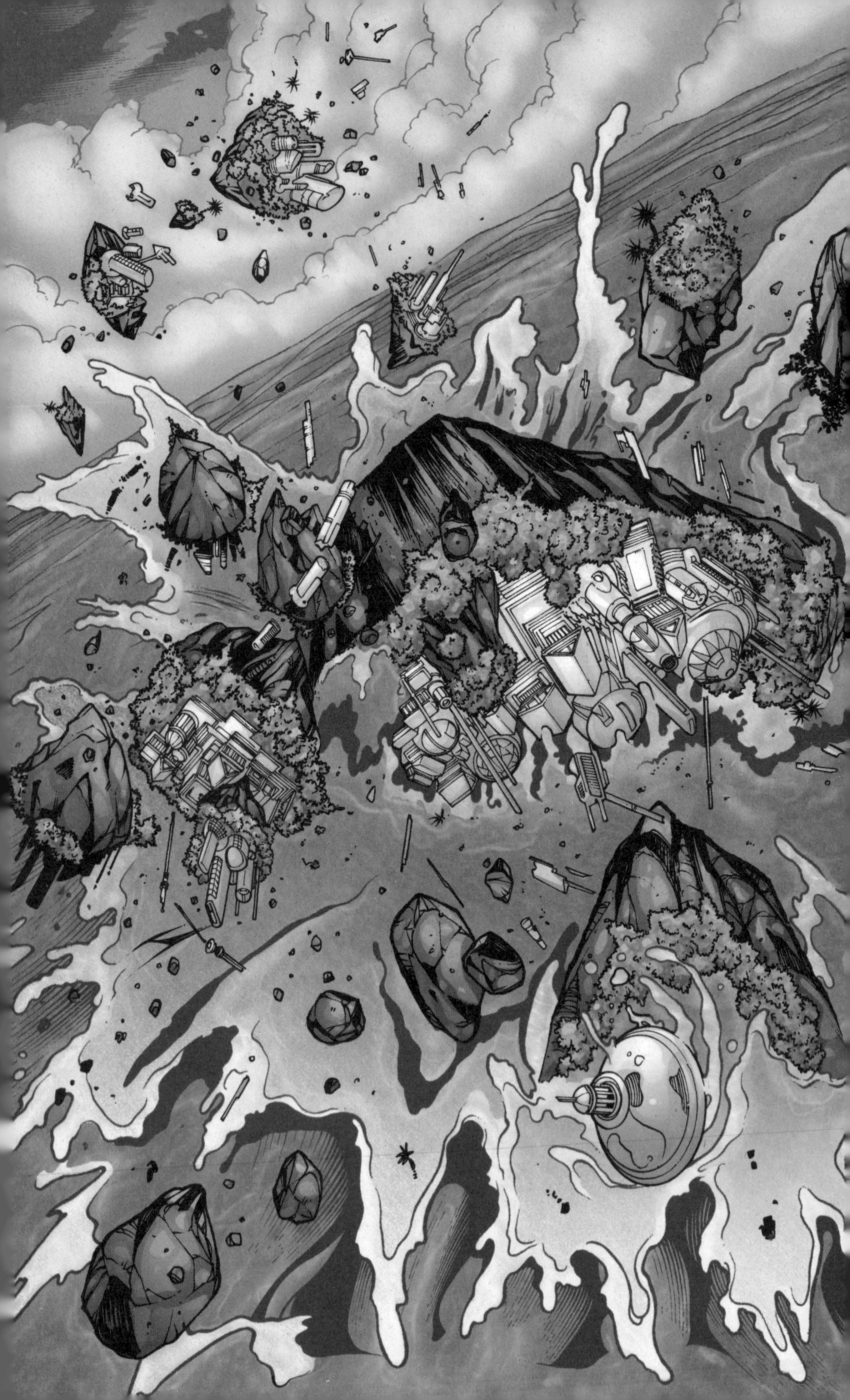

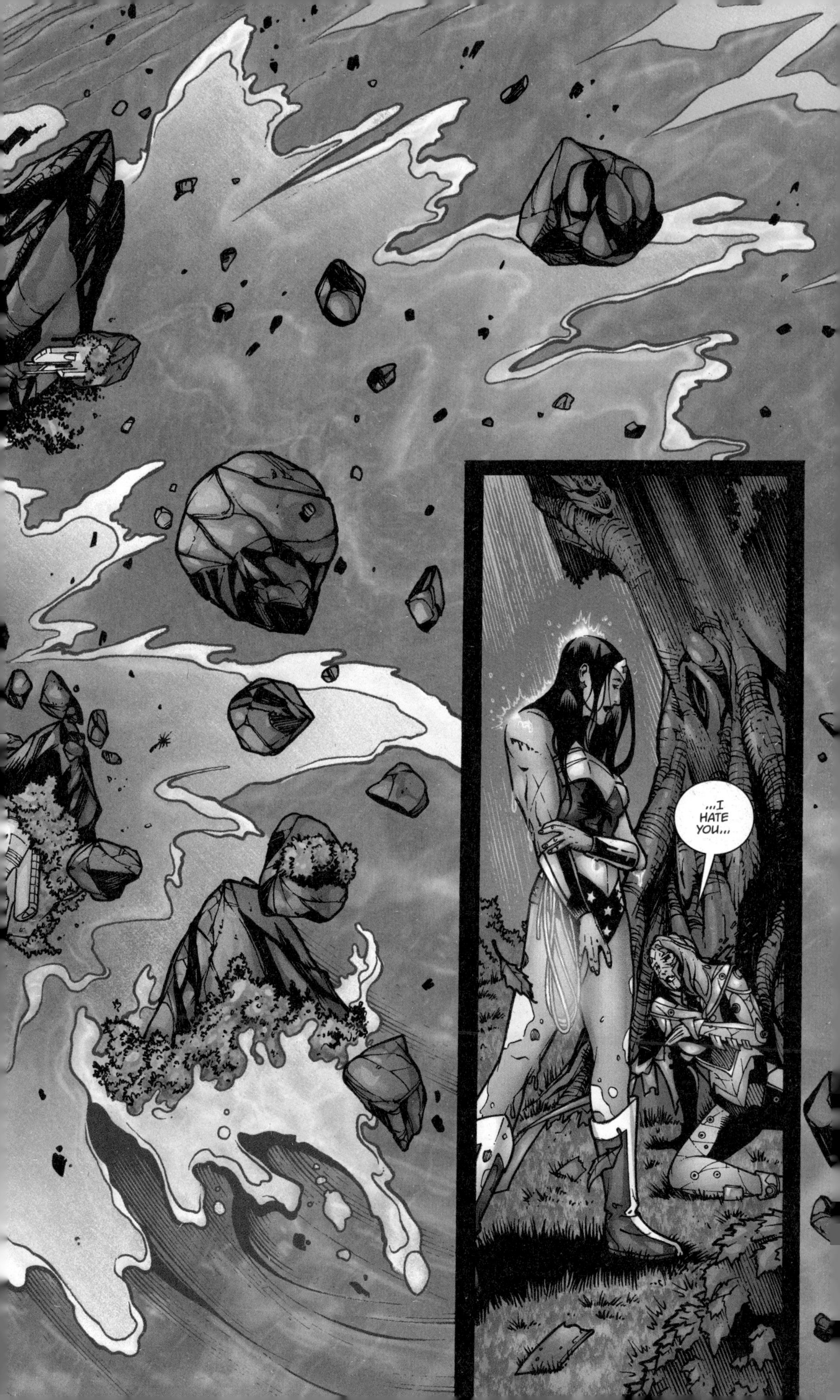
...I HATE YOU...

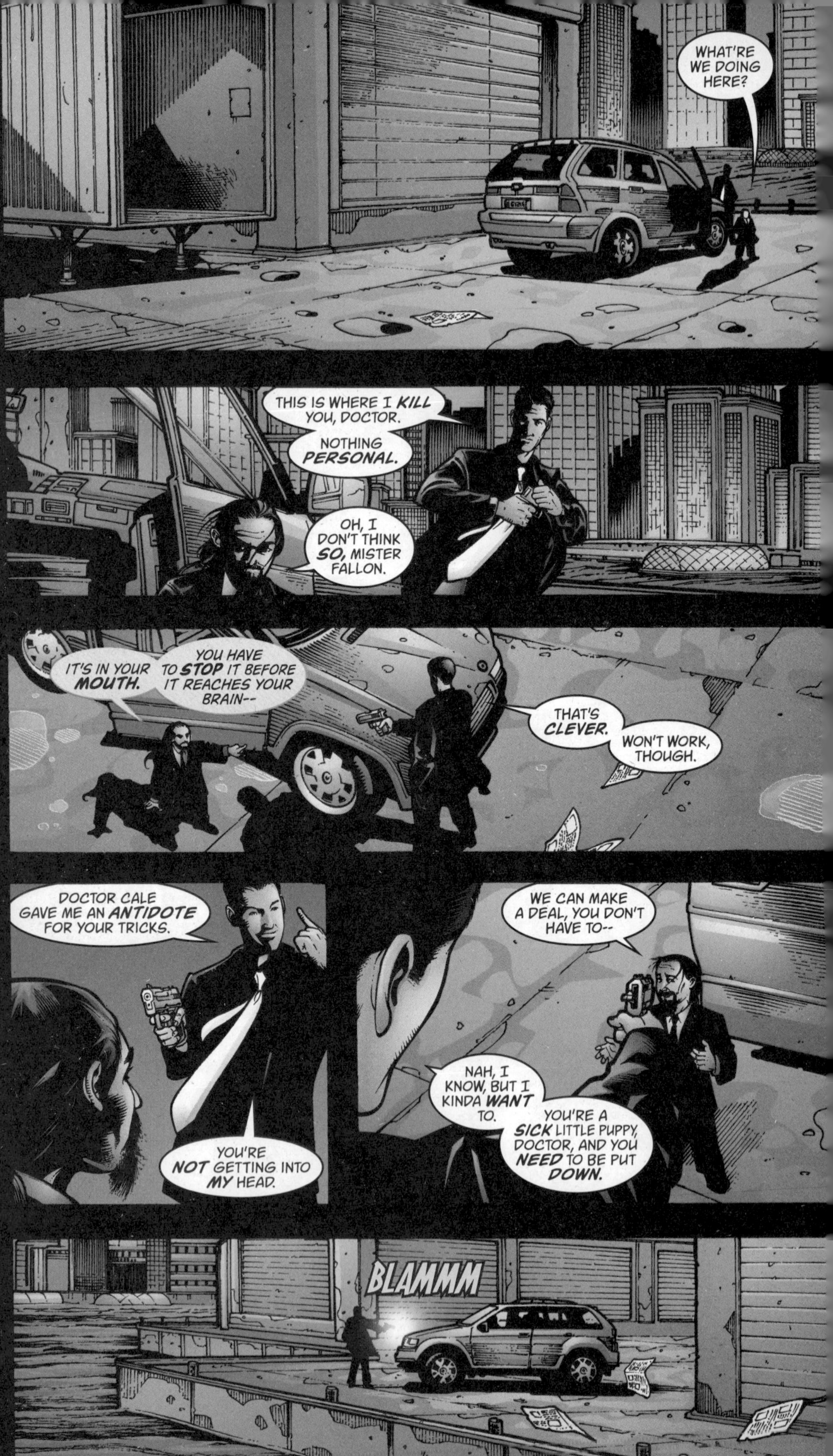
WHAT'RE WE DOING HERE?
THIS IS WHERE I KILL YOU, DOCTOR.
NOTHING PERSONAL.
OH, I DON'T THINK SO, MISTER FALLON.
IT'S IN YOUR MOUTH.
YOU HAVE TO STOP IT BEFORE IT REACHES YOUR BRAIN--
THAT'S CLEVER.
WON'T WORK, THOUGH.
DOCTOR CALE GAVE ME AN ANTIDOTE FOR YOUR TRICKS.
YOU'RE NOT GETTING INTO MY HEAD.
WE CAN MAKE A DEAL, YOU DON'T HAVE TO--
NAH, I KNOW, BUT I KINDA WANT TO.
YOU'RE A SICK LITTLE PUPPY, DOCTOR, AND YOU NEED TO BE PUT DOWN.
BLAMMM

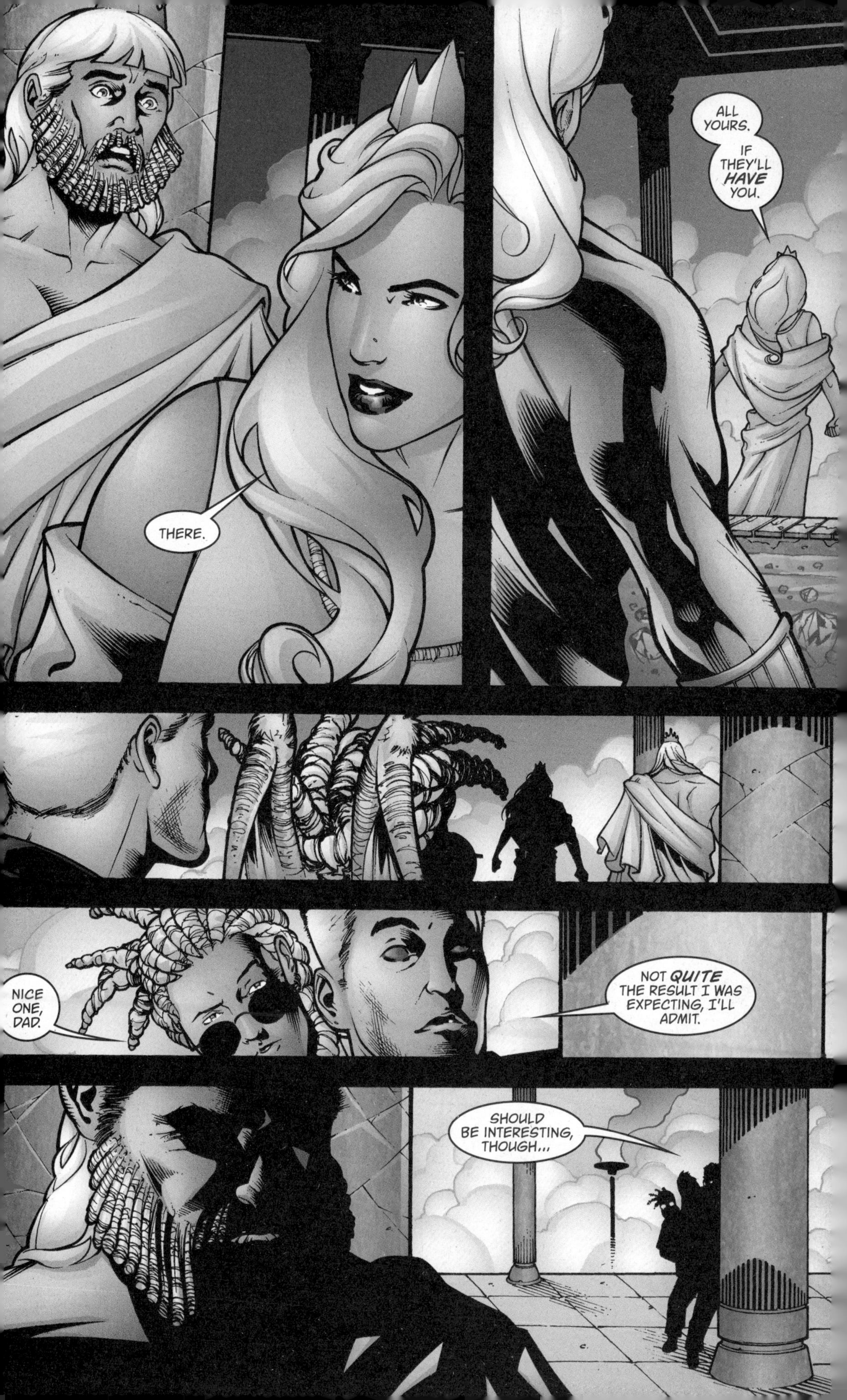
THERE.
ALL YOURS.
IF THEY'LL HAVE YOU.
NICE ONE, DAD.
NOT QUITE THE RESULT I WAS EXPECTING, I'LL ADMIT.
SHOULD BE INTERESTING, THOUGH...

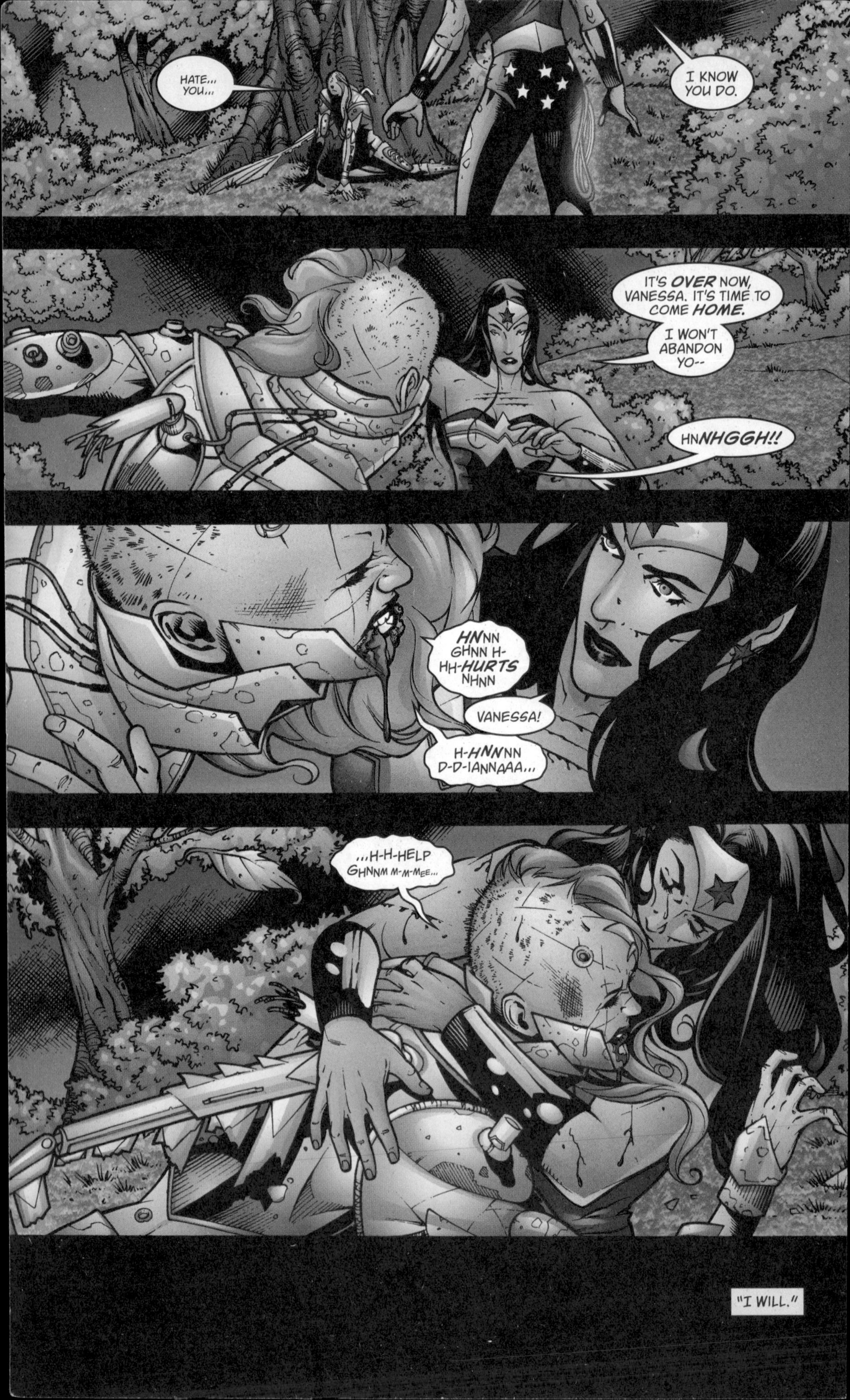
HATE... YOU...
I KNOW YOU DO.
IT'S OVER NOW, VANESSA. IT'S TIME TO COME HOME.
I WON'T ABANDON YO--
HNNHGGH!!
HNnn GHNN H-HH-HURTS NHNN
VANESSA!
H-HNNnn D-D-IANNAAA...
...H-H-HELP GHNNM M-M-MEE...
"I WILL."

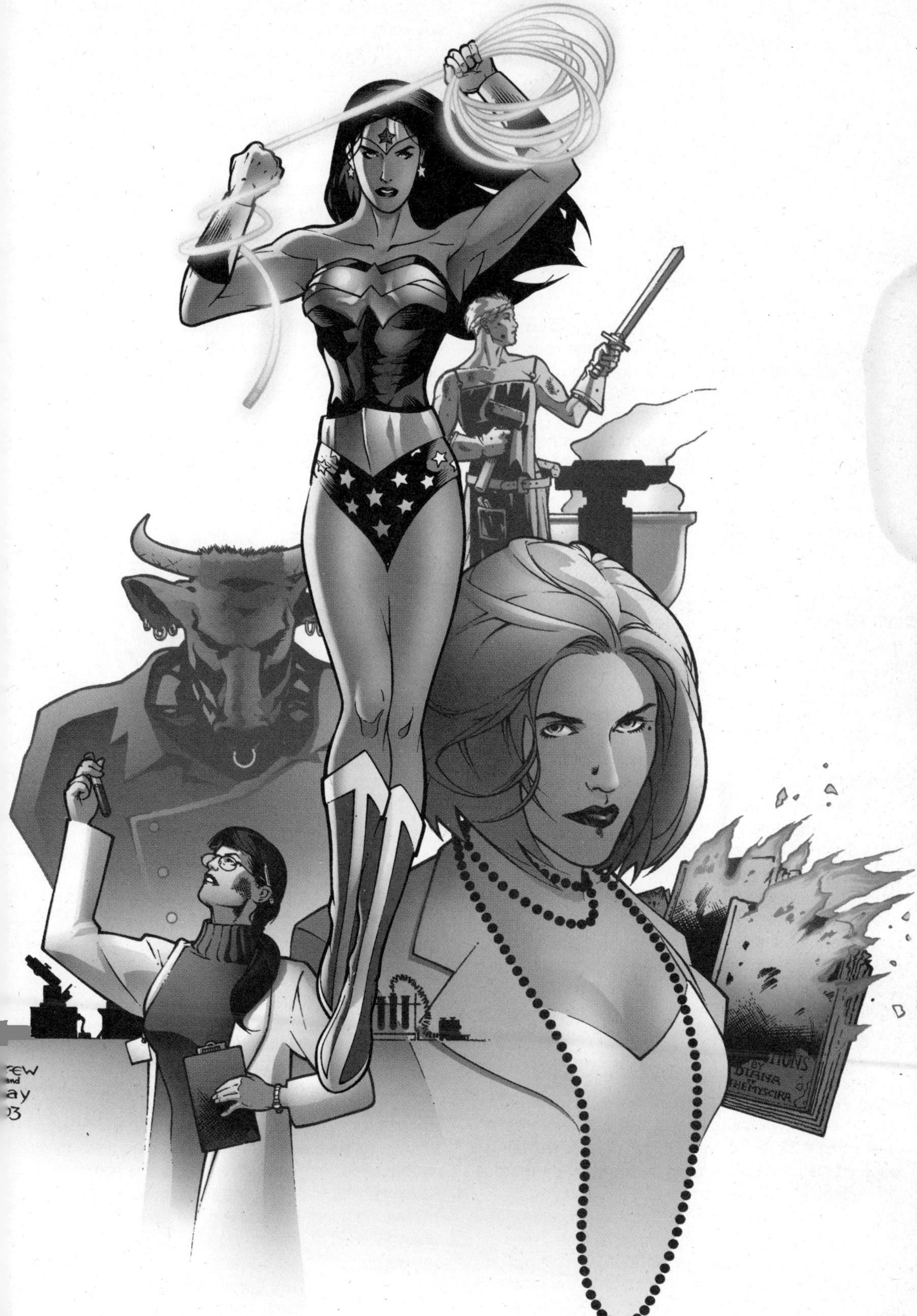
DIANA
THEMYSCIRA

ART BY DREW JOHNSON AND RAY SNYDER. COLOR BY WILDSTORM FX.

Calvin —
See attached.
Cale's not going
to be happy.
— Warren

this past w... and ... the ... of ... in a ... nder ... nto ... arm ... ut ... o ... d ... many and d... during the recent incide... thus raising the inevitable question of the place of so-called "metas" in global politics, and once again bringing the debate to the fore. The United Nations decision to call upon Wonder Woman to resolve the crisis and effect the arrest of General Abaku only further complicated the matter, since she was approached not in her capacity as a member of the Justice League, but rather as the Themysciran Ambassador to the United Nations.

"Clearly this was a unique case, and it required a unique solution," the Secretary-General told *Newstime,* speaking via telephone. "Of course this would not have been possible with the aid of any other ambassador. But we are speaking of the Themysciran Ambassador to the United Nations, Wonder Woman, a person who has been one of the U.N.'s most visible, and vocal, champions."

But was the decision to call upon Wonder Woman in her dual capacities — as both ambassador and metahuman — justified?

"Absolutely," the Ambassador responds. "The Security Council passed two prior resolutions regarding Itari and General Abaku, both of which the General ignored. The only other option was a military one, which would have resulted in the deaths of thousands — perhaps tens of thousands — of Itari citizens, not to mention countless soldiers on both sides of the conflict. There was an additional concern that an open conflict would have spilled over to neighboring countries, and perhaps drawn Umeci involvement."

Not everyone agrees with this assessment, however, and discussion since the event has continued, both within the U.N. itself, and in other governing bodies. Senator David Hale (R-Texas) is vocal in his concern for what he terms a "dangerous precedent."

"This isn't about the lives saved," Senator Hale says. "It's grossly simplistic to reduce the debate to just that. Was the Wonder Woman option more efficient than a military solution? Absolutely. Were lives spared? Beyond question. But once we turn to metas to solve problems of global conflict and politics, we're skating onto very thin ice. Where does it stop? When we turn to Superman or to Wonder Woman to solve those conflicts that we should be able to solve ourselves, we abdicate our authority, and our responsibility, both as human beings, and, speaking personally, for the people we represent."

Perhaps surprisingly, Wonder Woman shares the concern. In her book *Reflections: A Collection of Essays and Speeches,* she writes, "If there is one duty I must perform above all others, above my tasks as an ambassador of my people, above my responsibilities as an individual of great power, it is to teach… in action, to lead by example; in word, to inspire and energize."

Understandable, then, that many members of the international community claimed surprise, and, in some cases, alarm, at Wonder Woman's involvement in the arrest of Abaku. "No one believes she acted in a rogue or irresponsible fashion," says Hale. "Abaku's crimes shatter the imagination, and there's no question he had to be stopped, and brought to justice. Wonder Woman clearly acted on behalf of the U.N. But what if she had acted on behalf of Themyscira? What if it hadn't been a Third World dictator she'd apprehended, but a duly-elected First World official? The lines are blurring, and I'm afraid they're in danger of being erased."

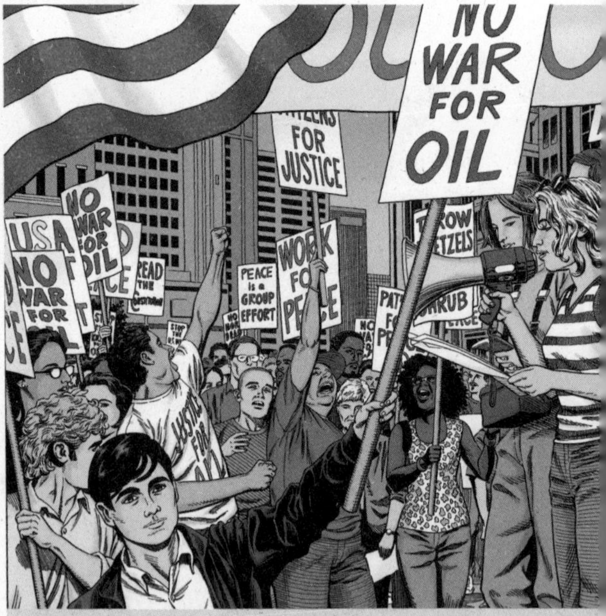
NO WAR FOR OIL
FOR JUSTICE
NO WAR FOR OIL
USA
NO WAR FOR OIL
PEACE is a GROUP EFFORT
WORK FOR PEACE

Ambassador Diana's book, *Reflections,* advocates public protests, like this one in New York's Times Square from spring 2003 *(S. Schreck/Airwave Studios)*

"If the Security Council had not specifically approved my part in the arrest of General Abaku, I would not have acted, it's as simple as that," the Ambassador responds. "We share the planet and our responsibility to it. For one person, any person, myself included, to presume that their way alone is the only way, or indeed the only best way, would be an act of supreme arrogance."

And should the situation arise again?

"I don't think it will," says Wonder Woman. "I pray that it doesn't."

It may be a faint prayer given the recent expulsion of U.N. Aid Workers from Umec this past

WE SAY: New York Wonder

She's beautiful, talented, and she saves the world from destruction almost daily. What's next for Wonder Woman? No less than inspiring a generation.

Cassandra Sandsmark, in torn and faded blue jeans and a gray T-shirt with the words "Property of Alcatraz" stenciled on the front, is brushing stray hair out of her eyes as she looks through the latest releases in the CD section. Ten feet away, Wonder Woman herself is struggling to decide between two boxed sets — Mozart or Beethoven.

And people are staring, and of course they are, because it's Wonder Woman standing there, the same Wonder Woman whose new book is stacked in the window displays all along the Lexington Avenue side of the store. Wonder Woman, wearing jeans and a wool sweater with sleeves that don't quite hide the shining bracelets at her wrists, and she's standing right there, in the Classical section, and yes, that really is Wonder Girl at the New Releases.

That's just not something you see every day.

"What about this?" Cassie asks, showing the latest by *McNamara Intact* to Wonder Woman. "Is this any good?"

"It's better than their last album," Wonder Woman says after a pause. "I think he'd probably like it."

When Cassie's asked who she's buying for, she shakes her head, grins, and says, "You'll need a lasso to get an answer out of me."

AMAZING AMAZONS

It's December 17th, almost a week before Christmas, and Diana and Cassie are engaged in a little holiday shopping. Not, perhaps, the most Amazonian of pursuits, but then again, who expects Wonder Woman to have even **heard** of *McNamara Intact*, let alone be able to comment on the relative merits of their latest album? Still, it's so mundane as to be almost unbelievable. An Amazon and her protégé shopping? Shouldn't they be out swinging swords or something?

"Right, because Amazons are all about blood, sweat, and tears," says Cassie with a laugh. "After this, we'll go castrate some men, don't worry."

"Don't say that," Diana says with a grin. "Someone's sure to take you seriously."

Ridiculous, perhaps, but then again, maybe not. Since the publication of Wonder Woman's book, *Reflections,* touched off a storm of public debate, the Themysciran Ambassador has been accused of everything from being a visionary to a subversive, and with a few more inflammatory stops along the way. It's a debate not without some merit. With chapters on everything from conservation (the Wonder Woman, a vegetarian, has strong views on the environment, and in particular the damage that comes from supplying the First World with beef) to the nature of love ("Aphrodite is one of my patrons," Diana is quick to point out. "What was it John Lennon said? *'Love is the flower you've got to let grow.'* Let it grow already, and quit trying to legislate it!"), the book has touched a nerve, and sparked everything from mild debate to public protest. "Which was precisely the point," says Diana. "Where's the purpose in sharing my views if people are just going to blindly and blithely accept what I have to say? That's called propaganda, not education."

Debate is one thing, but it hasn't stopped there. "I think it's ridiculous," Cassie says, clearly frustrated. "There's a handful of people who are

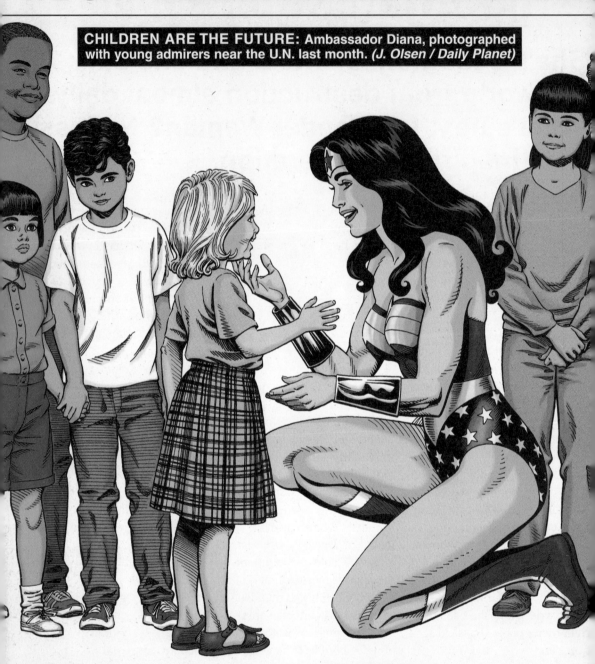

CHILDREN ARE THE FUTURE: Ambassador Diana, photographed with young admirers near the U.N. last month. *(J. Olsen / Daily Planet)*

AMAZONS

accusing Diana of trying to 'pervert' their kids, and that's just... that's just so *backwards*. Themyscira is the most socially and technologically advanced society in the world, they must be doing *something* right. But people hear the word 'Amazon'

and the phrase 'island of women' and they suddenly want to hide behind the couch. It's 2004, people, get over it! Stop being afraid of women!"

Diana smiles, listening to Cassie, her piercing blue eyes shining ("It's like looking into the most perfect blue sky," describes one embassy staffer who asked to remain name-

less). The fondness the two have for one another is obvious in the way they banter and joke while taking a break in the store's café — Diana drinks hibiscus tea, while Cassie downs a mocha latte — their relationship part mentor and student, part older sister younger sister.

So maybe this is more like

it? Maybe **this** is what being an Amazon is about?

"Do they have mocha lattes on Themyscira?" asks Cassie. "No, it's not, but it is, too… it's the comfort that comes from just, you know, hanging out with those who love you because they see the best in you, and they can forgive the worst. Being an Amazon — even an honorary Amazon — that's the coolest thing imaginable! To be part of that history, and to bring those ideas, those philosophies and beliefs to the rest of the world... that's about as cool as being a Titan."

"About?"

"Well, you guys don't have pizza," Cassie says.

Diana laughs. "We're working on it," she says.

Tea and latte finished, the two gather their purchases and make for the exit. It's a process that takes twenty-six minutes, as each of them is stopped several times for autographs and

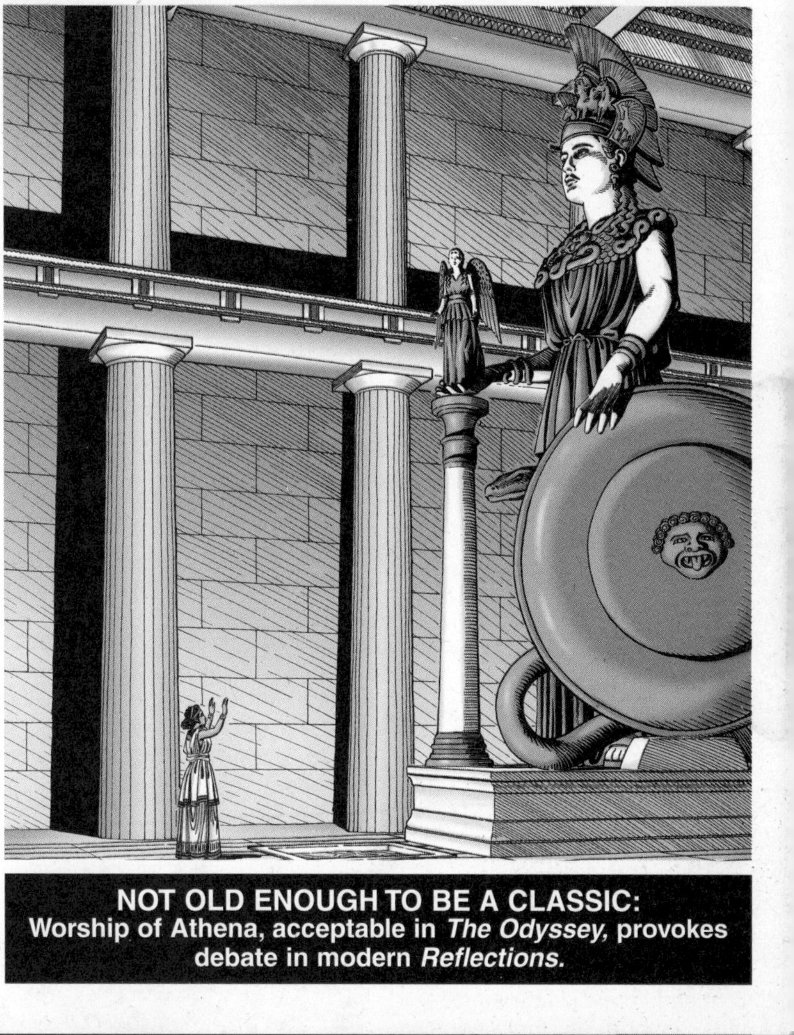

NOT OLD ENOUGH TO BE A CLASSIC:
Worship of Athena, acceptable in *The Odyssey,* provokes debate in modern *Reflections.*

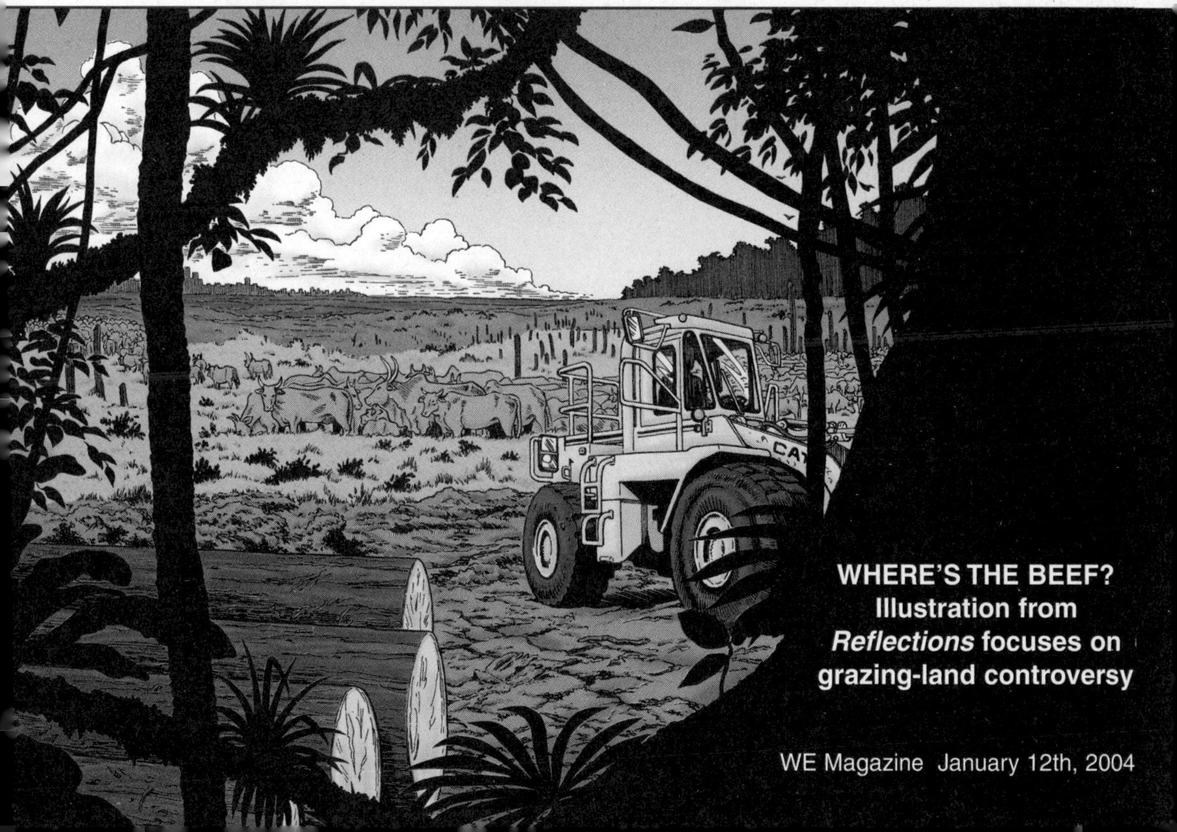
CAT

WHERE'S THE BEEF?
Illustration from *Reflections* focuses on grazing-land controversy

THEMYSCIRA:
MARGINALIZATION IN THE FACE OF MULTILATERALISM

BY RACHEL KEAST

Doctor Rachel Keast is the Legal Attaché at the Themysciran Embassy in New York and advises the Themysciran Ambassador in matters of United Nations proceedings and international law. She is the author of seven books, including the forthcoming Bullets and Bracelets: The Law of Themyscira, Then and Now.

The United States commitment to multilateralism as outlined in the September 2002 release of the National Security Strategy seems to have been swept aside in the recent debate on unilateralism and the efficacy of implementation of the Powell Doctrine. Globalization as such is here to stay, despite national interests to the contrary around the globe. In all this, Themyscira has effectively been reduced to a non-entity, coming lately as it has to the world stage. But examination of the Themysciran principals of diplomacy, sometimes referred to as the Hippolyta Doctrine, may shed new light on future diplomatic proceedings, insofar as multilateralism remains a pressing concern.

Separating those elements that remain well out-of-reach, that are unique to Themyscira, from those practices available to other nations provides a framework of discussion for further advances in diplomatic action and overtures that the United Nations, as well as other sovereign governments, could do well to adopt. With three thousand years of stable, peaceful governance to draw upon prior to its entrée into international global politics, Themyscira offers a unique diplomatic model.

Of course, there is always the issue of Themyscira's military might, which derives not from a strength of numbers, but from a combination of cultural imperatives and technological advantages unique to the nation. Themyscira is, perhaps, the only nation on Earth where not only do all of its citizens serve, but all of them do so willingly, and with pride, and remain at a state of readiness that is the envy of many armies. Presented as such, military action has always existed as a political option for the Amazons.

Yet, recent extraordinary conflicts not withstanding,[1] military force is an option Themyscira is ever loath to use. This is due in part to its self-imposed exile from what the Amazons call the World of the Patriarchy for so many centuries, but more in fact from the fundamental Amazonian understanding of all that a military option entails. As such, the Themysciran military option exists solely for the purpose of defense and is ever exercised only in such times and in such a manner as to insure the safety and continued protection and well-being of her citizens, a right shared by all sovereign nations.

---

[1] Referring of course to the global defense against Imperiex.

Ironically, perhaps, the presence of this military, backed as it is by the unique science and technology of Themyscira, has committed the nation to a path of peace that as yet stands unshaken. That its technology remains wholly proprietary is certainly of issue; while there are global interests who feel they, too, should have access to all that Themyscira has, it is the responsibility of the island nation's leaders to maintain a guarded stance that would prevent unchecked proliferation. In fact, it would be irresponsible in extremis for Themyscira to do anything else. This, along with many other factors, has further allowed Themyscira to maintain its status as an independent, neutral, and peaceful nation participating in global politics.

In fact, Themyscira's main export has been its ideals, in the form of its Ambassador to the United Nations, Diana daughter of Hippolyta, referred to more commonly as the Wonder Woman. These are policy stances that are offered rather than imposed.

Fig 1.1: Connection between "Homeric" Amazons and current Themyscirans controversy among scholars (Illo by Eric Shanower, used with permission)

WONDER WOMAN

SKETCHES BY DREW JOHNSON

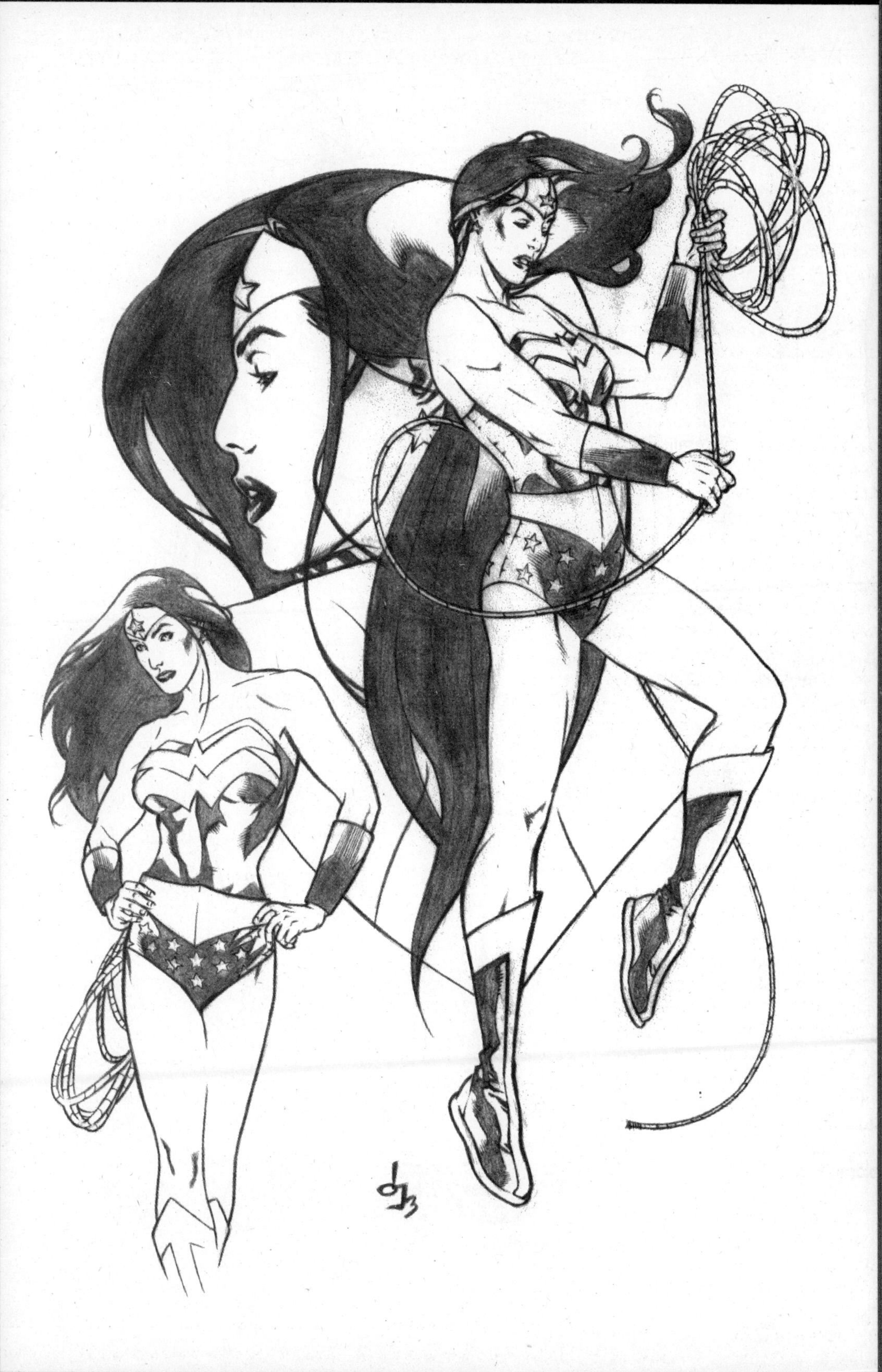

VERONICA CALE

NOTES ON CALE

• BEAUTY MARK BELOW LEFT
  EYE PROVIDES "VISUAL HOOK"

• COSTUME JEWELRY ROPE OF
  BLACK PEARLS GIVEN TO
  HER BY HER MOTHER — SHE
  ALWAYS WEARS THEM AND
  THIS PROVIDES ANOTHER
  "VISUAL HOOK"

drew
-3-

ARTEMIS

NOTES:

- FOLLOWS MATTHEW CLARKS PREVIOUS DESIGN

10

NOTES:

- SERIOUSLY BUFF ARMS + CHEST
- HEAVY GLOVES OVER AMAZON MANACLES
- HEAVY APRON OVER HER SHIRTLESS TORSO.
- TWISTED RAG TIED 'ROUND HER HEAD TO KEEP SWEAT OUT HER EYES
- WOVEN BELT AND LONG AMAZON LOIN CLOTH OVER HIP/PELVIC REGION
- ROLLED DOWN LEATHER BOOTS
- SHORT, SHAGGY, SELF CUT HAIR
- TALL- GIVES IMPRESSION OF OVERALL "BIGNESS"

Keep her simple lookin'

- More ragged hair -

- Chuck manacles

Linen drape light pants

lengthen apron

mid shin

LESLIE ANDERSON

NOTES—

· BLACK HAIR W/ BETTY PAGE
  BANGS — PULLED IN PONY TAIL

· BOOKISH GLASSES W/ YELLOW
  TINT

· CONSTANTLY HAS A PEN OR
  2 BEHIND HER EAR

· MODERATE FASHION SENSE

· SINCE SHE'S AT CAP
  SO MUCH — SHE'S OFTEN
  SEEN IN A LAB COAT

· OPPOSITE CALE'S LIGHTER
  HAIR + EYES — ANDERSON
  IS DARKER COMPLECTED
  AND MORE PRONE TO
  LOOKING STERN AND
  SHADOWY

drew 3

EMBASSY STAF

JONAH McCARTHY

Note —
· actually
  about 6'8

FERDINAND

NOTES:

· RINGS IN EARS AND NOSE
  CONTRAST "TOUGHNESS"
  AGAINST CHEF'S WHITES

· SLIGHTLY OVERSIZED
  HEAD AND HANDS

· LOOSE-FITTING, COMFORTABLE-
  LOOKING CHEF'S WHITES
  WITH BLACK RUBBER-
  SOLED SHOES — STANDARD
  CHEF'S GARB

· BLACK HAIR ON BULL-HEAD
  AND NECK DOWN TO ABOUT
  HIS STERNUM — THEN
  THE REST IS CAUCASIAN-ISH
  FLESH TONE.

· ABOUT 8 FEET TALL AND
  QUITE WIDE BODIED —
  IMPOSING, REALLY.

dj 3

ALANA DOMINGUEZ

NOTE—
...'s actually
...out 5'6"

RACHEL KEAST

NOTES:
RACHEL IS
ABOUT 5'4

PETER GARIBALDI with Martin and Robert

NOTES:
PETER IS
ABOUT 6'3

THE STARS OF THE
DC UNIVERSE
CAN ALSO BE FOUND IN THESE BOOKS:

GRAPHIC NOVELS

ENEMY ACE: WAR IDYLL
George Pratt

**THE FLASH: LIFE STORY OF
THE FLASH**
M. Waid/B. Augustyn/G. Kane/
J. Staton/T. Palmer

GREEN LANTERN: FEAR ITSELF
Ron Marz/Brad Parker

THE POWER OF SHAZAM!
Jerry Ordway

WONDER WOMAN: AMAZONIA
William Messner-Loebs/
Phil Winslade

COLLECTIONS

**THE GREATEST 1950s
STORIES EVER TOLD**
Various writers and artists

**THE GREATEST TEAM-UP
STORIES EVER TOLD**
Various writers and artists

AQUAMAN: TIME AND TIDE
Peter David/Kirk Jarvinen/
Brad Vancata

DC ONE MILLION
Various writers and artists

THE FINAL NIGHT
K. Kesel/S. Immonen/
J. Marzan/various

THE FLASH: BORN TO RUN
M. Waid/T. Peyer/G. LaRocque/
H. Ramos/various

**GREEN LANTERN:
A NEW DAWN**
R. Marz/D. Banks/R. Tanghal/
various

**GREEN LANTERN: BAPTISM
OF FIRE**
Ron Marz/Darryl Banks/
various

**GREEN LANTERN: EMERALD
KNIGHTS**
Ron Marz/Darryl Banks/
various

HAWK & DOVE
Karl and Barbara Kesel/
Rob Liefeld

HITMAN
Garth Ennis/John McCrea

HITMAN: LOCAL HEROES
G. Ennis/J. McCrea/
C. Ezquerra/S. Pugh

**HITMAN: TEN THOUSAND
BULLETS**
Garth Ennis/John McCrea

IMPULSE: RECKLESS YOUTH
Mark Waid/various

JACK KIRBY'S FOREVER PEOPLE
Jack Kirby/various

JACK KIRBY'S NEW GODS
Jack Kirby/various

JACK KIRBY'S MISTER MIRACLE
Jack Kirby/various

**JUSTICE LEAGUE: A NEW
BEGINNING**
K. Giffen/J.M. DeMatteis/
K. Maguire/various

**JUSTICE LEAGUE:
A MIDSUMMER'S NIGHTMARE**
M. Waid/F. Nicieza/J. Johnson/
D. Robertson/various

JLA: AMERICAN DREAMS
G. Morrison/H. Porter/J. Dell/
various

JLA: JUSTICE FOR ALL
G. Morrison/M. Waid/H. Porter/
J. Dell/various

**JUSTICE LEAGUE OF AMERICA:
THE NAIL**
Alan Davis/Mark Farmer

JLA: NEW WORLD ORDER
Grant Morrison/
Howard Porter/John Dell

JLA: ROCK OF AGES
G. Morrison/H. Porter/J. Dell/
various

JLA: STRENGTH IN NUMBERS
G. Morrison/M. Waid/H. Porter/
J. Dell/various

**JLA: WORLD WITHOUT
GROWN-UPS**
T. Dezago/T. Nauck/H. Ramos/
M. McKone/various

**JLA/TITANS: THE TECHNIS
IMPERATIVE**
D. Grayson/P. Jimenez/
P. Pelletier/various

JLA: YEAR ONE
M. Waid/B. Augustyn/
B. Kitson/various

KINGDOM COME
Mark Waid/Alex Ross

**LEGENDS: THE COLLECTED
EDITION**
J. Ostrander/L. Wein/J. Byrne/
K. Kesel

LOBO'S GREATEST HITS
Various writers and artists

LOBO: THE LAST CZARNIAN
Keith Giffen/Alan Grant/
Simon Bisley

LOBO'S BACK'S BACK
K. Giffen/A. Grant/S. Bisley/
C. Alamy

**MANHUNTER: THE SPECIAL
EDITION**
Archie Goodwin/Walter Simonson

**THE RAY: IN A BLAZE OF
POWER**
Jack C. Harris/Joe Quesada/
Art Nichols

**THE SPECTRE: CRIMES AND
PUNISHMENTS**
John Ostrander/Tom Mandrake

**STARMAN: SINS OF THE
FATHER**
James Robinson/Tony Harris/
Wade von Grawbadger

STARMAN: NIGHT AND DAY
James Robinson/Tony Harris/
Wade von Grawbadger

STARMAN: TIMES PAST
J. Robinson/O. Jimenez/
L. Weeks/various

**STARMAN: A WICKED
INCLINATION...**
J. Robinson/T. Harris/
W. von Grawbadger/various

UNDERWORLD UNLEASHED
M. Waid/H. Porter/
P. Jimenez/various

**WONDER WOMAN:
THE CONTEST**
William Messner-Loebs/
Mike Deodato, Jr.

**WONDER WOMAN:
SECOND GENESIS**
John Byrne

WONDER WOMAN: LIFELINES
John Byrne

**DC/MARVEL: CROSSOVER
CLASSICS II**
Various writers and artists

**DC VERSUS MARVEL/
MARVEL VERSUS DC**
R. Marz/P. David/D. Jurgens/
C. Castellini/various

**THE AMALGAM AGE
OF COMICS:
THE DC COMICS COLLECTION**
Various writers and artists

**RETURN TO THE AMALGAM
AGE OF COMICS:
THE DC COMICS COLLECTION**
Various writers and artists

OTHER COLLECTIONS
OF INTEREST

CAMELOT 3000
Mike W. Barr/Brian Bolland/
various

RONIN
Frank Miller

WATCHMEN
Alan Moore/Dave Gibbons

ARCHIVE EDITIONS

**THE FLASH ARCHIVES
Volume 1**
(FLASH COMICS 104, SHOWCASE
4, 8, 13, 14, THE FLASH 105-108)
J. Broome/C. Infantino/J. Giella/
various

**THE FLASH ARCHIVES
Volume 2**
(THE FLASH 109-116)
J.Broome/C. Infantino/J. Giella/
various

**GREEN LANTERN ARCHIVES
Volume 1**
(SHOWCASE 22-23,
GREEN LANTERN 1-5)
**GREEN LANTERN ARCHIVES
Volume 2**
(GREEN LANTERN 6-13)
All by J. Broome/G. Kane/
J. Giella/various

SHAZAM ARCHIVES Volume 1
(WHIZ COMICS 2-15)
SHAZAM ARCHIVES Volume 2
(SPECIAL EDITION COMICS 1,
CAPTAIN MARVEL ADVENTURES 1,
WHIZ COMICS 15-20)
All by B. Parker/C.C. Beck/
J. Simon/J. Kirby/various

**THE NEW TEEN TITANS
Volume 1**
(DC COMICS PRESENTS 26,
THE NEW TITANS 1-8)
Marv Wolfman/George Pérez/
various

TO FIND MORE COLLECTED EDITIONS AND MONTHLY COMIC BOOKS FROM DC COMICS,
CALL 1-888-COMIC BOOK FOR THE NEAREST COMICS SHOP OR GO TO YOUR LOCAL BOOK STORE.

Visit us at www.dccomics.com